G000270259

QUEER SAINT

ADRIAN CLARK AND JEREMY DRONFIELD

QUEER SAINT

THE CULTURED LIFE OF PETER WATSON, WHO SHOOK TWENTIETH-CENTURY ART AND SHOCKED HIGH SOCIETY

Published by John Blake Publishing Ltd,
3 Bramber Court, 2 Bramber Road,
London W14 9PB, England

www.johnblakepublishing.co.uk

www.facebook.com/johnblakebooks
twitter.com/jblakebooks

This edition published in 2015

ISBN: 978 1 78418 600 5

British Library Cataloguing-in-Publication Data:

A catalogue record for this book is available from the British Library.

Design by www.envydesign.co.uk

Printed in Great Britain by CPI Group (UK) Ltd

1 3 5 7 9 10 8 6 4 2

Papers used by John Blake Publishing are natural, recyclable products made from wood grown in sustainable forests. The manufacturing processes conform to the environmental regulations of the country of origin.

Every attempt has been made to contact the relevant copyright-holders, but some were unobtainable. We would be grateful if the appropriate people could contact us.

CONTENTS

Extracts from the letters and diaries of Cecil Beaton © The Literary Executors of the late Sir Cecil Beaton, 2015. Reproduced by kind permission.

Extracts from 'Voice From a Skull' and 'On the Photograph of a Friend, Dead' by Stephen Spender, from *New Collected Poems* (Faber and Faber) © 2004. Reprinted by kind permission of the Estate of Stephen Spender.

PICTURE ACKNOWLEDGEMENTS

Page 1: (above left) By permission of the Nagle family/ (above right) Private Collection; photograph by © Matthew Hollow/ (below) By permission of The Provost and Fellows of Eton College

Page 2: © National Portrait Gallery, London; private collection. Courtesy of Andrew Ginger

Page 3: By permission of Thomas Messel

Page 4: (above) © Hulton-Deutsch Collection/CORBIS/ (below) By permission of the Craxton Estate

Page 5: (above left) © Image Rights of Salvador Dalí reserved. Fundació Gala-Salvador Dalí, Figueres, 2015/ (above right) © Brussels, Centre for Fine Arts, Archives Philharmonic Society (1865-2001)/ (below right) By permission of Deirdre Levi

Page 6: (below) © Lee Miller Archives, England 2015. All rights reserved. www.leemiller.co.uk

Page 7: (above) © Estate of George Platt Lynes/ (below) © Press Association Images

Page 8: (above) © Lee Miller Archives, England 2015. All rights reserved. www.leemiller.co.uk/ (below) © Hulton-Deutsch Collection/CORBIS

ACKNOWLEDGEMENTS

Writers of biographies incur many debts. The principal debt here is to Professor Michael Shelden. He helped throughout the process, in ways which far exceeded anything one could have expected, providing information, advice, and material from his extensive *Horizon*-related archive. We are also very grateful to Hugo Vickers and Thomas Messel; they were extremely generous with their time and encouragement early on in this project.

Charles Rickett provided comments on Eton; as an Old Etonian himself, he saved us from committing any egregious blunders, as did Michael Meredith and Penny Hatfield from the Eton archives. Brian Sewell read Adrian's early drafting notes and provided insights which helped shape his thinking on Peter Watson.

From the Watson family, we should like to thank Peter Watson's great-nephew, Alasdair Nagle, who responded with great patience and courtesy to many detailed enquiries. Sir Rodney Touche, biographer of Peter's brother Sir Norman Watson, was also particularly helpful.

It is impossible to thank in detail all of the many individuals, institutions and libraries around the world that have helped. We would, however, particularly like to acknowledge the Master and Fellows of St

John's College, Cambridge, for providing access to the letters and diaries of Sir Cecil Beaton; many visits were required as we wrestled with Beaton's atrocious handwriting; St John's librarians Kathryn McKee and Mandy Marvin were exceedingly generous in giving practical help with the materials. Extracts from the letters of Lord Berners are used by permission of the Berners Trust, for which we are grateful. Information and photos were generously provided by Nancy Templeton, great niece of Waldemar Hansen. Dr Chris Fletcher, Keeper of Special Collections, Bodleian Library, University of Oxford, gave permission for use of material from the Stephen Spender papers; the Estate of Stephen Spender kindly gave permission to quote from these materials and from Spender's published poems. Professor Jonathan Gosling gave permission for use of material from the Keith Vaughan archive.

Michael Riordan of St John's College, Oxford, was very helpful in tracing Peter Watson's university career. Marc Masurovsky answered a number of enquiries on the workings of the Nazi ERR.

Vital archive material was provided by Chris Bastock (Tate Library), Beinecke Rare Book and Manuscript Library (papers of James Lord and Edith Sitwell), Michael Bloch (James Lees-Milne estate), Stephane Boudin-Lestienne (Association Villa Noailles), Ana Maria Bresciani (Henie Onstad Kunstsenter, Oslo), Sabine Coron (Sorbonne), Rebecca Daniels and Martin Harrison (Francis Bacon estate), Xavier Demolon (Tal-Coat committee), Elena Engelbrechter (Kurt Schwitters Archive), Vibeke Espholm (Nordic Library, Athens), John and Marilyn Gerry (Bushey Museum), Mary Gifford (Berners Trust), Emma Harrold (Oxford University Archives), Oliver Herford (Stephen Spender Trust), Moraiti Ionna (Benaki Museum, Athens), Stephanie Irlen (Neues Stadtmuseum, Landsberg), Christina Jansen (Scottish Gallery), Sharon-Michi Kusunoki (Edward James Foundation), Gemma McCallion (Public Record Office of Northern Ireland), Charlotte McKillop-Mash (Stephen Spender papers, Bodleian Library), Alexis Marotta (Calder Foundation), Roger Nougaret (BNP Paribas Archives), Michael Phipps (Henry Moore Foundation), Jennifer Ramkalawon (British Museum), Diana Rawstron (Lucian Freud estate), Richard Riley (John Craxton estate), Dr Maria Teresa Tosi (Fondazione Marino Marini) and Renate Wuersch (Universität Basel).

The following kindly answered Adrian's questions regarding Norman Fowler's activities in the British Virgin Islands and Nevis: Dr J. S. Archibald, Julian Clarke (who was hugely generous and helpful in particular by putting Adrian in touch with others), Steve Dickinson, John Everitt, Penny Haycraft, Vincent Hubbard, Michael O'Neal, Dr Alson Percival, Christopher Varlack and Dr Pearl Varlack.

The following people also helped in all sorts of ways: Edward Allcard gave an account of his transatlantic voyage with Norman Fowler, and Alexander Fitzroy-Clarence (formerly Alex Leslie) described in fascinating detail his relationship with Peter Watson; advice, information and feedback were received from Oliver Bernard, Sandra Boselli, David Clare, Ian Collins, the late John Craxton, William Cross, Charles Duff, Anne Dunn, Patrick Elliott, William Feaver, Clive Fisher, Jonathan Gathorne-Hardy, Jonathan Gibbs, Victoria Glendinning, Richard Greene, the late Richard Hamilton, Martin Hammer, Lady Selina Hastings, Gill Hedley, Anthony Hepworth, Michael Holzman, Justine Hopkins, Richard Lannoy, Jeremy Lewis, Andrew and Angela Lownie, Nigel Macdonald, Muriel Marseille, Jean-Yves Mock, Jeremy Musson, Melanie O'Rourke, Janetta Parlade, Antony Penrose, Michael Peppiatt, John Powell, David Pryce-Jones, John Richardson, Fred Sharf, Dr James Smith, Matthew Spender, David Taylor, Professor Mark Watson-Gandy, Francis Wheen, Professor Brian Whitton and Sofka Zinovieff.

We are both grateful to our agent, Andrew Lownie, for bringing us together, and to Anna Marx at John Blake Publishing for believing in the book.

Finally, Adrian would like to thank his long-suffering wife and daughters for putting up with the spirit of another man in the house; they now know more about Peter Watson than they could possibly want to.

... Some are, and must be, greater than the rest,
More rich, more wise; but who infers from hence
That such are happier, shocks all common sense.

Alexander Pope, *An Essay on Man*, Epistle IV

PREFACE

A PORTRAIT OF MORTALITY

In New York's Museum of Modern Art there is a strange and haunting portrait of Peter Watson. It was painted by Alberto Giacometti in Paris in 1953, three years before Watson's death. The picture seems to hint at the sitter's impending mortality: the formally suited figure stretched, stiff, and blank-eyed – translucent as a ghost.

There is a foreboding of doom in the picture; is this just hindsight, or was Giacometti seeing a true vision of his subject's future? Watson knew the artist well. Each day he put on his suit and tie and took a taxi from the Hotel Pont Royal, where he stayed whenever he was in Paris, and travelled to Giacometti's cramped, dirty studio at 46 rue Hippolyte-Maindron. Each day he had the same experience. Giacometti liked his sitters to come in the afternoon and stay late into the evening. We know from photographs of Giacometti at work that Watson would have been seated close to the painter, at an angle to his easel, facing the window so that the subdued light fell upon his face.

His view would have been of the detritus that characterised Giacometti's studio: half-finished plaster sculptures, some swathed in material to hide them from view; some raised on plinths; tall, mysterious sculptural presences on the studio floor; canvases stacked against the walls; an unused bed; a table cluttered with artist's materials; the dirty window obscured by a loose piece of curtain. Behind Watson we can make out a broken door, or perhaps the stretchers on the backs of canvases.

Giacometti's portraits are hard and intense. He preferred subjects with whom he sensed some empathy, and his pictures were reflections of his own disturbed and depressed soul. So they do not suit all his sitters. There is no such mismatch in the picture of Peter Watson. Three short years away from his physical death, Watson appears in the artist's vision of him already emotionally dead. He is a husk, both in the image and in the reality of his life as expressed through his letters. The emptied face, with its blank eyes, stares at the painter, and at us. Giacometti had found his subject.

Peter Watson had not always been this way. A legendary figure in the English cultural world of the mid-twentieth century, he was alive with energy: collecting, promoting, creating, organising. He was also propelled by a prodigious sexual drive. And yet he was barely detected by the popular radar; his reputation (cultural and personal) was confined within his own social circle.

A portrait of his life draws together pieces from many interconnected scenes. We find him in the Eton of the 1920s – the Eton of A. J. Ayer, Cyril Connolly, Tom Mitford, George Orwell, Anthony Powell and others. He passed briefly through Oxford at the right time to be caught in the aroma of Brideshead Revisited. The intense aesthetic sensibilities and the open, exuberant homosexuality that characterised both worlds had their influence on his development and the direction of his life. His background, as the son of a self-made man, made him an outsider in some people's eyes, but he had magnetism, and his sophistication won him a place within the social elite. His hard cash helped.

The path of his life wasn't always easy. Aged twenty-one and seeking the looser sexual mores of Europe, he travelled to Vienna with his boyfriend, the artist Oliver Messel, who introduced him to Cecil Beaton. Beaton fell in love with him – the beginning of an intense, passionate love that never wholly abated. Peter Watson preferred men from the more disreputable end of the social spectrum. He had affairs with male prostitutes, and involved himself in the gay goings-on in Weimar Germany in the early 1930s, before the decadent subculture of the cafés and cabarets was brutally and decisively swept away by the Nazis.

Peter Watson's hungry sexuality became notorious, and he was used as the protagonist in at least two satirical novels. The dangerous choices he made were eventually to lead to his premature death.

His lasting legacy came from the other side of his character: his abiding passion for the arts. He used his wealth to support young painters such as Lucian Freud, John Craxton and Francis Bacon. He put money and hard work into the cultural magazine *Horizon* and the founding of the Institute of Contemporary Arts. The pictures and sculptures he owned at various times in London and in Paris – including works by Bacon, Braque, Dalí, de Chirico, Ernst, Freud, Giacometti, Klee, Miró, Moore, Nicholson, Picasso, Renoir and Rodin – constituted an amazingly wide-ranging and impressive collection of works by the leading artists of the time.

His social circle encompassed the cream of the contemporary arts: he was friendly with Picasso and Giacometti; with Cocteau and Sartre and Camus; with Christian Bérard, Gertrude Stein and Olivier Larronde. His status also gave him an entrée to the lofty circles of Parisian aristocracy.

And yet, despite his ascendancy, as a character he left behind him as much shadow as substance. At times he slips almost entirely from our grasp, receding into near-invisibility – hollow and translucent, as in Giacometti's portrait. At Peter Watson's heart lay a shadow; his character was a phantom; it faded and changed.

The events of the wider world through which Peter Watson lived, combined with the increasing desperation of his emotional life, slowly crushed him. His own life was a reflection of the conflict he perceived between civilisation and humanity's rush to destruction; we see the result of the conflict in Giacometti's portrait of the hollowed-out man – whom Beaton called a 'queer saint', other-worldly, melancholic and just a few short years away from death.

This is the story of how he came to that state.

1

A VIOLENT QUARREL

1956

At about three o'clock in the morning of Thursday 3 May, a police constable was on routine night patrol in West London. His beat took him through the small triangle of South Kensington that lies like a wedge between Hyde Park and Knightsbridge. It was a solidly respectable area, and in the quiet middle watch of the night there was little for a beat constable to trouble himself with. London was sound asleep. He stopped a moment and savoured the sense of peaceful solitude. Even the weather had turned blessedly mild at last, England's spring having arrived late, held back by an abnormally bitter April.

The constable's peace of mind was blasted to fragments by a frantic shout and a clatter of running feet. He fumbled instinctively for his whistle and truncheon, but he'd barely got a hand on either before a figure hurtled out of the pre-dawn gloom, nearly knocking him off his feet. The figure resolved itself into the shape of a young man, all dishevelled shirtsleeves and hair awry. In a state of terrified panic, he yammered incoherently into the constable's face. Shaken, the embodiment of the law gathered his wits and dignity and tried to calm the man. It was hopeless: all he could get from him was babble about a friend called Peter.

It was clear that something somewhere was badly wrong. The constable allowed the young man – he was handsome and athletically built, his voice sounded American, and his clothes, despite being in disarray and inadequate to the early morning hour, were expensively cut – to lead him to the scene of the crisis. They ran all the way.

They came to a terrace of elegant Victorian townhouses overlooking the square at the bottom end of Rutland Gate. The front door of number 53 stood wide open, and light spilled out through its pillared portico onto the pavement. The young man ran up the steps, through the door, and on up the stairs.

Like many of the houses in this district, number 53 had been made down into flats. The young man took the stairs three at a time, the constable puffing in his wake. Outside flat 3 they found the porter in his night attire and a state of bewilderment. From him the constable at last got some information. The young man's name was Norman Fowler, and he was a known ... er, *friend* of Mr Watson, who was the tenant of flat 3. Fowler had been staying with Mr Watson for some time.

The flat door was locked. Fowler claimed he'd run out in search of help without bringing his key, and the door must have slammed shut behind him.

This was all rather odd. Frowning, the porter told the policeman that Mr Watson had gone away for a few days. They both looked inquiringly at Fowler. In a state bordering on aggressive hysteria, he swore that Peter was at home, and in horrible danger. The constable had taken a dislike to Fowler already, and not only because he knew full well what 'er, friends' got up to – he sensed that under the panic there was an unpleasant customer, spoiled and petulant. A muscular fellow, too. The constable braced himself and approached the door.

After several jarring attempts, his solid middle-aged bulk proved superior to the frame: it splintered and gave way. With the porter following cautiously and Fowler urging him on, the constable entered the hallway.

He could smell trouble before he even noticed the pool of water seeping beneath the bathroom door. He tried the handle; it was locked too, from the inside. He called out, but there was no response. Peering through the keyhole (it didn't occur to him to wonder why the key wasn't in the lock) he could see nothing but a tiled wall through a haze of steam.

The door gave way to his shoulder more easily than the outer door had. As it swung inward, a billow of soap-scented steam enveloped him. Through it, he saw the bath, tap running, water spilling over the rim. Lying in it was a man, naked: a long, slender figure, thin knees bent up; his face was beneath the water, and he was very obviously dead.

The porter, his face grey, stared boss-eyed past the constable's shoulder. Yes, he murmured hoarsely, that was Mr Peter Watson all right.

* * *

Robert Jolliff was a sober-looking man, bespectacled and on the grey downward slope of middle age. He stood in the centre of the sitting room of the Rutland Gate flat and surveyed the scene. A couple of hours had passed, and it had quietened down considerably. The police had finished their business and the medics had departed. Dawn light was glowing through the three tall windows at the end of the room.

Jolliff's placid gaze roamed over the elegant furnishings and the clutter of paintings: canvases large and small were hung on the walls and stacked in corners, competing for space with strangely angular, globular sculptures. Modern stuff. Young Peter was known for his taste in art – and other things. He'd spent a small fortune on his collection of paintings, but it was the 'other things' that Jolliff was concerned with at this moment. Those other things could have all manner of repercussions.

He had arrived just under an hour ago, to a scene like a galloping field day: neighbours were loitering on the stairs, roused by the hubbub, hoping for a sight of something scandalous. They were rewarded by the spectacle of the body, swathed in a blanket, being taken downstairs to a waiting ambulance: it was being manoeuvred through the hallway just as Jolliff came up the steps from the street. He stepped back and watched it pass. Evidently the situation was precisely as grave as he had anticipated. He had been despatched to the scene by his employer, Sir Norman Watson, elder brother and next of kin to the deceased. Sir Norman, who'd been informed immediately of the death, wasn't in town, and had sent his man to manage the situation.

Alone at last with his thoughts, Jolliff stooped to examine the corner of a canvas: amid what looked to him like daubings was a signature that meant nothing to him. He sniffed, wiped his glasses on a linen handkerchief, and walked to the bathroom.

Peter's body was gone, but the water was still in the bath. He pulled the lever and, as the water gurgled away, noticed something glinting on the floor. He bent and picked it up. A key. He looked at the splintered door frame, and tried the key in the lock. It fitted.[1] His impassive gaze went from the key to the bath and back again. Why in the world would a man preparing to bathe lock the door, then remove the key and drop it on the floor? For that matter, why would he lock the door at all? The only other person in the flat, if Fowler's account was to be credited, was Fowler himself. They were lovers, were they not? Particularly intimate lovers – intimate enough that Peter had made Fowler the principal beneficiary of his will.

Leaving the key in the lock, Jolliff moved on to the bedroom. Disarray, almost as if there had been a fight. Fowler had been kept in here, sodden with grief, after the discovery of the body. He was gone now – sent off to hospital with hysterical shock. Some friends were attending to him. Good luck to them.

There was even more art on the bedroom walls. Jolliff might know little enough about this bizarre modern stuff, but he understood that there was a good deal of money tied up in it, and he knew that Peter had a comfortable sum in the bank, even after a quarter-century that had been all spending and no earning. The man Fowler was going to be pretty well off. Even without the capital sum, which was tied up in a trust, he'd be able to live affluently for what remained of his life.

Jolliff glanced round the room again. He could almost swear that there *had* been a struggle in here. There was a suitcase discarded in the corner, half unpacked, and more untidiness than would be accounted for by one bereaved homosexual, even one as strong and athletic as he knew this Fowler to be. More than strong enough, indeed, to have broken the bathroom door down himself rather than waste time running for a policeman.

He went back to the sitting room, where he picked up his bowler hat and the parcel of papers he had gathered. Discretion. That was the watchword. Sir Norman required it; business required it; together they would ensure it. Complications, untidy deaths: they could cause impossibly vexing repercussions for a man in Sir Norman's position, an ageing bachelor who, some whispered, had certain … *foibles* in common with his deceased brother. Putting the bowler on his head and the papers in his briefcase, Jolliff took one last look around. There could be no doubt about it: a simple case of accidental death. Tragic. He left the flat, nodding to the policeman who was standing sentry outside, and walked out into the warming May morning.

* * *

The death of Peter Watson reverberated through the social circles he had moved in like the detonation of a bomb. The waves of shock and grief spread out from their epicentre in Rutland Gate, carried by telephone and by scribbled, disbelieving letters from one friend to another.

All over London, in Paris, in New York, painters and poets, critics, artists and friends and former lovers were stricken; Christopher Isherwood and Truman Capote were shocked; Henry Moore wondered what artists would do now without Peter Watson's support; Sonia Orwell told Stephen Spender that in Paris everyone was saying that Peter had killed himself.[2] Lucian Freud, one of the young painters who were indebted to Peter Watson for his patronage, contributed to this impression; he felt that Peter had become disillusioned with art, and that life had lost its meaning.

The blast echoed most violently just a few streets away from Rutland Gate, in Pelham Place, where Cecil Beaton had his London residence. He had been hoping to invite dear Peter down to the country for a few days of bucolic ease, taking advantage of the fine turn in the weather and a rare interlude in his hectic working life. Instead he received a heart-stopping telephone call. 'The terrible news was given to me', he wrote in his diary, 'that Peter was dead.' He let out a moan like a bull in agony. He felt like fainting; he tried to persuade himself that it couldn't be true, and when he could not do so, he despaired.[3]

The following day, Beaton had calmed himself enough to write to Greta Garbo: 'I have been crying like a hysterical child most of the day and night. My lifelong friend Peter died yesterday.'[4] Everyone knew that Peter had been more in Beaton's heart than a friend; he was the love of his life. That Peter did not return that love – at least not in the way Cecil wanted – was his life's tragedy.

While Cecil Beaton moaned and mourned, the last of the string of volatile young men to whom Peter *had* chosen to give his love was recovering from the shock. Norman Fowler had been released from hospital and taken in by friends. On the Monday following the death,

Stephen Spender visited him at their house in Chelsea. Spender found him difficult to talk to: he broke down continually, believing that he would be blamed for Peter's death.[5] It didn't cross Spender's mind that Norman's sense of guilt might bear more than one interpretation, that it might not be merely the common self-accusations of grief.

Not all who were affected were given to such operatic remorse. Far from the opulence and gleam of London society, quieter echoes of the explosion in Rutland Gate were felt in a little terraced house in a backstreet in Workington, Cumberland, where the elderly Miss Mary Atkinson heard of her nephew's sudden death, and (some time later) of the annuity that was left to her in his will. In all the glamour of his adult life, Peter had not forgotten his mother's kindly elder sister, a constant reminder of the humble, unpretentious root stock from which he came.

* * *

The day after his visit to Chelsea, Stephen Spender walked through the soot-blackened archway that led into the modest brick-built Coroner's Court in Horseferry Road, Westminster. Looking around the lobby, he counted about a dozen people who had come for the inquest, aside from the police.[6]

He noticed Peter's brother, Sir Norman Watson; like Peter he was tall and slender, had the same eyes, the tendency to stoop, the same peculiar pattern of wrinkles at the back of his jaw; but as far as Spender could discern he had nothing else in common with Peter – certainly neither taste nor temperament. (Spender was not privy to the same rumours as Robert Jolliff.) Peter would have been particularly disgusted by his brother's conservative pinstripe suit. Years ago, in Switzerland, Peter had given Spender a ticking-off for purchasing just such a hideous garment with money that he, Peter, had given him. Spender had never been able to wear the wretched thing.

Norman Fowler was present at the court, as key witness. Spender was surprised to see him deep in whispered conversation with Sir Norman Watson and Peter's doctor. Moving closer, Spender gathered that the three men were agreeing with each other about how obvious it was that Peter must have died accidentally, by simply falling asleep in his bath.

The coroner, when he arrived, was only too happy to go along with this ready conclusion: Spender felt that he had the air of a man who had come to solve a problem rather than one whose job it was to adjudicate a cause of death. After hearing the police and medical evidence, he returned a verdict of accidental death. Spender noted how emphatically he ruled out any possibility of an alternative – such as suicide, for instance. That should put paid to the Parisian gossip. (It didn't.)

If Spender was taken aback by Fowler's conversation with Sir Norman at the court, he was even more surprised the next day to discover how irate Fowler had been that Spender had attended the inquest – so angry that he could not be reasoned with. Ever charitable, Spender put it down to the jealous possessiveness of love.[7]

As time passed and friends traded snippets and scraps of information, the misgivings of Stephen Spender and Cecil Beaton germinated ... but somehow never took root. How could Peter manage to fall asleep in his bath when he'd had such trouble sleeping lately? What was the true cause of the row between Norman and Peter on the night he died? Was it true that Peter had been away on mysterious business, refusing to tell his lover where he had been? Was it true that Peter had been planning to throw Norman over for somebody new? Why did Norman, replete with his inheritance, decamp so abruptly to the far shore of a remote Caribbean island? Was Lucian Freud right about Peter's state of mind: was it true that the one thing that mattered more to Peter Watson than anything else – art – had begun to turn pale and die?

The obituaries were written; the memorial concert was held; the questions went unanswered and were slowly forgotten, and a veil was allowed to fall over the whole episode. Peter Watson receded ever further into shadow.

2

BETWEEN THE PRINCE AND THE FROG

1921–1926

The note appeared at some time during morning school. Quite how it came to him, Alan Pryce-Jones didn't notice; it was simply there about his person. It was perfectly clear, however, from which boy it had come: Peter Watson.

Pryce-Jones was intrigued. He rather admired Peter – a long, thread-thin boy with pleasing, delicately sculpted features and large eyes that had a tendency to bulge. He had a face 'equally poised between the prince and the frog'. Pryce-Jones was beguiled by Peter, and a little in awe of him; although still only fifteen, Peter had fashioned himself into the very spirit of refinement and elegance – 'one of the most sophisticated beings I ever knew'.[1] Some Eton boys found this intimidating; others found it fascinating.

The note Peter had slipped into Pryce-Jones's possession was an invitation to come to his room during the midday break. It didn't say what for, but it seemed to offer something quite extraordinary – something not to be missed. It would be well worth breaching the rule that forbade boys from different houses congregating with each other.

When the lesson ended, Pryce-Jones made his way to Peter's house. He was rather envious of the boys in this house; old Arthur Goodhart, the housemaster, was an eccentric and easy-going fellow, ideal for boys who preferred to live outside the bounds of good behaviour. Pryce-Jones had to make do with the duller, stricter Whitworth.

With an air of mystery, Peter welcomed Pryce-Jones into his room. He had a broad, slightly protruding mouth, and a way of smiling that could vary from a froglike smirk to a faint, almost ethereal glimmer – in this mood the traces of ugliness that marred his features vanished and he appeared quite beautiful. It was this mysterious depth that Peter's acquaintances seemed to be drawn to, and that Pryce-Jones found so enchanting. He was wearing that exquisite smile now, and Pryce-Jones wondered what marvel could be afoot.

As senior boys, they were allowed to decorate their rooms however they chose, but they all had the same rose-trellis wallpaper, the same small grate, the same scarred, black-varnished furniture with the names of past inhabitants engraved on its surfaces, the same writing desk and bookcase, the same small window that was kept open at all hours in all seasons (if any boy shut his window, Matron would open it again when she made her round).[2] One boy, part of the same set of aesthetes as Peter, had turned his room into a sultan's tent by hanging it entirely in gold lamé. Few went that far.[3]

Peter closed the door and led Pryce-Jones over to the bookcase. The atmosphere of anticipation heightened as Peter levered out some Latin dictionaries and reached in behind. He drew out a small oval bottle filled with an amber liquid. 'Smell this,' he said, removing the glass stopper and sighing ecstatically as a light, penetrating floral aroma rolled up towards the boys' nostrils. Peter's speech was slow and sleepy with delight: 'It's called *Quelques Fleurs*,' he breathed reverently, inhaling the perfume deeply.

Pryce-Jones watched the performance with amusement; for him, this would always be the epitome of Peter Watson, the aesthete, the divine sophisticate, the indulger of sensory pleasure.[4]

Although still a boy, he stood out as a person of refinement. Eton College in the early 1920s suffered no lack of aesthetes and sensitive souls. There were other, less delicate, blooms as well: fiercely creative and intellectually pugnacious. Peter was not one of them, but there was a sinewy stem beneath the fragrant petals; perhaps it came from his ancestry, which was closer to the soil than that of most of his hot-house peers.

His background was mysterious. Despite his elegant manners and seemingly effortless air of assurance, some people claimed to detect an odour of *trade* from the fastened cupboard that was Peter Watson's family background. The words *nouveau riche* were occasionally murmured, and some claimed that his father had been a peasant costermonger who'd started out pushing a barrow around the backstreets of some grim provincial town.

Peter had arrived at Eton in 1921, aged thirteen. His provenance was obscure – while most boys had come from one or other of the larger, better-known prep schools, Peter had gone to an obscure and struggling little Eton feeder called Evelyn's, at Hillingdon in Middlesex.[5] In later life he never spoke of his time there; it was isolated in a stretch of countryside, a miserable place of dormitories and confinement, home to around forty boys aged between nine and twelve. A near-contemporary, Jo Grimond (later a Liberal politician), also chose to draw a veil over his time at Evelyn's when recalling his childhood, mentioning only that he pleaded with his parents to take him away.[6]

Eton seethed with class. The sons of earls and viscounts mingled with the heirs to vast fortunes, a few of whom had already inherited great estates that were held in trust for them. In Peter's house were several 'Honourables' and two boys with titles: Viscount Ockham (son of the Earl of Lovelace) and William Lygon, who was son of the 7th Earl Beauchamp and had the courtesy title Lord Elmley. (A few years later, at Oxford, Lygon became friends with Evelyn Waugh, who used him as the model for 'Bridey' in *Brideshead Revisited*; his family were the basis for the Flytes, and Madresfield Court, the Lygon family's country seat, was the model for Brideshead itself.[7])

Because Peter kept quiet about his background, other boys were all the keener to sniff out the *nouveau* aroma. When Peter's parents, Sir George and Lady Watson, came to the Fourth of June – Eton's annual gala day of sports, speeches and boating – they arrived in a huge, gleaming Daimler limousine. One sharp-eyed boy, whose father was an earl, noticed that the car had two bud vases either side of the back seat, and another attached to the glass partition separating the passenger seats from the chauffeur. Standard enough fittings for such a car, but these were of embossed silver rather than the usual glass, and it really wasn't the done thing to actually *use* them, especially not as the Watsons had, stuffed full of sweet peas and carnations.[8]

Evidently there was something not quite *au fait* about such people; they were not quite of the class they pretended to be.

* * *

At the end of each summer half, the Daimler would collect Peter and take him home for the holidays.

With its high, square roof of gleaming black and its curved, coach-built flanks in glossy plum, the Daimler would drive sedately down from Eton, through Windsor and Reading towards the tiny village of Sulhamstead Abbots. Just before the village, it would turn off and follow a winding lane that ran alongside the Kennet and Avon Canal and then cut across between the gravel-pit lakes of Theale. At the corner of Bottom Lane stood the entrance to the Sulhamstead estate, guarded by a small and rather dainty white lodge. The Daimler rolled in and took the long drive that curved round the gentle slopes of the park. Peter, alone in the capacious back seat, would gaze out at the rolling parkland and the woods in the distance. Outside of school, this had been his world for as long as he could remember. And the house, coming into view as the drive rounded its last curve, had always been his home.

Sulhamstead House was an elegant Georgian mansion – hardly modest, but tasteful, and quite restrained for a family as rich as the Watsons. It was a classically simple Palladian block of white stucco fronted by a huge pillared portico. Its lofty windows gazed serenely out on hundreds of acres of green park bordered by woodland, beyond which were the estate farms and cottages.[9]

The Daimler would halt before the pillars, where footmen would be waiting to take the young gentleman's luggage. His mother would perhaps be there to greet him. Peter rarely spoke or wrote of his youth – little about Eton, nothing about his prep school, and barely a word about his home life or his parents. The sneers and insinuations of other boys at school – which would continue into adulthood – must have wounded and shamed him. The tiny traces of evidence that did survive, however, prove that he secretly retained a fond attachment to his home and childhood.[10] It had been a solitary life; as the youngest sibling by a full decade, Peter had led the life of an only child, with the spoiling and attention-hogging that went with it.

His sister, Florence, had married in 1916, when Peter was just eight;

her husband was an Irish army officer called Nagle, whom she met when Sulhamstead House served as a convalescent home for wounded soldiers. Sir George had objected to the match – Nagle was a drinker and a gambler – but it went ahead anyway, causing frictions that would linger in the family for years. Florence and her husband lived away now, and she devoted all her time to bringing up their two children and breeding Irish wolfhounds. Peter's brother, Norman, had preceded Peter to Eton, part of the last public school generation before the war. In 1914 Norman had gone straight from school into the army. He took a commission in the King's Royal Rifle Corps, then moved to the Royal Flying Corps. He survived, and came out of the war with a taste for adventure and aviation.

Even if Peter's parents weren't there to greet him in person when he came home from school, at least Sir George and Lady Watson's images were present in the great hall in the form of their portraits, painted by Sir John Lavery before the war.[11]

It was his mother whom Peter resembled. Lady Watson had the same pleasing features – the same large, liquid hazel eyes, the long nose in a slender face, the high cheekbones, strong chin and full lips; Lavery had painted her in a pale blue gown and fur stole, gazing distractedly over the viewer's left shoulder. Peter was his mother's favourite, the most like her in temperament and taste as well as looks; she loved the opera, and encouraged Peter to take an interest in music.[12] Sir George Watson was a stouter, more solid-looking gentleman than his sons. His fine, fairish hair was silvering and prone to turning up in wisps. He had a warm, affable countenance; his small eyes crinkled humorously in his round, heavy-jawed face. He was the very picture of Edwardian prosperity. Thoroughly established in county society, he had served his year as High Sheriff of Berkshire from 1920 to 1921,[13] and now, in his sixties, was looking forward to a quiet semi-retirement.

Peter's friends and acquaintances claimed that Sir George Watson – lord of the manor and filthy-rich baronet – was a *self-made man*; undoubtedly an inferior form of manufacture in the opinion of the people who lived in young Peter's world. They said that Sir George had made his money by inventing margarine (pronounced with a hard *g* in those days, which somehow made it seem all the more disreputable) and had purchased his way into the nobility. Having apparently begun as an urchin trundling a handcart through the streets, by some entrepreneurial alchemy he had built this tiny concern into a vast margarine fortune. And as for the so-called 'Lady' Watson, for all her beauty, her strings of pearls and Lavery portrait, she was said to have been a mere *nursery maid*.

It was true that Sir George Watson had begun in obscurity and built up his riches through sweat and acumen, but his origins weren't quite as lowly – nor indeed as romantic – as rumour claimed.

William George Watson had been born on Boxing Day 1861 in Warwickshire, the second child of a well-to-do farmer, who owned a sizeable set of acres near Coventry and was prosperous enough to employ three servants and a governess. By the end of the 1880s, young George was well along the path that would lead him out of provincial obscurity; he had become a butter merchant, and his teenage brother Albert was his assistant.[14]

The quaint image of the humble handcart was a myth. George Watson's relations had been growing prosperous in the Midlands dairy trade for decades, and George didn't have to begin at the bottom; he joined in a going concern. At the age of sixteen he began working for the dairy business that had been founded by members of the Watson family in Birmingham in the early nineteenth century. It was now owned and run by a man called Jackson, although the Watson family connection was maintained.

Jackson and young George eventually fell out over the trade in margarine. Contrary to the myth, George did not invent it, but he did pioneer the marketing of it. Jackson opposed the move; margarine was regarded as too downmarket for a business whose customers were mostly middle-class. When Jackson refused to make him a partner, George decided to go his own way. His brothers, who had also been working for Jackson, joined him. There were three of them altogether: George, the eldest, then Charles, then Alfred. (Albert was too young yet to join the enterprise fully.) In 1887, George and Alfred Watson opened their own independent dairy shop in Wolverhampton, selling butter, margarine and cheese – the Maypole Dairy Company was born. They strove to make it pay; Alfred developed a drive for opening up new branches across the Midlands, while George masterminded the business strategy. Meanwhile, their brother Charles moved north and founded his own dairy firm in Lancashire, which he later merged into his brothers' firm. By the end of the century there were more than a hundred Maypole Dairy Company shops across England. They went on multiplying, spreading into Scotland and Wales. The brothers also acquired creameries and factories in England and Ireland, and absorbed Jackson's old company, which brought another eighty shops into the empire. By the First World War there were nearly a thousand Maypole shops across Britain, with a new one opening every week between 1905 and 1914.[15]

The Watson brothers were 'minting gold', people said. They had concentrated their whole strategy on selling just five products: eggs, condensed milk, tea, butter and margarine, all produced under their own Maypole brand. One third of all Britain's margarine was supplied by them, and George Watson was called upon to advise a government select committee on the butter trade. The result was a huge boost to the business with the passing of the Butter and Margarine Act 1907, which regulated what could be sold as 'butter'. The elimination of disreputable competition helped Maypole's profits to triple between 1904 and 1910.[16] It was a progressive company; the brothers invested in technology and designed an advanced business model. They were socially progressive too, pioneers of profit-sharing.

While George Watson's business grew, so did his family. He was married twice, both of his brides coming from the northwest of England, where Maypole had its first major expansion. He married his first wife, Mary (who was either a distant cousin or just happened to share the surname Watson), in 1887, the year of the founding of the company. She died within a year. George remained a widower for six years before remarrying. His second wife was Bessie Atkinson, elfin-pretty and thirteen years his junior. Bessie was the daughter of a steelworks manager from Workington in Cumberland, and employed as a schoolteacher (not a nursery maid).[17] In 1894, aged nineteen, she married George in the church at Stretford in the suburbs of Manchester.

By the turn of the century George and Bessie had migrated to Essex and had two children, Florence and Norman. They were growing very rich, and edging their way into the Home Counties. In 1908, George made his first move into the landed gentry, purchasing a country estate: Chilton Lodge near Hungerford, a large mansion with a couple of thousand acres, for which he paid £82,000. The family never moved in, and by the end of that year George had sold Chilton on.[18] Perhaps his decision was connected with the fact that Bessie, a full decade on from the birth of Norman, was pregnant again.

The baby was born on 14 September 1908, in a large house in a leafy road beside the Thames in Maidenhead, Berkshire.[19] He was christened Victor William, but would always be known as Peter. Why his given names were abandoned is one of the small mysteries that followed him through life. A young Scottish nursemaid was hired to care for him.[20]

When Peter was still an infant in arms, his father finally got his country estate, purchasing Sulhamstead House in August 1910.[21] Then, in 1912, he crowned his achievement with a baronetcy. George and Bessie became Sir George and Lady Watson, and George styled himself Lord of the Manor of Sulhamstead Abbots. With the title came a grant of arms, for which Sir George chose the motto '*Esto quod esse videris*' – 'Be what you seem to be'. Acutely appropriate for a man donning the apparel of the upper class, but there may have been another, more subtle, purpose in Sir George's choice: the same motto was used by the Earls Sondes, whose family name had once been Watson. He might have intended that a family connection be inferred by those who knew their heraldry.[22]

The estate was a huge investment. Beyond the mansion and the parkland were six estate farms and dozens of tied cottages. There were two thousand acres in all, sprawling across three parishes. The property included shooting rights and five miles of prized trout fishing on the Kennet. Despite these assets, the rent rolls would never be enough to make the estate self-supporting; for the rest of his life George would be obliged to inject a steady supply of money into it.[23]

Inside, the house had two drawing rooms, business rooms and a dining room around a great hall; upstairs were eight bedrooms and five dressing rooms, as well as servants' rooms; downstairs were kitchens, pantries, housekeeper's and butler's quarters; outside were larders, a dairy, a brewhouse, a wash house, stables and garages.[24]

The newly ennobled Sir George plunged enthusiastically into the role he had taken on. He had the money, the cars, the country estate, the title, and a brood of offspring being schooled alongside the children of the mighty. His likeness had been rendered in oils by both Lavery and by Sir Hubert von Herkomer RA.[25] Now he turned his attention to patronage. If there was one thing the old aristocracy was willing to like about the *nouveau riche*, it was their cash.

On 6 December 1919 there appeared a leading article in the *New York Times* headed 'Sir George Watson gives £20,000 to found a chair in Kingdom's Universities', with the subheading 'Prince of Wales pleased'. The article described how, in response to an appeal by the Anglo-American Society, Sir George had donated the entire sum required for the foundation and endowment of a chair in American history, literature and institutions. The Duke of Connaught (president of the society) received Sir George's cheque with gushing gratitude, and passed the glad news on to the Prince of Wales (the future King Edward VIII), who wrote enthusiastically to Sir George. The prince politely declined Sir George's flattering suggestion that the chair be named after him, and insisted that it ought to carry its benefactor's name instead. And so it did. The first holder of the Sir George Watson chair was Viscount Bryce, Liberal politician, diplomat and former professor of civil law at Oxford, who gave his inaugural lecture in June 1921.[26]

Thus stood Sir George Watson's public persona in the year Peter went up to Eton. He had everything a rich gentleman should have, apart from the most important thing – the luck of having been *born* a rich gentleman, to a father who had also been born a rich gentleman.

If there was any common ground between Peter and his father, it must have been slight. Even in adulthood Peter would have little interest in business, and his tastes were forward-looking, avant-garde and sophisticated. He adored music from the earliest age (long before he learned to love art), and perhaps shared this impulse with his father. The first thing Sir George had done when he purchased Sulhamstead in 1910 was order a huge pipe organ for the hall. It was built in America by Garwood of New Jersey and imported via a company in Middlesex that supplied organs to many wealthy households in Britain. This one was said to have a pleasingly 'smooth, orchestral' tone, and, what was more, it didn't require a skilled organist: Garwood's organs included an automated mechanism like that of a pianola.[27] Quite what Peter's music-loving soul thought about this behemoth, one can only speculate.

As old age approached, Sir George began delving back into his agricultural roots, and developed a sideline in pig breeding. Throughout the 1920s, his name cropped up occasionally in the papers as the winner of prizes for his Wessex Saddleback sows at agricultural fairs across the country.[28] He could hardly have chosen a pursuit less in tune with his younger son. If any of these announcements ever came to the notice of Peter's school friends, they must have added some cruel twists to the remarks about his background. His precocious sophistication gave him some defence – and had perhaps been cultivated and refined for that very reason – but he was still a boy, still vulnerable in an environment that was hypersensitive to nuances of class and could react venomously against interlopers.

Peter Watson was, and always would be, an outsider. Unlike many of his contemporaries, he would never look back fondly on his schooldays.

3

'NOTHING IS MORE AWFUL THAN TOO MUCH REALITY'

It could have been worse. Of all the houses at Eton, the easy-going Goodhart's was the one that most suited a boy like Peter, who disdained sport, wasn't academically distinguished, and who liked to go his own way.

There were two categories of pupil at Eton College. In the minority were the seventy King's Scholars – a fixed quota of boys of exceptional ability who were educated free of charge. They lived in the College building in the heart of the school, and tended to regard themselves (with some justification) as a cut above the rest, not just intellectually but historically; their heritage went back to the school's founding in 1440, and they saw themselves as its true core. Cyril Connolly and George Orwell (or Eric Blair, as he then was) were among the older 'Collegers' who were in their final years at Eton at the beginning of the 1920s. Being a Colleger – and thus part of the centuries-old lineage of the school – was a rather splendid thing.[1] The other boys, of whom there were more than a thousand, were fee-paying 'Oppidans'.[2] Peter Watson was among them.

Oppidan boys lived in various parts of the town, accommodated in the school's two dozen houses. Each house was presided over by a master. It was an ill-regulated system, ripe for abuse. The housemasters were, in effect, hostel-keepers, each renting his house from the school and running it as a business, charging the boys' parents huge fees. A housemaster was entirely free to select the boys he admitted; the school's headmaster had no say in selection, or in the fees charged, or how the boys were accommodated.[3] Greedy and unscrupulous housemasters could grow rich, and the school benefited by charging them steep rents. The business was lucrative enough that some housemasters invested their own money in extending their houses or building new ones. A housemaster who wished to develop his reputation and attract pupils might feed his boys lavishly, and then starve them at times when money needed to be saved. By 1919 the corruption and profiteering had grown so out of control that one of the schoolmasters complained about it to the provost, M. R. James, lamenting 'our horrid desire for more money', which infected the running of the school at every level. Oppidan boys were selected according to the plumpness of their parents' wallets, and the masters grew fat on the fees.[4]

The character of each Eton house was absolutely defined by its housemaster. When one of them retired or moved on, he would bequeath (or more likely sell) his business to a successor. His current batch of boys would be part of the deal, and would usually have to move *en masse* to new premises. Because of this, each house was known by its master's name rather than by that of the building in which it resided.[5]

Despite the endemic venality, there were conscientious housemasters; most cared sincerely about academic standards, almost all placed a high value on sporting success, and many were strict disciplinarians. Peter's housemaster was different; the amiable A. M. Goodhart fitted into none of these categories. His house had few standards, and no discipline at all.

Goodhart had dedicated his life to the school; by the time the thirteen-year-old Peter Watson arrived in September 1921, he was well into his mid-fifties and beginning to look towards retirement.[6] He taught classics, although his real love was music, and he wrote settings for school songs. Goodhart was a gentle-looking man, with a steep forehead and a rather fine nose nestling on a profuse growth of moustache. He gave a constant impression of 'slightly unreliable benevolence, an awareness of being always prepared for the worst, and usually experiencing it'.[7] His character was widely agreed to be utterly lax and tolerant, but opinion differed as to whether this was a good or a bad thing. One sober boy thought him 'a deplorable figure – perfectly futile', incapable of enforcing elementary good behaviour in his house.[8] Anthony Powell, a contemporary of Peter's, wrote that Goodhart's was 'not merely a "bad" house, but universally agreed to be far the "worst" house in the school'. His every utterance was prefixed by 'a curious little purring sound', which the boys mimicked. He was sometimes bullied by the boys – tales ran around the school of rowdy pupils rolling their hip-baths against his study door in the middle of the night (this was in the days before the house acquired proper bathrooms), or hurling objects at his back when he made his nocturnal rounds. He found it quite impossible to identify, let alone punish, the culprits; with Goodhart, a boy could escape detection by the universal ploy of leaping into bed and pretending to be asleep.[9]

When Peter Watson first arrived in the house, it had calmed down somewhat since its heyday of misrule. It was accommodated in Walpole House, a block of elegant Edwardian redbrick two street corners away from the College. It had three storeys and a garret, and its protruding bay windows resembled the quarter galleries of a man o' war, giving the building a maritime air, as if it might run guns out of the boys' windows, sail off down Eton Wick Road and sink Keate House with a broadside.

The atmosphere within had mellowed into a kind of congenial, tolerant anarchism. Anthony Powell, noting the house's complete failure to win trophies for any kind of sport, felt that he 'could not have been more fortunate' in his choice of house. Likewise Peter Watson; if there was anything Peter couldn't bear, it was to be ordered about, controlled and confined. Many years later, during the Second World War, he shuddered at a friend's description of army life, and rejected his claim that it did one good to live with people with whom one wouldn't normally have chosen to associate, because it tended to 'expand one's experience of reality and humanity'. Peter commented tartly, 'I did enough of that at school. Really nothing is more awful than too much reality – I must say I'd rather have a little fantasy for myself than all this deadly dull reality.'[10]

A. M. Goodhart had the great virtue of imposing the minimum possible of dull reality on his boys. But still Peter disliked it, and rarely talked about his schooldays in later life.

Outside Goodhart's house, life at Eton was all about order, control, discipline and work. Divisions (as lessons were called) began at 7.30 in the morning, before breakfast, and the last one ended at 5.45 p.m. There were two periods of PE or military drill each day, and services in the school chapel. Diligent boys spent every spare hour studying, and all ended their day with a long period of prep (the boarding-school equivalent of homework) until bedtime and lights-out at 9.50 p.m.[11]

The school timetable devoured the whole week, dominating everything, and boys could only express themselves by breaching the rules – not a safe course in a regime where discipline was enforced with the cane. Corporal punishment could be administered by masters, but also by a select set of senior boys in each house. Some boys with a bullying streak relished the power of being a prefect, while some declined to engage in it. Peter, who managed to achieve prefect status despite his lack of academic or sporting distinction, claimed to get satisfaction from beating bad boys – perhaps there was a trace there of the sexual callousness that would become a part of his adult character.[12] He wasn't a bully, but he liked to dominate; he was capable of dealing out punishment, and there was a cold spot in his character that enabled him to do it quite calmly.

At least with prefects it was possible for a charming boy to flirt his way out of a beating. David Herbert, the wayward, truanting second son of the Earl of Pembroke, learned to escape punishment through sexual charm, but with the headmaster that wasn't possible. Instead of a cane the head used the much more painful birch. The instrument of punishment was kept on display in the headmaster's assistant's office, and the ritual associated with it was as perverse as it was cruel:

> You were taken up to a special room in Upper College where you waited with your heart thumping against your ribs, watched over, silently, by the head's assistant ... The door opened and in walked the headmaster dressed in a black gown and wearing a black mortar-board with a silk tassel; you were then given a lecture on whatever misdeed you had committed. When this was over your trousers and underpants were removed by the assistant and you were left shivering with your arse bare ... then you were led, quaking, to the block. The assistant handed the headmaster the birch, placed you on the 'guillotine', and sat on your head.[13]

The strokes of the birch took off skin and left injuries that would hurt for weeks. At the end of the half, the boy's parents would be billed 10/6d for the cost of a new birch (itemised as 'School Medicine').

Even without physical punishment, the Eton regime (which was no more brutal than other public schools, and milder than some) was capable of breaking sensitive boys; one of Peter's contemporaries (and later his friend), Edward James, was among them. He had several things in common with Peter: he came from a hugely wealthy family with a mixed aroma of trade and aristocratic pretensions; he was bright but not exceptionally so; and would grow up to patronise the Surrealist art movement. Unlike Peter he was delicate and failed to develop a defence against the system; intimidated by the aura of Peter and the other sophisticates, James was also bullied by his housemaster, and eventually had to be taken out of school.[14]

There were some bright spots in the school. Boys delighted in taking breakfast with the provost, M. R. James, a 'genial and amusing super-uncle' who allowed the boys to talk freely and joke about the masters, and who loved to discuss his celebrated ghost stories.[15] The College dining hall had a 'respectful comfort which made each mouthful taste historical'.[16]

Despite the toughness of the regime, Eton was changing. Peter had come up at a time when boys were beginning to take control of their own schooldays in a way their fathers and older brothers never had. Perhaps it was significant that this change coincided with the end of the First World War. So many of the previous generation of public schoolboys, who had embodied the tradition of 'play up and play the game' for the honour of the side, had ended up as names on the long rolls of war dead.[17] The first post-war generation, it seemed, was determined not to go the same way – at least not without making their mark and asserting their identities. Between 1918 and the late 1920s an unusual number of would-be writers, artists and other expressive, outlandish characters passed through Eton, and the place was never quite the same again.

Among them was Cyril Connolly, who in later life would be one of Peter's closest friends; several years old than Peter, as the 1920s began Connolly was emerging from his miserable period as a fag. As they became senior, he and some of his civilised contemporaries brought about a kind of velvet revolution against the school's militaristic culture, its beatings by fagmasters and the feudal fagging system itself. The new generation sought to replace these antiquated values with reason, humane treatment and democracy. It began among the Collegers and spread through some of the more liberal houses. The result was a more liberal environment, in which art and self-expression – the essence of cultured civilisation – could flourish.[18]

In 1922 a group of boys founded the Eton Society of Arts, an open club for boys with yearnings after art and literature. It was a vibrant and successful movement, thronged with adolescent poets, would-be novelists, artists, dramatists and aesthetes. Among the founding members were Anthony Powell, Henry Yorke (who later wrote novels under the pen-name Henry Green) and Robert Byron. Also on the founders' roll were Harold Acton and Brian Howard; both would have careers in literature, but their lasting contribution would be when Evelyn Waugh combined them in the flamboyantly homosexual Anthony Blanche in *Brideshead Revisited*.[19]

Of the two, Brian Howard was the more outrageous and, in some ways, unbalanced. He had some characteristics in common with Peter Watson (later in life they became close friends). Anthony Powell, who didn't like Howard, saw that he was as much interested in himself as in art. Although he had been the driving force behind the establishment of the Eton Society and considered himself a genius, Howard had a wayward streak that was 'likely to obstruct, rather than encourage, an interest in the arts'. But like Peter Watson, Howard's 'confidence and sophistication were both startling in a boy of that age'. Howard's appearance was striking, with 'a dead white face', and his 'full pouting lips' and 'huge eyes that seemed by nature to have been heavily made-up' gave him 'the air of a pierrot out of costume'.[20] He enjoyed dressing up in women's clothing, and with his naturally effeminate looks he made a very passable girl.

He wasn't the only cross-dresser at Eton. One boy, recorded only as 'R' by Alan Pryce-Jones, disguised himself as a girl, rode up to the school in the family's Rolls-Royce, and, introducing himself to his tutor as his sister, interviewed that gentleman about himself.[21] On at least one occasion Oliver Messel (another extravagant character who later became intimate with Peter Watson) dressed himself as a young lady and walked through the school; boys tipped their hats to him, and the trick was only discovered when the 'lady' was followed to Messel's room and found to be taking tea there alone.[22] David Herbert (the sharp-eyed son of an earl who spotted the faux pas of the flower vases in Sir George and Lady Watson's Daimler) also made a hobby of cross-dressing; his favourite turn was to dress up in ladies' clothes and, smoking scented cigarettes in a jade holder, take a hired limousine up to London to see a matinée. He encouraged friends to join him, and on one occasion three of them spent an evening as the 'Dolly Sisters', drinking and dancing with unsuspecting men in a bar in Bray.[23]

One important thing Brian Howard and Peter Watson had in common was dubious ancestry; Anthony Powell commented with a dash of snideness that Howard's father had origins that were 'enigmatically imprecise' but 'largely American'.[24] But at least his parents weren't obviously *nouveau*, and his father was not apparently self-made.

No evidence survives of Peter having participated in the Society of Arts. He may have had an interest, but as a boy he hadn't acquired a love of art, still less an understanding. But he understood self-expression. For him, aesthetic and mannerly sophistication were, in combination with his father's money, a bridge into the world of the cultured, civilised classes. He was an outsider, far more so than the poor King's Scholars or Anglo-American sprigs like Brian Howard.

If a boy wanted to stand out for his sophisticated air, he had stiff competition in post-war Eton. The boys, recalled the writer John Lehmann, 'developed our eccentricities together, making fantastical characters out of one another'.[25]

According to another contemporary, Henry Yorke, all these boys who were unable to excel at manly games were retreating into femininity – either literally, in the case of the cross-dressing incidents, or figuratively through self-conscious display. 'We were feminine,' he wrote, 'not from perversion ... but from a lack of any other kind of self-expression. Also we watched the effect we produced on others in the way women do and ... we screamed and shrieked rather than laughed and took a sly revenge rather than having it out with boxing gloves ...'[26]

Peter took a different approach to gaining distinction, similar to that of another contemporary, Ian Fleming, who was the same age as Peter and similarly unable to achieve success through games or cleverness; Fleming cultivated an air of supreme sophistication, opulence (he had his own car) and pomaded dandyism; unlike Peter, he had the misfortune to be in the house of the strait-laced E. V. Slater, who abhorred his entire character. ('I'm going to break you, Fleming,' Slater told him – a remarkable sentiment for a pastoral carer to express to one of his boys.) Also unlike Peter, Fleming hotly pursued girls out of school.[27]

Cyril Connolly also pursued the line of cultivated sophistication, despite having the intellect not to need it. Anthony Powell thought Connolly a 'formidable entity' and noted that he used his physical ugliness as 'one of his several means of imposing a fascination on people'.[28] Connolly's room in College was notorious: young Colleger John Lehmann would recall that 'the perfume of Sin that seemed to rise from it was compounded ... from the curling smoke of Turkish cigarettes, powerful liqueurs produced from secret hiding-places, risqué discussion of avant-garde books ... and lurid stories of the forbidden world of cabarets, night-clubs and dancing girls.'[29] Unlike Peter Watson and most of his contemporaries, Connolly was already thinking beyond the realm of school; he was determined to turn himself into a legend: 'Conviction of his own "genius", that virus of the Twenties', had infected him, according to Powell; he wanted to be 'Baudelaire and Rimbaud, without the poverty and suffering'. Connolly had been told by a schoolmaster, 'You can't be fashionable and first-rate', but he was apparently determined to prove him wrong.[30]

The sophisticated set were quite the wrong sort for a good boy to mix with. Another contemporary, James Lees-Milne, distinguished between two related sets of boys – the intelligent, sensitive boys and 'the enchanting, unserious raffish boys, whose parents were for the most part cosmopolitan and rich'. Lees-Milne, who was one of the former set, yearned to be part of the latter, but 'was in no sense grand or sophisticated enough to adorn their colourful company'.[31]

Peter Watson had managed to make himself one of them; he had the wealth and the sophistication to match them, but his background was insufficiently grand and not at all cosmopolitan. And so he studied his contemporaries and refined his manner. He was exceptionally good at it. Alan Pryce-Jones summed up the way Peter looked upon the world – 'a face lit by inner amusement and a kind of reluctant practicality, the face of a born professional who preferred to be an amateur'.[32] Being an amateur, of course, was the mark of the civilised upper-class man. Meticulously distancing himself from the professional and mercantile classes, Peter affected the weary languor of the aesthete, but 'behind the assumption of permanent slight fatigue a keen mind was working, a keen eye looking'.[33] Later in life he would turn that keenness of vision to productive use; for now it was fully occupied in finding the chemistry that would launder the aroma of margarine from his money and gain him admittance to the leisured upper class.

Sexuality was intimately and intricately tied up with the arts and aestheticism at Eton, and lurked in other areas too, from sport to physical punishment. The constant homosexual undertow of the English boarding school exerted its pull on all boys, for good or ill, whether they were themselves homosexual or not.

Goodhart's house had its own particular sexual flavour. Anthony Powell believed that Goodhart was a closet bisexual, attracted to good-looking boys, 'but not to excess'. 'A touch of kinkiness was added by a fervid preoccupation with ladies' shoes ... which Goodhart made no attempt to conceal.' At the same time, he struggled with the conflicted, phobic view of homosexuality shared by all the masters and most of the boys – he called 'sodomism' the 'most loathsome form of dual vice', and could work himself into a foaming rage if he detected any trace of it (or even a flippant attitude towards it) in his boys.[34] In the exclusively male environment, odd friendships developed, in which the deep bond of youthful companionship was mingled with physical feelings. Younger boys became a substitute for girls, and the prefects and fagmasters would pimp for each other, sending attractive pubescent specimens to each other on bogus errands.[35] Eton, like any other public school, was alive with love affairs and 'more brutal intimacies'. Those boys who abstained did so from personal fastidiousness more than moral distaste; they were all conscious that, 'at best, this was a very makeshift release for those who had other objectives in view.'[36] For the minority of boys whose natural orientation was homosexual, it must have been a confusing environment in which to come to terms with themselves.

Between 1925 and 1927 the environment was made even more confusing by the presence of movie star Tallulah Bankhead – she of the drowsy eyes, sulky beauty and Alabama drawl – who was enjoying a break from Hollywood, acting on the British stage, and had taken a house not far from Eton. Tallulah grew friendly with a number of the boys, including Peter's friend Alan Pryce-Jones, who visited her home, where Tallulah 'gave us a Sunday cocktail before evening chapel', despite the masters who 'lined the streets by her house to protect the morals of the school'. Pryce-Jones and his friend Tony Wilson smuggled themselves past the patrols by hiding under a rug on the floor of a taxi.[37]

Tony, who was nineteen, became romantically involved with Tallulah, which led to a damaging scandal in which it was alleged that the actress had lured several Eton boys to a hotel and had a sexual romp with them. Tony Wilson, despite his age, 'was so worldly,' she recalled, 'so urbane, I was sure he was all of thirty. Those English youngsters confuse you.'[38]

Hardly surprising – they confused each other.

* * *

Peter Watson left Eton at the end of 1926. He had sat his final exams in July, and came 163rd out of 208 boys in his year. He returned for the Michaelmas half, and left at Christmas. He was eighteen years old, and still in the midst of his formative period.

Goodhart had retired by this time, and gone to live in his native Brighton. He passed on his house to a younger master, R. A. Young,[39] a maths master and successful cricketer who refashioned the house in his own image; by 1925 it had begun to build up a small collection of sporting cups. The house must still have been short of boys of sound public school character, though, since it was under Mr Young's tutelage that Peter became a prefect and exercised his cane on bad boys' backsides.

He was captured in a house photograph in 1926: tall and thin behind the row of trophies. His hair was meticulously parted and slick with lotion, his face serious but expressionless, head tilted to one side. The boys around him, in their tailcoats and striped trousers, gazed into the camera with an intimidating array of confident, arrogant expressions.

Some boys gained a lot from Eton, such as James Lees-Milne, who came from a poorer 'philistine background' and was thankful for the friends he made there, and for the induction into 'a love of literature, the arts and above all civilized living'.[40] Peter was quite different; although many of the friends of his adult life were old Eton boys, they weren't his contemporaries. And although his love of music seems to have been a lifelong thing, and might have been encouraged by Goodhart, he played no known part with the Eton artistic set. But what he did undoubtedly acquire was a love of civilised living, and a superlative knack for doing it with exquisite taste.

His sexuality is another matter; it may have been stimulated at Eton, toyed with and titillated, but in an environment where homoerotic behaviour was a many-headed (and only occasionally two-backed) beast, it must have been bewildering for the minority of boys like Peter whose alignment was deeply and permanently homosexual. In that sense, Eton probably didn't give Peter a sense of his sexual identity; that, it seems, came during the next episode in his life, when, along with others of his class and kind, he moved on to Oxford.

4

THE FREEDOM OF THE WORLD

1927–1930

In 1945, during the closing months of the Second World War, languishing in London and frustrated at being unable to travel abroad, Peter Watson sent his friend Cyril Connolly an Egyptian postcard. He entertained himself (and hoped to annoy the censors) by writing it in a mixture of hieroglyphics, Tibetan, Persian, ancient Greek and Arabic. Above a little sketch of a house, labelled in Greek *Οξφόρδ* (Oxford), he wrote in Greek, 'In this house I was born.'[1]

He didn't elaborate, but the allusion was fairly plain. Although Eton had given him the key that opened the door into the cultured upper class, his own true identity was unlocked by a key that he found at Oxford. What Peter seemed to be saying was that his adult self, fully formed and unashamed of either his heritage or his sexuality, came into existence there.

Unlike most of his contemporaries, who were formed by their public schools and would spend the rest of their lives struggling with the baggage they had been encumbered with, Peter Watson stepped out of Eton quite lightly. Perhaps because he was an outsider, an observer and mimic who didn't engage very deeply in the lives and pursuits of his schoolfellows, he didn't become dependent on that world. Connolly had suffered from his schooling; he had become institutionalised, and believed that most of his friends had been wrecked by it. As a young man in the 1930s, he came up with his 'theory of permanent adolescence', which he wrote down memorably in *Enemies of Promise*:

> It is the theory that the experiences undergone by boys at the great public schools, their glories and disappointments, are so intense as to dominate their lives and to arrest their development. From these it results that the greater part of the ruling class remains adolescent, school-minded, self-conscious, cowardly, sentimental and in the last analysis homosexual. Early laurels weigh like lead and of many of the boys whom I knew at Eton, I can say that their lives are over. Those who knew them then knew them at their best and fullest; now, in their early thirties, they are haunted ruins.[2]

Peter Watson went up to St John's College, Oxford, in October 1927. He was nineteen years old and intended to read modern languages.[3] St John's wasn't a popular choice for Old Etonians; of the boys who went up at the same time as Peter, fifteen went to Christ Church, twelve to Magdalen, and about half a dozen each to Balliol, New College and Trinity.[4] Only Peter Watson and one other boy went to St John's.

The influences that governed the passage from public school to Oxbridge were many – family tradition, housemasters' connections, and fashion. Until the 1920s Eton had maintained a relationship with King's College, Cambridge, which amounted to a closed shop. But that was changing; many Oppidans were now choosing Oxford, and some Collegers were too. The same trend was affecting boys at other public schools, although there were exceptions: Cecil Beaton (who had been at Harrow) had bucked the trend in 1922 by choosing St John's, Cambridge (and spent his first days there worrying that he might have chosen unwisely).[5] Some made their choices through necessity. In 1922 the impecunious Evelyn Waugh, who had schooled at Lancing, went to the low-key Hertford College (known mainly for its Bridge of Sighs). James Lees-Milne, who had flirted with the raffish set at Eton, involving himself with David Herbert in the escapade of the 'Dolly Sisters', was denied the chance to go to Cambridge by his choleric father, who 'had run up debts in the nineties', and Oxford was ruled out because 'there were three niggers at Balliol'.[6] Lees-Milne eventually made it to Magdalen with his mother's support.

For most young men it made little difference which college one went to. To those who were interested in social life, the arts, or in personal aggrandisement, collegiate identity had little relevance; these were arenas that cut across college boundaries, and one's college mattered little unless one were a serious scholar. Peter Watson was certainly not that.

Cyril Connolly dreaded the move to Oxford – the rooms at Balliol were less comfortable than those at Eton, and the society seemed colder. Having dealt with the trauma of being sent to boarding school by building up 'a private civilisation of reason and love at a temperature warmer than the world outside', he felt desolate at having it shattered and having to start all over again. 'The world of matey young men with their pipes and grey bags, the blokeries to which we had been allotted, filled us with despair ...'[7]

For Peter, who was perhaps more self-sufficient and loathed being restricted and regimented, the increased liberties of undergraduate life must have compensated for the upheaval. As for having been 'born' at Oxford, it was probably here that he first recognised his homosexuality for what it truly was – an inextricable, inherent part of him. Boys who had taken part in homoerotic play at school through peer pressure or sheer hormonal imperative were freer (though not entirely free) to mix with young women. Alan Pryce-Jones recalled:

> In this life women, and especially Oxford women, played a very small part. We were proud if we found our invitations accepted by Elizabeth Harman or Anne Huth-Jackson, but in general we associated girls with London, and moved in a strictly masculine but not necessarily homo-erotic world. It was *chic* to be queer, rather as it was *chic* to know something about the twelve-tone scale and about Duchamp's 'Nude Descending a Staircase'.[8]

Meanwhile, those like Peter who had been naturally homosexual all along must have become fully aware of this fact about themselves – that they were different from other boys, even from other aesthetes. This might well have traumatised some of them, but not Peter Watson. He was self-confident by nature, and his family's wealth gave him freedom. He would never make any attempt – aside from routine public discretion – to conceal or compromise his sexuality.

The image of Oxford between the wars would always be dominated by the memoirs and novels of the aesthetes – *Brideshead Revisited* being the preeminent example. It was a skewed vision, scarcely representative of the time and culture. The aesthetes and intellectuals were a rare, heady spice which was sprinkled extremely sparingly into Oxford's thick, stodgy meat-and-dumplings stew of rugger-loving, cricketing hearties and dusty, tweedy scholars. For every dainty blossom or screeching queen there were dozens of sportsmen and hundreds of studious young men whose purpose was to get their degrees and go dully to work. Statistically, some of these men must have been homosexual, but they kept it hidden.

When Peter went up to Oxford, much of the gay scene that his immediate predecessors had enjoyed had disappeared. There had been two principal centres. One was the George Restaurant, popular with undergraduates and with homosexual ones particularly. The other, much more vital, had been the Hypocrites' Club; located above a bicycle shop in St Aldates, it was a drinking club for aesthetes – camp, witty, eccentrically dressed and rich. Young men who sought acceptance among this circle – which included people like Brian Howard and Harold Acton – adopted their chic homoeroticism. Evelyn Waugh, who wasn't homosexual but desperately wanted to be accepted by the upper-class aesthetes, was famously seen kissing a male friend there. However, the Hypocrites' Club, having grown too audacious for its own good, was closed down by the university authorities in 1924, and the aesthetes had dispersed.

By 1927 the Waugh generation had moved on and their successors took their aestheticism a little more lightly, but in much the same spirit. They were different from the generation of the First World War. 'We felt ourselves bottled up by our elders, and bored to extremity by their tales of Passchendaele and Mametz Wood,' Alan Pryce-Jones recalled. 'And so part of our silliness was in reaction against the repetition of abstracts like victory, patriotism, never-say-die endeavour. We preferred to make horrible cocktails … of ingredients like Crême de Cacao, Parfait Amour, or Vieille Cure …'[9]

Culturally and intellectually, 1927's Oxford aesthetes spurned the realism, the sentimentalism, the patriotism and the strenuous progressivism of the Victorian and Edwardian eras. Kipling and Galsworthy were shunned, along with Arnold Bennett and H. G. Wells.

The Pre-Raphaelites and George Frederic Watts were spurned, as were Wagner and Elgar, Sargent and Puvis de Chavannes. Ronald Firbank was salvaged from the wreckage of the nineteenth century, and placed alongside the Sitwells. Aldous Huxley, D. H. Lawrence and Gertrude Stein were admired. Many of these would later become personal friends of Peter Watson, but for now they were distant figures of worship. The contemplative music of Erik Satie and the sketchy art of Christian Bérard were in. The enthusiasms which inflamed the Oxford aesthetes were arbitrary and informed as much by fashion as intellect. 'We were utterly inconsistent,' Alan Pryce-Jones wrote. 'We admired El Greco and Delacroix because they were suddenly *chic*, although we rejected in them the sublime at which they aimed. We sought out the small, the rare, the sketch rather than the finished masterpiece.' He went on:

> We were in many ways a silly generation, with the exception of a few stern spirits, such as Wystan Auden, Christopher Isherwood, Stephen Spender, who kept a little aloof and mixed their own blends of medicinal high spirits and rather governessy doctrine. Not that we were silly in the sense of being blinded by the ease of life as displayed by the British and American rich ... By the end of the Twenties, most of us were coming to terms with an impending *Götterdammerung*: it was only a matter of when and from which quarter the blow would fall.[10]

Peter Watson certainly took on the 'silliness' of his generation – at least for a time. Eventually he would migrate towards the 'governessy' set of Auden, Isherwood, Spender and Connolly; but as a nineteen-year-old in Oxford, that change was far in the future, and for a long while he would be as frivolous as the worst of them – while remaining several degrees more chic and elegant than the best.

Of all the things that Oxford might have provided him with, what Peter seems to have got from it is confidence – confidence in his place among the upper class and about his sexual identity. But it gave him little in terms of successful education, and certainly didn't give him a degree. Peter's time at Oxford was short, intermittent and, in academic terms, unfruitful. He went up in October 1927, and came down again a little over two years later, having made several attempts to sit and re-sit his first-year exams.

Information about his time at Oxford is sparse, but his career seems to have paralleled that of Alan Pryce-Jones – in whose final downfall Peter played a part. By the end of his first year at Oxford, Pryce-Jones had become 'uncomfortably conspicuous'. He dined at the George Restaurant, lived beyond his means, had unpaid bills in college, had been reported in the university newspaper, the *Cherwell*, and was 'an eighteen-year-old riding for a fall'. His father was called in to see the college president. He paid his son's college bills, and Pryce-Jones was gated (confined to college after nine in the evening). He treated his reprieve with typical irresponsibility; having made a prior arrangement to attend a dinner-dance outside Oxford, that very first evening he sneaked out of a window and set off across Christ Church Meadow, where he was arrested for trespassing. Having failed to bribe the police constable, Pryce-Jones was hauled off to the cells.

After his release, he managed to hide out in a hotel for a few days, but eventually his mother told him to come home. At this point, his friend stepped in and kindly made things several degrees worse.

> Peter Watson, saying that I could not possibly leave Oxford on a third class one-way ticket, appeared with a Rolls-Royce and drove me to London, insisted on greeting my parents with an air of hearty geniality and left just before the storm broke.
>
> The Rolls-Royce was the last straw. Had it been John Betjeman's Morris Cowley my welcome might have been less blighting.[11]

The university merely rusticated Pryce-Jones for a term, but his parents decided that his student life was over.

Meanwhile, over at St John's, Peter's own career was faltering. At the end of Trinity (summer) Term 1928, he sat Pass Moderations (the preliminary exams for students who were not seeking honours degrees). He failed them all. He came back in Michaelmas Term (autumn) to re-sit them, and managed to pass Greek, Greek history and logic. A few months later he succeeded in passing French.[12] In Trinity Term 1929 he transferred from reading modern languages to philosophy, politics and economics.[13] Returning to Oxford at the end of the year for one more stab at his exams, he didn't pass anything. In four attempts over two years, he'd passed only four first-year tests.

* * *

Peter's persistent failure must have been due to misbehaviour rather than inability. In 1929 he and a fellow undergraduate, the Hon. Hamish Erskine, gave a party in their rooms. It began with lunch, which was followed by what the *Daily Mail* called 'the largest cocktail party ever given'. The festivities ran on all day, and a constant stream of chauffeur-driven cars filled the road outside the college, depositing Bright Young Things in great numbers.[14]

Between failed exams, Peter spent time in Munich at a language school, apparently with a view to improving his German and boosting his performance at Oxford. In practice, what he actually gained was a love of Bavaria and the Alps, along with a stimulating taste of Munich's wildly erotic homosexual nightlife. The scene was in its heyday during the 1920s, and drew priapic, gay young Englishmen irresistibly to it. W. H. Auden, Christopher Isherwood, Stephen Spender and Brian Howard were just a few of Peter's contemporaries who went to Germany and found their kicks among the muscular, handsomely blond working-class German boys who drove a thriving trade in the night-cafés and bars.

Many of these settings were far from decadent in appearance – they were 'plain and homely and unpretentious', according to Christopher Isherwood:

> Its only decorations were a few photographs of boxers and racing cyclists, pinned up above the bar. It was heated by a big old-fashioned iron stove. Partly because of the great heat of this stove, partly because they knew it excited their clients (*die Stubben*), the boys stripped off their sweaters or leather jackets and sat around with their shirts unbuttoned to the navel and their sleeves rolled up to the armpits.[15]

This mode of display became part of the language of homoeroticism; a few years later, Peter would be painted and photographed by Cecil Beaton dressed in exactly this manner, smiling slyly into the lens at the man who desired him beyond all treasure.

Germany and its boys provided an unparalleled freedom for the Englishmen. Christopher Isherwood (writing about himself in the third-person) 'felt a marvellous freedom in their company'. Having hesitated and stammered in English, he 'could now ask straight out in German for what he wanted'.

> At school, the boys Christopher had desired had been as scared as himself of admitting to their desires. But now the innocent lust which had fired all that ass grabbing, arm twisting, sparring and wrestling half naked in the changing room could come out stark naked into the open without shame and be gratified in full. What excited Christopher most, a struggle which turned gradually into a sex act, seemed perfectly natural to these German boys; indeed, it excited them too. Maybe because it was something you couldn't do with a girl ... Maybe, also, such mildly sadistic play was a characteristic of German sensuality; many of them liked to be beaten, not too hard, with a belt strap.[16]

Some of the young Englishmen – certainly including Peter Watson – had learned at school to beat boys and to enjoy it. Most of the Englishmen treated their affairs for what they were – a titillating, liberating entertainment – but a few, such as Brian Howard, fell deeply in love with their German beaux, letting themselves in for a world of heartache years later when the Nazi regime came to power and the war began.

Peter Watson was one of those who took it lightly –a relish added to his enjoyment of the countryside and the culture. Any immediate educational benefit in terms of academic languages was apparently wasted.

And yet he went back to Oxford, term after term. It might have been paternal pressure keeping his nose to the grindstone (or at least pointing in the vague general direction of the grindstone). Sir George Watson clearly valued education, and Peter was the first of his offspring to go to university. Florence had been thrown out of school (apparently for hiring a car to visit Worcester Cathedral without permission) and then married young, while Norman had gone straight from Eton into the army on the outbreak of war.

The university – perhaps because of Peter's apparent determination to pass, perhaps with an eye on Sir George Watson's wealth and influence and his evident willingness to fund academic chairs – had given Peter many chances, but its supply of patience was exhausted. The inevitable news spread among Peter's friends – in January 1930, Nancy Mitford, who had been visiting her boyfriend in Oxford, reported that 'Poor old Peter Watson has been sent down.'[17]

* * *

The end of his university career wasn't the only major change in Peter's life. Immediately after his expulsion and one year after he had come of age, everything altered for Peter Watson. From being merely the son of a tycoon, he became a wealthy man in his own right. And yet his path to riches had some surprising twists in it.

Having felt the onset of old age and sensing the approach of mortality, Sir George Watson had revised his plans for the disbursement of his fortune. In late 1929 he had been diagnosed with bowel cancer, and although it wasn't necessarily terminal, it apparently made him consider the future of his children. He was thoroughly disgruntled by Peter's failure to show any interest in business or any application to his academic studies. Left to himself Sir George might well have given him a reduced inheritance or even cut him out altogether. But Lady Bessie would not let that happen; she believed that her favourite child should be allowed to develop as a connoisseur of the arts, and in order to do so he must have a good financial settlement.

Bessie must have had considerable influence over her husband because, on 6 January 1930 Sir George created a settlement for Peter – an extremely generous one whereby an enormous sum of money was placed in trust for him. With trustees managing it, it should be enough for him to live in luxury for the rest of his life. From his father's point of view, the settlement was a symbolic cutting-out of the wayward son, for when Sir George created a new will some months later, Peter was excluded entirely from it.

Whatever the feelings behind it, the settlement gave Peter the freedom of the world. His trust fund is estimated to have been about £1 million, roughly equal to the share of the fortune Sir George would be leaving to each of his other children. At the rates of return prevailing at the time, the trust would have yielded an annual dividend of about £50,000 – an income that placed Peter among the richest young men of his generation.[18] In practical terms it made him richer even than those with similar incomes, since he had no burdens – no wife, no children, no houses, no legions of servants to pay; no businesses or estates to drain his personal wealth (Sulhamstead, for instance, despite its tenanted farms, always ran at a loss,[19] as did most similar estates, and was kept afloat with cash from Sir George's pocket). All Peter's income was his own to spend. In the unlikely event of his needing more, he could apply to the trustees and they would provide from his fund.[20]

Sir George's settlement on Peter and the new will were undoubtedly precipitated by Sir George's knowledge that he might not have long left in the world. In July 1930, less than six months after putting his signature to Peter's settlement, he was admitted to a London hospital for an operation to treat his cancer. A few days before going under the knife, he signed his new will. Something went wrong; immediately following the operation, he suffered cardiac failure, and on 12 July 1930 he died in the Manchester Street Nursing Home in Marylebone.[21]

His body was taken back to Berkshire, where he was buried at St Michael's Church in Sulhamstead Bannister. His brothers and sister came to the funeral, and Mary Atkinson, Bessie's spinster sister, travelled down from Cumberland, where she still lived in the little terraced house in Workington in which she and Bessie had grown up. Aside from family, the mourners were a colourful mix of Maypole Dairy business associates and members of the Berkshire county set.[22]

Sir George was reported as leaving an estate with a value just north of £2 million with over £800,000 to pay in estate duty. It was divided equally between Norman and Florence. The baronetcy went to Norman, along with a trust fund of £200,000 and ultimate possession of Sulhamstead and other properties. Bessie was left with a trust fund, £10,000 in cash, and life tenancy of Sulhamstead. There were various other bequests to Florence's children (£10,000 each), academia (£10,000 for the National Institute for Research in Dairying at Reading University), servants, tenants, and charities (including £5,000 to the Royal Berkshire Hospital and £1,000 each for the Salvation Army and Dr Barnardo's).[23] In the middle of the will there was a clause stating that his younger son, 'Victor William' Watson, was left nothing because 'adequate provision' had already been made for him.

It can be said with some certainty that the £2 million Sir George was reported to have left was only a part of his whole fortune. According to standard practice at the time (and since), the bulk of his wealth would have been kept in trusts to avoid duty. The £2 million would have been a kind of working capital (one could even regard it as petty cash) used to generate annual income and pay for the running of the houses and estate.[24] The family wealth had been locked in place in 1924, when Sir George sold his share of the Maypole Dairy Company. Since the war, times had become tough in the dairy trade, and Maypole's profits – which had hit a peak in 1919 – went into decline in the early 1920s; showing the same astuteness with which they had built up the business, the Watson brothers got out of it with their wealth intact before Maypole's slippage turned into a fall.[25]

Despite all this careful management, Sir George managed to leave a bit of a mess behind. During the final years of his life, he had been attempting to trade his baronetcy up to a full barony, and had spent tens of thousands of pounds in the attempt. So-called honours-trafficking had been rife in Britain since before the First World War. One of the most prolific brokers – certainly the most notorious – was clergyman's son and professional liar John Maundy Gregory, who made a fortune selling honours and titles on behalf of the Lloyd George government. In 1923 he began negotiating with Sir George Watson for the purchase of a barony. The business was interrupted by the crisis of the General Strike in 1926. At least, that was Maundy Gregory's excuse – in fact he was losing influence in the government, and by 1927 had lost it altogether. Not only that, the sale of honours had been made illegal in 1925.[26] But he carried on taking money from gullible clients, including Sir George, who paid him £30,000 as late as March 1930. Either Sir George was tipped off about Maundy Gregory's real status or became suspicious, because shortly before his death Sir George began demanding his money back. It was eventually returned after his death, when his executor took legal action. In 1933 Maundy Gregory was arrested on suspicion of obtaining money for titles; he went bankrupt and the extent of his honours trafficking scheme came scandalously to light.[27]

Sir George's willingness to hand over such a huge sum illegally to a man of doubtful character can be taken as a measure of how important rank and position were in the rarefied social stratum he had fought his way into, and in which he hoped his children would fit naturally.

In fact none of them fitted entirely; all three were outsiders or eccentrics in their various ways. Norman – or Sir Norman, as he now was – had inherited their father's business drive, and had a passion for long-distance skiing that was entirely his own. He spent part of his inheritance on developing a new ski resort at Lake Louise near Banff in Canada. Cows were imported from Switzerland to make the scenery more Alpine. (Surprisingly, it flourished.)[28] At the same time, Norman's love of aviation, acquired during the war, led to his taking over the chairmanship of an ailing British aircraft manufacturer and knocking it into profitable shape, and from 1934 until his retirement he remained chairman of the Heston Aircraft Company.[29]

Meanwhile, Florence followed her own path, breeding racehorses and Irish wolfhounds. She had adored big dogs since her father had bought her a wolfhound when she left school in 1913; he was called 'Sir Michael of Sheppey' and cost Sir George £5. From that moment Florence's course was set. In 1928 she had divorced her unreliable husband after he ran off with a kennel maid, and she never remarried.[30] Some have speculated that, like Norman, who lived at home with his parents as a young man and didn't marry until well into old age, Florence wasn't attracted to the opposite sex. It may be that Peter was far from alone in his sexual orientation, and that the only thing that distinguished him from his siblings was his refusal to conceal it.[31]

Peter certainly had little else in common with his brother and sister. And there was a touch of irony in the fact that it was he alone who inherited his father's single-minded determination to join the genteel upper class. And, despite the whispers of *nouveau riche* that had surrounded him at school, he succeeded. When he embarked on his new life as a fully independent man of means in 1930, it was with an élan which was all of his own making and exquisitely honed. His wealth was vast, and his life completely unencumbered.[32] He didn't even buy a house or a flat. When in England he stayed with his mother or with his friends. His travels in Germany had awoken a restless spirit in him, and from this moment on, Peter would spend most of his time travelling. He had little liking for dull old, drizzly old London, and the cultural and sexual sunshine of Europe was his for the taking.

5

A SWOON OF ROMANTIC LOVE

1930–1931

Things were working out well for Cecil Beaton.

The summer of 1930 found him on a soaring high. Every strand of his life bore pearls. He was twenty-six years old and the world was opening all its doors for him; his love of photography and devotion to aesthetics had come together, and he was becoming known as a photographer and designer. The previous year, Cecil had made his first trip to America, and Hollywood was already recognising his talent; film stars were posing for his lens and liking the results. His faultless eye for elegance of line and monochrome *chiaroscuro* brought the stars into a new, modern age of sophisticated high-society glamour.[1]

It had been a long and hard journey. Born well beneath the topmost reaches of society, since his schooldays at Harrow and his brief period at Cambridge he had fought his way upwards. During the 1920s, through flair, charm and talent he had become part of the most chic and rarefied circle of the young upper class – the so-called Bright Young People.

In August 1929, the same year as his first visit to America, Cecil had taken his first book project, *The Book of Beauty* – a scrapbook collection of his photos, drawings and writings – to the Covent Garden offices of the publisher Duckworth (recommended to him by his friends Edith and

Osbert Sitwell), where it was accepted on the spot. Now, in summer 1930, *The Book of Beauty* was in production and would soon be out.[2]

Cecil, who had been living in the family home in Sussex Gardens until now, had also found a house of his own upon which to exercise his eye and designing pencil. It had happened quite by accident. He had taken the material for his book down to Wiltshire, seeking advice from his friend Edith Olivier, hostess and mother figure to a generation of artists and writers. His fellow artist and designer Rex Whistler was there too, an almost permanent resident in Edith's house on the Earl of Pembroke's Wilton estate. Cecil was entranced by the air of idyllic rural calm exuded by Rex and Edith:

> At the end of lunch one day, the three of us were sitting at her small round table on the chairs Edith had covered with needlework pictures of the various rectories in which she had lived her full, if secluded, life. We had eaten trout caught from the river outside the bay-window; we had drunk white wine out of Edith's tall green goblets. After strawberries from her garden, and coffee, we were extolling the glories of Wiltshire. I wondered aloud if I could find a cottage nearby, and if I, too, might not be able to achieve this peace of mind?[3]

Edith recalled having heard of a place nearby – a deserted house with a grotto. Cecil insisted that she drive him there immediately. After some searching along winding country lanes, they eventually found the place 'in an utterly isolated, remote, and almost hidden valley'. Cecil fell in love at once. 'Sleeping among the drooping ilex trees stood a small cluster of cedarwood-coloured brick buildings, elegantly faced with stone. From the moment I saw this haunting, haunted sight, in its aura of lazy beauty, I knew Ashcombe would belong to me.'[4] It needed work; the house was uninhabited, and the buildings had been used for storage, stabling, and hatching pheasants. Cecil rented the place and with the help of his friend Michael Rosenauer (a Viennese architect) and a local tweed-clad builder, as well as his own sketchbook and fecund imagination, he began turning it into his ideal country retreat and studio.

With his reputation rising, his first book on the shelves, and his future domestic peace of mind assured, Cecil decided to take a holiday. He chose Vienna, where he joined up with another of his friends, the American writer Anita Loos, author of *Gentlemen Prefer Blondes*. Cecil was aflame with enthusiasm for his new house, and together they searched Viennese antique shops for cheap baroque furnishings. Cecil's aesthetic taste was all his own. He didn't follow the Deco fashion; instead he went for its antithesis: colour and elaboration, either classical or baroque, often trimmed and punctuated with a quirky Punch-and-Judy gaudiness which came from his background in amateur theatricals. His designs were the very opposite of his photographic style.

While in Vienna, Cecil met up with yet another friend; Oliver Messel happened to be something of a rival – a fellow artist and stage designer. Oliver and Cecil were of an identical age, but possessed quite different styles and temperaments (although their sexual orientations were similar and both had taken a youthful delight in dressing in women's clothing). Where Cecil cultivated an air of aloof dignity, Oliver was fun. On first acquaintance, the waspish Cecil had thought Oliver Messel's art 'rather nasty and trashy', although it had 'a good deal of brilliant superficiality'.[5] Unlike Cecil, Oliver had some formal training in art and design; after Eton, he had gone to the Slade School of Art, and was working professionally on costumes and sets for ballets and revues by the age of twenty-one, while Cecil relied on self-study, an assured sense of his own good taste, and a talent for weaving himself into society and gaining patronage. They were different physical types – Oliver's solid build and dark, boyish good looks contrasted with Cecil's slender, delicate form.

During their time in Vienna that summer, the mild rivalry that existed between the two young men would take a new turn, evolving into a deeper and more meaningful sexual jealousy. Oliver had not come to Austria alone. With him was a much younger friend, a fellow Old Etonian who had recently come into a great fortune; Cecil thought him unremarkable – 'a tall, gangling young man, with the face of a charming cod-fish'. His name was fittingly ordinary – Peter Watson.[6]

Cecil had not the slightest apprehension that he was looking at his destiny in that face, no conception of how momentous this meeting would be. Initially Peter Watson appeared in Cecil Beaton's eyes merely as 'a quiet fawn coloured person who on first acquaintance did not strike me as being at all interesting'.[7] It didn't occur to Cecil that his life, which had been going swimmingly until now, was about to turn against him. Everyone has his cross to bear, and Cecil was about to put his shoulder under the one that had been allotted to him.

The lack of interest was mutual. Peter and Cecil were civil to each other, but no more. The three young men went to fêtes and beer halls rather than to the more elevated cultural highlights Vienna had to offer – probably on the lookout for the kind of muscular male company that could be found in Germany's more decadent cities. Cecil, unable to detect anything remarkable about Peter, wondered why Oliver was so interested in him; they were clearly not lovers. 'Do you not think him a bit of a bore?' Cecil asked one day.

Oliver did not. He was not merely interested but intrigued by his new friend – especially by the fact that he was prodigiously rich, and generous with it. He had bought Oliver some very nice books on architecture. But there was more to his interest than that.

Cecil was incredulous. 'Do you *like* him?' he asked.[8]

Oliver's face, ordinarily rather bright and boyish, with an open, innocent way of smiling, was capable of expressing a quite unboyish delight, and it did so now; there was a flourish to his dark, fine eyebrows and a twist at the corner of his mouth.

'Yes,' Oliver said, and winked. Cecil was quite shocked at his 'louche and tarty' manner. A new element in their rivalry was born. Oliver's interest in Peter so intrigued Cecil that it began to stir an interest of his own. Oliver noticed this, and it sharpened his own appetite for Peter.

What Peter himself thought of his companions' behaviour – or if he even noticed it – was never recorded. He was busy enjoying Austria, a place he believed he loved more than any other in the world. At the age of twenty-one he wasn't very well-travelled – Germany and Austria were about the limit of his experience.

Cecil would always remember vividly the precise moment when the cool civility thawed. Peter had agreed to go with him on a sightseeing walk around Vienna's side streets. Travelling down in the hotel lift, they stood in awkward silence. The lift had a mirror, and Cecil, glancing surreptitiously at Peter's reflection, noticed Peter doing the same. Cecil would always recall how 'as I looked at him he shot me a glance of sympathy, of amusement.' The two burst out laughing, and when they emerged from the lift they were walking arm in arm. Cecil traced everything to that glance in the mirror – 'it went straight to my heart – and from that moment I was hypnotized by him.'[9]

Sexually, Cecil Beaton was a man who painted on both sides of the canvas with equal delight (and torment), capable of losing himself in adoration and passion for either female or male. Among the many breakthroughs he had achieved on his second trip to America the previous year, he had lost his virginity, deliberately and calculatedly sleeping with two obliging women in the space of a few days. One was Marjorie Oelrichs; described by Anita Loos as a sort of high-society version of Mae West, Marjorie was 'plump and beautiful' with a voice that was a 'sexy wheeze' and a brain 'like a bag of popcorn'.[10] Cecil's second sexual encounter was with Adèle Astaire, dancer and sister of Fred, who was eight years older than Cecil. He had first seen the lithe but plain-looking Adèle dance with Fred on stage in Birmingham in 1924, and been awestruck – he found her 'so American and perfect and slim and graceful and smart ... I adore her ugly face'.[11]

Neither of these women awoke any feelings of adoration in Cecil. But Peter Watson did; Cecil could hardly tear his gaze away from him.

He would always struggle to describe what it was about Peter that exercised this hypnotic effect. His strange, *jolie-laide* looks, his long body, the lankiness of which was concealed in the fashionably baggy suits he wore. Cecil noted his broad shoulders, and was aroused by his large hands. Like Oliver, he was fascinated by Peter's wealth, and the opulent style in which he travelled, accompanied by a chauffeured Rolls-Royce, a large collection of suits and 'a grand electric gramophone'. Anita Loos 'faded from the picture'; Cecil was interested only in Peter.

Perhaps they recognised something in each other – the ultra-refinement of young outsiders who had made it into society – and the vulnerability that went with it. Each had his disadvantages to bear. Peter's grandfathers had been a farmer and a steelworks manager, whereas Cecil's grandfather, Joseph 'Jossie' Sisson, was even lower down the scale – a village blacksmith – and his Beaton grandfather had made his money in trade.[12] But at least Peter had the compensation of great wealth. Cecil, despite his privileged upbringing, would always have to work for a living.

Oliver and Peter intended to travel on from Vienna to Venice. They invited Cecil, and he needed no persuasion. The three of them took a small house on the Grand Canal, redolent with the dank, genteel squalor of historic Venice. There were only two bedrooms, one of which was a double. With painful civility Oliver and Cecil discussed who should share with Peter (apparently without consulting the man himself).

'Of course you must, Oliver – I don't want to barge in.'

'No, you'd like to – you sleep with him.'[13]

So it went, back and forth. To his lasting regret, Cecil allowed Oliver to take the lead. There was nothing outré about the arrangement – this was an age when men travelling together commonly shared a double bed and thought nothing of it. But in this particular party everyone was acutely aware of the undertone. While Oliver and Peter grew more intimate, all Cecil could do was stew in his jealousy and forage for antiques in the alleyway shops.

The house was suffused with the odours of the Grand Canal, German songs played on Peter's gramophone, and sexual tension. For Cecil, one particular record, played over and over again, 'had a haunting line which became the theme song of my increasing besottedness'.[14] He kept Peter's discarded handkerchiefs 'for their glamour' and purloined a pair of his socks with his name tag inside, which he wore with 'joy and pride'. When Peter was out, Cecil stole into his room and, simmering with sexual frustration, tried on one of his jackets – which he had 'known the look of so well from outside, to know it from inside and to feel the bulge of the handkerchief in the breast pocket'.[15]

He concealed his feelings in front of Peter and Oliver, but felt as if he were wired for electric shocks, which jolted him continually as the days passed. He photographed Peter and Oliver together, he took them to visit Baroness Catherine d'Erlanger – a formidable society hostess with whom he had gained an entrée during a previous trip to Venice.[16] When Peter fell ill with a fever, Cecil brought him white tuberoses, adding their thick scent to the house's canal *mélange*, and hurried home from each day's outings to nurse him.

Cecil's one consolation was that Peter and Oliver did not seem to be growing any closer romantically. He still had hope.

When the time came for Cecil to leave for England, he did so with deep reluctance. Peter and Oliver were staying on for a while, intending to travel back via Florence and visit Alice Keppel (former mistress of Edward VII, now living quietly with her husband in a villa near Florence).[17] But the proofs of *The Book of Beauty* were awaiting his attention, and there was Ashcombe to attend to, not to mention the bric-à-brac he had been sending back from Vienna and Venice.

He departed in an odd mood – the contentment that sprang from the book and the house and his budding love for Peter mingled with apprehension and frustration.

After a while longer in Venice, on the last evening before their departure, something clicked into place between Peter and Oliver. Alone in their double room above the Grand Canal they consummated their relationship.

Later, back in England, Oliver wasted no time in telling Cecil what had happened – that he and Peter were now lovers. Cecil was deeply upset, but not disheartened. He believed that Peter was destined to be his. 'Surely no one could appear so sympathetic and beguiling,' he reasoned, 'unless they were slightly taken by me?'[18] What had begun as a romantic fancy had grown insensibly deep. 'I had never come into contact with anyone with such charm,' Cecil would recall. 'We got along so well together – surely that meant a great deal to him? Of course he was by now wildly intrigued by Oliver – and they saw a good deal of each other – but this didn't prevent me from being utterly overwhelmed …'[19] Oliver, though, seemed to take the relationship lightly, a dog in the Watson manger.

For Cecil, having to observe Peter from the intimate vantage point of a close friend 'made me only more lost in a swoon of romantic love'. He determined that one way or another he would win Peter's love – even if he had to use calculation and manipulation to do it.

* * *

Back in London, Peter resumed his extravagant and irresponsible life. When he wasn't staying in hotels or with friends or when he fancied a period in the countryside, he carried on living at Sulhamstead.

He spent time with Cecil, who began trying to introduce him to art. During their weeks in Vienna and Venice Peter had educated Cecil about music (Cecil admitted to a profound ignorance on the subject, having been unaware, for example, that there was more than one Strauss). Now he returned the favour, taking Peter to the Leicester Galleries, then at the heart of London's modern art world. There Peter took his first close look at a piece of modern painting – a work by Henri Matisse.[20] He didn't record what he thought of it at the time, but it fertilised a seed in him.

Although it made an impression on him, it wasn't enough to make him change his life. Culture was all very well, but for the time being in Peter's immature mind it couldn't hold a candle to opulent living.

In late autumn he took delivery of a new Rolls-Royce he had ordered before the Vienna trip, described by Cecil as 'a vast black and orange thing that he giggled about'.[21] The car was a kind of statement – a splash, a thing to be noticed and talked about. Nancy Mitford, exasperated by his flamboyance, wrote to her brother Tom that Peter 'has just bought a coral-coloured Rolls-Royce inlaid with gems & with *fur* seats. I love him quite a lot but it is no use ...'[22] Perhaps trying to maximise the effect, Peter also took to driving the Rolls himself rather than relying on a chauffeur. His skill left something to be desired, and the danger of being driven by him became almost as much a talking point as the car itself.

His ability, and presumably Oliver's nerves, were put to the test at the end of October, when they drove down to Wiltshire to visit Cecil. The builders had at last made Ashcombe habitable, and it was ready to receive its first weekend guests.

It was a small party – just Peter with Oliver Messel, along with Rex Whistler and Edith Olivier. Rex and Edith, who had been present at the birth of the Ashcombe project, were thrilled with the result, and Cecil revelled in the attention: 'We savoured the chill smells of paint and freshly carpentered wood, combined with the warm smell of calico, new rugs, and crackling log fires.' The once-abandoned, lonely house had become 'unlike any other abode, admittedly fantastic and strange with its bright colours and silver trumpery but to me ... infinitely charming'.[23] It was a magical time and place for Cecil, the young man in love: 'The house seemed to be heavenly and the surrounding countryside lovelier than any I have ever seen since. It was an idyll for me and the presence of Peter made everything that much more outstanding.'[24]

(Edith disagreed – possibly feeling slighted by Cecil's obsession with him, she took a dislike to Peter from the very start, and saw 'no excuse for his presence except as chauffeur'; she thought him 'sinister' and 'gauche'.[25])

Cecil felt that if he could separate Peter from his friends – especially from Oliver – he would surely be able to win him for himself. Accordingly, he had hatched a plan. During that weekend, he coaxed Peter into taking a short walk with him along the steep chalk valley in which Ashcombe lay. They sat on a tree trunk, admiring the view, and Cecil broached the subject. He was planning a return trip to America in the New Year, and would Peter care to come with him? They could visit Mexico, Honolulu – wherever he wished ...[26]

It was a doubly clever plan. Not only would it separate Peter from his friends, it would also put him in a position where he was beholden to Cecil, where he could be dazzled by Cecil's knowledge of the land of glamour and his familiarity with its celebrities and high society. To Cecil's delight, Peter was enthusiastic. He would love to see America, and was charmed at the prospect of doing so in Cecil's company.

With indomitable optimism, Cecil was now sure that Peter would be his, despite the presence of Oliver. Innocent and courteous to the last, Cecil had put the two of them in one of Ashcombe's double bedrooms. On the last morning of their stay, he rose from his bed, full of life and excited by the forthcoming journey back to London (they were all travelling together in Peter's Rolls). He hurried to their room, intending 'to breeze into the double bedroom to wish my friends good morning'. He turned the handle and found, to his dismay, that the door was locked.

There was only one possible interpretation, and Cecil's throat dried and his heart 'went to stone'. Thwarted, cut out, humiliated, he cursed himself for his naivety – 'it was ridiculous of me to put them together and not to expect them to make love – they had done so already before – yet somehow I thought they could not possibly do such a thing under my nose.'[27]

The journey back to London was fraught. Cecil could barely speak, and with his mood and Peter's inexpert driving, the atmosphere in the Rolls must have been tense. (On the Monday, Edith, who wasn't with them but had been driven previously by Peter, wrote an anxious letter to Cecil. She could tell that Peter was 'finding it a strain to drive the car and was made nervous by the wet roads. I hope he got you back safely ... I felt it was rather beyond him, as he isn't yet I expect altogether used to the Rolls – it's a big thing to manage.'[28])

Oliver noticed Cecil's black mood. Later that day, when they were alone together, he asked Cecil if he was very sad. Cecil immediately confessed his love for Peter, and how upset he was about the incident that morning. Oliver, who had apparently intended merely to stick a barb in his rival's side, was astonished by the depth of Cecil's emotion, and seemed genuinely sorry. Cecil could scarcely believe his own feelings – 'it was as if I had contracted some terrific virus.' He could only hope that the voyage to America would make everything right.

* * *

On New Year's Eve 1930, the vast, elegant mass of the ocean liner RMS *Majestic* lay berthed at the White Star Line dock at Southampton, her crew and shore-hands preparing her for departure. This was the same dock from which *Titanic* had set sail two decades earlier. Aboard the *Majestic*, seething with anxiety, was Cecil Beaton, as worried as if he were about to sail on the ship's notorious predecessor.

He had motored down to Southampton, fully expecting to find Peter – who was catching the boat-train from Waterloo – already aboard and waiting in their cabin. There was no sign of him; no luggage, no Peter, just a pristine, unoccupied cabin. Cecil's heart fell, and as the hours ticked away towards sailing time and Peter still didn't appear, he began to despair.

It looked very much as if Peter wasn't going to come; Cecil had given a farewell cocktail party for his friends the previous night, and Peter hadn't turned up to that either. Cecil had telephoned Sulhamstead, but Peter wasn't there. Cecil discovered later that he had decided to spend the last night in London with Oliver – the beastly, jealous rival, who Cecil was sure was deliberately trying to keep Peter from him. Peter had departed London for Southampton in the morning, intending to call in at Sulhamstead on the way ...[29]

Cecil stood on deck, disconsolately watching the comings and goings on the dockside. With only an hour until sailing time, Peter had still not arrived. Gradually all traffic ceased, and the hands prepared to withdraw the gangway. It seemed that Cecil would be travelling to New York alone. Then, at the last possible moment, when Cecil had given up on him, Peter appeared on the dockside, laden with parcels and hastening up the gangway – when he joined Cecil he was 'all giggles'.[30]

Throughout that day, as the *Majestic* steamed towards her first stop at Cherbourg, Cecil never took his eyes from Peter; he watched over him as he lay sleeping in their cabin that night.

It was a six-day voyage to New York, and throughout it Cecil remained fixated on Peter, believing that they would be lovers before this trip was over. He believed also that Oliver had deliberately delayed Peter in London – what a triumph it would have been if Peter had missed the boat.

There were acquaintances aboard, but none of their close friends, and they spent their entire time together. Peter was buoyant, given to hilarity and 'ragging the fellow passengers in a most obvious and rude way'.

There were few of their own kind to socialise with; among their fellow first-class passengers were the popular Irish tenor John McCormack and a few obscure Hollywood people, but for the rest it was a stodgy mix of bankers and industrialists.[31] It was hardly an intoxicating blend.

But the social make-up of the voyage was barely noticed by Cecil, who was full of nothing but Peter. 'Titania was never so besotted of her Bottom than I with my travelling companion.'[32] They walked around the deck arm in arm, they gossiped, talked seriously, played backgammon, or sat in companionable silence. They acquired their own private language and jokes, based on a kind of cod-Tudor courtliness ('Nobody can compare with ye in wytte and kyndlinesse,' Peter would write to Cecil in a later letter[33]), and created many pet-names for one another – Kekil, Cess, Celly-boy and Cee-Cee; Petee, Pitt and Petsy. They stood on the top deck at midnight in the light of a huge moon as the wind whipped the spray into a silvery flume. In the privacy of their cabin they shared baths and tussled together on their beds, and each evening they kissed goodnight. But there it halted. Peter brushed away all Cecil's attempts to steer their intimacy towards romance and sex; he became Cecil's poppet and his sweet, but there was no sex. Cecil wasn't discouraged, and when they disembarked at New York he was as happy as if there had been.

Peter was 'an accomplished and bright traveller,' Cecil wrote in his diary, 'and takes in a place at a glance.' His initial reaction to New York was amusement – 'he laughed uproariously and thought the whole place like a child's place made of toy bricks.' They plunged immediately into the social life of the city. As soon as they were in their hotel suite Cecil called Anita Loos – 'And from that moment a wild rush – both of us in fine fettle ... spruce and dandy. I holding Peter's arm showing him all I could.'[34]

They went with Anita to watch Fred and Adèle Astaire (Cecil's one-time lover) perform at the Ziegfeld Theatre; it was one of the last performances of the musical comedy *Smiles*, which had been a flop and was about to close its run.[35] Cecil and Peter were welcomed backstage, and from there they went on to a speakeasy and a nightclub.

Cecil spent the following days almost constantly on the phone. This was a working trip for him – his social circle of celebrities coincided with his professional circle of photographic subjects. He had an exhibition to arrange, and work to do for *Vogue*, but had been neglecting it in favour of spending time with Peter. Before leaving England he had arranged for a bouquet of lilies and violets to be delivered for his beloved – 'the first definite realization of the fact that I love him very much'. There were social teas with Condé Nast, a visit to Bessy Marbury, the veteran lesbian literary agent (whose clients had once included Oscar Wilde), and another to the house of the banker and art collector Jules Bache. There were drugstore ice creams on Broadway and black dance bands in Harlem.

And everywhere there were celebrities. Cecil couldn't get enough of them; they were a personal delight and the lifeblood of his career. A few days after he and Peter arrived in New York the film star Tallulah Bankhead – the exotic associate of Peter's schooldays at Eton – returned aboard the *Aquitania* from her period immersing herself in British theatre and high society. In the demi-mondes of Piccadilly and Broadway it was rumoured that she had been deported for her behaviour – particularly the alleged seduction of Eton schoolboys.[36] Cecil was well acquainted with Miss Bankhead; he had photographed her, and had included her in *The Book of Beauty*; his summing up was a typical blend of honey and acid – her luscious face was 'accentuated by the superfluity of make-up – for this silver-blonde's *maquillage* is done in a most baroque manner'; her cheeks 'are like huge acid-pink peonies, her eyelashes are built out with hot liquid paint to look like burnt matches, and her sullen, discontented, rather evil, rosebud of a mouth is painted brightest scarlet and is as shiny as Tiptree's strawberry jam'.[37] Tallulah had come back to the States to star in a new talkie. She denied that she had acquired an English accent, and 'declared that her "Alabama drawl" had helped to win her success in England'.[38]

Peter, it seemed, despite the air of frivolity in which he had begun the voyage, and which had continued through the early days in New York, began to find the whirlwind somewhat hollow and stupefying. He would never acquire Cecil's addiction to celebrities, and told him that he 'would go mad in this place' if he were here for long. At bedtime, when they rode up together in the 'scented glitzy elevator' or when they dressed together in their room, Cecil craved Peter's body – its almost emaciated thinness 'with minute hips and long flagpole legs, but strong with flat wide shoulders and torso' and those big, strong hands.[39]

He knew that Peter had been getting around New York on his own, seeing people Cecil didn't know. He was also finding Cecil's over-attentiveness wearing and boring. Cecil sensed this, and was embarrassed.

'Lover situation unsatisfactory,' he wrote; 'outward trappings of poppet and my sweet ... but no real spark except on my side ... I pay no attention to anyone else at any party. I sigh and moan to myself when alone.' His confidence that he could win Peter's love was crumbling. 'I mustn't be a fool,' he wrote, 'it's nonsense to give everything – the more you do the more they loathe and despise you.'[40]

It was time again to lever Peter away from the social crush and get him alone. From New York they travelled south by train, eventually making their way to Mexico via the Caribbean. They spent time in Palm Beach, Jamaica, Haiti and Havana. Nothing changed, except for the worse. By the time they reached Mexico the relationship had grown brittle with tension. Cecil found himself living in a constant state of uncertainty and jealousy. Peter would go out alone, refusing to say where. But although he claimed to be irritated by Cecil's attention, he didn't like it when the attention went elsewhere. One day, when they were walking on the beach in Haiti, Cecil was accosted by a group of holidaying debutantes who knew him by reputation, and Peter was suddenly, unreasonably angry, falling into a morose sulk.

At other times, Cecil would arrange for them to dine with acquaintances, only for Peter to cry off at the last moment. 'I'm not going to that dinner tonight,' he would suddenly announce in the lazy Oxford drawl that Cecil suddenly found irritating. 'I can't face it – I've got a headache.' Cecil would have to make excuses, confining his fury to his diary – 'oh the ungratefulness of the bastard!'

It had all gone wrong. During the voyage from England and the rail journey down from New York, Cecil had delighted in watching Peter sleep, lying close to him, sketching a portrait of him. Now the sight disgusted him. 'Peter asleep – how I loathed him – sleeping looking hideous like a pig – head leaning far backwards – huge fluffy fat mouth open. I hated – hated – hated him.'[41]

And yet he couldn't let go. Peter's cruel indifference repelled but also magnetised him; one night in Palm Beach they had talked until late while Cecil worked on some drawings for *Vogue*; it was one of the very rare occasions when Peter spoke about his time at Eton. He told Cecil about being a prefect and beating the bad boys. 'I was very impressed,' Cecil wrote, apparently with a frisson of masochistic arousal; 'so commendable.'[42]

Meanwhile the weather turned bad. In Haiti Cecil suffered 'the despair of whisky sodden colonials ... the rain has been pouring – wind blowing and I am left alone – no one here I know – no one to confide in and I am really miserable. Peter quite insensitive to why I am temperamental – I long to loathe him permanently but can't – I long to love him but it will never be a success.' By the time they reached Havana, Cecil had decided that he was no longer in love, and no longer miserable: 'It only annoys me to realise how badly I have played my cards.' He had been wrong about Peter – 'he is charming with a delightful taste and sense of humour' but 'he loves no one – he is fond of no one – he despises people who are too nice.' Working himself into a frenzy of deprecation, Cecil concluded that Peter only liked 'ruthless people who make their own way over others' and that he was 'independent, selfish, rude, insolent, conceited – young and silly and completely unimportant' and a 'fickle, facetious cad', but at the same time 'secretive as the grave' and 'a braggart'. In short, Peter Watson was everything and nothing to the lovelorn, tormented Cecil.

* * *

Santa Fe, an unimpressive trail town between the edge of the Sangre de Cristo Mountains and the New Mexico desert, had once been a blessed haven for migrants who had survived the dangerous trails through Indian country. Now, in March 1931, only eighty years on from the days when the westbound wagon trains used to roll in from the great trails, it was a haven for one very rich eastbound Englishman.

Peter was alone at last. He had left Cecil behind, and was on his way home. The mainline railroad didn't come through Santa Fe, but since the turn of the century the town had developed a community of artists and writers. Peter made a stopover, took a room in the La Fonda hotel – a huge Pueblo-style place in white adobe that was a hangout for local artists – and liked what he found there (including an unnamed 'marvellous Indian painter'[43] – his earliest recorded enthusiasm for an individual artist).

He was still smarting from his last contact with Cecil. Their journey together since leaving England had been a long and sometimes arduous one. New York had been exciting but bewildering; the Caribbean an emotional torment of gaiety alternating with misery, and by the time they reached Mexico things were positively sordid.

Peter had grown weary of acting a part in Cecil's self-directed drama of love, alternately the object of adoration, of jealousy, and of petulant loathing. He had enjoyed Cecil's company more than Cecil had appreciated, and even after it reached the limit of tolerability in the Caribbean, Peter's affection for him still held, and he gave him one more chance. 'I *adored* Haiti too,' he jotted on a postcard while they were sailing to their next destination, 'but you mustn't really be so naughty in Jamaica as you are being on the boat.'[44]

In Nassau Cecil had become worse: sulky and depressed. In Mexico they spent some time driving through the mountains, but the crisis came when it was time to travel north to California. They had heard horror stories about Mexican planes, and on the day before they were due to fly, Peter got cold feet. Cecil was 'dumbfounded, aghast'; he had work to do in Hollywood, and *had* to take the flight, but Peter refused. Not only that, Peter didn't offer to pay for Cecil's ticket (despite apparently having paid for the whole holiday thus far). Fuming, Cecil went by train.[45]

Peter joined him in Hollywood four days later. They got on equably for a short while, mixing with members of the Hollywood set whom Cecil was photographing – Gary Cooper, Fay Wray, Loretta Young and Lillian Gish. Mary Pickford – 'America's Sweetheart' – invited them to an intimate dinner at Pickfair, the mock Tudor mansion in Beverly Hills she shared with her husband, Douglas Fairbanks.[46]

But soon Cecil's neediness pushed Peter away again. And then he made the grave error of writing Peter a letter describing all his woes and hardships, all his grievances; and he compounded his error by making the even worse mistake of talking indiscreetly to several friends about Peter, including Adrian Greenberg (known to the world simply as 'Adrian'), the celebrated costume designer for Greta Garbo, Jean Harlow and Joan Crawford.

That did it. Peter had finally had enough; not only of Cecil's clinging and self-pity, but also the tactic of cold-shouldering he had begun to adopt in a clumsy attempt to play hard-to-get. Peter insisted that they leave Hollywood and begin heading for home. They travelled by train as far as the Grand Canyon, but then Peter went on alone, leaving Cecil to make his own way to New York.[47]

In Santa Fe Peter found the peace and quiet to think the situation over. He was never a vigorously communicative man, as Cecil had noted many times; in high emotional states he preferred to withdraw and think things over – or brood – a trait that had contributed to Cecil's view of him as stand-offish and cold. In his hotel in Santa Fe, Peter sat down and wrote Cecil a letter of measured, considered anger. 'I was too angry after I received your letter to reply to it right away,' Peter wrote. 'I am puzzled by imagining what satisfaction you could have from it. You must realise how absurd it was. I am really not a recalcitrant housemaid to be snubbed and written to in such a manner.' What seemed to hurt most was Cecil's underestimation of Peter's own feelings. Peter thought of Cecil as a valued and loved friend – whereas Cecil seemed to be revealing himself as a careless, manipulative would-be lover. Peter went on:

> The whole question of my affection, admiration, respect for you is too absurd to go into. My respect is certainly not increased by this last behaviour. You know perfectly well I have always had affection for you. Your own technique has made it uncommonly difficult for me to deal with you, such as your never talking to me if anyone else is about, never telephoning to me but always leaving it for me to do ...
>
> Friendships do not fade away as you say they do. I have behaved far more as a friend to you than you have to me.

The power in this relationship still resided with Peter, and the conclusion of his letter confirmed it.

> Yes, my boy, you just spend a few days alone and think it over and then write me an apology to London.
>
> Until you do this you cannot be happy because it is most important for you not to be on a false basis with me. This causes you to pile on my head the blame for many things in your life ...
>
> We all have our tragedies. I have just as many as you, perhaps more, but we must all solve them ourselves. This entails compromise which can be employed without losing integrity. If we cannot see ourselves as victims of others we have to realise we are victims of ourselves.

(Quite what Peter felt his own 'tragedies' were, he never said, but from the context one might infer that they were romantic.)

Peter was also vexed by Cecil's gossiping. 'I have never done this about you or about anyone else in my life. This cheapens you and me in the eyes of the world.' He finished with a pointed reminder that 'the sentiment of love is a very much subtler and more complicated thing than you give it credit for.'[48]

* * *

They met again precisely where their journey had started – on the dockside at Southampton. Peter travelled down with Cecil's sisters, Nancy and Baba, to meet him when he sailed in on the SS *Europa* on 5 April.[49]

Cecil had wept himself to sleep each night after Peter left. In New York, he had gossiped acidly about him to all his friends, and was encouraged when they joined in. But he was tired when he disembarked at Southampton, having not slept at all the night before. They were civil to each other – 'How are ye?' Peter asked, reviving their private joke – but when he told Cecil that he had hardly seen Oliver since his return, and that indeed Oliver had written saying that he never wanted to see him again, Cecil was unmoved.[50]

At least, he tried to be. A short while later, he lunched with Oliver. Together they picked over Peter's faults. Oliver reiterated what he had said in his letter – 'I never want to see him again – he's so vague and casual and conceited.' Cecil, perhaps seeing himself in Oliver, didn't believe it for a moment; indeed, as soon as Oliver saw that Cecil and Peter were still friends, his jealousy stirred and he began to want 'proprietary rights' again. One evening, Cecil implored Oliver 'to give Peter up for me', but this was the worst possible line to take with Oliver Messel. 'He couldn't help being first and foremost a bitch – he does not wish to make anything better and so the time passes with my trying to keep these two apart without making myself guilty of any real mischief.'[51]

Cecil didn't merely want Peter – it was as if he wanted to *be* him, to meld with him. Unconsciously he adopted Peter's mode of dress, his poise, his manner of speaking. He overheard his sisters remarking that they spoke so alike, 'we were virtually indistinguishable on the telephone.'[52] Nancy and Baba weren't the only ones to notice this chameleon transformation; some claimed that it had even affected his physical form, the couturier Charles James commenting, 'It's extraordinary: you used to have a rump like your mother – rounded and curved – now you've got a flat backside like Peter Watson.'[53]

Such an obsession couldn't be shed easily. Peter was very fond of Cecil, and having made peace with him after the return from America, he believed that they could continue as friends – close, intimate friends – but no more. He even admitted that he had behaved badly towards Cecil in America.

And yet there was a deep fissure of misunderstanding between them. For Peter Watson, a close friendship could be physically intimate without being sexual – which wasn't unusual among men at this time, whether homosexual or heterosexual – but his personal boundary where intimacy transitioned into sex was idiosyncratically located, far closer to sex than was generally regarded as proper, and Cecil was probably not the first and certainly not the last to misjudge it. He blamed everything on Peter's capricious temper; and so, when the intimacy resumed, poor Cecil believed that so had his chances.

6

PINING FOR GRANDEUR

1931–1933

Peter Watson was, in Cecil Beaton's view, 'the most unperturbed bastard'; he was 'uninfluenceable' and, Cecil added with his heart breaking, 'I shall never alas be his lover.'[1] It was the end of October 1931, and Cecil was aboard ship again, sailing for New York, alone this time, brooding over the summer just past.[2]

It had seemed to start so promisingly, with a trip to Paris; they shared a bed, and Peter was kind, but he kept the two rivals – Oliver and Cecil – simmering throughout the summer. He involved himself in the social calendar, attending Ascot, going to the opera, and spending time with his family at Sulhamstead.

He was rarely happy there as an adult – sometimes in his youth he had been driven to go abroad just to get away from his family. Although he loved his mother, the atmosphere within the family, which was composed of individuals with strong, largely incompatible personalities all pulling in different directions, could be extremely tense.

Lady Bessie was finding life as a widow somewhat restricted; while Sir George had been alive, the couple had stayed in hotels – Claridge's or the Carlton – when visiting London,[3] but that must have seemed less proper now that Bessie was alone. Accordingly, she intended to buy a house, and Peter, as her favourite and rather more apt to urban living than his brother, helped her to choose.

Between his family, Ascot and all the other calls on his time, Peter travelled and spent time with Cecil. At Ashcombe, which Cecil was turning into a nexus for the young generation of aesthetes and artists, Peter was the most welcome guest, but also the least reliable. Following the trip to Paris, Cecil arranged a weekend party, planning it so that Peter should be the first to arrive: Cecil would meet him romantically at the top of the downs and escort him back to the house, which had been made ready for the party. In fact Peter motored down late and was the last to arrive. He missed the tomato juice and cocktails, and dinner was eaten without him. While Cecil and his friends (including Lord Berners, the humorist and gossip, who observed the relationship between Peter and his homosexual male friends closely and with great amusement) were playing party games upstairs, the horn of Peter's Rolls was heard honking in the courtyard. Cecil went down to greet him, and found him in the darkened dining room, picking at leftovers, chuckling to himself.[4]

Cecil recalled what Christabel Aberconway (another of the guests) had said earlier – 'Oh how lovely it would be to walk in the moonlight on the top of the downs' – and after everyone had gone to bed, he and Peter slunk off into the darkness. They walked for hours under a bright moon, and it was four o'clock before they returned to the house. Like errant schoolboys they raided the larder for ginger cake, and Peter remarked that they had better watch what they ate, since they would be sharing a bed. Cecil felt a thrill of anticipation. After a hot bath, he took Peter to his bedroom.

It was a fantastic room, and Cecil was immensely proud of the design that had gone into it. It was decorated in a vivid circus theme, with harlequins and animals on the walls, fabulous furnishings and a striped pole as a picture rail. The centrepiece was an incredible circus-themed bed: pelmeted, curtained, with carousel poles as posts and carved, painted horses and fantastical patterns at the head and foot. Cecil, who was practised in the art of self-portraiture, took many photographs of himself with his circus bed, sometimes reclining on its pillow, sometimes in costume, and on one occasion in his gingham dressing gown, sitting at the foot of the bed, a half-smoked cigarette in one hand, gazing down with smouldering, possessive longing at Peter, fully dressed in suit and tie, who looked inscrutably back at him.

That night, after bathing, Peter and Cecil gossiped and giggled in the circus bed, and 'fought gaily', tickling, ravaging the bedclothes. Cecil worried in case Christabel, sleeping in the next room, should be woken by their squeals. Afterwards he and Peter lay blissfully in one another's arms. But still there was no sex. Nonetheless, Cecil was 'almost completely happy – as completely as I ever will be with this poppet'.[5]

The next night, Peter went with Cecil's sister Nancy to visit the Melchetts;[6] Cecil waited up for Peter's return, with the circus bedroom lit with candles, sleeping drowsily, but 'each time I woke there was no poppet'. Getting up in the middle of the night, he discovered Peter in the bedroom which had just been vacated by his sister Baba. The poppet was fast asleep, naked as a suckling pig. Cecil returned sadly alone to his circus bed, consoling himself with the thought that he could take Peter his pyjamas in the morning and wake him with a kiss.

* * *

In August, Peter and Cecil set off together on another grand trip. They started at St Moritz, where they again walked arm-in-arm in the moonlight and cuddled in bed last thing at night and first thing in the morning.[7] Cecil, who had resolved not to pressurise Peter any more but to let things flow naturally, was blissfully happy. In the ice cream-pink hotel bedroom Cecil marvelled at how good he looked in his scarlet pyjamas, his skin browned and hair curled by the sun, and his poppet in his arms.

From St Moritz they motored to Germany, stopping off for an idyllic picnic in a Bavarian mountain meadow. As they drove 'through Wagnerian mountain passes, through lush fine woods of extreme delicacy, through musical comedy rickety villages with a million highly coloured flowers in window boxes', Peter was radiant; he 'sniffed every nuance of every smell – he was so happy – he likes this country more than any other in the world'. Peter even took delight from the sight of a farmer struggling to control a wayward cow. 'Gracious,' he said as they passed the scene, the cowbell jangling, 'and I believe it's a bull too!'

'Is it?' Cecil asked.

'Yes, I think I saw some balls!'[8]

He was enjoying himself immensely. Peter loved Germany – especially Bavaria and the Alpine country; he loved it so much, he was reluctant to notice the shadow that was creeping across it in those early years of the 1930s.

A shadow was falling between Cecil and Peter too as their holiday progressed. Cecil's ardour was growing – he thought Peter 'looked stunning and had more male chic and grace than ever – there seems to be nothing inside the baggy long trousers. The coat hangs in straight lines from very broad shoulders, hands are enormous.' Cecil – who since his teens had made himself the very embodiment of male elegance – felt inferior and ungainly beside him. He was impressed by Peter's culture, too – his ability to sit through five hours of Wagner with unbroken concentration and a connoisseur's ear – 'completely unlimited in his interests and knowledge'.[9]

In Munich, to Cecil's dismay, Peter plunged into the nightlife – the beer halls and cabarets where liaisons with young men could be arranged. Neither Cecil nor Peter was a stranger to the sexual underworld, but the last time they'd delved into it, it had been as mere acquaintances, with Oliver between them. Now Cecil 'felt nervous and sick in trepidation' at the thought of going to the 'queer places' – 'I hate going to these sort of places with anyone I like and I was anxious in case I should be made agonisingly jealous or furious.'[10]

Over lunch one day, Peter tried to explain his feelings to Cecil. He was deeply fond of him, and appreciated his kindness. Oliver, by contrast, was naughty and bitchy (which made Cecil 'swoon with delight'). That evening, when they went out to the 'night haunt' – which to Cecil's surprise turned out not to be sinister but 'a dark brown room filled with pipe smoke and jolly pub people' – Cecil was so pleased, he didn't even mind the presence of the young 'boyfriend' Peter picked for the night.

But by the end of the holiday, and more so as the summer progressed, Cecil slumped back into despondency, still unable to give up the hope that Peter would become his lover, and still unable to make it happen.

* * *

Peter, meanwhile, taking a lead from Cecil, had become fixated on selecting a home and furnishing it – not yet for himself, but for his mother. By the end of November Lady Bessie had settled on 36 South Street in Mayfair, just off Park Lane. It was a relatively modest four-storey townhouse, disproportionately tall and thin, as if the swollen magnificence of the mansion at number 38 was squeezing it hard against its neighbour. Peter took upon himself the task of decorating and furnishing it, and although it belonged to his mother, it was in effect Peter's house; he moved in, while Lady Bessie went on residing at Sulhamstead.[11]

'I pine for grandeur,' he wrote to Cecil, who was in New York on one of his working trips. Peter was thinking of the places he had seen that year – from the scaled-down splendour of Ashcombe to the grandiose mansions of Beverly Hills, the apartments of New York and the palaces of Munich. He declared that when he took a house of his own it would have to be larger than 36 South Street. Even so, he despaired of filling his mother's house up; there just weren't enough beautiful things to go round. 'I was in an antique shop yesterday,' he told Cecil, 'fancied a piece, in sallied the Queen and snicked it. Imagine Her August Majesty & I tussling!'[12]

He also asked Cecil to send him some records from Marconi's, including two of 1931's hits – 'White Heat' by Leo Reisman and his Orchestra, featuring Fred Astaire, and 'Can't You See' by Paul Whiteman (the 1920s 'King of Jazz', who commissioned Gershwin's 'Rhapsody in Blue' and made its first recording). This would become a regular part of their friendship over the years; Peter's hunger for music – especially for avant-garde and jazz – couldn't be satiated from the shops in London, and whenever Cecil was in New York, Peter would send him a cheque for £10 and ask him to pick out ten records. On this first occasion, the choice seems almost calculated to taunt Cecil – the lovelorn lyric of 'Can't You See (How I Love You)' could have been written specially for him.

Inside, Peter was yearning for an aesthetic satisfaction which his mother's house and London's music could provide. He had just that evening come from a performance of William Walton's new cantata, *Belshazzar's Feast* (receiving its London premiere conducted by Adrian Boult and broadcast live on the BBC). 'It is glorious fun,' Peter wrote, 'the end left me sopping wet', and yet he longed 'for one minute's romanticism' among the dazzle and drama, because 'one mustn't starve the soul, must one?'[13] He was in a flighty, fidgety mood. 'Oh I envy you so terribly,' he told Cecil. 'I pine to come out and join the *dazzling* society in N.Y.' (This was a change from January, when he'd felt he'd go mad if he were there for long.)

With *Belshazzar's Feast* still clashing about in his brain, Peter was reminded of a sight he'd seen recently, and he couldn't resist twisting Cecil's jealous tail with it. He had been granted a preview of Oliver's set designs for a new production of Offenbach's *opera bouffe*, *La Belle Hélène* (restyled for the modern age as *Helen!*); it was due to open at the Adelphi in January. Peter told Cecil that he thought Oliver's designs marvellous. So did the critics; nobody seemed to share Cecil's snide opinion that Oliver's style was showy and trashy.[14]

But although he liked to tweak Cecil's feelings from time to time, and never hesitated to put him down if he thought he deserved it, Peter loved him. And although Cecil copied Peter's style and manner, Peter less obtrusively imitated Cecil's sense of decor. Thanking him for a weekend at Ashcombe, Peter admired its beauty – 'oh but Cecil how disheartening for me. How can I expect to arrange my house so charmingly ... Bless you my sweet and *please* ask me again.'[15]

Cecil scored a point when he gave Peter a clock for the new house in South Street. 'Dearest Celly-boy,' Peter enthused, 'I can only gaze and gaze at it more and more ravished ... and it is certainly far the nicest thing in the damned house and always will be. Bless you – you are so sweet sometimes!!' (Only sometimes.) Giving Cecil his 'dearest love', he admonished him: 'You are *not* to give me expensive gifts.'[16] (This prohibition evidently didn't go the other way.)

From the very beginning Cecil had confided his feelings about Peter to one of his closest acquaintances, Stephen Tennant. Son of a Scottish baron and, some said, the brightest of the Bright Young Things, Tennant had been a vital stair in Cecil's climb into the high reaches of the fashionable set, and they had become intimate friends. They resembled each other as closely as brothers – Stephen's gracile features were fashioned from the same fine porcelain, and his wilting gaze was the very model for every fashionable young aesthete of the age. Cecil had told Stephen all about Peter in the rush of his first infatuation, and Stephen was duly titillated. 'He sounds perfect – I adore little behinds too – and am always drawing sailors with tiny tight behinds like terriers.'[17] He longed to meet the owner of this exquisite seat for himself, and accordingly Cecil took Peter over to Wilsford Manor, Stephen's country home, which was close to Ashcombe.

Like Cecil, Stephen was a keen artist and designer, but like Peter he had an inherited fortune and didn't need to work (although his income, at about £15,000 a year, was a mere third of Peter's).[18] They had other things in common, including being the object of the obsessive love of an older man: in Peter's case the slightly older Cecil, in Stephen's case the much older Siegfried Sassoon, who was twenty years Stephen's senior and absolutely in love with him. (Unlike Peter with Cecil, Stephen had a sexual relationship with Siegfried.)

Peter and Stephen took to each other right away. Stephen was charmed, and undoubtedly found Peter's rear as tight and adorable as he'd anticipated, and Peter was bowled over by Stephen. (He was as acutely aware as Cecil how important Stephen Tennant was among the fashionable upper class, and this may have influenced his admiration.) As soon as he got home Peter wrote to Cecil to thank him; he'd found Stephen 'absolutely marvellous. I adored him. It was a great treat.'[19] Tennant didn't always inspire such affection; people were divided between those who adored him and those who found him spoiled, pretentious and narcissistic.[20] Peter Watson was in the former camp, and that first encounter was the beginning of a long and affectionate (though probably not sexual) friendship.

The same could be said of his relationship with Cecil – although it wasn't for want of Cecil trying. Even after years of close friendship, poor 'Celly' struggled to understand what it was about Peter that so captivated him. He was 'shy and childish about telling anyone his plans or private thoughts'. And his physical attractions were as puzzling to Cecil as they were to everyone else. Years later, Peter's friend Lord Berners was asked by somebody 'if Peter Watson had been very beautiful in his youth'? Berners replied ironically, 'My dear, he is just as beautiful today as he has ever been.'[21] In Cecil's eyes Peter was 'the most exquisite and lovely looking person I have ever met. His looks seem to me to be abstracted contemporary ... He is hideous often but possesses beastly beauty that is subtle and so much more important than pink cheeks and eyelashes – and his buttocks, leanness and long stringy legs and arms, buttery neck and big hands make for me the ideal.' Cecil also marvelled at how Peter had grown since that first summer in 1930 – 'He seems to have developed so much character and a great deal of knowledge.'[22] This change in character and knowledge would gradually send Peter down a path in life that would deviate from Cecil's.

Besides weekends at Ashcombe, the two friends travelled together. And Cecil still wished – with a forlorn desperation now – that romance would bloom. As Peter grew more attached to Cecil, he was more willing to endure his moods and jealousies and other foibles, but as he grew insensibly away from him intellectually, the friendship continued to be strained – sometimes explosively.

In summer 1932, at Peter's suggestion, they travelled to Paris, Barcelona and back to their old haunts in Venice. Along the way there were parties with friends at Le Touquet and Monte Carlo, a Manet exhibition in Paris, visits to Cannes and Parma. Peter, who enjoyed his affectionate intimacy with Cecil, continued to indulge it, only to recoil in unguarded moments when he felt that Cecil had crossed a line. Lying on their bed one day, Cecil took a tuberose stem, and tickled and stroked Peter's skin with its delicate white petals – the soles of his feet, his hairline, 'the creases where the arm bends, the folds in the eyelid ... the hands – the breasts and flat hard tummy.'[23] In the mornings, Cecil studied Peter asleep, 'twitching like a dog – agonised jerks of arms and legs', unconsciously moistening his mouth and dilating his nostrils as he began to wake; and then his eyes would open and see Cecil scrutinising him. 'Go away,' he would say peevishly. In the evenings, if Peter went out alone – as he often did – Cecil would suffer physical pain, constantly back and forth to the lavatory.

In Venice, where the crowded epicentre of the summer social scene was to be found, Cecil's jealousy came to a head. On 29 August, Lady Diana Cooper gave a big party on one of the islands to celebrate her fortieth birthday. Among the guests were Peter, Cecil, and Oliver Messel, in company with Randolph Churchill. The trouble started with a scene that had nothing to do with any of them. There was an incident between English baronet Sir Richard Sykes and Miss Doris Duke, a sly-eyed, captivating nineteen-year-old American tobacco heiress. Some days earlier, Sykes had attempted a fumble with Doris in her car. Unable to make him desist, Doris had had her chauffeur stop the car and throw the lecherous young baronet out into the road. Sykes was furious, and at Lady Diana's birthday party, brimming with spite, he deliberately burned the back of Doris's hand with a Lucky Strike cigarette (one of the brands her father's American Tobacco Company manufactured). Randolph Churchill, who also fancied Doris and, like everyone else, had been drinking heavily, leaped violently to her defence.

There must have been something more than booze in the atmosphere that night, because the fight between Churchill and Sykes instantly escalated into an all-out wing-ding brawl. Lady Diana recalled that 'wives were clinging to their men to stop them joining in.' Amidst the violence, Cecil Beaton seized the opportunity to slake his jealousy, which had been stoked up all year by Peter's rebuffs and his enthusiastic praise for Oliver's set designs; the tender bloom of Ashcombe leaped into the fray with claws and fists flying. Lady Diana, who might have been expected to lament her ruined party, was impressed: 'Oliver Messel and Cecil Beaton were fighting like bears,' she recalled, 'and, as I thought, doing *splendidly*!'[24]

Peter and Cecil travelled on for a few days. When the time came for them to part and for Cecil to head back to England, Peter was 'sullen and mulish'. He asked carelessly, 'What are your plans?'

Cecil replied that he supposed he would leave by the six o'clock train that day. He hoped that Peter might – like all his other friends – implore him to stay on, but Peter was silent. Receiving no reply, Cecil asked outright, 'May I stay?' Peter didn't object, and so they had one last – surprisingly happy – evening together. The next day Peter came with him to the railway station. As the train pulled in, Cecil felt cold and tearful. Inside, he still told himself, 'Peter is so devoted to me, but the outward forms are never shown.'[25] They waved as the train drew away – 'We held our arms high, too sad to wave,' Peter's figure dwindling to a sliver.

Feeling 'forlorn and wretched at the prospect of returning home' to a house where it would be cold, with the leaves blowing in through the windows, Cecil stopped off at Le Touquet, where he stayed at Maison Elisa, the villa belonging to Syrie Maugham (ex-wife of W. Somerset Maugham). There he wrote Peter an apologetic letter. 'I loved our holiday so much. You were so sweet and kind and I can't thank you enough for being so divinely generous.' He hoped they could do it all again sometime. 'Please dearest Petee let's always be friends – I shall try not to make it difficult.'[26]

On Peter's birthday, Cecil's anxious jealousy returned. 'I wonder where he is by now and who with – I dread to think who may have taken command as soon as I left.'[27]

Peter had travelled on via Trieste, where he had a brief encounter with his brother, Sir Norman, then Germany and Austria. When he reached Landeck, in the Austrian Tyrol, he received Cecil's letter.

His reply was equivocal. For the sake of love, he was perfectly willing to forget all the clinging and the pettish sulks, but since leaving Venice he had discovered that Cecil had been blabbing about him again, and had chosen as his confidante the elderly American-born Princess Jane di San Faustino, a notorious gossip. 'It really was terribly unwise of you,' Peter wrote. 'I heard about it in both Vienna & Munich. She is renowned for being mentally incapable of retaining anything she thinks of interest.' She was also inclined to twist and re-interpret what she was told, and by the time it had been Chinese-whispered across the Alps, the story had quite turned on its head. Peter suffered the humiliation of having friends tell him knowingly that they'd heard he and Cecil had spent a '*very happy last night together*' in Venice.[28] Despite his exasperation, Peter thanked Cecil for being the only person to remember his birthday. He also added cryptically that 'poor Oliver seems to have absolutely mucked things this time', and, knowing that he was tickling Cecil's most sensitive spots, mentioned that he had seen Greta Garbo in Munich.

Cecil was obsessed with Garbo; he had tried to meet her ever since his first trip to America in 1929. Finally, earlier this year, he had succeeded with the help of his friend Eddie Goulding, the disreputable British director, who had just directed her in *Grand Hotel*. Cecil met her at Goulding's Hollywood mansion; he spent time alone with her, and claimed that he had managed to kiss her. She gave him a yellow rose she had picked, which he pressed in his diary and later hung in a frame above his bed at Ashcombe.[29]

Garbo had been in Europe since early August; she had come to visit her native Sweden, and there were rumours that she would visit England before going back to Hollywood.[30] Cecil must have prayed that he would get another meeting, but it was to be many years before they met again. The mere mention of Peter having seen her in Munich – his two objects of devotion, together! – must have made his heart stop.

As for who had 'taken command' of Peter once Cecil left him, the answer, innocuously enough, was his mother. Lady Bessie Watson was alone in Baden-Baden (Sir Norman presumably having abandoned her there), 'having a cure', and Peter had agreed to spend some time with her. He wasn't looking forward to it ('It is a *horrifying* place') but he was fond of his mother and did his duty.[31]

* * *

Back in England, his friendship with Cecil resumed its bumpy course. It wouldn't be long before they hit another big hole in the road, and Cecil really would have cause to be jealous.

In the meantime, Peter occupied himself with home-making. While he laboured to fill up his mother's house and make it beautiful (in between his long jaunts abroad), he kept an eye open for a place of his own. Living his social life among the Bright Young People (no longer quite so young nor quite so brilliant as they had been in their 1920s heyday), he considered moving out of Mayfair and into fashionable Chelsea. His friend Diana (*née* Mitford) and her husband, Bryan Guinness, had a house in Cheyne Walk, and Peter took a fancy to it.

The Mitford sisters – particularly Diana and Nancy – were fond of Peter. But like all the other frivolous, irresponsible and sometimes louche young men they mixed with, he attracted the disdain of their choleric father, Lord Redesdale, known to his children as 'Farve'. Farve was caricatured by Nancy as 'Uncle Matthew' in her novel *The Pursuit of Love*, and was every bit as unbalanced in real life as in fiction. He threw one young man out of the house for openly carrying a comb in his breast pocket, and another was offered a horsewhipping for daring to put his feet on the sofa. 'Damned sewers', he called these contemptible young sprigs of modern manhood. When Peter telephoned on one occasion, hoping to get Nancy, he had the misfortune to be answered by Farve, who bellowed, oblivious to the fact that Peter could hear him clearly, 'That hog Watson wants to speak to you!' For ever after, Peter was affectionately known to the Mitford girls as 'Hog'. It stuck so firmly that when the younger sisters acquired a pet hedgehog from Harrods, it was christened Hog Watson in his honour.[32]

By the autumn of 1932, Diana and Bryan's marriage was under severe strain. Diana had met and fallen in love with Sir Oswald Mosley, the former MP and Fabian socialist who had recently undergone a political conversion and was in the process of launching his new party, the British Union of Fascists. By November, Diana's husband was growing jealous of her friendship with Mosley, and tried to separate them, but Diana 'insisted upon my right to choose my own friends ... Mosley had become indispensable to me.'[33] Even though Mosley stuck by his wife, Lady Cynthia – known to everyone as Cimmie – Diana's marriage was finished.

Like many of their social circle, Peter was close to both Diana and

Cimmie. (Indeed, Cimmie was so fond of him that Cecil, who adored her and valued the patronage she had given him, was jealous.[34]) Peter didn't take sides – indeed, there was no open enmity between the two women. Diana waited unobtrusively to see what would happen; she and Bryan separated, and by January 1933 the household at 96 Cheyne Walk was being broken up and the servants let go. Peter had his eye on it, and rather fancied it for himself.

It had a distinguished history – it was made from the end wing of a seventeenth-century mansion that had been remodelled and made down into separate houses in the eighteenth century. Number 96 had once belonged to James McNeill Whistler, and was similar in size and shape to the house in South Street – narrow with four storeys – and was capped by a quaint mansard roof with arched windows overlooking the Thames. In March the house was put up for sale, and in a welter of indecision Peter wrote to Cecil (who was on another of his American trips) asking for advice. The house, he wrote, 'tempts me exceedingly but I am sure I should cool within a year'. He was also concerned about the propriety of taking it under the circumstances. 'Would anybody care?' he wondered.[35] Impatient for Cecil's opinion, he followed the letter up the next day with a telegram: 'COME BACK SOON MISS YOU TERRIBLY WOULD YOU ADVISE TRYING BUY GUINNESS CHEYNE WALK HOUSE BEST LOVE PETER'.[36]

Cecil's reply was not preserved; perhaps he advised against it, or perhaps Peter thought better of seeming like a vulture, circling above the Chelsea Embankment with his talons full of cash. He didn't buy the house, which was just as well, because the tragedy that followed might well have cast the purchase in an even worse light.

In April, Mosley and Cimmie visited Rome, where the Fascist baronet admired the efficiency of Mussolini's new Italy. On their return to England in May, Cimmie was taken ill and was operated on for appendicitis and peritonitis. She was a popular figure, and the society pages in *The Times* reported her condition daily. On Saturday 13 May there was 'slow but definite progress', but by Monday her condition said to be 'very serious'; things brightened the next day, when she was 'slightly better'.[37]

That evening, Peter went with Doris, Viscountess Castlerosse, to visit Diana. (Doris Castlerosse was a current flame of Cecil's; she was noted for her sexual zest, and Cecil had begun an affair with her the previous year, partly in the hope of making Peter jealous.[38] In fact Peter was quite comfortable with the situation.) Diana had made a new home for herself at 2 Eaton Square, Belgravia, where she waited out the process of her divorce and wondered whether her lover would ever be free to marry her. That evening events took a dramatic turn; while Peter and Doris were with her, their mutual friend Robert Byron arrived, bringing devastating news: Cimmie Mosley had just died.[39]

'Isn't it really horrifying,' Peter wrote to Cecil. 'Existence just fails utterly when such a thing happens. Like all of us I was so very fond of her.' Diana, he wrote, was 'nearly off her head – poor Diana'.[40] The mistress's grief and anxiety at the death of the woman who was her rival might seem surprising – but Diana believed that Mosley, already guilty about the effect of the situation on his children, might now turn away from her. His daughter Vivien, in fact, would always believe that Diana had effectively killed Cimmie ('with Diana there, she didn't want to live').[41] A memorial service was held at St Margaret's, Westminster, on the following Friday, but despite saying that everyone would be going to it, Peter was not among the long list of mourners; neither, significantly, was Cimmie's bereaved husband or any of the Mitford family.[42]

Conveying the sad news to Cecil – who was holidaying in Rome with friends, the chattering Princess Jane and a Mr William Odom (according to Beaton's biographer, 'a mysterious, very rich American with a smile like a snarl, whose only attraction was his willingness to pay for the entire trip'[43]) – Peter ended on a determinedly upbeat note; 'Love also to ye,' he closed, signing himself 'Petee'. In between the sad news and the jocose closing, Peter couldn't help mentioning that Oliver was back in town – 'looking much better than when he left'.[44]

If this barb was intended to provoke Cecil's jealousy, it was wasted. Cecil was jealous all right (Doris Castlerosse notwithstanding), but no longer of Oliver Messel. Since February there had been a new and much younger spark in Peter Watson's life – a spark that Peter had been trying to keep concealed but which would quickly drive Cecil to a pitch of hysterical grief unlike anything yet seen.

7

UNDER SOME STRANGE INFLUENCE

1933–1934

Some weeks had passed since Cimmie Mosley's death, and things ought to have calmed down in Peter's social circle. Instead they had suddenly become even more stressful.

On a Saturday afternoon in June, at around teatime, Peter, anxious and heavy-hearted, sat down at the desk in the house in South Street. Taking a sheet of headed notepaper and a fountain pen (which had a pronounced tendency to run dry after every few words), he wrote:

> My dear Cess,
> This is really a nightmare and please let us be sane and friends again ...[1]

He paused. What to write? How to express his confused thoughts?

Earlier that day he had been to the Beaton family home in Sussex Gardens, ostensibly for lunch with Cecil; in fact he had found himself subjected to an emotional performance like nothing he had ever seen, even from Cecil. He could still picture vividly the tears, the anguished face and tragic voice as Cecil read out his prepared statement.

'My dearest Darling,' it began. 'This is so much the saddest thing that has happened in my life. It is *so* serious for me to make the painful wrench but I *cannot continue* being made miserably unhappy constantly by your peculiar vagaries.'

The farewell eulogy was long and densely written over two sides of a sheet of paper. Cecil's invariably spidery handwriting was unusually agitated – the close-set lines wavered up and down, the words degenerating into scrawl as the power of his feelings unbalanced his hand: '... after all that we have been through with each other, when we should be enjoying the results of our experiences together, and though I have become much less jealous and difficult, and in spite of the fact that when giving any confidences you are always assured of my sympathies, you have become, under some strange influence, less intimate and sincere, more elusive and not only my pride but my heart is dreadfully wounded by your secrecy, casualness and evasions from the truth.'[2]

Peter had been discovered; he had been – in Cecil's eyes – unfaithful to their love, and it was more than the suffering, unrequited lover could bear. It was the crowning insult, the last straw, the final curtain.

It all went back to the beginning of the year, when Peter was holidaying in Austria, where he'd met a person who had become rather special to him. His name was Robin, and he was only seventeen years old.

Peter had been minding his own business, 'spending a quiet and healthy life', when Marjorie Oelrichs arrived with a couple of friends, a Mr and Mrs Ramos.[3] Peter had been acquainted with Marge since they were introduced in New York by Cecil. She was an American high-society miss – bubbly and pretty despite a rather masculine set to her jaw – and had given Cecil his first real sexual experience some years earlier. Marge had been trying for over a year to get Peter to come with her to the ski resort at St Anton in the Tyrol; not liking the sound of the company she kept there, he had resisted until now.[4] This time he gave in, and, as he'd expected, he hated it; his feelings were only expressible in violent inky capitals: 'I LOATHED St Anton,' he wrote to Cecil. 'It was absolute torture there – a big FLOP.' The place was full of people who detested each other. One lady ('that awful woman you like', Peter described her to Cecil), one Mervie del Valle, was suing the hotel because they had thrown her out for slapping one female guest and biting another.

But amidst the prevailing ill will there was a bright spot. Marge had brought with her a young cousin, Robin May Thomas, an appealing teenage boy who caught Peter's attention immediately. Peter thought

Robin a 'peach', and a friend described him as 'the sweetest little creature you could possibly wish to see, with hair the colour of corn, lovely light grey eyes and a winning smile'.[5] His mother was Marge's aunt, the wayward, erratic Blanche Oelrichs, who was bisexual and wrote plays and poems under the pseudonym 'Michael Strange'. Blanche was currently on her third husband – the first had been a banker's son called Leonard Thomas (Robin's father), the second was the actor John Barrymore, and the current one was a New York lawyer called Harrison Tweed.

Peter befriended Robin, and, loathing St Anton as he did, escaped with the boy to St Moritz. Marge Oelrichs remained in St Anton with her friend Mrs Ramos, while Mr Ramos came with Peter and Robin and spent his time going to bed with every woman he could find.[6]

Writing to Cecil about the trip, Peter loaded his letter with gossip, mentioning Robin carefully, saying only that he liked him, nothing more. However, when he returned to London and met up with Cecil at the Royal Opera House, Cecil noticed that Peter was wearing a ring, which wasn't at all like him. But when he tried to find out the reason behind it, Peter was taciturn and uncommunicative. Marge Oelrichs, who knew well enough what Peter had been up to at St Anton and St Moritz, had warned Cecil (without going into details) not to see Peter anymore, but Cecil had chosen not to listen.[7]

Soon Cecil set off on his own travels with Mr Odom – the tour of the Continent during which he heard of Cimmie Mosley's death. From Rome Cecil travelled to Paris, where he met up with his mistress, Doris Castlerosse, with whom he enjoyed a 'great sex interlude'. Cecil's treatment of Doris was frivolous and had a dark underside – she was in love with him, but he felt 'no emotion whatsoever' for her, and he consciously enjoyed the superior position this gave him, which was an antidote to his subjugation by Peter: 'I become a peacock and feel so self-assured and even beautiful.'[8]

Then Peter suddenly appeared in Paris. Somehow, so did the news of the true nature of Peter's relationship with the teenage Robin Thomas. The best friend, the friend to whom Cecil 'would go if I were dying', had broken his heart yet again. Harsh words were exchanged between them, and this time, Cecil swore, it must be the end of his tortured, hopeless devotion.

Back in London, in an extremity of passion and self-pity, Cecil wrote his letter and, inviting Peter to the house on the pretext of giving him lunch, made him sit and listen to a recital of it. 'I cannot weep anymore,' he emoted piteously; 'my eyes are swollen and my face almost unrecognisable from so many tears and so much hysteria.' He recalled the fond memories of their relationship – 'the taste of the breakfast of honey and rolls' in Venice, 'and when you returned to London I had made you into God and I met God at the Ritz – and we went together to buy the car which later took us on so many eventful trips.' But it was all over now; Cecil declared that 'it is best for me to say goodbye to the Peter who has been the most loved person in my life.'[9] From now on they would be mere acquaintances.

It was true that Peter Watson could be selfish, that while ever sensitive about his own needs and emotions, he was inclined to disregard other people's feelings or discount their value as it suited him from moment to moment. He was quite capable of coolly using people – a trait that would grow more pronounced as he aged and hardened. But there were some people Peter really loved, and Cecil was one of them; the thought of losing his friendship genuinely distressed him.

> For heaven's sake let's meet next week and don't feel so down. Nothing warrants such depression I assure you on my part. If you feel it does and you do not want to see me please tell me.
>
> I am extremely sorry that you have been so deeply affected by my errors in Paris. When my life was rather unhappy and now when otherwise I feel extremely happy it seems a pity you cannot be too.[10]

Cecil gave way, and their friendship was restored. But it didn't last long – not even for the whole duration of the summer.

By late August Peter was once more in his favourite part of the world with his (current) favourite person – in Salzburg with Robin, who had turned eighteen: not quite a child now, but not yet of age in any person's eyes. On this visit – to Peter's intense frustration and dismay – Robin was accompanied by his mother, Blanche. Peter detested her, citing her 'wild and communistic personality' and her drunkenness.[11] Blanche's 'communist' views mainly consisted of feminism – she had been a suffragist and, along with many other celebrated American women (such as Anita Loos, Amelia Earhart and Georgia O'Keeffe), was known to be a supporter of the Lucy Stone League, a group that advocated for women to be allowed to keep their own names when they married. This was enough to make her seem eccentric in the social world she inhabited. Despite what he said of her, Peter's dislike of Blanche was probably entirely to do with her standing between him and the object of his desire, her teenage son.

One evening, probably at the Österreichischer Hof hotel, where Peter was staying, Blanche got really drunk and said things to him that he would not repeat but which undoubtedly touched upon his relationship with Robin. Deeply upset, Peter poured out his heart in a letter to Cecil, who was holidaying at Cannes with Doris. Referring to Blanche with pointed spite as 'Mrs Tweed' (her married name), Peter wrote that she had 'succeeded in making me more unhappy than I have ever been in my life. Her whole personality and outlook has absolutely shattered me for the moment.' Perhaps conscious of how his current state of mind over Robin must echo Cecil's over him, he added, 'I know it's ridiculous to let oneself be so influenced but I really am rather sad.' Peter was intending to travel to Venice for a few days. 'Do please come if you would like,' he told Cecil. 'I long to see you and not because I now feel down.'[12] (Significantly, Peter did not mention how Robin might be feeling about the whole affair.)

At Cannes, despite Doris's devoted efforts to cheer him up, Cecil too was feeling rather down, and Peter's letter galvanised him.[13] Rather than waiting to meet Peter at Venice, he caught a train to Salzburg – the devoted friend rushing to the rescue. But Peter didn't meet him at the station as planned, and Cecil was dismayed to find a brief note from him at the hotel. Marge Oelrichs had shown up, and Peter – evidently much more cheerful now – had gone on an excursion into the mountains with her. 'I have asked for a room for you,' said the note, scrawled on a hotel memo sheet. 'Longing to see you.'[14]

Despite that longing, they spent a chilly first evening together, and before many days had passed, Cecil, let down and disregarded once more, left for Venice.

* * *

Robin Thomas wasn't the only recipient of Peter's affections that year, although he was the most important. Perhaps because of the effects of being in love, Peter started throwing his money about more extravagantly than ever.

His social circle included several interesting individuals who were happy to take advantage of it. His friendships with Cecil, Oliver Messel, Nancy Mitford and her sister Diana brought him into range of the hugely eccentric Lord Gerald Berners (Gerald Hugh Tyrwhitt-Wilson, 14th Baron Berners), writer, composer and social satirist, whose idea of decor included dyeing the pigeons on his country estate in bright colours so that in flight they resembled confetti, stencilling the lining of his Rolls-Royce with butterflies and installing a four-and-a-half-octave clavichord inside it.[15] Peter holidayed from time to time with Berners' set in Paris, Munich, Florence and Venice. Berners had a long-term 'companion' (or boyfriend), Robert Heber-Percy, who was some thirty years younger than himself – about Peter's age. He was as eccentric as Berners, but with a violently reckless streak that earned him the nickname 'Mad Boy'. His milder escapades included riding, naked, on horseback into Berners' country house at Faringdon.

Berners and Heber-Percy were joined by Peter for a tour of Europe in late 1933, during which the Mad Boy's exploits included nearly killing a woman in Salzburg by hurling a glass tankard into the street from a restaurant balcony and attempting suicide in Venice (while wearing full Tyrolean costume). He was drugged so heavily that his friends were forced to carry him into the hotel in Florence (still semi-conscious and still in costume) before the stupefied gaze of the other guests.[16] Berners feigned exasperation, but admitted that these little outrages delighted him. In Amalfi, Heber-Percy 'woke up in a Neapolitan mood, put on a scarlet shirt, a blue jumper, green trousers and a yellow belt' and suggested that he and Berners go down to breakfast on the crowded hotel terrace. Berners refused to be seen with him. 'Whereupon the creature flew into a rage and hit me over the head with a button-hook.'[17]

Peter became intimate with Robert Heber-Percy, but didn't have any long-term relationship with him – more likely because of the Mad Boy's commitment to Berners than any disquiet about his tempestuous character or any sense of loyalty to Robin. As he matured, Peter's tastes in men would swing between two poles – on one side were relatively mild young fellows like Robin; at the other were those with violently eccentric temperaments like Heber-Percy. Although his relationship with the Mad Boy was never very serious, Peter did become smitten enough to buy him expensive gifts, ranging from a motor car to a golden retriever called Pansy Lamb.[18] He was currently in the grip of a gift-giving mood, and that same year he gave Oliver Messel a Rolls-Royce. Oliver drove it down to the family home at Nymans, and received a tremendous roasting from his father, who ordered him to return it immediately.[19]

When Cecil heard about Peter buying cars – *cars!* – for such people, his jealousy was piqued, and he made no secret of it. It was all one to Peter, and he casually bought Cecil a car too. Cecil fancied something small and sporty, and Peter obliged. 'Do please select any roadster which catches your fancy,' Peter wrote to him as he was about to set off on holiday with Berners, 'for which I forward a discreet cheque.'[20] The cheque was lodged with Cecil's father, who wondered innocently what Cecil could have done to deserve it – 'On account of your blue eyes?' he asked. The roadster Cecil chose was an Alvis that cost £1,000.[21] Flushed with excitement, he wrote to Anita Loos, 'Peter has given me a car and a dressing case which makes me very happy but he still has me on the end of a piece of string.'[22]

* * *

It wasn't obvious at the time, but this outburst of generosity marked the peak of Peter Watson's frivolity. A change was coming over him during those middle years of the 1930s; his social, sexual and cultural lives were so intricately intertwined that the signs of it would have been unnoticeable to those around him, but the hedonistic, trivial, self-obsessed social world that had been his life since at least as far back as Oxford was beginning to lose its hold on him. At the same time, the life of the mind and the higher senses was growing more important.

The worlds of the arts and of high society had always been linked. Artists, after all, must have money, and the rich must have culture – or at least the illusion that they have it. Although he didn't have the creative spark himself (as Cecil, Oliver, Stephen Tennant and so many of his other contemporaries did), Peter Watson's mind wasn't content with the mere illusion or outward display of culture. As he passed the midpoint of his twenties he showed signs of a deep and serious devotion to the cause of art.

Music had always been important to him, as long as he could remember, and his fine aesthetic sensibilities had been notable when he was a schoolboy, but it was only through his relationship with Cecil that he had learned about art, and begun to discover the thrilling things that were happening within its modern movements.

Others helped him on his way. Among the first was Surrealist painter Pavel Tchelitchew. Peter was introduced to him sometime in 1933, possibly by Cecil, having already become enthusiastic about his work, which he began to buy in 1932.[23] Tchelitchew had been born in Russia in 1898, and escaped the country in 1920 while the Bolsheviks were consolidating their stranglehold on it. He settled eventually in Paris, where he became part of Gertrude Stein's salon circle. Tchelitchew incorporated Surrealism and Cubism in a distinctive style that would later be labelled Neo-romanticism (entirely separate from the earlier neo-romantic movements in music and literature). His homosexuality induced a powerful strain of homoeroticism in his work, and an inclination towards the male figure and penetrative, provocative explorations of masculine physique. He took a sexual interest in Peter, but it wasn't returned; Peter was only interested in the art.

In Paris, Tchelitchew had formed a relationship with the American poet Charles Henri Ford, a dark, beautiful young man from Mississippi. Peter met Charles Henri for the first time in 1933 on the terrace of the restaurant Les Deux Magots in the Place Saint-Germain-des-Prés in Paris – the hangout *de rigueur* for the artistic set.[24] Peter was thrilled. Apparently oblivious of the fact that he was addressing the boy's lover, he thanked 'Pavlik' (the Russian diminutive of Pavel) for giving him 'un des grands plaisirs de ma vie' in introducing him. (Tchelitchew's English wasn't strong at this time, and he and Peter communicated largely in French.) 'Il est merveilleux!!' Peter enthused, going on to describe how charmed he was by Charles Henri's liquid eyes, his voice, and everything he said. Truly, the young man had greatly astonished him, he wrote – adding anxiously, 'Qu'est-ce qu'il a pensé de moi?'[25] (Charles Henri claimed later that Pavlik had introduced them as a sort of gentle revenge against Peter for his own rejection, knowing that Peter would fancy him.)[26]

Peter's ongoing affair with Robin Thomas and now his bewitchment by Charles Henri Ford marked the beginning of a lifelong penchant for good-looking young Americans, against which Cecil stood even less of a chance. No evidence would survive of any affair between Peter and Charles Henri, but from time to time there would be hints that things were not always cordial between Peter and Pavlik ('Your last letter wasn't very nice, Pavlik,' he wrote from New York in 1934. 'Why? Are you ill?'[27]). But most of the time their friendship was close and affectionate.

Pavlik himself was not at all like his boyfriend. When he wasn't in his studio he favoured smart suits, often pinstriped, and with his sombre air and august profile he looked more like a statesman or a banker than a radical painter. He grew very attached to Peter Watson, and painted his portrait at least twice – or three times if one includes a cartoon he sketched in a letter, showing Peter at the wheel of his Rolls-Royce cabriolet, flying through the air and delivering 'merveilles de gourmandise' to Pavlik, Charles Henri and Cecil.[28] In one of the formal portraits, rendered in gouache and sand on paper, and perhaps made during one of their periods of friction, Peter is a rather sour-faced Tudor nobleman in ruff and doublet – the costume perhaps related to Peter and Cecil's faux-Tudor private language of 'wytte and kyndlinesse'. In the other portrait, Peter is a pretty, fresh-faced boy encased in a huge suit of armour – a painting that Christian Bérard called 'the English Joan of Arc done by the Russian Botticelli'.[29]

Cecil was present when this portrait was painted (as was Charles Henri), and caught it on camera – a treble portrait of the sitter, artist and painting together. Cecil was fond of this kind of double portraiture; he also painted Peter, reclining on the lawn at Ashcombe and feeding the white doves from his hands, and photographed him with the painting in the background. This was a particularly suggestive group of images – Peter wore his shirt open to the navel and sleeves rolled up to the armpits – like the German boys in the 'queer places' in Munich – and smiled into the lens with such provocative amusement that he was obviously conscious of the effect he must be having on Cecil.

In spring 1934, Peter and Cecil were in America again. Cecil had gone over in January (as he did every year), and Peter joined him in March. He hadn't particularly wanted to go, but his attachment to Robin Thomas was still strong – so strong that, despite all the trouble it had caused the previous year, he had written to Cecil in New York asking about him. There had been some kind of row between Peter and his young lover, and Peter had been through a bout of depression and was longing for news: 'Please tell me truthfully what he is up to,' he wrote. 'He preserves with me still an outraged silence which is silly. But I know so well how silly he is and I am still very fond of him.'[30] In his impatience, Peter gave the letter to his brother (to whom he always referred sardonically as 'Sir Norman'), who was sailing to New York the next day, to deliver by hand.

Peter managed to put up with the strain for another month. Then, in March, he travelled down to Plymouth and caught the SS *Île de France* for New York. Aboard, he made friends with the young French art dealer Pierre Colle, whose Galerie Pierre Colle in the Rue Cambacérès in Paris specialised in Surrealist and Dada art, exhibiting works by Dalí, Duchamp, André Breton, Max Ernst, Miró, and Man Ray. (The previous year he had been the first exhibitor of Man Ray's iconic 'Object to Be Destroyed'.) Colle was still only twenty-five years old, and already a significant name in the Paris art world. 'Je le trouve si gentil,' Peter wrote to Tchelitchew, 'et je l'aime beaucoup beaucoup.'[31] Possibly it was this friendship that gave Peter the impetus to rebuild his life around his new love of art collecting; indeed, on the forms for his previous voyage to America, as a wealthy, directionless playboy, he had listed his occupation as 'nil', but now he described himself as a 'student'.

In New York, Peter took a room at the Waldorf Astoria, and was thrilled and astonished to find himself on the forty-second floor – 'C'est vrai,' he told Pavlik, 'bonne vue!'[32]

If Peter managed to meet Robin while he was in America, he didn't record it; however, he did tell Pavlik that he believed he was happier than he had ever been in his life before – 'and if it is true, one day I will tell you why'.[33] There is no evidence that Pavlik ever heard why, and Peter's relationship with Robin Thomas would never amount to much.

Once again, most of Peter's time in America was spent with Cecil. New York was a different city than it had been three years earlier; Prohibition had been repealed in 1933, the speakeasies were gone, and drink could be had easily at all times of the night. Between his hectic working life and socialising, Cecil had become ill – he was on prescribed drugs, and when he first met Peter off the ship in New York, he was a 'jittering wreck'.[34] Apparently in an attempt to alleviate the strain on Cecil, the two friends retraced their earlier, ill-fated journey down to the Caribbean. (Meanwhile, Pierre Colle embarked on a road trip from New York to New Orleans, which Peter thought the most hideous route in the world.[35])

It was the rainy season in Haiti, and it bucketed down every night. Cecil tried to relax by painting, and, according to Peter, intended to begin his 'période Gauguinoise', while 'moi, je regarde les nègres'.[36] Cecil discovered a butterfly farm and obtained a batch of what he believed were chrysalises, and infiltrated them into Peter's room one night; the intention was that Peter would awake to find his room filled with the flutter of beautiful tropical butterflies; instead his beloved woke up to find himself crawling with half-developed caterpillars.[37]

This holiday lacked the friction and fractiousness of the previous one, but Peter's presence still made Cecil restless and lovelorn, and Peter had to persuade him away from the rum bottle. Eventually they returned to New York, and, following another intense period of work for Cecil, sailed home together. Pierre Colle was aboard too; he and Peter both felt able to breathe again as soon as they were out of America, and they both looked forward to seeing Paris again.[38]

For the son of a man who had given a huge sum to found a chair in Anglo-American studies, Peter Watson would never be particularly at ease in America, despite his penchant for American men.

* * *

The change that was coming over Peter continued. He was tiring of British upper-class society, with its public school mentality and its triviality. In November 1934 he moved another step closer to the art world, when he went to stay in Paris with Marie-Laure de Noailles.

Dark, elegant and handsome in a long-faced Virginia Woolf kind of way, Marie-Laure was only a few years older than Peter, but she was a giantess in the contemporary arts in France. Born into a family of French-German-Jewish aristocracy and descended from the Marquis de Sade, she was a powerful and radical patron, having backed films by Dalí, Man Ray and Jean Cocteau (with whom she had an affair before her marriage to the Vicomte de Noailles) and compositions by Poulenc, as well as holding court to the cream of the Parisian artistic set. She and her husband lived in the huge, palatial *hôtel particulier* (mansion) at 11 place des États-Unis, off the avenue d'Iéna, near the Arc de Triomphe. It had become a sort of élite commune for the rich and artistic set.

By late 1934 Peter was finding his feet amid this circle, but was already taking a dislike to those elements of it that reminded him of the shrieking childishness of the Bright Young Things at home. On this visit, he found – without naming names – the house full of people behaving 'like desperate children'. He was fond of Marie-Laure, and it distressed him to see the way some people played on her nervy temperament and drove her to hysteria. 'I think it disgusting,' he wrote to Cecil, and considered shortening his intended stay.[39]

But he held on, mingling with the great, wealthy and radical and at the same time acquiring a reputation as 'the most elegantly attired Englishman in Paris'.[40] His dress was beautiful – he wore exquisitely cut, flawless double-breasted suits and long coats in dark wool or light tweed, fashionably long shirt collars and silk ties carefully puffed out between the jacket lapels. His thick, dark hair was clipped in a taper to the nape of his neck (the nape which Cecil so loved to stroke) and on top was slicked neatly with Frances Fox ointment, an American brand popular with celebrities that could be bought from a shop in Regent Street.[41] His manner varied to suit his environment; he was known for a cool, placid elegance, but at parties he could take on a camp persona, his voice swooping gaily.[42]

Peter spent time with the artist and designer Christian 'Bébé' Bérard – who had become one of his favourites and was an influence on Cecil – and Bébé's boyfriend, the dancer Boris Kochno. Peter also had 'a pleasing and quiet time' riding in the Bois de Boulogne with Marie-Laure's little daughters, Laure and Nathalie, aged ten and seven. He enjoyed concerts featuring the Russian cellist Gregor Piatigorsky and the teenage prodigy Yehudi Menuhin ('which sounds impressive but isn't'). And, perhaps the highlight of his stay, he went to visit the great Fauvist painter André Derain and his friend Pablo Picasso, 'who has done the most incredible lithographs you could imagine in the Greek pagan style'.[43] (These were the remarkable etchings making up the 100-piece Vollard Suite, which Picasso had begun in 1930.) One morning he rose at dawn to escort Princess Natalia Paley to the Gare Saint-Lazare. Natalia – sometimes known to her friends, including Peter, as Natacha – was sailing for New York that morning. She was a society celebrity and a budding film star, and there were 'batteries of cameras and mercury lamps for her' at the station, and also for others catching the same boat-train: French actress Lili Damita, composer Johann Strauss III and figure skater Sonja Henie.[44]

But, engrossed as he was by Paris, Peter was drawn back towards England by two concerns. One was Cecil's health; he had been seriously ill, and was scheduled for an abdominal operation. Peter was anxious – although didn't express himself very tactfully, asking Cecil in every letter to specify when he was going 'on the board' to be 'knifed' and 'sliced' so that he could be back in England when it happened. His second concern was that he had finally, after putting it off for three years, bought himself a house in London. Lady Bessie had moved into her house at 36 South Street; she and Peter had shared it for a year, but now he was moving on to a place of his own. It needed furnishing and decorating to a standard commensurate with his reputation for exquisite taste and style. The most elegantly attired Englishman in Paris needed a fitting English home.

'Although Paris is crazy about me,' he wrote to Cecil, 'I shall be back tomorrow.'[45]

8

THE ART OF LIVING

1934–1935

Long, sleek, in dark green winged with gleaming black, a Bentley murmured past Marble Arch and through the press of traffic under the winter-bare trees lining Park Lane. In the back seat were Peter Watson and Cecil Beaton, chatting gaily as they motored along; Cecil had felt a pang of regret as they came in along the Bayswater Road and passed the familiar turning to Sussex Gardens. The Beaton family household, which, like that of the Mitfords, had been a throng of social activity, no longer existed; after Baba's marriage Cecil's parents had moved out and taken rooms at Notting Hill Gate.[1] But Cecil couldn't be downhearted now; he was with his poppet again, and was being taken to stay in poppet's new house for a few days so that he could shop and brace himself for hosting a family Christmas at Ashcombe.

Peter had been delightful company lately – 'kind and sweet as possible' – coming back from Paris, sending Cecil rosebuds when he was in hospital, and driving him (or having his chauffeur drive him) wherever he wanted to go.[2] They had spent time in Cornwall, visited Ashcombe, and were now returning to London. They had reached a new understanding, and in December Cecil had noted in his diary that although he was still in love, and needed to give up the habit, it no longer hurt as much.[3]

The chauffeur steered the Bentley off Park Lane into Upper Brook Street. The car was a new addition, and was in keeping with Peter's maturing sense of style. The gay coral Rolls, with its gems and fur, was gone, and in its place was the dark-green Bentley, the latest benchmark of motoring chic. Bentley had been renowned for its sporting models – well-built, noisy and uncomfortable (it was said that Bentley made 'the world's fastest lorries'), but they had now introduced a new model which was sleekly styled and as quiet as rustling leaves, but could do a clean eighty if you had the nerve for it. Marketed as 'The Silent Sports Car', it was a dream to drive, and *the* model for a fashionable young man who loved to motor.[4]

Just before reaching Grosvenor Square, the chauffeur swung the car left into a side street leading to Lees Place. Here, secluded – almost hidden – among the rows of Mayfair townhouses and mews was a tiny private courtyard where Peter had made his home.

Shepherd's Close was a brand-new build: a row of three neo-Georgian houses whose small front gardens faced a secluded private lane – Shepherd's Close itself – and whose rear elevations faced Shepherd's Place, the narrow alleyway linking Upper Brook Street and Lees Place. The three houses had been begun in 1933 and were now more or less complete.[5] Peter had acquired number 1 for himself, and now – a week or so before Christmas 1934 – had finished making it fit to show to friends.

Peter and Cecil and their luggage were dropped in the close while the chauffeur took the Bentley off to its underground parking nearby. The cases were collected by the maid and Peter's valet – a redoubtable, taciturn man called Walter Cox – and the two friends went indoors into the warmth. The expensive electric gramophone in the drawing room was already playing Sibelius at a low volume, with a clarity 'as though a muffled orchestra were playing in the room' – a novelty in the days when raucously loud horn gramophones were still the norm. Cecil relished the luxury of a homecoming without the bustle of a large family household, mountains of correspondence to deal with, and his secretary presenting him with work.

Cecil was delighted by the house; so was everyone who came there, and it became noted for its chic, but Cecil was the first to see it. The style

Peter had gone for was low-key grandeur with moments of surprise, similar to that created by Cecil at Ashcombe and Stephen Tennant at Wilsford Manor – a restrained version of Edwardian drawing-room elegance, with vibrant touches here and there. Peter stopped short of Cecil's circus gaiety, and his splashes were confined to subtle touches, such as bedrooms painted in pink or plum, and an ornate jardinière in the drawing room. That aside, the house was designed to give comfort to the body and solace to the soul, with soft sofas, central heating, books everywhere, and walls hung with art.

Peter's collection was already growing, and even the bathrooms were well provided with art. There were many works by his British friends, including Cecil, but also Pavel Tchelitchew, Christian Bérard and some of the more eminent artists he had begun to collect: André Derain, Salvador Dalí and – his nod to the nineteenth-century aesthetic that informed his interior design – Renoir. (Later that year he would start expanding his horizons with a growing enthusiasm for early Renaissance art – particularly the works of the fifteenth-century German painter Konrad Witz. 'I have gone mad over German painting,' he would write to Cecil; 'every Witz gives me a thrill, and I crave one for the Close. Do you think a nice Crucifixion scene for the dining room?')[6] Only a few months had passed since Peter took the house, but already it had attracted enough notice that British *Vogue* sent a photographer round to capture it.[7]

There were three servants in residence – aside from Cox the valet, there was a maid and a cook,[8] whose cuisine Cecil thought superb. All the senses were catered for with everything an aesthete could want.

So began one of the pleasantest times Peter and Cecil ever spent together – certainly since Cecil's crisis the previous year. It wasn't without its trials. Cecil was still weak after his illness – on one occasion, while out Christmas shopping, he fainted in Woolworth's. It was also costing him a good deal of mental stress suppressing his desires for Peter and controlling his behaviour towards him. Peter allowed him the same intimate liberties as ever, but Cecil knew now that it must stop short of sex, and knew not to let himself be petulant about it. They talked late into the night, lying together in bed, Cecil stroking Peter's back and the nape of his neck until he fell asleep, then tiptoeing back to his own room, leaving the connecting doors open. They woke simultaneously in the morning, and Cecil, in bliss, knew once again that 'this is where most in the world I wish to be.'[9] At the same time he felt his impossible hopes rising again, and struggled to keep them subdued. Desperate to please, he spent wildly on Christmas gifts for Peter from Harvey Nichols – which that year came in the very popular gift-box packaging Cecil himself had designed for the store, decorated in seasonal patterns and character cartoons.[10] The gift Peter most wanted – a pet dog – was already being provided for; he acquired a long-haired Skye terrier who was christened Bone and was a constant presence throughout the house.

It was during this stay that Cecil acquired the idea – whether confided to him by Peter or inferred or imagined by Cecil himself – that Peter was conscious of his own lack of a contribution to art, that he 'feels himself inwardly to be an inferior person' because 'he practises no art'. And yet, as Cecil further reasoned, Peter's own art was existential – he was his own canvas, upon which he had diligently been painting since he was a schoolboy trying to obliterate the shadow of his family background. In doing so, by this point in his life – he was now twenty-six – he had made himself a connoisseur among connoisseurs. Furthermore, in Cecil's view, Peter had an 'art for being alive every moment of the day', noticing and commenting on the aesthetics of the scenery – the growth of a stand of trees, the bend in a river path, the textures of the earth, the fleeting colours of the sky. 'I am put on my mettle to keep my end up,' Cecil wrote, 'and he can beat me hollow on architecture, music, and as regards human relationships he considers I am but a child.' Cecil considered the art of living the greatest of them all, and himself a 'sluggish and incompetent' practitioner compared with Peter. Jean Cocteau had called Cecil 'Malice in Wonderland', and Cecil had to admit that he had 'succeeded in spending my life in an unreality made up of fun ... and my interests are limited to the joys of certain intellectual forms of beauty, to sensual delights only to a blunt degree', and had done 'too many light, quick sketches ... and photographs galore'. When he was with Peter he felt as if he were an apprentice in what Nietzsche had called the art of living.[11] 'One thing is needful,' Nietzsche wrote in 1882: 'To "give style" to one's character – a great and rare art!'

> It is practised by those who survey all the strengths and weaknesses of their nature and then fit them into an artistic plan until every one of them appears as art and reason and even weaknesses delight the

> eye ... Here the ugly that could not be removed is concealed; there it has been reinterpreted and made sublime ...
>
> 'It will be the strong and domineering natures that enjoy their finest gaiety in such constraint and perfection under a law of their own.'[12]

When Cecil was with Peter, he tried to learn from him – 'for he is the best person at the art of living that I know'.[13] And yet Peter still had some way to go before he reached the position he was (perhaps unconsciously) driving towards. There was too much frippery still, too much inconsequential, joyless 'fun' in the society he and Cecil lived in, but they were both still habituated to it. Cecil would never leave it behind, but for Peter the coming year – 1935 – would be the one in which he completed his transition from frivolous schoolboy aesthete to serious patron of the arts. (At the same time, in Peter's best-loved part of Europe, other ideas of Nietzsche's concerning the nature of man were being bent to violent political purposes. Despite being a frequent and vulnerable visitor to the heartland of Nazism, Peter hadn't been affected by it; that was another thing that would change during the coming year.)

Approaching Christmas, Cecil grew irrationally worried about Peter. Elinor Glyn, the elderly author of risqué romantic novels, had gained some notoriety by claiming to be able to experience visions of the future when in a trance, and some of her predictions had been found to come true, which seemed to reinforce her claims. Cecil thought Glyn 'extremely tiring and pretentious', but in early 1934 had been disturbed when she developed an obsession with Peter, and claimed to have had one of her trance visions about him: 'I see Peter Watson,' she said, 'and he's bad – really bad – bad all through and he'll come to a bad end – he won't see another Christmas Day.'[14] Cecil regarded her as a monstrous old hag and insisted that he didn't believe in her, but her foretelling still worried him, and when Boxing Day came he was relieved to hear Peter's voice on the telephone.

What remained with Cecil from this experience was that he had been forced to think about the possibility of Peter dying, and was 'horrified to realise how mixed my feelings would be'. He didn't confide those feelings even to his diary, but they can be imagined – terrible, lacerating grief at the loss of his beloved, mixed with a sense of release from the bondage of being unremittingly in love with him. Peter would later confide to

Stephen Tennant his belief that 'the predominant urge beneath our daily life is the half-submerged wish for a perfect companion.'[15] Cecil believed he had found his, and lived out much of his life in anguish because he couldn't have him. Peter himself would spend a good deal of emotional energy in the same pursuit, but with the difference that he didn't fixate upon a single person but upon a succession of them. This drive would lead – indirectly and more than two decades late – to the end foretold by Mrs Glyn.

* * *

In early 1935, two incidents occurred – one utterly trivial, the other more serious – which respectively eroded Peter's attachment to the English smart set and shook his love of Germany.

In January, he set off on one of his frequent and lengthy tours of Europe, beginning with the snowy slopes of Austria and Switzerland. Meanwhile he left Cecil, still convalescing and without a home of his own in London, with the run of Shepherd's Close and its servants – including Cox the valet, who didn't accompany Peter abroad. ('Keep Cox on the move,' Peter advised, 'and give lots of balls. The ones I shall never give.')[16]

The uncongenial English social scene that Peter had despised so much in St Anton a couple of years earlier had spread to St Moritz. At first, Peter had a delightful few days skiing with Baron Nicolas de Gunzburg (a wealthy Franco-Russian dilettante and friend of Princess Natalia Paley, renowned for his theatrical costume balls). Then the arrival of a couple of English friends drew Peter into St Moritz's British circle, whose ringleader was Mrs Janet Campbell, daughter of Lord Beaverbrook. The new arrivals were Sir Alfred Beit, nephew of a South African mining tycoon, and the Hon. William Drogo Sturges Montagu, younger son of the 9th Earl of Sandwich. Alfred had inherited his fortune around the same time as Peter, along with a baronetcy, and had promptly become Conservative MP for St Pancras. His statesmanlike dignity was severely at risk in St Moritz. Following a party given by a Mrs Selwyn, a drunken riot began, whipped up by Janet Campbell and 'a lot of hungry women', who seized poor Drogo and publicly debagged him. They tried to do the same to Alfred, but failed.[17]

This marked the end of Peter Watson's ability to tolerate the useless, witless public-schoolishness of English society – 'the most awful bums', he called them. They had made St Moritz unbearable, 'so I am going to Kitzbühel with Niki, stopping each night somewhere different'. Although Alfred had escaped the public debagging, he was 'full of gloom and sadness as these bums ransacked his room and have behaved to him like school bullies and he seems to feel very lonely'.[18] Alfred's woes were complete when a couple of weeks later he fell off his skis and broke his leg in two places.[19]

Kitzbühel, in the Austrian Tyrol, was no improvement. The town was 'full of English public schoolers and their children' and the valley was full of rain and mud, so that skiing could only be had on the very highest slopes. Peter's misanthropic ill temper was driven to boiling point when the fashion photographer George Hoyningen-Huene (a friend of Cecil's who had recently defected from Paris *Vogue* to *Harper's Bazaar*) telegraphed asking Peter to meet him off the train at Kitzbühel and then failed to show up. Then, to crown his miserable mood, Peter was bedridden for days by 'an eye-splitting attack' of influenza exacerbated by the mountain altitude.[20]

After a few days on his back he felt better. The sun was shining too, and in an uplifted mood he decided to pay a flying visit to Munich. This was when the second – more serious – incident occurred.

There might be a variety of reasons why a young man alone would travel all the way from Kitzbühel in Austria to Munich in Germany (via a bizarrely long detour north to Frankfurt) just for one day, but, in the account of the visit he told to Cecil,[21] Peter didn't mention any of them. He loved Munich, and there was one thing about it – one particularly exciting thing – that Peter couldn't get in any other European city save Berlin. Germany's sexual licentiousness was in the process of dying – the new regime was cutting open society's underbelly and eviscerating its decadent elements – and Peter must have known it, so perhaps he was hoping for one last fling before the lights went out.

At three o'clock in the afternoon, Peter was sitting in a Munich café with an unidentified young German who (he wrote, apropos of nothing) was 'coming into a lot of money'. Whether Peter was proposing to help him go abroad and take his money out of the country, or whether a more sexual negotiation was taking place (more probably both, *quid pro quo*), the next thing Peter knew, Kriminalpolizei officers descended out of the blue, arrested him and marched him off to the police station.

There they took down details of all the registered Reichsmarks he had cashed that day in Frankfurt and Munich. (The Nazi regime was relying on the mark to bolster its military rebuilding, and had strict exchange controls in place.) Then they told him to go back to his hotel – the Vier Jahreszeiten – and wait.

He went back to the hotel, but he didn't wait – instead, 'I whipped my grip out of the Vier Jahreszeiten *immediately*' and took it to the Hotel Regina. Then, after hanging around there for a short while, 'I took the next train for Kitzbühel.'

It occurred to Peter that the police 'had thought I was a Communist spy'.[22] However, this didn't quite add up with the currency trouble, which in turn conflicted with his statement in the same letter that he'd been arrested 'for talking to a German'. There seems to have been confusion in Peter's mind about why exactly he had been arrested, and no explanation at all of why he fled so precipitately. Panic seems the most likely explanation – the panic of a homosexual man in a once-friendly country that had suddenly turned vehemently homophobic. The days of Peter Watson's love affair with Germany were all but over.

Arriving back in Kitzbühel to find it raining again, he retreated to Vienna. There he found the solace his soul needed. He purchased a (presumably original) edition of Fischer von Erlach's seminal 1721 volume *A Plan of Civil and Historical Architecture*, and yearned over German and Italian Renaissance paintings.[23] After a disappointing evening of 'bad ballet' followed by 'an hour of Gitta Alpár in a pretty lousy operette peppered with swooners', Peter attended a Jäger ball – part of Vienna's celebrated season of fabulously opulent dances – which was 'one of the most heavenly evenings I have ever spent'. It was held in a vast hall of pillars and chandeliers, 'beautifully decorated with swags of Xmas tree all in green and painted scenery of mountains', in which 'the atmosphere was so divine with two enormous bands playing heavenly waltzes.' Of the four thousand present, all 'were gay and charming'. The English upper class might be riddled with crass, overgrown schoolchildren, but the Viennese knew how to be civilised.

And yet Vienna depressed him. 'The association of Robin in this place is terribly strong and at times frightfully upsetting.'[24] The relationship, which had made him happy for such a brief time the year before, was now virtually over, and it would be years before Peter fell in love again.

The only lasting value, it seemed, was to be found in art. Back at

Shepherd's Close, Cecil was still having a crisis about the value of his career as a photographer. Peter tried to console him. 'Poor Cecil,' he wrote from Kitzbühel, 'photographs cannot be dog's work when they are taken as well as you take them.' Thinking of his own approach to life and style, he added: 'Anything that is well done is in itself a chef d'oeuvre, from a pudding to Schönbrunn, and a delight to everyone.'[25]

In the coming year, he would begin putting his money and influence behind this principle, with his first major act of patronage.

* * *

In early 1935 Peter was visited in London by Marie-Laure de Noailles. She told him about a brand-new work by a promising young Ukrainian composer, Igor Markevitch, a prodigy who had been discovered in 1929, aged just sixteen, by Sergei Diaghilev, impresario and founder of the Ballets Russes. Markevitch was already an accomplished composer, and Diaghilev had commissioned a piano concerto from him and invited him to work on one of his ballets. Arranging for a performance of the concerto in London in summer 1929, Diaghilev had promoted the concert in a letter to *The Times*: Markevitch's music, he wrote, 'is dear to me, because I see in it the very birth of that new generation which can protest against the Paris orgies of the past few years'. His composition 'tolerates no compromise. ... The insistence of his dynamic rhythm is particularly surprising ... and all his themes are well hidden in contrapuntic valises. His music is next door to pleasure.'[26]

By 1935, now aged twenty-two but still a prodigy, Igor Markevitch was in Paris as a protégé of Marie-Laure de Noailles – and more than that: it was said of their relationship that Marie-Laure had 'trouvé son Chopin' and cast herself in the role of George Sand; they had become lovers.[27] The new piece, which she described to an excited Peter Watson, was an oratorio, *Le Paradis perdu*, based on Milton's *Paradise Lost*. Marie-Laure, having introduced the composer to the poem, had taken a lover's and mentor's interest in its development; plans had been made for a premiere in Brussels, but the organisers would not allow enough time for rehearsals. On the strength of Marie-Laure's description of the work, Peter flew to Paris to meet the composer and they quickly became friendly.

Igor Markevitch was a striking young man to look at – delicate and weirdly beautiful, his face was a perfectly slender inverted triangle, with cheekbones sharp as knuckles, dark almond eyes and swooping brows, and a shock of thick, waved hair. He made Cecil Beaton and Stephen Tennant look like brawny farmhands. Possibly his looks intrigued Peter, but his music interested him more. From their very first introduction, Peter asked Igor to play him the *Paradis*, which he did. Even in its rudimentary form, Peter was so overcome by it he could hardly describe his feelings. What he found in it was probably that thread of romantic melody he desired, woven into the dissonant avant-garde fabric (Diaghilev's 'contrapuntic valises'), which he had failed to find in Walton's *Belshazzar*.

As soon as Peter learned about Igor's difficulties with the Brussels premiere, he decided to step in. He would fly the young composer to England and speak to the BBC about mounting a performance. Igor barely had time to agree before he found himself aboard an Imperial Airways biplane, heading for London.[28]

Igor stayed with Peter at the house in Shepherd's Close, which delighted him – despite its modest proportions, it 'breathed comfort'. Each morning, they breakfasted together in Peter's bedroom – an echo of his friendship with Cecil – and discussed Peter's plans for tackling the BBC. Through these morning conversations, the two young men quickly became close friends. Peter at twenty-six was four years older than Igor – almost exactly the ages he and Cecil had been when they first met. Igor was delighted by Peter's 'generosity, humour and passion for music'.

It was the only kind of passion between them – Igor Markevitch wasn't homosexual, and despite his beauty Peter showed no sign of being sexually attracted to him. Quite possibly Igor simply wasn't Peter's type – although he never went for butch men, he did like lovers with a masculine strength in their physiques and jawlines.

However, 1 Shepherd's Close that summer wasn't devoid of romantic passion. For some time Igor had been in a halting on-off romance with ballerina Kyra Nijinsky (daughter of the great Vaslav Nijinsky). She was currently working in London, dividing her time between a C. B. Cochran revue and the Ballet Rambert; left alone in the house one day, Igor called her on the phone. 'I was waiting for you,' she told him. 'I shall always be waiting for you.' Within an hour she appeared at Shepherd's Close; Igor would always recall 'this moment of emotion when the fever entered our veins'.[29] For the time being he kept the liaison secret from Marie-Laure, either from a reluctance to hurt her feelings or from a fear of her 'hysterical' temperament and loss of her patronage.

Meanwhile, there was *Le Paradis perdu*. Edward Clark, head of the BBC's classical music department, was invited to dinner, and the plan for a British premiere put to him. Clark was a conductor as well as a producer, and a champion of modern music who had given BBC coverage to new works by Shostakovich, Kurt Weill, Bartók, Anton Webern, and Schoenberg. The three men enjoyed an exciting evening of erudite musical conversation. (Peter wasn't trained in music, but, in Markevitch's view, there were few amateur connoisseurs who could equal his musical sensibility.) Clark was enthusiastic about the oratorio, and agreed to fix a date in December for the performance.

Igor was fascinated and impressed by the famous elegance of Peter's attire, whose studied carelessness the Ukrainian, acclimatised to the values of Paris, saw as an essentially English trait; there was a view among fashionable English aesthetes that one needn't attempt to match or coordinate one's dress – if one's garments, handkerchiefs, ties, socks and shirts were beautiful in themselves, then they would naturally go together. Thus, each morning's dressing was an exercise in trusting to chance. Peter would glance out of his bedroom window and, depending on what seasonal scene was happening outside, he would choose the appropriate outfit. Then, with music playing, and sometimes talking on the telephone at the same time, he would throw open cupboards and drawers, pulling out socks, ties and shirts by the dozen, along with trousers and jackets, holding them up, selecting at random and tossing the discards carelessly onto the bed or the floor. As the day's outfit fell haphazardly into place, Cox the valet would follow him about the room, breathless and red in the face, picking up, folding, stowing away and bringing order to the chaos, and never uttering a word beyond 'Yes, sir.' All the while, Bone the terrier stood by, wagging his tail and eating Peter's slippers.[30]

At the end of June, Peter took Igor to stay with Gerald Berners at Faringdon, his country estate. Among the other guests that weekend were Tilly Losch and Italian diplomat Mario Pansa (first secretary to the Italian legation in Copenhagen and described by *Life* magazine as 'the most fascinating man on the Continent'[31]). Exotic dancers, Fascist diplomats and avant-garde composers: a measure of the mixed company that was to be had at Faringdon. Signing the guest book, Peter gave his 'profession' as *animateur* (patron, sponsor),[32] probably at Berners' prompting and in honour of Igor's presence, the only occasion on which he is known to have described himself so, despite its being what he fundamentally was – *animateur*, enabler, promoter and supporter.

* * *

After his experience in Munich in January, Peter's relationship with Germany had been badly marred. Even so, shortly afterwards he visited Germany again, now sourly referred to as '卐-land'.[33] This time he was going to Weimar rather than Munich; he didn't record his reasons for the visit, but the fact that he referred to the city as 'Goethestadt Weimar' (Goethe's city) implies that his reasons were cultural. It was a dangerous place to go – although Berlin was the capital and Bavaria the heartland of Nazism, Weimar was still one of the seats of power – it was heavily garrisoned, and the first concentration camps had been established nearby in 1933 (chiefly for political prisoners).

That visit passed without incident, and in September Peter visited again – but on his way out of Germany, making for Venice, he was arrested again. This time it was the border police who took him; they held him for two days, without access to his belongings, before letting him go.[34] Telling Cecil about the incident, he didn't mention the cause, and reported it as an irritating rather than a frightening experience, but whatever the cause, that was to be his last recorded visit to Nazi Germany.

It wasn't for lack of invitations. The infection of Nazism had got hold of a handful of his closest friends, including Diana Guinness (*née* Mitford). After Cimmie Mosley's death, Diana had started living with Oswald. Inspired by her Fascist lover's politics, Diana went to Germany with her sister Unity – already an enthusiastic Nazi – and in March 1935 Unity introduced Diana to Hitler. It was the beginning of a long and intense friendship. In September – right after his last arrest – Peter was recovering from his ordeal in Venice when he received a phone call from Gerald Berners. He and Diana were going to Nuremberg to attend Hitler's Parteitag – the seventh of the increasingly popular, bombastic and belligerent Nazi Party congresses, better known as the Nuremberg Rallies. The previous year Leni Riefenstahl had filmed the rally for

Triumph of the Will; this year she would create another landmark in *Day of Freedom: Our Armed Forces*, commemorating the rally at which Hitler's intention to make Germany a conquering force came out into the open, with the repudiation of the Versailles Treaty and the unveiling of the Wehrmacht's scale and power. (In response Britain increased its spending on armaments and France scaled up its military conscription.)

Gerald Berners, ever the eccentric, seemed to regard Nuremberg as another diverting event in the giddy social calendar. Peter saw things differently, and declined the opportunity to go. 'It was lovely meeting Hitler,' Berners would write in a postcard to 'Mad Boy' Heber-Percy.[35] Perversely, Berners disliked the Nazis but liked Hitler, who he thought was 'a good honest man' who had been 'corrupted by the German people's beastliness, their alternately cringeing and arrogant sentimentality'.[36] Diana felt differently; for her, Nazism was the hope of the future. The following year she married Oswald Mosley in Germany, in a secret ceremony at Josef Goebbels' house, attended by Hitler.

Safe for the moment in Venice, and acutely conscious of what Nazism had to say about people with his sexual orientation, Peter noted gloomily, 'If there is a war I suppose I shall be taken across the Bridge of Sighs', alluding to the days when the bridge served to link the Doge's palace with the city prison and echoed with the dolorous cries of the prisoners who were taken across it.[37]

* * *

Gerald Berners rarely took anything seriously – least of all his friends. To be acquainted with him was to expose oneself to the risk of satire, practical jokes and even ridicule. In 1935, during a stay in Rome with Diana prior to their trip to Nuremberg, Berners started writing a novella called *The Girls of Radcliff Hall* – a *roman à clef* in which the characters and love lives of several of his friends were parodied with vigorous glee. He cast them as lesbian schoolgirls – Cecil Beaton, Oliver Messel and Robert Heber-Percy were prominent in it; Cecil was cast as the heroine ('Cecily Seymour'), and the plot revolved around his obsession with Peter Watson ('Lizzie Johnson') and Peter's fling with Robin Thomas ('May Peabody'), all presided over by Berners himself, cast in the role of the lesbian headmistress, 'Miss Carfax'.

The title was a play on the name of lesbian author Radclyffe Hall, whose novel *The Well of Loneliness* had been a sensation in 1928; an attempt to portray the difficult lives of 'sexual inverts' in Britain at the time, it was suppressed by its publisher after a campaign against it by the *Sunday Express* and threats of criminal prosecution from the Home Secretary. Many contemporaries thought *The Well of Loneliness* a turgid, dull book; *The Girls of Radcliff Hall* was altogether different in spirit – one could see it as a celebration of male homosexuality enacted through the medium of a lesbian comedy, written by a man who was himself gay (in all senses of the word). But above all it was a parody.

Cecily, the heroine, is charming and talented – 'as clever with her paint brush as she was with her needle'. Lizzie (Peter), 'in spite of her capricious nature', is genuinely fond of Cecily, but is constantly having crushes and pashes with other girls ('How she manages it with that tow-coloured hair and that awful complexion I just can't imagine,' says a girl whose character is based on David Herbert). One of Lizzie's crushes is on Millie Roberts (Heber-Percy), but it is the arrival in the school of May Peabody – an adorably pretty American girl based on Robin May Thomas – that inflames Lizzie's adoration and causes heartache for Cecily. Cecily tries to make Lizzie jealous by having a fling with Mr Vivian Dorrick (Doris Castlerosse), but it is futile; Lizzie devotes all her attention to May, and doesn't even go to see Cecily in the school play ('Cecily, though her heart was breaking, put up a brave show. Never before had she seemed so gay, so brilliant ... But when Miss Carfax went round afterwards to congratulate Cecily she saw that there were tears running down her cheeks'). Little May is warned that 'your friend Lizzie Johnson is not at all a nice girl. And I want you, dear, only to have very nice girls for your friends.'[38] The plot progresses, involving a blackmail attempt against Lizzie by little May (the source of this in real life is obscure, but may be connected to the 'outraged silence' Robin maintained towards Peter in early 1934 and Peter's efforts to conciliate him). Lizzie has affairs with other girls, but eventually becomes a nun.

Diana, who was present during the writing, recalled: 'Every morning Gerald read me the latest chapter; sometimes he had to stop reading he laughed so much. It was wonderfully funny if you knew the characters and their foibles but perhaps less so for the general public.'[39] Accordingly, the book was privately printed in a limited run and passed around from hand to hand.

Besides Diana, the effect on the author's friends wasn't invariably positive. Cecil Beaton – who with neither a fortune nor an aristocratic title was in the most vulnerable social position – threatened to sue Berners for libel. Backing down, instead he attempted to single-handedly eradicate the book by collecting copies and destroying them.[40] Noël Coward – whose lover Jack Wilson was portrayed in the book as having a fling with Peter – said, 'Oh dear! What a beastly little book.'[41]

If Peter himself had any feelings about *The Girls of Radcliff Hall*, they were not recorded. Although the book was deeply embarrassing for Cecil, it was Peter whose character was most mercilessly traduced by it. And yet there is no evidence of his having been particularly offended or put out; perhaps because by this time he was confident enough in himself not to feel the slur the way Cecil did, but perhaps also because he was less involved with that particular British social circle now; he would never completely remove himself from it, but with his friendships with Pavlik, Marie-Laure, Bébé Bérard, Igor Markevitch and others, and his growing devotion to the cause of art, it had ceased to be the centre of his world. The new centre would be Paris.

9

LE PARADIS PERDU

1935–1936

By the end of 1935 the increasing power of Nazism had put Germany out of bounds for Peter, and Austria probably felt less comfortable than it had. There was still Switzerland, but Paris was the place to be. Peter's reputation as the most stylish Englishman in Paris now began to evolve into a role as a Parisian patron of art.

For Peter Watson, the era of pure frivolity was over; he was becoming part of a world in which style, entertainment and society were serious business. English friends such as Cecil Beaton and Stephen Tennant understood this, but they were rare, and chose to confine themselves largely to England and – in Cecil's case – America. Cecil was put off trying to make an impression on Paris society – 'Peter has had so much success there that it might be important for me to have success there also.'[1]

One man who did try to gain an entrée to Peter's Parisian circle was Charles James, a designer and couturier who was a close friend of Cecil's. Peter found him exasperating and embarrassing. During one visit in early 1935, James 'behaved with incredible stupidity'; on the day of his arrival 'he telephoned to Cocteau and to Bebe saying he was sick of not meeting who he wanted and could he come to tea? He has got madly on my nerves with his hysteria and stupidity.' To crown it all,

Charlie had to have an operation (in a back room of his hotel) on 'the most appalling boil on his tummy' and insisted on Peter coming to 'hold his hand'. Peter called it 'one of the worst ½ hours I ever spent'. With infuriating ingratitude, 'now he writes me insulting letters and behaves like a schoolgirl just in love' (Berners was evidently not the only one to make this kind of comparison). 'When with him I get so mad because I so despise his point of view.'[2] This can have done nothing to sustain Peter's attachment to his English acquaintances – indeed, in the same letter he couldn't even bring himself to describe 'the sort of thing that has been going on in London which I took good care to steer clear of'.

But the shift in Peter's centre of gravity didn't mean an end to partying – nobody did that with more verve than the French – and neither had Peter's hunger for sex lessened in any way. Spending more time in Paris gave him access to its liberal homosexual subculture as much as its high society and its arts.

Few can have known it then, but Paris was enjoying its last season of greatness, its final act on the centre stage of the artistic world; within a few years the curtain would fall, and when it rose again the great drama of modern art would have moved elsewhere – much of it to America. (Pavel Tchelitchew had already anticipated this shift, migrating to the USA with Charles Henri Ford in 1934.) But, for the time being, Paris was the place to be; the unique culture of radicalism and aristocratic splendour, the refinement of the salons and the depravity of the demimonde, remained as alive as it had been in the previous century, now dominated by the disconcerting principles of the twentieth-century avant-garde: Dada, Surrealism, Cubism, and Fauvism. Although he continued to lobby for a strain of Romanticism in modern art and music, Peter Watson was an enthusiastic patron of the new European movements, and would remain a near-permanent fixture of the Parisian scene until the long-anticipated war drove him out.

* * *

Although Paris would be his favoured place, Peter retained his house in Mayfair and continued to travel. In the summer of 1935 he visited Igor Markevitch at his home at Corsier-sur-Vevey in Switzerland – they were still preparing for the scheduled premiere of *Le Paradis perdu* – and planned a tour of Greece for September. Their friendship was blooming.

Peter visited Salzburg and found it intensely crowded with people 'of every possible kind' – Oliver Messel was there, as well as interior designer Sybil Colefax (known as 'Sybil Colebox' to Gerald Berners and Peter); Edward James and Tilly Losch were present simultaneously, despite having been divorced the previous year (on grounds of her adultery; she had tried to make his homosexuality a feature of the divorce, but failed), and Edward was gravitating into Gerald Berners' circle. Musical talent was represented by the soprano Olga 'Oggie' Lynn (a long-time friend of Peter and Cecil) and the composers Kurt Weill and Fritz Kreisler (both of whom Peter admired), as well as Igor Markevitch, who was there with Marie-Laure; she evidently didn't know yet about Igor's trysts with his true love Kyra Nijinsky. English high society was represented, in Peter's dismissive account, by '2 Duchesses of Westminster' and '3 Skeffington Smyths'.[3]

Digging deeper into the arts, during that summer Peter ventured into Italy, where an unimaginably heavenly Correggio exhibition in Parma was 'perhaps what impressioned me most of all'. In Milan he stayed with Count Luchino Visconti, who was just embarking on his career as a film-maker. He had a house and racing stable at Milan, described by Peter as 'a fantastic place consisting of seven houses round a big garden with green roofs'. Visconti had recently been employed as assistant director on Jean Renoir's influential proto-neorealist film *Toni*, which was notable for using 'real' people rather than actors. Visconti had been inspired by the experience, and would go on to make neorealism a coherent movement. 'We spent the afternoon in the swimming pool,' Peter wrote to Cecil, 'asking strangers with vague enough faces if they would like to act in the films.'[4]

Moving on to Geneva, Peter was delighted by it, and understood how right Voltaire and Stravinsky had been to make it their home; over the years, Switzerland would replace Germany in Peter's affections. Travelling on again with an almost feverish restlessness, he spent a few days yachting in the Adriatic, and visited Pavlik Tchelitchew and Charley Ford at Lake Garda, where they spent the day with Salvador and Gala Dalí,[5] but for Peter the highlight of that summer was his travels in the Mediterranean with Igor.

They met at Bologna and sailed from Brindisi for Athens on 13 September, the day before Peter's twenty-seventh birthday.[6] In Greece they hired an old Studebaker limousine, along with a young chauffeur called Niko, who would become more of a travelling companion than a servant. A resourceful and stylish young man who wore a pink handkerchief in his pocket, Niko had driven Gerald Berners and several of Peter's other friends, and was full of stories about their adventures, which he recounted wittily to his passengers. For Igor, the journey was a great spiritual adventure, discovering the diminutive scale of mankind in proportion to nature and antiquity; the Parthenon by moonlight and the amazing acoustics of ancient amphitheatres astonished him.

A plan to travel on to Rome was abandoned due to the worsening political situation. There was diplomatic tension between Mussolini and Britain over Ethiopia, and British travellers were being advised not to visit Italy. Instead Peter and Igor travelled further east, to Salonika. They had experienced the rusticity of Greek villages, but this was altogether different – Peter's lasting impression was of 'dusty roads, nauseating food with nothing but high goat's milk and butter to cook with' and 'beds seething with fleas'. 'I have never been to such a primitive country in my life,' he wrote. But his irrepressible friend took delight in it all. 'Igor has been a heavenly companion and has enjoyed everything madly'[7]

* * *

By the autumn Peter was back in England. He was scheduled to sail for New York in November, but squeezed in a visit to Cecil at Ashcombe and the hosting of a small party at Shepherd's Close, with guests including Pavlik Tchelitchew, Stephen Tennant, psychoanalytic anthropologist Geoffrey Gorer, and Charlie James (presumably recovered from his boil). Gorer must have been there in his capacity as one of Pavlik's many patrons; he can have had little else in common with Peter, or with the other male guests. He had recently published a book on the Marquis de Sade in which he aired some subtle but clearly homophobic views. (He appeared to coincide with de Sade in classing homosexuality as perverse, and believed that it had become more popular in the twentieth century due to bourgeois men's 'neurotic fear of life and responsibility.'[8]) Nonetheless he sat on Peter's sofa, with Tchelitchew at the other end and Stephen Tennant between them clutching his glass of milk while Pavlik slipped pieces of chocolate cake between his lips.[9]

Stephen, who still rather fancied Peter, noted that evening that his dark hair had been lightened by his recent sun-drenched tour of the

Aegean; Stephen was also taken with his adoption of fashionable Austrian touches such as short jackets with rounded lapels (presumably the shortness of the jacket set off his ever-delectable rear).

On 13 November Peter sailed from Southampton aboard the RMS *Berengaria* (still giving his occupation on the boarding list as 'student').[10] For the first time he was visiting America without Cecil's company. (Cecil had taken on the set design for a new Frederick Ashton ballet, which would be opening in December.) This was just as well, because although the 'official' purpose of the trip was to visit Pavlik and Charles Henri at their new home,[11] one of the items on Peter's New York itinerary was a reunion with the lovely Robin Thomas – now twenty years old.

Perhaps because of this liaison, or perhaps because of some spat at Ashcombe (Cecil was going through another phase of feeling that only a permanent break could cure his hopeless love), Peter wrote no letters to Cecil during this stay, and little trace of it would have survived if Stephen Tennant had not joined Peter in New York later in the month. Dining with Rex Whistler at the St Regis – the absurdly splendid Beaux Arts hotel built by J. J. Astor on East 55th Street and 5th Avenue – Stephen was surprised and thrilled to find Peter there, hosting a dinner with Russian-born composer Nicolas Nabokov and ballet costumer Barbara Karinska – both had worked for the Ballet Russe de Monte Carlo (an offshoot of the original Ballets Russes), which made Stephen feel faint with awe. But despite Peter's entreaties to join the party, Stephen was feeling too tired and delicate to stand the strain.[12]

Peter and Stephen – along with young Robin – were reunited a few days later at a party hosted by Peter's old acquaintance Tallulah Bankhead. Rex Whistler, who'd had a fling with her in England, was still smitten, and Stephen was excited to distraction by the prospect of meeting film stars. He brought her several enormous bouquets of flowers, but they were put in the shade by the gardenia tree brought by Robin Thomas. Tallulah, who (as Peter and his school friends could attest) had a proven penchant for boyish men (and boys), spent the evening trying to seduce Stephen, not realising that he wasn't susceptible to her magnetic allure. He escaped with his virtue, if not his nerves, intact. 'I was deeply ill at ease with her,' he recalled. 'I felt she was a man-eating vampire, really.'[13]

* * *

Back in England, Peter's first major act as a patron of modern arts came to fruition on the evening of 20 December 1935, with the live BBC broadcast of the premiere performance of *Le Paradis perdu* by Igor Markevitch, done as part of the regular 'Concerts of Contemporary Music' series. It took place before an audience in the concert hall at Broadcasting House, with Igor conducting the BBC Chorus and Orchestra; the soloists included soprano Oda Slobodskaya and tenor Hugues Cuénod, whose repertoires ranged from Bach to Stravinsky and Shostakovich.[14]

Le Paradis perdu was a bold piece, and inevitably received a mixed reception. The *Observer* critic likened the work to Stravinsky's *Firebird*, while noting that 'the technique is altogether more extravagant.' His verdict was equivocal: 'That the oratorio is dramatic, that it has vitality and imagination and consistency, will not be denied.' But 'the score is too thick, too feverishly mechanical and of destructive, disintegrating complexity'.[15] The critic seems to have been listing, as if they were faults, the very qualities that made the work appeal to Peter.

Having overcome its birth pangs, the piece finally had its European premiere at the Beaux Arts in Brussels the following May, and in Paris shortly after. And thus Igor's aspirations were complete. A few weeks before the Brussels premiere, on 20 April 1936 in Budapest, he and Kyra Nijinsky were married. Igor had at last written to Marie-Laure to tell her about Kyra, and was rewarded with an imperious, frigid silence. Peter, who was best man and didn't wish to cast a blight on the happy day, kept quiet about the fact that the heartbroken Marie-Laure had summoned him and ceremoniously laden him with all the presents that Igor had given her, with instructions to return them. Eventually she forgave Igor and, last of all his former lovers, made peace with Kyra.[16]

Later that year, Igor and Kyra had a son, named Vaslav after his famous grandfather. But it couldn't last; the marriage fractured and they were eventually divorced. Igor and Peter would remain friends for several years, but by the outbreak of the war they had grown apart. Peter felt that Igor, under Italian influence, 'was becoming a cultural Fascist'.[17] Igor left Switzerland, settled in Italy and served as a partisan during the war. They met again in London in 1947, when Igor had turned aside from composing and built a career as a conductor. Peter was excited by the reunion with his old friend, and, in spite of the breach, Igor would always retain very fond memories of Peter, who, along with Diaghilev, had been one of the strongest supporters of his art.

* * *

In December 1936, Peter sailed again for New York.[18] Part of his purpose this time was to catch up with Cecil, who had gone there a week earlier and was preparing for an exhibition due to open in January. But Peter had another purpose in America – a purpose he had deliberately kept secret from Cecil. He had a new lover, and had fallen deeply, desperately in love. Robin Thomas was gone and forgotten, but like Robin the new lover was young – twenty-two to Peter's twenty-eight – and American; he had returned from Europe to his home country in August, and now Peter was following him.

As it happened, Cecil had been conscious for months that Peter had been behaving oddly and secretively, and he suspected that something was afoot. He had decided again that the time had come for a final break with his beloved tormentor. This time, he swore, it was over.

The new lover was called Denham Fouts, an American Peter had met in Europe. Denham was described by one person who knew him as 'a fascinating figure, a male whore, a kind of dark angel of the Paris nighttime streets'.[19] Peter had fallen madly for him, and it would be a long time – years of mingled joy and anguish – before he would struggle free from the net.

10

DARK ANGEL

1936–1938

Truman Capote, who was one of the long and illustrious line of men who would be captivated by Denham Fouts during his short lifetime, famously called him the Best-Kept Boy in the World. His reputation as a male whore and courtesan of extraordinary beauty spread far and wide during the 1930s and 1940s: 'Denny,' recalled Capote, 'long before he surfaced in my cove, was a legend.'[1] Peter Watson lived through the making of the myth, and bore the emotional scars to prove it. He'd had his first brief erotic encounter with the dangerous, crookedly beautiful 'dark angel' in a nightclub in 1933, and after staying apart for several years they came together again in London and then set up home in Paris.

Thus Peter would consummate his Parisian odyssey with a destructive love almost worthy of a Zola novel. Of all the men who are known to have loved and kept Denham during his brilliant career, Peter Watson was the first, almost the last, and certainly the most constant, as well as being the most bruised by the experience.

Peter never knew the full facts about Denham Fouts – nobody did. Denham's story was and is obscured by a mist of rumour, legend, half-remembered fact, and fantasy. Many of the legends were of Denham's own telling – such as his claim to have been kept by a German ace fighter pilot who was a relation of the Red Baron, and to have been a member of the Hitler Youth. And his tales had a disconcerting habit, when subjected to scrutiny, of turning out to be true. Gore Vidal, who knew him in the 1940s, was convinced that 'Denham never lied'. When Denham claimed, rather implausibly for a migrant American good-time boy, that he was intimate with King Paul of Greece, Vidal was sceptical. It had just been reported that King Paul was suffering from typhoid fever – 'I must send him a telegram,' Denham said. 'The next day,' Vidal recalled, 'Denham showed me the reply: "Darling Denham, so wonderful to hear from you. Why haven't I heard from you before? ... Love, Paul."'[2] And yet it would always be difficult to sift truth from the myths.

His origins remained obscure, although he told a picaresque version of his story. The bare facts are that he was born Louis Denham Fouts in Florida in May 1914. The story was that he came from the sprawling Atlantic city of Jacksonville and that his father was a baker. In fact, although he grew up in Jacksonville, he was born in Boca Grande, a needle-thin island that lies across the glittering blue mouth of Charlotte Harbor on Florida's west coast. His father, Edwin Louis Fouts, was a Yale graduate from Denver who worked in management, at various times presiding over a broom factory in Jacksonville and managing a branch of Sherk's Ice Cream Company in Atlantic Beach, and in later life was an estimator (quantity surveyor) and building contractor.[3]

According to the story told to Truman Capote, around 1930 the sixteen-year-old Denham 'was living in a Florida crossroads cracker town and working in a bakery owned by his father. Rescue – some might say ruin – arrived one morning in the fattish form of a millionaire driving a brand-new built-to-order ... Duesenberg convertible.' The 'bakery' was probably Sherk's Ice Cream parlour, where he was a clerk, but if his later performance is any guide, the Duesenberg and the millionaire were probably as described. And so began the adventure – 'that night, without having returned home for even a change of underwear, Denny was a hundred miles away in Miami.'[4]

The gorgeous boy learned to sell himself, and to travel. By 1933, aged nineteen, he had put thousands of miles and a whole ocean between himself and Jacksonville, and was living in the newly Nazifying Germany, plying the courtesan trade with the panache of a seasoned professional. It was here, in a nightclub – one of Germany's 'queer places', probably in Berlin – that he met Peter Watson. 'He took me back to his hotel,' Peter recalled, 'where he gave himself cocaine injections.'[5] It was a one-night stand, but a seed had been planted. Peter was attracted and fascinated not only by Denham's looks but by his cynicism, and wondered if he could become the only person in Denham's life to win his trust and love. But after that one striking encounter in gay Berlin, they didn't see each other for several years, and Denny went on with his adventure.

It might well be true that he was in the Hitler Youth – everyone who knew him believed the story, and he certainly had the physique and the blond looks for it. He was a Nazi's Aryan wet dream made flesh – indeed, the one definitely apocryphal story about Denny was that the Führer himself lusted after him; the composer Ned Rorem remarked that, 'if Fouts had slept with Hitler, as Hitler wished, he could have saved the world from the Second World War.'[6] It was said that Denham's regular keeper during his time in Nazi Germany was the fighter ace von Richthofen – not the Red Baron himself (who had died in action in 1918) but his cousin, Wolfram Freiherr von Richthofen, a First World War ace who had survived and was now a high-ranking officer in the resurgent Luftwaffe.

Everyone – from the businessman in the Duesenberg to princes and kings – was captivated by Denny's beautiful but off-kilter looks. He had been made in the same matinée-idol mould that had produced Rudolf Valentino and Cary Grant – but in Denny's case it had gone slightly askew. He had the fair features, the straight, sharp, handsome nose, the jawline, the full underlip, the lozenge-shaped cheeks and the smouldering eyes – but there was an asymmetric fault-line in his face. Christopher Isherwood, who knew and loved him in the 1940s, was fascinated and repelled simultaneously by his appearance – 'the lean, hungry-looking tanned face, the eyes which seemed to be set on different levels, as in a Picasso painting ... His handsome profile was bitterly sharp, like a knife edge. And goodness, underneath the looks and the charm, how sour he was!' Like Peter Watson, Isherwood was drawn by the darkness of Denny's personality, which 'could sometimes be wonderfully stimulating and bracing, especially as an antidote to sweetness and light'. But Isherwood 'learned by experience to take it in cautious doses. Too much of it at one time could make you feel as if you were suffering from quinine poisoning.'[7]

Isherwood felt that the erect, physically fit Denham had a body that was too perfect: 'You couldn't say it wasn't good-looking, lying there in the sunshine, very dark brown and gleaming with oil ... And yet it repelled me slightly; it was slender in the wrong way, and somehow too elegant, too wearily sophisticated in its movements ... Perhaps it had lost its unself-conscious animal-grace in the process of acquiring the negligent-arrogant art of being looked at.'[8] It is entirely possible that Denny learned to apply this layer of elegance over his 'animal-grace' by observing Peter Watson at close quarters.

Denham's age was uncertain – he was nineteen when Peter first met him in 1933, and yet he had already begun to lie about his age, consistently knocking off two years.[9] Perhaps this was how he managed to gain admittance to the Hitler Youth. His motive for joining can be guessed at, and if the guess is correct, it was almost as sinister as the organisation itself; although he whored for older men, and relied on them to keep him, Denny's own sexual preference was for adolescent boys.[10]

After his fleeting encounter with Peter Watson, and having broken up with von Richthofen, Denham hiked to Venice, then settled in Capri for a while, and eventually made his way back to the United States with a new lover and keeper. Retaining a firm hold on the social ladder, this time he had captured a British peer of the realm; Evan Morgan, 2nd Viscount Tredegar, a thin, melancholy-looking man who came from one of Britain's most eccentric aristocratic families (his mother was said to have made a hobby of building human-size birds' nests). Evan was a keen occultist, a chamberlain to Pope Pius XI, and, despite having married for form's sake, was exuberantly homosexual. He had picked Denham up in Capri, where the intriguing lad was being arrested for non-payment of hotel bills. 'Unhand that handsome youth,' Evan ordered the police, 'he is mine!'[11]

They began an intermittent affair (most of Denny's affairs were like that). In 1935 Denham spent some time in England while Evan holidayed in the Bahamas. Possibly he dallied briefly with Peter Watson again, but in March he sailed for New York, where he joined Evan at his suite in the Plaza Hotel. Denny's stay in his home country was short; a few days later they sailed for Britain, where they were intending to stay at Evan's Welsh country seat, Tredegar Park, near Newport in Monmouthshire. Travelling with them was the man who would soon replace Evan as

Denham's gentleman of the purse-strings, the balding, gnomish Prince Paul of Greece.[12]

These affairs were brief. Eventually, Denny's instinct pointed him towards the person who could be best relied on to keep him; thus he drifted back to the man he had fleetingly met and docked with in that German nightclub. He and Peter had corresponded sporadically ever since, and now – probably at some time in the middle of 1936 – Peter took him in. For some time they lived together very discreetly (and probably intermittently) at Shepherd's Close, but by the following year they would be looking for a safer love-nest – in Paris.

Having had to endure Cecil's jealousy over Robin, Peter attempted to keep his love affair with Denham secret from his best and truest friend. In fact, he kept it largely away from the attention of most of his English friends – as Capote put it, they were dismayed (though some were probably cruelly delighted) that the elegant, personable Peter had become 'infatuated with the notorious Denny Fouts, an "exhibitionist playboy", a drug addict, an American who talked as though his mouth were busy with a pound of Alabama corn mush'.[13] So for the time being Peter kept Denny under wraps, especially concealing him from Cecil.

Peter was drawn to Denham's physical attractions, but more so to the idea of being needed by the 'terribly neurotic' younger man; Denham 'had no confidence in anyone', Peter recalled; 'this stimulated me and I thought if I took trouble he would [have confidence] in me.'[14] In later years, Peter would come to understand himself, and realise that 'my greatest need is to love rather than to be loved.'[15] In that respect he was perhaps more like Cecil Beaton than he knew. But, as Cecil could have told him (and indeed *had* told him many times), the need to love would not protect him from suffering when his love was not requited.

* * *

Even if it had been possible to keep Denham secret from society, Peter should have known by now that Cecil was too sensitive and perspicacious a creature to be deceived. In November 1936, Cecil, feeling 'devitalised' by his work, which now seemed trivial to him, and in a constant state of anxiety and drugged haze from the treatments that were supposed to help him cope with his overwhelming workload, began to realise that something was going on. He wrote in his diary that 'this month my relations with Peter have reached a dull impasse. In each other's presence our speech is halting and evasive ... and there is such disturbance and so many secrets between us now – and such lack of understanding.'[16]

Cecil didn't know what the big secret was, but experience told him it was something dire, and that the damage to his own emotional well-being would be severe. The time had come – again – for a permanent severance.

He had made occasional attempts to snub Peter during the past couple of years, and had been gratified by how upset Peter was – it was 'galling to his vanity', Cecil noted. Peter, who loved and valued Cecil, was hurt by these snubs – such as his failure to write during one of his stays in America; 'It's a pity you can write to Johnny McMullin and not to me. I will efface myself when you come back so as you can spend your time with your other friends. Cheerioh, Peter.'[17] McMullin was fashion editor of *Vogue*, and only a slight acquaintance of Cecil's, so the snub was particularly acute.

These minor tiffs had not disturbed the course of their friendship. But by the end of 1936 Peter's secretiveness – almost certainly indicating the existence of a serious lover – had driven Cecil to the brink (again). In New York he made the acquaintance of Miss Bathsheba Askowith, actress, acting coach and – most importantly for Cecil – self-styled clairvoyant. She listened patiently as he poured out his vaguely disguised story, and concurred that a break from his friend was both necessary and justifiable, and that indecision was the worst thing.[18] But the really decisive advice came from his close friend Nicolas Nabokov, the composer, who knew Peter quite well. They talked through the night in Cecil's New York hotel room, until Cecil 'groaned with exhaustion and unhappiness' and Nabokov was 'rolling from side to side in painful exhaustion'. He empathised with Cecil's plight – he had been there himself, madly in love for years with a woman who spurned him. The answer had been to remove her from his life – an act of 'terrible force, tremendous bravery' that caused him weeks and months of anguish and pain. But in the end, he told Cecil, he had found strength and freedom. 'You will find it too,' he promised; in order to grow, one must prune.[19]

So Cecil summoned his courage and resolved – again – to excise Peter from his life. The opportunity to begin the pruning occurred very soon. On 7 December 1936 Peter arrived in New York and booked into his regular haunt, the St Regis.[20] He had come to America to meet up with Denham, who had sailed over in August, ostensibly to visit his family in Jacksonville.[21] (Despite his financial dependency on Peter, which would increase over the next few years, Denham would never feel beholden to him or obliged to spend time with him.)

Peter had come to New York at a time when America – and indeed the world – was agog over the abdication crisis in Britain: on 10 December King Edward VIII brought his brief reign to an end in a blaze of press excitement. Every newspaper in the civilised world wanted photos of the scandalous Wallis Simpson, and Cecil Beaton had several that he'd taken the month before in England. He could have named his fee for them, but he was loyal to *Vogue*, and the photos appeared in the magazine on 1 January 1937.[22] It garnered attention for the exhibition of his photography at the Carroll Carstairs Gallery in New York, which opened on 4 January. Salvador and Gala Dalí were there, as was Marjorie Oelrichs (now married to the Jewish bandleader Eddy Duchin, which had caused her to be cold-shouldered by America's fastidious high society, whose anti-Semitism made England's pale by comparison) and the ever-reliable Doris Castlerosse.[23]

Peter Watson was not at the opening; Cecil had not invited him. He had been pruned. When Peter inquired, he found that Cecil had gone away. Peter was shocked and grieved, especially as Cecil had sent him a Christmas present a couple of weeks earlier. He waited for Cecil to return to New York – still a frigid silence – then contacted him again. 'My dear child,' he wrote plaintively from the St Regis, 'I do not understand why you didn't telephone me when you came back. Also why didn't you ask me to your exhibition? It is all very strange and can help none of us – please use a little more of your understanding. Life is difficult enough as it is.'[24]

Cecil eventually replied from Palm Beach, telling Peter that he had broken off their friendship and did not wish to hear from him.

Given his past behaviour, Peter might have guessed that Cecil wouldn't have the stamina to keep it up, but that didn't make it any less upsetting. Peter and Denham travelled back to Europe, where they began making plans to establish a home together. Shepherd's Close would do at a pinch, but Peter was yearning for Paris. He was happy with Denham, in love and looking forward to the future.

* * *

Peter found the future waiting for him in Austria, in the plump, ugly and decidedly unlikely form of Cyril Connolly, formerly of Eton and Oxford, now a part of the wandering British literary set, with one foot in London and the other in Paris. Peter and Denham were spending the summer in Peter's habitual manner – touring Europe. They stopped off in Kitzbühel, which Peter had last visited in early 1935, his stay blighted by rain, muddy ski slopes and English public-schoolers. On this visit he found an old public-schooler whom he was prepared to like – Cyril Connolly and his young American wife, Jean.

Connolly was five years older than Peter, and their overlap at Eton had been brief. Peter must have known his name at school, as during Peter's first year Connolly had been a member of the august and powerful Eton Society (informally known as 'Pop'), one of the strata of senior boys with the power to beat younger ones. And he was probably also familiar with his career since school. Just a year earlier, in 1936, Connolly had published his first and only novel, *The Rock Pool*, a satire set among a group of decadent arty types; it had been deemed too obscene for Britain, and had instead been published in Paris.

Paris had been lucky for Cyril Connolly – in 1929 he had met nineteen-year-old art student Jean Bakewell there, a lively and attractive American with a big income. They went to New York together and were married in 1930. They toured Europe on Jean's money, took a flat in the King's Road, and built up a small and diverse salon of writers that included Evelyn Waugh, Elizabeth Bowen, Dylan Thomas and Anthony Powell. Their circle intersected with Peter Watson's, and they had presumably at least heard his name and knew of his reputation for wealth and style.

When Cyril and Jean met Peter and Denham at Kitzbühel, all four of them hit it off right away.[25] Cyril, like most artists and writers, had a keen eye for a rich source of cash, and Peter was a particularly charming and generous one. But Cyril also appreciated his intellect – or at least his taste, which was finely judged and flawless in every department, from ties and handkerchiefs to cars, wine, concertos and paintings. But the strongest attraction was between Peter, Denham and Jean. She quickly became very friendly with both of them. They had things in common – Denham was a fellow American migrant in Europe, and Peter was a gay, hedonistic youngster who had inherited a large income, as had she (albeit much smaller than Peter's).

That bond would cause trouble later, but for the time being the four had an enjoyable time together and became firm friends. Eventually Peter and Cyril's friendship would blossom into a creative partnership, with the help of another wandering British aesthete, the poet Stephen Spender, whom Peter had first met in Paris in 1935.[26] But on that summer's day in Kitzbühel, that project was still (as it were) out of sight below the far horizon.

These new friends aside, Peter continued moving further away from Britain spiritually, intellectually and, he hoped, physically. He had decided to settle in Paris, and set about looking for a home. The same sense of anticipation and the longing for a place of his own that had gripped him in the early days of his wealth, while furnishing his mother's house in South Street, took him over again. So did the same fastidious notion that it must be the perfect 'heavenly dwelling'. And after weeks of searching, he despaired. 'I have worked myself to a nervous breakdown looking for apartments,' he wrote to Cyril, who was going through a bout of depression in London, 'and have found nothing.'[27] The only place he had seen that was suitable in terms of aesthetics and comfort was in the same building as Léon Blum, the former and future prime minister, which was 'always *surveillé* by 12 policemen'. That wouldn't do at all.

Meanwhile Peter continued to enjoy Parisian culture and society from his suite at the Ritz on the Place Vendôme. The cultural palette was mixed that year – he was 'terribly bored' by the opening night of Jean Cocteau's new play *Les Chevaliers du Table Ronde*, but delighted by sneak previews of ballet designs by Bébé Bérard and Dalí. And like all of Paris he was knocked back on his heels by the impact of Picasso's new 'Spanish picture' (as he called it), an enormous mural canvas portraying the bombing of Guernica by General Franco's German allies in April that year. The painting, commissioned by Spain's Republican government, was first exhibited at the Paris Exposition Internationale des Arts et Techniques dans la Vie Moderne. But Peter was disappointed to discover, at a private viewing, that the sketch studies for the painting seemed 'terribly harsh and crude, quite lacking the power of the big picture'.[28] It was an interesting glimpse of the gap between the mere layout and draughtsmanship of a picture and the totality of the artist's vision brought to life on the canvas.

Knowing Peter's love of Picasso, Cyril bought him a copy of the artist's new engravings, a series that prefigured *Guernica*, depicting in savage monochrome the violence and terror perpetrated in Spain by Franco's insurrection; it was titled *The Dream and Lie of Franco*, and was a sensation – there was a plan to reproduce it as a series of postcards so that the proletariat could buy it. Peter was touched, but already had a set of prints, so he told Cyril to keep them, and admonished him affectionately (as he had Cecil Beaton some years earlier): 'You are *not* to give me presents.'[29]

At around the same time, Peter made a much more significant Picasso acquisition, buying the 1934 canvas *Reading at a Table* (also known as *Girl Reading* or *La Femme lisant*), a portrait of the artist's lover Marie-Thérèse Walter – an unusually serene and beautiful work by Picasso's challenging standards – from the London gallery of Parisian dealer Paul Rosenberg.[30] It was a large canvas – more than a metre and a half high by over a metre wide – and must have taken up a lot of room in the already crowded house at Shepherd's Close.

Peter still had no place in Paris to hang his paintings. He was living out of expensive hotels, with no place to make his own, no place to live with Denham and house his art collection, which was burgeoning (he had begun to consider himself a dealer rather than merely a connoisseur[31]). But he was immensely picky, and it became clear that 1937 was going to end without the heavenly dwelling manifesting itself.

At least one other trouble was resolved; while his new friendship with Cyril and Jean Connolly came into existence, his old friendship with Cecil Beaton revived. Cecil believed that at last he had gained the freedom that Nicolas Nabokov had promised would come from the 'pruning' of Peter, and without the cost of losing his friendship. For the first time since that summer in Vienna in 1930, he could be friends with Peter without suffering pain. ('Hurrah! Oh how happy I am!' he wrote in his diary.)[32] In September 1937 his latest book came out – *Cecil Beaton's Scrapbook*, another take on the collage technique he'd pioneered with his *Book of Beauty* in 1930 – and in recognition of the new phase in their friendship it was dedicated simply to 'Peter'.

Peter, whose patience with Cecil's moods and changes of heart was seemingly limitless, was moved; he declared that the *Scrapbook* was 'a triumph, a hundred per cent success and *must* have a bigger circulation than the Bible'.[33] He alluded coyly to the dedication: 'And Peter? Who is he? If I don't know him may I meet him – if I do I am very proud.' Cecil would be leaving for America soon, and Peter suggested, 'Wouldn't it be nice to meet before you go? I should love to so much.' He disclaimed any selfishness, insisting that he would not suggest it if he thought it bad for Cecil. 'Or am I a bore?' he wrote. 'Or are you a bore? Or did I do something terrible? If so please tell me exactly what.'[34]

Cecil didn't trust himself to see Peter yet, and replied by telegram: 'Am really glad you liked my book which naturally was dedicated to you. I miss you very much but perhaps 'tis better so.'[35]

Cecil's love life was moving on in every way. That year, he had dumped the stopgap Doris Castlerosse for the more exquisite Greek charms of Lillia Ralli, who, despite lacking Doris's blonde looks, had the double advantage of being tremendously chic and a close friend of Prince George and Princess Marina, the Duke and Duchess of Kent – glamorous royalty *par excellence* – whose circle Cecil was anxious to penetrate.[36]

He had created a space between himself and Peter, yet it would be some years before they would settle permanently into a friendship that was comfortable for both of them. Perhaps indeed it was better so.

* * *

With winter creeping over Europe, Peter and Denham departed for a thrill-seeking tour of the Far East. Having failed to find a home in Paris, Peter was desperate to avoid a winter in England. 'I am so thankful to be out of London and to be going far away,' he wrote to Cyril from the Paris Ritz shortly before departing.[37] He had been getting restless even in Paris, wearying of city life, 'and London is to me the worst city I have ever stayed in.'

It was an odd moment to choose for a first trip to the Orient. A few months earlier, in July 1937, the Second Sino-Japanese War had broken out with the full-scale Japanese invasion of China. Even now, as Peter and Denny prepared to sail, a ferocious battle was being fought for possession of Shanghai. Chinese commander Chiang Kai-shek threw everything he had into the defence of the city, in the hope that Western military aid might come. But the world's governments were preoccupied with the deteriorating situation in Europe, and all that came was two gay adventurers in search of hot weather and disreputable fun.

Peter and Denham sailed from France via the Mediterranean and Suez, and by December had reached their first port of call: Colombo, capital of British Ceylon, which was sweltering in a steamy tropical summer of heat and rain. Peter was surprised to find, in this modern age, a 'complete musical comedy colony with tea, good manners, racing and rickshaws'. The Ceylonese natives were 'very fine, polite and utterly subdued'. Peter was very disappointed by his first glimpse of society east of Suez – it was stiflingly male and heterosexual. 'My sallies into Consular society,' he wrote to Cyril, 'have been rather disappointing. No drugs, no women, no boys as far as I can see although slight signs of drink. Otherwise I can't think *what* they do. In the town there isn't a bar open after 11 – not at all what I came to the Orient for.'[38] This was as much Denham as Peter speaking. Unlike Denny, Peter's tastes did not run either to drugs or to young boys. It was possibly during this tour, in fact, that he discovered his concubine's pederastic tendencies; at the time he viewed them with perplexity, and only later would he come to regard them with horror.[39]

Everything in Ceylon was expensive, and although to Peter's eyes the British colonials all looked poor, he guessed they must be rich. The hotel food was ghastly, but the Indian curry was 'to die from it's so wonderful ... yum-yum'.[40]

The newspapers from home worried him – 'civilisation in collapse is not an edifying spectacle.' It seemed that a war might erupt while he was still in the East, but he assured Cyril that 'I feel I shall come back to be gassed with all of you.'[41] Peter viewed the impending war with gloom for the sake of civilisation, and with the antipathy that was the hallmark of his generation; he and Cyril both approved Aldous Huxley's new collection of essays, *Ends and Means*, which was eloquently anti-war; Cyril had reviewed it for *The Sunday Times*, noting with approval that 'Huxley's great point is that the Means are never justified by the End. That violence in any cause, right or wrong, begets more violence. He is the complete pacifist.'[42] Peter strongly concurred, but felt that Huxley's book was 'a very tiny voice crying in a wilderness'.[43]

There was a war already boiling away ahead of the two lovers, and for all his avowed pacifism Peter sailed blithely towards it. From Ceylon the travellers voyaged on to Singapore and Java aboard a Japanese ship, which Peter reckoned had the advantage of being unlikely to get torpedoed by its own Imperial Navy. Observing Japanese efficiency at first hand, comparing it to the damp British colonials and presumably recalling Nazi Germany, Peter was prompted to wonder why energy and efficiency were only found in 'aggressive and Fascist states'. This seemed a feature exclusively of the modern world, which had not affected the ancient civilisations and would puzzle him always. The only exception was the United States, whose vitality he admired but whose frenetic atmosphere he could never stand for more than a few weeks before it exhausted him.

In Singapore they stayed at the Raffles Hotel. Peter had intended to remain in Singapore until January, but stayed only long enough to obtain a visa for the USA.

By the time he and Denham reached Shanghai the fighting had ended and the city was firmly in Japanese hands; the Chinese had retreated and were now in a hopeless fight for Nanking. Shanghai was a wreck. The battle had gone on from August to November, and the fighting had been intense; the 'Bloody Saturday' bombing by the Japanese – alongside Guernica, one of the first uses of modern bombers against a civilian target – caused worldwide outrage and left whole areas in ruins.[44] But as in all war-ravaged cities, no matter how violent the suffering or how extensive the destruction, the first thing to revive in the aftermath was the nightlife – pleasure, however desperate, always finds a way to cling on and survive. Delving into the Shanghai underworld, Peter ran into an old German friend – Freddy Kaufmann, who had run a bar called the Jockey Club in pre-Nazi Berlin. He now had a bar of his own on the Shanghai waterfront. Denny took to the place with great enthusiasm, and when Peter departed for Hong Kong to catch a ship for America, Denny stayed behind, apparently with the intention of taking a job in Freddy's bar.[45]

Peter didn't seem perturbed by the parting (Denham Fouts could be intense, and would be wearing company on a long voyage). Peter sailed alone from Hong Kong on Christmas Eve 1937 aboard a Canadian liner bound for Hawaii. It was a long voyage of two weeks, calling at the Japanese ports of Kobe and Yokohama (where Peter saw in the New Year), and finally arriving at Honolulu on 6 January.[46]

Hawaii was adorable; the perfect blend of American vitality and the exotic South Seas, well-stocked with muscular young men: 'incredibly luxurious hotel, wonderful beach with surf to ride and beach boys at every step ... flowers everywhere and everyone gay and singing with ukeleles.'[47]

But there was no escaping society. On his very first day he bumped into Doris Castlerosse and a crowd of movie people. It seemed that Doris had not given up her fantasy of being in films – several years ago Peter had remarked to Cecil that she fancied herself as a film star and would go off to Elstree for screen tests. He was irritated by her: 'My God, Cecil, isn't she unnerving, I go nearly mad at her sometimes.'[48] Cecil had believed Peter's dislike was caused by jealousy, and indeed Peter seemed to tolerate her well enough now that Cecil had ditched her for Lillia. Perhaps both having been recently shoved away by Cecil gave them a bond.

Doris was in company with producer Samuel Goldwyn and Broadway lyricist and MGM publicist Howard Dietz. Peter was already acquainted with Dietz's wife, Tanis, who had formerly been married to Peter's friend Drogo Montagu (victim of the great debagging in St Moritz two years earlier). They discussed films, which depressed Peter – 'I have realised the hopelessness of expecting a really intelligent film coming out of Hollywood.'[49]

After two weeks in Hawaii, Peter and Doris sailed together for Los Angeles.[50] Doris took an adobe villa on Roxbury Drive in Beverly Hills at $1,000 for the month (which would be about half a year's rent in London or Paris) and Peter stayed with her for a while.

Peter dined several times with director George Cukor – the one movie person he really liked – who was then bogged down to his heavy brows in the seemingly hopeless task of adapting the hit novel *Gone with the Wind* for the screen. Production was being delayed by the impossibility of writing a script concise enough to be commercial; but it was producer David O. Selznick's determination to get the reluctant Clark Gable for the lead role (and Sam Goldwyn's refusal to release him from his MGM contract) that was really holding the film up. Peter's conversations with Cukor confirmed his opinions about Hollywood – that 'the whole business is a world unto itself built on its own fantastic financial success.' As a serious source of art, it was hopeless.[51] Peter had never taken to Hollywood, and now he liked it even less. Other than Cukor, most of his old friends there bored him now.

There was one old friend who was far from boring – Erik Charell, the German choreographer and producer, who was visiting California from his base in New York. He was a relatively respectable stage producer now, but had once been the doyen of German vaudeville. Back in the 1920s Charell had put on stupendous shows for Max Reinhardt's celebrated Friedrichstadt-Palast nightclub in Berlin, hub of the decadent cabaret scene, which throbbed with jazz, bared flesh and eroticism of every flavour. In the 1930s Charell had fallen foul of the Nazis on two counts: the crackdown on the 'degenerate' nightclub jazz culture, and his Jewish descent. He departed Berlin for Paris and London, producing for the West End stage and later for Broadway. When Peter caught up with him in California, he was on a break, renting a house in the desert for six weeks. Peter, who liked Erik a great deal, stayed with him twice, and fell in love with the bright beauty of the desert.[52]

But there was no getting away from the movie business; when Peter eventually sailed for home from New York at the beginning of April, he was accompanied on the ship by his old acquaintance Mary Pickford (now divorced from Douglas Fairbanks) and Olivia de Havilland (who was lobbying hard that year for the role of Melanie in *Gone with the Wind*).[53]

His visit to America had not been wholly discouraging, though. In New York he had visited (as he always did when in town) Pavlik Tchelitchew and Charley Ford. Two things came out of his visit. First, he arranged to finance the publication of Charley's first book of poetry, *The Garden of Disorder*, which came out later that year. (Peter, who still wasn't entirely confident as a judge of literature, consulted Cyril Connolly about the merit of the poems before going ahead.)[54] Second, he had a conversation with Charley about the idea of founding an arts magazine. Charley would edit it, assisted by his friend and literary collaborator Parker Tyler, and Peter would provide the funding. The idea inspired both of them, and although their magazine never came into existence, they would each carry the idea forward separately and bring it to fruition on opposite sides of the Atlantic.[55]

* * *

Back in England, Peter paid a visit to his family at Sulhamstead before heading back to France. Then in May he travelled down to Marseilles to meet Denham, who had finally slouched back to Europe, presumably having satiated his appetite for Chinese boys and Shanghai waterfront life.[56]

The situation in Europe had moved on since their trip to the Orient. The German annexation of Austria had occurred on 12 March, and the face of Europe had changed. Another Englishman in Paris at the time, the Surrealist poet David Gascoyne (who became friendly with Peter and Denham later that year), felt 'constantly haunted by the shadow of this most recent crime of fascism ... How can one's mind escape any longer from the constant menace ...? It is beyond my understanding how anyone can remain indifferent and undisturbed.'[57] Peter Watson was not indifferent, but he showed no sign of being particularly disturbed by the Anschluss, even though it meant that Kitzbühel, Salzburg and Vienna were now out of bounds to him along with Berlin and Munich. Just as he had been conscious of the war in China but had not let it interfere with his pursuit of pleasure, he was now aware of the monster of Nazism but refused (at least for the time being) to let it obstruct his enjoyment of Paris.

And yet he didn't close his mind to the threat. The Germans he had met recently in America believed that Nazism was already doomed, but Peter wasn't convinced. He had heard of the Nazi regime's policy on art, and saw it as symptomatic of their insanity. They were debating, he had heard, whether to suppress the religious pictures of Matthias Grünewald (a German Renaissance painter who employed the same unbeautiful realism as his Flemish contemporaries) because they were 'not heroic enough'; Rembrandt was also under suspicion as 'not sufficiently anti-Jude' and Van Gogh was seen as representing the degenerate so-called *Kultur Bolschewismus* (cultural Bolshevism, the Nazi catch-all for modernism in art). 'Isn't it crazy?' Peter commented.[58]

But Paris was still alive with art, vibrant with creativity – unlike England. While in America, Peter had been distressed to hear a rumour that Wystan Auden was going back to schoolteaching (which had kept him going from 1930 to 1935). 'I admire his freshness so much,' Peter had written to Cyril, 'and deplore the English tendency towards the classroom.' He wondered whether homosexuality explained this tendency (faintly foreshadowing the very words that Cyril would use in *Enemies of Promise* later that year to condemn the British ruling class). 'I must say I never felt the urge!' As for Wystan, Peter thought 'a few days in Shanghai would do him good.'[59]

No, there was no living in England for Peter. It was time for a decisive change – he would turn thirty in September, and must have been acutely conscious of it. His home *must* be Paris, with its artists and its stylish *haut monde*, as well as the nightclubs, like the hyper-fashionable, ultra-decadent Boeuf sur le Toit or the claustrophobic *boîtes*, the tiny underworld clubs where young men could be picked up. He had a few valued British friends who were frequent visitors to Paris, and his circle of French friends had grown (he became such a frequent visitor at Marie-Laure's Riviera home at Hyères that the gardener there recognised him instantly when he revisited the place a decade later).[60]

And so he dedicated himself once more to finding a Paris home for himself and Denham. By the end of the summer he had fixed on an apartment – it was on a lively, fashionable street, it had an artistic pedigree, and it belonged to one of France's most prominent patrons of the arts.

11

A HEAVENLY DWELLING

1938–1939

The stepping-stone that carried Peter Watson the last yard into the swim of Parisian society was Comte Étienne de Beaumont. Designer, aesthete and arts patron (he had commissioned works by Picasso, Braque and Satie, among others), de Beaumont was a legendary figure. Anyone who attended one of the annual *bals masqués* at his Parisian mansion throughout the 1920s and 1930s would have a memory to illuminate the rest of their life.

Fantastically wealthy, Étienne de Beaumont was another rung up the social ladder from Marie-Laure de Noailles, and occupied an altogether higher plane of magnificence. He was the very heart and soul of Paris's artistic society in the twenties and thirties, and his masked balls were among its highest expressions, attended by the stars of the artistic world – from Marcel Proust to Christian Dior, by way of Erik Satie, Jean Cocteau, Man Ray, Pablo Picasso, Coco Chanel, Serge de Diaghilev, Pierre Cardin and a host of others. De Beaumont's parties were never thrown – they were carefully, intricately staged. Each had specially arranged music and décor; the mansion – including the courtyard and garden – would be decorated with uniquely created scenery, and there would be choreographed dancing, rehearsed *entrées* and *tableaux vivants* featuring the costumed guests. Each ball had a different, amazing theme – the sea, the baroque, the tales of Perrault, kings and queens, automobiles and machines – and the costumes were to match.[1]

De Beaumont was an imposing and self-consciously serious-looking gentleman. In silvery middle age, he was a debonair exquisite with a fine Roman profile and a sense of poise that the likes of Cecil Beaton could only aspire to. Peter Watson had first met him at St Moritz in 1933 (on the same occasion he first encountered Robin Thomas) and discovered a playful spirit beneath the sober, aloof pose: 'Étienne de Beaumont, believe it or not, is a riot,' Peter wrote.[2] Now, in the summer of 1938, he learned that de Beaumont had an apartment to let in the rue du Bac. It needed some modernisation to bring it up to Peter's standards of comfort, but its location was ideal.

The rue du Bac was a bright, lively street – situated close to the Seine on the Rive Gauche in the 7th arrondissement, it connected the Boulevard Saint-Germain to the Pont Royal, which crossed the river to the Louvre and the Tuileries gardens. Number 44 was a fairly plain four-storey block, probably eighteenth-century, with shops on the ground floor and wings running back from the street to enclose a small courtyard. André Malraux had an apartment in the building in the early 1930s, and wrote his novel *La Condition humaine* there, and the flat Peter rented had some artistic history too.

Consisting of two bedrooms, drawing room, dining room, kitchen and bathroom, it was at the rear of the building, overlooking the courtyard on the first floor. It had been fitted out by Étienne de Beaumont in the 1920s as a studio apartment for Picasso, but the artist hadn't liked the light from the windows, and never moved in. Instead, de Beaumont let it cheaply to the American poet Archibald MacLeish, who described it as having big rooms, but 'everything else about it crowded'; yet its size mattered little because it was on the rue du Bac, 'which is a wonderful street'.[3] MacLeish was part of the community of American writers in Paris that included Ernest Hemingway (who visited him at the apartment frequently), Gertrude Stein and F. Scott Fitzgerald. (Fitzgerald wrote *The Great Gatsby* while in France during 1924 and it is likely that the descriptions of the fabulously opulent parties given by Jay Gatsby at West Egg owed more than a little to the great *bals* of Étienne de Beaumont.[4]) By the late 1930s the American community had moved on, but Gertrude Stein was still around, and continued to visit 44 rue du Bac during Peter's tenancy.

Installing himself in the apartment – for which he paid a modest rent of 28,000 francs a year (about £150)[5] – Peter set about making it the centre of his own Parisian world. It would serve several purposes: as a salon for Peter's Parisian socialising and a home for the new additions to his art collection; but more importantly it was a permanent home for Denham, a place where he could at last settle and be loved by Peter, who hoped that he could cure him of his erratic, self-destructive temperament and his drug addiction. It would be a hard struggle – Denny had returned from his stay in China with a new habit: on top of the cocaine he had been using since his time in Berlin, he was now also addicted to opium.[6]

Over the following months, the apartment's walls began to fill with art. Peter acquired paintings by Georges Braque, de Chirico, Paul Klee, Joan Miró, Max Ernst, Picasso, Dalí and others. Some pictures were probably brought over from London when in September 1938, having apparently decided that Paris was his permanent home, Peter packed up the house in Shepherd's Close and disposed of it.[7] He had put a great deal of thought and energy into fitting and furnishing the house just so, but no matter how exquisite he made it inside, there was nothing to be done about the city it was in, and so it had to go.

Some paintings went into storage, and some were probably transferred to his mother's house in South Street. Styling himself as a dealer as much as a collector, he tended to keep only his choicest pieces on display in his homes – the best and most interesting work he could lay his hands on from each artist – while others were sold on. Some pictures he loaned to galleries for special exhibitions, and they went as far afield as London, Edinburgh and New York.

One of the most striking works in the Paris flat, kept on permanent display in Denham's bedroom, was Pavel Tchelitchew's *Bathers*, a group nude that was a nod to Cézanne and Matisse.[8] Peter had given the painting to Denham – one among several valuable works he bestowed on him. It was a striking and weirdly erotic view of three naked bathers standing facing each other (one was a portrait of Charles Henri Ford); the view was from ground-level looking up between the muscular, parted legs of the central figure, at the apex of which hung a great cock like a rope's end. Denham hung the painting above the bed, and sometimes liked to alter the view by hanging it upside-down or even fixing it to the ceiling. Other works Peter gave him included a still life by de Chirico and Picasso's *Reading at a Table* (which was kept in London for the time being).

The ménage at 44 rue du Bac began coming to life in late summer 1938, but Peter still had work to do before the apartment would be up to his standards. There were servants to be hired, the hot water system needed replacing and the bathroom required renovating ('rushing around choosing lavatories isn't such fun,' Peter wrote to Jean Connolly following a week with her in Antibes).[9] It would be Christmas before the place was fit to be lived in properly.

But even before then, the flat was teeming with life, most of it British, or at least Anglophone. Peter hadn't wholly abandoned his British friends, and the rue du Bac became a magnet for them. The Connollys visited – especially Jean, who had quickly grown close to Peter and Denham. Stephen Spender and his wife Inez came to stay several times, and Brian Howard and W. H. Auden visited. Downstairs was a small apartment, which Peter had somehow acquired as part of his arrangement with Étienne and which he sublet to the American abstract expressionist painter Buffie Johnson;[10] through her, the young poet David Gascoyne drifted into the Peter Watson circle.

Gascoyne initially became acquainted with Denham, of whom his first impression was of 'a sumptuous, spoiled young man with a lot of frail and rather hard-worked charm'.[11] But by December he had begun to change his mind. One evening, following a lecture on poetic drama at the Sorbonne, Gascoyne joined up with Peter Watson's party, which included Denham, Brian Howard and his German lover Toni Altmann, the writer James Stern and his wife, and W. H. Auden. As they squeezed into a car to go to the Brasserie Univers, Denham suddenly exclaimed to Gascoyne, 'You're just the person to come with us on my trip tomorrow!'[12] Denham's 'trip' turned out to be a motoring tour to Megève in the French Alps. He was going with the American artist Edward Melcarth; Peter, who was busy with the apartment and had no desire to cling to Denham – who was going through one of his calm periods – was not coming. Gascoyne accepted the invitation and, to his surprise, by the time the trio returned to Paris he had become 'genuinely fond' of Denham, and from that moment became almost a fixture at 44 rue du Bac.[13] His friendship with Peter would be much slower to develop.

Peter's friendship with Stephen Spender had also been a slow grower. They had known each other since 1935, but it was only in late 1938 that they became close. Stephen was a few months younger than Peter, already a renowned and well-connected poet, with oceans of political chic attained through his reporting on the Spanish Civil War. He was bisexual, and as a friend of Auden and Isherwood had explored the German gay scene at the beginning of the thirties. Now he was pursuing the straight side of his nature. Although he found young men more attractive, he had decided that sex with a woman was 'more satisfactory, more terrible, more disgusting, and, in fact more everything ... more of an experience.'[14] In 1936 he had married Inez Pearn, an Oxford postgraduate. She was handsome, with expressive, wide-set eyes (not unlike a female Peter Watson, in fact), and had a formidable mind; although she was friendly, some found that her intellect made her chilly.[15]

Stephen was an occasional recipient of Peter's patronage. He was touched by the way Peter supported artists, and by his humaneness; Peter helped people in 'a personal way ... first because he thought they had talent, and afterwards because he remembered that they were human beings who simply needed help'.[16] Spender spoke for many when he wrote that Peter 'had a burning and passionate love of the arts. His judgement was good, though perhaps slightly modish, but what is more important ... is the fact that for him the pursuit of art was a quest.' And, perhaps even more important than that, 'In my own friendship with him,' Stephen would recall in later years, 'there seems absolutely no cloud.'[17]

Of all the people who were close to Peter Watson (without being his lovers) Stephen Spender was one of the most smitten by him, second only to Cecil Beaton. Indeed, Peter once told Stephen that he reminded him of Cecil in some ways. 'I do see a certain resemblance,' Spender admitted, 'because there is something ascetic about his appearance and character, in spite of his affectations.'[18] Stephen did, in a sense, fall in love with Peter, but it was a platonic love, without complications.

The Spenders stayed with Peter and Denham in December 1938 and again in January. In between, the Connollys spent Christmas at the flat. Jean caught flu and was forced to extend her stay over New Year, while Cyril left for London; their marriage had been under considerable strain for more than a year, and the coming months would test it to destruction.

Peter went away at about the same time as Cyril, possibly to visit his mother, whose health would trouble her during the years that followed. Peter had been given a reminder of his own mortality the previous November, when during a visit to Britain he stayed with Sir Michael Duff (writer, godson of Queen Mary and nephew of Diana Cooper) at his country home, Vaynol, near Bangor in North Wales. The only other guest was Peter's old acquaintance and nemesis, the novelist Elinor Glyn, who had so frightened Cecil back in 1934 by predicting that Peter was 'bad all through' and would come to a bad end within the year. At Vaynol Peter took the opportunity to twit her about her foretelling, and point out that it had been a few years now and he wasn't dead yet. 'God will save you,' she told him solemnly.[19] (Wrong again.)

Still happily alive, with the home he had yearned for in Paris and a partner to love, Peter was still restless, and as soon as Christmas was over he was off again.

Back at the flat, Jean Connolly nursed her flu on a couch beside the fire. Reclining on the opposite couch was Denham, housebound with a bad foot. With Peter away, David Gascoyne spent much of his time in the apartment, taking advantage of the luxuries on offer, a break from the deprived state he normally lived in. 'Everything here is crazy,' he wrote in his diary on New Year's Eve. 'The big central salon has the air of a stage-set. The most extraordinary collection of people wander in and out all day long: dubious friends of Denham's, English pansy or sub-society friends of the Connollys, the actor Jean Marais, Melcarth, servants ... and odd, unidentifiable individuals with beards and hats, carrying ladders or portfolios or pieces of furniture about.'[20]

Without Peter's restraining hand, Denham wasn't coping well with his confinement. On New Year's Day, after several hours of drinking with David Gascoyne, he got the idea in his head of going to visit Jean Marais, who was acting in Cocteau's new play, *Les Parents terribles*, at the Ambassadeurs theatre. He couldn't be dissuaded, and ordered David to call a cab. When it arrived, Denny emerged 'wearing simply a fur-coat over his pyjamas and clutching a decanter of brandy, two glasses and a large silver cigarette box. He staggered into the taxi and we drove off to the theatre at top speed.'[21] There, making a dramatic entrance in the lobby and resisting attempts to throw him out, Denny demanded to see Monsieur Cocteau. He and David were taken backstage to Marais' dressing room, 'where Cocteau received us with, at first, puzzled surprise, and then ... with the most charming understanding. "Mais naturellement," he assured us, "la pièce était écrite pour être vue en pyjama!"'[22] He then proceeded to do what he could to calm Denham down.

Later that night, back at the flat, Denham got into an argument with Brian Howard, who had been out with Jean Connolly for the evening. Denham let slip that he had been a member of the Hitler Youth, 'whereupon Brian went off the deep end'. Brian was part Jewish, and he condemned Denham root and branch, promising to tell Wystan Auden and Stephen Spender, who were sure to be disgusted. (Spender, who was also part Jewish, had once gone chest-to-chest with a young Nazi in Germany, unable to contain his rage at the stupid hatefulness of the man's beliefs.) In the face of Brian's shrill denunciations, Denham stormed off to his bedroom, and a few moments later there was a gunshot. David and Brian hurried in to find Denham lying face-down on the bed, a smoking revolver on the bedside table. 'Denham lay there sobbing, did not speak. I took the revolver into the sitting-room, turned the light out, and when Brian had gone away, went back and sat on the bed for a while. It was difficult to find anything to say.'[23]

When Peter came back a week later, the household regained some stability, and David Gascoyne made himself scarce. He was present in late January, though, when Peter gave a lunch for Gertrude Stein and her partner Alice B. Toklas.[24] The two women, elderly now, had become a fixture of the Paris avant-garde, staying on after their fellow American literati drifted on; nothing could separate them from each other or from France – not even the subsequent German invasion would prise them out. The Spenders were staying again, and while Peter talked quietly with the shy, diminutive Alice, the stentorian Gertrude held forth to the Spenders on politics and literature, overriding their polite arguments by 'making preposterous statements and simply barking "What? ... what?" when anyone asked her questions'. Nobody could resist her. 'Everyone relaxed when she had gone; one felt that a natural force had left the room.'[25] Even Denham faded into the background in her presence.

Peter's relationship with Denham continued on a remarkably steady course – even after two years they got along well enough together, despite Denham's erratic behaviour, perhaps because they were often apart, but more likely because Denny was just unbalanced and self-destructive enough to excite Peter's urge to love and mend him, but not beyond the reach of all self-control and sanity. When Peter was around, he seemed to be relatively stable – it was when Peter was away that the trouble tended to occur.

As a couple, they were certainly more stable than some of the heterosexual partnerships they knew. The cracks in Jean and Cyril Connolly's marriage had been widening since 1937; Jean had been tolerant of his frequent affairs in the first years of their marriage, but when he got himself involved in a much more serious relationship with Diana Witherby, a budding writer who was twelve years his junior, it was the beginning of the end.[26] Jean attached herself more than ever to Peter and Denham, finding comfort in their friendship. At the same time, Stephen and Inez Spender's relationship was tense; Inez had fallen in love with another man, the poet Charles Madge, and the marriage wouldn't last out the summer.

* * *

In early summer 1939, leaving his troubles at home, Stephen Spender joined Peter for a tour of Switzerland.[27] They motored around the country in Peter's Bentley – the same sleek, dark-green tourer (or at least one just like it) in which he had taken Cecil to and from Cornwall some years earlier. On this occasion it was driven by a chauffeur who had (Stephen was told) worked for HRH the Prince of Wales before he became king.

Peter took Stephen to visit the painter Paul Klee at his home in Bern, where he had settled after fleeing Germany in 1933 (his 'degenerate' artworks were even now being destroyed by the Nazis). Klee was one of Peter's favourites, and he enthused about him to Stephen, telling him that Klee did something that had never been done before – 'to paint interior light shining outwards'.[28] Although he was in the terminal stages of scleroderma – a debilitating illness causing hardening of the skin and organs – he was still working, and received Peter and Stephen 'with the utmost kindness' and spent the afternoon with them. He showed them some gouaches he'd recently painted and which Peter was particularly interested in. They returned the next morning, and Klee's wife, Lily, showed them the loft of a nearby garage that was stacked with his paintings. Stephen asked the price of one that took his fancy, a Hindu goddess – it was £75, which was far beyond his means. Even the gouaches, at £15 each, were too expensive for him.[29]

During that tour, Stephen acquired his first deep and lasting impression of Peter as an aesthete and as a person:

> At this time Peter was one of those rich people who without seeming at all dependent on his wealth ... manages to get the utmost in the way of pleasure and beauty out of riches. When I think of him then, I think of his clothes which were beautiful, his general neatness and cleanness ... [and] his knowing that the best food in Switzerland is often to be obtained at the buffets of railway stations. Of course his most wonderful quality as a companion was his complete frankness, that of someone who tells you everything he admires, and who in his private life has no respect for conventions and therefore nothing to hide. He was not uncritical of people's morals, but to him genius and intelligence were far more important than morals, and when they were combined with immoral behaviour he regarded this simply as tiresome and tried to ignore it. He was always very intelligent about other people, and for that reason to be alone with him among a lot of other people was always amusing.[30]

As well as visiting Klee, Peter's tour of Switzerland took in a viewing of Spanish art stored for safekeeping in bank vaults, and meetings with fellow art patrons and dealers. Some of the dealers had become close, dear friends – such as Christophe Bernoulli of Basel – and the trip was part business, part social, and wholly about art.

Stephen, whose habitual attire was of the literary-hobo variety, was not fit to be seen in company with the dealers, so Peter gave him some money to buy a suit. Having little idea about sartorial style and thinking it would be appropriate for business, he chose a pinstripe. Peter's sensibilities were outraged by this garment, and he told Stephen off. 'I was never able to wear it,' Stephen recalled, still feeling the sting of Peter's rebuke many years later.[31]

That same summer, Peter's friendship with Cyril Connolly came under strain. Cyril greatly admired Peter's wealth, style and elegance, and, as one biographer would put it, he 'liked to imagine that he could live as well if he had been blessed with the means' and that Peter Watson's existence 'seemed to embody many of Connolly's daydreams about a life of ease and independence'.[32] But as Cyril's marriage to Jean deteriorated, he began to see Peter as a malign force. As is often the case with blithe adulterers, Cyril could be jealous about his wife's friends and apt to lay blame anywhere but upon himself. Jean had abandoned their flat in London at the end of 1938 and begun living in Paris, where she saw more than ever of Peter and Denham. Cyril didn't like it – he felt that both Peter and Jean were drifting away from him. In July 1939 Jean wrote to Cyril suggesting a separation and mentioning that Peter thought it would be good for the marriage.

Immediately the philandering Cyril cast Peter in the role of marriage-wrecker; he conceived the idea that Peter was attempting to break them up, and wrote furiously to Jean: 'I don't think I ever want to see Peter Watson again, such counsel he gave to you.'[33] He communicated his anger directly to Peter as well, who by this time was holidaying at the Tunisian resort of Hammamet. Cyril inquired pointedly where Jean might be, and accused him of trying to destroy his marriage (overlooking the fact that his continuing relationship with Diana, which he refused to give up, might have something to do with it).

Peter Watson was not a man to be hectored; he responded coolly with the same *don't-be-a-silly-boy* directness that had greeted some of Cecil Beaton's outbursts. 'My dear Cyril,' he wrote. 'Please get the idea out of your head that I want to see you and Jean separated. I do not and I should be very sorry if it happened.'[34]

He guessed that Cyril's problems and his unhappiness were caused fundamentally by frustration over his career as a writer. The previous year Cyril had published his memoir of youth, *Enemies of Promise*; poignant, memorably written and powerful as it was, the book was in effect a long and elaborate explanation for his failure to become the great novelist he had promised to be. Public school, and its lifelong emotional effects on all who went through it, had killed the spark of daring. But Peter could see that Cyril was 'more liable to be happy if you are working at writing' (and therefore, presumably, less likely to take hasty pot-shots at friends). 'I certainly do not think you should do journalism,' Peter added, 'knowing how you hate it if you have other ideas.' He was right – Cyril had been reduced to writing book and film reviews for the *New Statesman*, and was in despair. Evidently he needed some large creative project in his life – but what should it be? Privately, Cyril was contemplating the idea of an erudite arts magazine, with himself presiding over it. All he needed was someone rich to fund it.[35]

'I expect to be back in Paris about Sept 20th,' Peter concluded drily.

'Write me there and tell me if your crisis is finished. It deserves to be by now.'[36]

Peter intended to round out his summer travels with a visit to a friend in Corsica and then meet up with Stephen Spender and motor back to Paris for late September. But within two weeks of his letter from Tunisia, all his plans were thrown to the winds by the sudden spate of European events. On the first day of September, Germany smashed its way into Poland; Britain and France reeled in shock for two days, and then reluctantly declared war.

Peter's life would never be the same again. Nobody's would.

12

A TIME OF BARBARISM

1939–1940

It was as if they hadn't even seen the juggernaut coming. For two years, everyone travelling Europe had expected there to be war at any moment; but when it did erupt, it caught most of them entirely by surprise. Or perhaps it wasn't surprise – perhaps it was mere carelessness. Those few who were most conscious of the direction in which Europe was heading retreated to England before the summer reached its height. David Gascoyne was one; another was Stephen Spender. But for many, including Peter Watson, it was as if the invasion of Poland and the Allies' response to it were completely unexpected.

Two years earlier, Peter had sailed into the midst of a war in the Far East, knowing he was doing so. So perhaps it was the same kind of blithe spirit that made him go on making arrangements for his European travels. In the middle of August, while Germany's forces were massing secretly on the Polish border, he anticipated being in Paris for late September. Denham, who was characteristically even more careless, had gone to Finland 'to fish for salmon among the silver birches'.[1]

Despite his apparent lack of concern about the situation, some factor – perhaps some intuition, or more likely just the chance turn of events – drew Peter back to Paris earlier than he had anticipated, and he was there when the news broke. Within a few days he was making hasty arrangements to leave. The French government's war contingency plans had been activated, and the prospect of evacuating the city was in the air. Number 44 rue du Bac was closed up by the authorities, who intended to allocate it for use by the French Red Cross.[2] Peter had no choice but to leave his paintings – now numbering dozens of valuable works – where they were.

They wouldn't be completely abandoned. Peter made an arrangement with an acquaintance, the Romanian art critic and literary scholar Sherban Sidéry, who would take care that no harm befell either the apartment or the paintings. How well Peter knew Sidéry isn't recorded, but he was a friend of both Marie-Laure de Noailles and Picasso, so must have seemed trustworthy. Peter later made arrangements for some of his art to be transferred and stored in a vault of the Banque Nationale pour le Commerce et l'Industrie, including over thirty works by Dalí, Braque, Picasso, de Chirico and others. But at least twenty paintings were still in the apartment, including three by Klee, three by Max Ernst (including his eerily vivid *Marais aux Songes*), a Miró, two Picassos, two Dalís and a Francis Rose view of the port of Toulon.[3] This last was one of the paintings given to Denham, who was fond of it because Toulon was where he sometimes went to buy opium.[4]

Telling himself that his collection would be safe, Peter left Paris on a train bound for Calais.[5] For perhaps the first time in his life, he was unable to travel in luxury – all Europe's armies were on the move, and the train was packed with troops. Peter sat squeezed in among them, alone and wondering what the world was coming to. The sudden, unlooked-for intrusion of war into the midst of his peaceful summer plans had a profound effect on him; he would never quite get over the coming of war to Europe, and even in years to come when the war was long over, he would be haunted by a feeling of a huge and sinister threat waiting to engulf the world.

Denham, meanwhile, was making his way slowly back from Finland. How he managed it, he never said, but it must have taken all his considerable powers of persuasion and brass neck to circumnavigate the war zone and get back to England. At the same time, Jean Connolly left Paris for London, but barely paused there long enough to say a frosty hello to Cyril before departing for Yorkshire. Brian Howard was lingering on the Côte d'Azur with his German lover – Toni was now an enemy alien and faced the threat of internment by the French government. Brian was the only one of his generation of gay Berlin thrill-seekers to have kept his nightclub score as a long-term boyfriend, and was now paying the price for it.

Another Englishman who was in the South of France when the war began was Cecil Beaton, just down the road from Brian at Tamaris-sur-Mer. Feeling that in a time of war he should put away his personal troubles, Cecil wrote a short letter to Peter.

> At such a time as this I want you to know how much I regret not having seen you all these many months. Although it has been impossible to meet on such terms of happiness as we used to ... I have only thought of you with more tenderness and devotion than I have had for any other companion in my life. The blame for so many of our complications must rest entirely with me and I am deeply sorry ...
>
> If we are both to be preserved I pray that one day we shall both find that the break in our friendship has been but a severe pruning from which may grow greater strength. May God bless you always during these times of barbarism.
>
> Love from your Cecil[6]

Having put down these deepest feelings on paper, Cecil boarded a train for Paris en route for England.

* * *

Back in London Peter faced the immediate problem of finding somewhere to live. He had got rid of Shepherd's Close a year earlier, and his ageing mother was about to give up her Mayfair house and retreat to the peace and fresh air of Sulhamstead. Besides, his relationship with Denham required somewhere private. Peter took a suite at the Hyde Park Hotel and, flushed with the urge to do his bit for the war – preferably in a pacifist manner – took on what was almost certainly the only job he ever had in his life: in the offices of the Red Cross in Grosvenor Crescent.[7]

He found himself working alongside another temporarily useful soul, Eddy Sackville-West (cousin of Vita and heir-apparent to the Sackville barony). He and Peter had a love of modern music in common, and Eddy had used his position as music critic for the *New Statesman* to promote young British composers such as Benjamin Britten. He also supported Michael Tippett, as did Peter, who became a friend and patron to the young composer.[8]

While Europe busied itself with going to war, Cyril Connolly applied himself to realising his private dream. In the brief interval between Peter's return to Paris at the end of August and the outbreak of war, Cyril met him for lunch at a pavement café and broached the subject: how would Peter fancy funding a British-based arts magazine? Peter wasn't enthusiastic; right down to the last minutes of peace he still believed that he was settled in Paris for the long term, and had no interest in anything British – he couldn't bear England. He would as soon go to Arizona and take up orange farming, he said.[9] Anyway, he was already considering backing a French arts magazine. Cyril scoffed at the idea – there was already a surplus of arts papers in France. 'Instead of hating England in Paris,' Cyril had written, Peter 'should bring his hate to London, where it would do some good. He should leave the whale, like Jonah, and return to blast Nineveh.'[10]

Now Peter was back in Nineveh against his will, but Cyril still couldn't convince him to blast it with the organ of Cyril's proposed magazine. But he was weakening. Being confined to Britain and doing office work for the Red Cross were not going to be fulfilling. But he wasn't won over; he and Stephen Spender were considering supporting an existing journal, *New Writing*, which was run by Peter's old schoolfellow and Stephen's sometime close friend John Lehmann and which badly needed an injection of cash.[11]

In late September, Peter and Cyril both attended a party at the house of Anglo-Irish novelist Elizabeth Bowen in the neo-Palladian splendour of Clarence Terrace, overlooking Regent's Park. Cyril pressed Peter again; he suggested that running a magazine would count as war work, and might get the support of the government. Peter still wasn't keen, but he had run out of arguments. Finally, reluctantly, he said yes.[12]

Despite their relatively short acquaintance, Peter had got to know Cyril Connolly well, and had a very good understanding of his faults, which included laziness and vanity; he was unsure of his own judgement and (by Cyril's own admission) 'unable to finish what I have begun'.[13] Peter, generous though he could be, wasn't about to put his money into a pet journal that might be defunct within months or never even brought to press. Cyril could not be allowed sole charge of the magazine; therefore Peter asked Stephen Spender to co-edit.

Stephen was in the process of pulling his life back together. Inez had finally left him in July, casting him into a despair from which he was only just beginning to awaken. He was trying to revive himself with writing, spending much of his time in the quiet glooming of the worm-eaten old timber house he had bought in the somnolent Suffolk market town of Lavenham, pushing himself to write.[14] He was interested in working on Peter and Cyril's magazine, but he only took on the co-editorship on the condition that he be anonymous; John Lehmann was still under the impression that he would work for *New Writing*, and would be grossly offended if Stephen were to support a rival publication.[15]

Peter agreed, and Stephen and Cyril began meetings to discuss their plans.[16] They played with titles – *Sirius*, *Scorpio*, *Equinox* and *Centaur* were all considered before settling on *Horizon*. More importantly, they considered the content – Spender argued that 'there should be features on the subject of Culture and War, so that we should be able to keep a constant criticism of how broadcasting, publishing, music and art are going.'[17]

It was all very new and exciting. To Stephen's odd state of mind, London in those early days of war seemed weirdly cheerful:

> The blackout time gets a few minutes earlier each evening, so one notices more than ever the drawing in of the autumn evenings. Actually, the weather has been particularly fine lately. The streets glitter a biscuit yellow all day. The crowds waiting at the bus stops for the few buses give the town an air of festivity. The sandbags on the pavements, the strips of paper on the windows, the balloons in the air, are sufficiently new in the bright sunlight to be interesting and almost gay.[18]

The sinister reason for it all was still sufficiently far off to seem unreal. Art and culture were imminent and important, and war could still be viewed entirely through their prism.

Peter signed a contract formally committing himself to the magazine in October 1939. The only explicitly stated cost was £33 a month for printing and distributing 1,000 copies; on top of that he would be paying for premises, salaries and contributors' fees (two guineas a page for articles, one guinea a page for poems).[19] Although Peter took on the role of art editor, he was content to step back and let Cyril and Stephen run the whole show. His name would not appear on the magazine itself, and with Stephen's anonymity it would appear to be wholly a Cyril Connolly production. Peter's name appeared discreetly on the magazine's letterhead ('*Horizon* – V. W. WATSON, C. V. CONNOLLY. Edited by Cyril Connolly'), but nowhere else except on the cheques that paid for it all.

In that early period, before the magazine's emergence, Peter was quiet and reserved about it; when soliciting a contribution from Parker Tyler he referred to *Horizon* as 'a sort of pamphlet'.[20] Perhaps this was an affectation, a reluctance to be seen to be enthusiastic about an English arts project; or maybe he recognised the significance of what he was doing; after years of putting his money and influence behind a select handful of artists and composers, he was now involving himself directly in creating something of substance, and making the commitment that an artist makes – with the concomitant risk of rejection. His coolness may have been an insurance against failure, calling upon the relaxed, sophisticated insouciance that had got him through school.

Stephen's anonymity – and therefore his precarious friendship with Lehmann – would be the first casualty of Connolly's editorship. In early October, while he and Stephen were still in discussions, Cyril wrote a clarion piece for the *New Statesman*, intended to herald and justify the creation of *Horizon*; he pointed to the Munich betrayal of 1938, the victory of Fascism in Spain and the eruption of war in Europe as evidence that the political mission of writers was dead; they were trapped now 'on an island from which the sun is hourly receding'; it was no longer their job to fight Fascism. There were signs, he declared, 'not merely of a bitter disillusionment about the real power and meaning of democracy in England, but also a bitter revulsion from all political platforms'. Too much trust had been placed in parties and slogans, and now 'a withdrawal is necessary in self defence.' Connolly predicted that 'nostalgia will return as one of the soundest creative emotions, whether it is for the sun, or the snow, or the freedom which the democracies have had temporarily to discontinue.'[21] The venue *par excellence* for such discourse, he declared, would be his magazine.

This was enough to alert John Lehmann to the imminent existence of *Horizon* – a rival to his embattled *New Writing*. And he further realised that Stephen Spender was involved. The sense of betrayal was shattering, and he viewed Spender now as 'my enemy in the deepest sense'.[22] Virginia Woolf – whose Hogarth Press published *New Writing* – was also dismayed and felt let down by Stephen, of whom she was fond (she had been deeply concerned about him after Inez left). Stephen spoke to Woolf, but she declined to contribute to *Horizon*, and so did E. M. Forster, T. S. Eliot and Hugh Walpole.[23] It would be a long time before the wounds healed, when eventually Penguin stepped in to prop up *New Writing*. For now, there was open hostility towards the upstart journal before it had even been born.

It was as if there were a malign hoodoo at work. Only two days after the *New Statesman* article appeared, Cyril and Diana were in a taxi, passing near Sloane Square, when a military lorry, speeding out of nowhere, rammed into Diana's side of the vehicle. Cyril was unhurt, but Diana was hospitalised for six weeks, and would take months to recover. As Cyril gnomically expressed it: 'He released, sorry a mistake, she crossexamined by death, handed over to pain for further questioning.'[24] Cyril had hoped that Diana would work on *Horizon*, but that would be out of the question for a long time. Jean came back to live with him out of sympathy, but their marriage was still moribund.

Things could have been worse; poor Brian Howard was stranded at Sanary on the Côte d'Azur, his lover Toni having been interned at Toulon, along with the painter Max Ernst and many other German expatriates. Brian wrote pleading letters to everyone he could think of – including Peter Watson – asking for intercession. 'It's out of the question that T. should remain where he is. I cannot let him emerge, though, into an empty and possibly hostile world alone.'[25] It would be a long struggle and would end in bitterness; Toni was eventually released, spent a while in the British Pioneer Corps, then in 1942 made his way to the United States, where he married a rich American woman. Heartbroken, Brian crawled even deeper into the bottom of a bottle. By comparison, Peter's dramas with Denham – most of which were still to come – were perhaps not so dreadful.

By the end of 1939 Peter had found a new London home for himself and Denham. He took a flat in a small block at 40 Berkeley Square, Mayfair. The paintings that had been in storage or at his mother's house (which had now been sold) were moved into the flat – there were works by Miró, Klee and Picasso. He had Dalí's *Moment of Transition* and the

Renoir bronze head *Coco*. Some of his paintings had been shipped to the United States. His Picasso *Reading at a Table* – the painting gifted to Denham – was on loan to the Museum of Modern Art in New York for an exhibition opening in November,[26] and his Renoir *Woman and Child* was in New York on sale (it was picked up by an American buyer in October for £1,000).[27]

That Christmas, Peter took an unusual step: he bought his first major work by a British artist. He'd owned British pieces already, but they were all by friends such as Beaton, or eccentrics like Sir Francis Rose.[28] All his serious purchases had been of European artists – German, French, Swiss, Spanish ... but now, in December 1939, he bought his first Graham Sutherland from the Lefevre Gallery in London: *Damp Tree Roots*. It was followed shortly afterwards by a Ben Nicholson, and then another Sutherland, *Entrance to a Lane*, bought from the artist via the Leicester Galleries – a dark, dreamlike spiral painted at Sandy Haven in Pembrokeshire.[29]

This was the first inkling of a change in direction for the avowedly European connoisseur.

* * *

It wasn't the only change. The first issue of *Horizon* – the January 1940 number – appeared in December 1939. Despite the Woolf-led boycott there was no shortage of material. There were essays and short stories by Cyril Connolly, J. B. Priestley, Herbert Read, H. E. Bates and Stephen Spender, and new poetry from W. H. Auden, John Betjeman, Walter de la Mare and Louis MacNeice. Connolly's editorial laid out the magazine's ethos – its aim was 'to give to writers a place to express themselves, and to readers the best writing we can obtain. Our standards are aesthetic, and our politics are in abeyance.'[30]

Despite this editorial forswearing of politics, most of the pieces in that issue made some commentary on the war – but they were apolitical in terms of parties and ideologies. Auden's poem 'Crisis' was laden with doom and guilt and approaching menace, while Priestley wondered what the war was for, and whether it was a sign of a fundamental change in mankind, and Spender's essay asked 'How Shall We Be Saved?'. For the thirties generation of writers, in its first months this new world war looked like an utter failure of civilisation on every front – a failure of the politics of both conservatism and radicalism. 'At the moment civilisation is on the operating table,' Connolly's editorial went on, 'and we sit in the waiting room. For so far this is a war without the two great emotions which made the Spanish conflict real to so many of us. It is a war which awakens neither Pity nor Hope.'

There were non-political contributions too – Betjeman's typically bucolic churchyard meditation 'Upper Lambourne', for instance; but even this was tailed by MacNeice's 'Cushenden', which continued the bucolic imagery before subverting it with the closing line, 'What a place to talk of war.'

A couple of olive branches were extended towards Lehmann and Woolf – Cyril's editorial acknowledged approvingly her dislike of conventional literary reviews, and promised proper critical essays, and a favourable review was given to the latest Christmas number of *New Writing*; John Lehmann was said to have a 'conjuror's power' to obtain good articles from unknown writers. (Admittedly this might have been a slightly backhanded compliment.)

One item that was absent from *Horizon*'s table of contents was a piece by Gertrude Stein. Peter had written to tell her about the magazine and invited her to contribute something; he'd been dismayed to receive what he described to Cecil Beaton as '3 pages of the most arrant balderdash I have ever read, a poem-opera-play about Lucrezia Borgia. It sounds much funnier than it really is, so I don't know really what to do with it now ... She just wasn't trying.'[31] Stein had just published a children's book, *The World is Round*, illustrated by Sir Francis Rose, and Peter supposed that 'she "gave" herself for that and has nothing left.' Musing on the current vogue for 'child literature', he thought he understood the reason for it – that 'perhaps even idiocy is the best way out of this appalling life.'

That first issue of *Horizon* met with bitter disdain from the older generation of literati. The magazines of *their* Great War generation, the critics said, had brought to light the likes of T. S. Eliot and James Joyce, whereas all *Horizon* could rustle up was a roster of here-today-gone-tomorrow scribblers like J. B. Priestley, H. E. Bates, W. H. Auden and John Betjeman. Virginia Woolf noted privately that the magazine was 'small, trivial, dull' and declined to read it.[32] Even its cover was picked on – plain and unfashionable. The critics had missed the point. *Horizon* was deliberately stepping away from fashion; its aims were serious. A fashionable cover, with photography and sans-serif typography, would be like 'a rubber topped chromium table in a neon lit cafetéria'; *Horizon*'s dowdy frontage was intended to be like the outside of an old restaurant where the paintwork was shabby but the food was first-class.[33]

And, despite the resoundingly dismissive *pah!* from the Bloomsbury generation, *Horizon* was an immediate, astonishing success. The print run of 1,000 copies sold out within a week, and in his editorial in the February number Cyril crowed that copies of the first issue were 'now a collector's rarity'.

Peter was delighted, exhilarated, and not only because his investment seemed safe. (Morally safe, that is. He would never make a profit from it, but at least the money he lost would be worth it.)[34] Aside from a few diffident stabs at soliciting contributions, he had confined his involvement to supplying the cash; but with the success of the launch, he couldn't sustain his detachment for long. Having been so reluctant to back the magazine, and so unwilling to be publicly associated with it, he was now unable to resist getting involved, and in February 1940 he wrote a four-page memorandum on the second issue, directed towards everyone involved in it (but mainly at Cyril).

'I find the magazine *excellent*,' the memorandum said. 'But I feel like writing about it in greater detail so listen.'[35] He approved almost everything, but noted that certain contributors needed to write with '*More guts*'.

Certain things he picked out for particular praise. One was an extract from Stephen Spender's diary giving his thoughts on Germany before Hitler and how its personal freedoms had been destroyed. (Peter had underlined Stephen's observation that 'satisfactory personal relationships exist when the people who enjoy them have a satisfactory relation with society.'[36])

Peter approved of Cyril's editorial, in which he tackled the prickly issue of Auden and Isherwood having decamped to America. The critics, Cyril said, were 'quite right to link up *Horizon* with a sneer at the English emigrés in California, for the departure of Auden and Isherwood to America a year ago is the most important literary event since the outbreak of the Spanish War.' Cyril contended that 'Auden is our best poet, Isherwood our most promising novelist ... They are far-sighted and ambitious young men with a strong instinct of self-preservation, and an eye on the main chance, who have abandoned what they consider to be the sinking ship of European democracy.' And Cyril made a prediction which, for its time, before the war had got properly under way, was stunningly accurate: 'Whatever happens in this war, America will be the gainer. It will gain enormously in wealth, and enormously (through the refugees) in culture. England will be poverty-stricken, even in victory.'[37] Cyril placed *Horizon* exactly in line with the young writers' view of Europe and the failure of its pre-war aesthetic, which had been dominated by the social realism of writers such as Woolf and Forster (although Cyril refrained from naming names).

Peter strongly approved: 'Congratulations,' he wrote, 'for the courage in these times to say out loud such things. Bravo!'

Another piece that pleased him was a review article on the subject of war by a very confident author of whom Peter had never heard. 'Please tell me who is George Orwell?' he wrote. 'His article is *splendid*. What else has he written? I hope he will write often in *Horizon*.'[38]

The only thing Peter really disliked was a short story by G. F. Green, 'Room Wanted', which he thought '*quite second-rate*'. Regardless of the story (which was actually rather good), he was irritated by Green's use, without attribution, of the poem 'The City' by the modern Greek poet Constantine Cavafy; Peter was familiar with it and was intrigued by the particular translation Green had used:

> In these same streets you shall wander,
> and in the same purlieux you shall roam . . .
> There is no ship to take you to other lands, there is no road.
> You have so shattered your life here, in this small corner
> that in all the world you have ruined it.

Peter noted irritably that 'it is a poem I like and means something quite different to what G. F. Green thinks.' In his story, Green seemed to have taken it literally as representing urban despair, while in fact its author – a writer of homoerotic verse – intended the city to represent the burden of one's inner life, a personal albatross. It could have been applicable to Denham's addiction to drugs or Cecil's addiction to a hopeless love; whatever its significance might be taken to be, it struck hard with Peter.

On the arrangement of works of art and literature, Peter gave a rare insight into how he viewed their station in human life:

> Each work be it an article or a whole book is situated in the life of the man and the literary life of a nation. We have the right to change the places of things and works according to our own estimate of values but a work is never beautiful *only in itself* but in what it brings with it, *memories* and *hopes* ... A work can never be completely detached from its spiritual environment.[39]

Hence, perhaps, one of his never-discussed reasons for leaving his art in Paris rather than shipping it to London: out of its proper environment it would be diminished.

'As for policy,' Peter wrote, returning to the subject of *Horizon*, 'I hope you manage to have one soon and I hope to agree with it.'

* * *

During that peaceful first winter of the war, the returned aesthetes tried to settle into life in London, fidgeting about from place to place like a person trying to find a comfortable position in a lumpy armchair.

Peter and Denham's residence in the Berkeley Square flat was a brief one. Cyril stayed sometimes, and in January 1940 David Gascoyne was put up there for three weeks, having bumped into Peter at a New Year's Eve party, and for a short while it was almost a recreation of the *ménage* at 44 rue du Bac.[40] There were sparks, just as there had been in Paris – Cyril upset David by telling him that he should resign himself to 'never being anything but what he called a "literary" writer' and that he was in fact 'much *worse* than *literary*, really'.[41] Denham, uncharacteristically, tended to drift about in the background during this period. The only thing he did to attract attention was to grow a moustache, which in David's eyes made him look 'extraordinarily like Errol Flynn'.

By February, Peter, Denham and Peter's art collection had moved south to Piccadilly, taking a two-bedroom flat in Athenaeum Court, a modern Art Deco block overlooking Green Park, at four guineas a week.[42] Cyril, who was now living well on his *Horizon* salary (paid by Peter), eventually took a flat there for a while. (Later that year Cyril tried to bump up his money by getting Peter to pay his rent as a *Horizon* expense; Peter told him firmly but not unkindly, 'I do not think it a good idea.')[43]

Horizon continued to put out its monthly issues, gaining confidence and new writers as it went, adding Cecil Day Lewis, V. S. Pritchett, Laurie Lee and Dylan Thomas to its list of contributors. There were occasional art contributions commissioned by Peter – drawings by Osbert Lancaster, an article on Frances Hodgkins by John Piper, a review of American painting by John Rothenstein (director of the Tate Gallery); these were few in the early years, but would grow in number as *Horizon* developed.

The magazine also acquired new drains on its finances in the form of impoverished writers – among whom Dylan Thomas was the most forthcoming and enduring. In spring 1940, with creditors pursuing him hard, he turned to *Horizon* for help. Stephen Spender had a whip-round among friends, and some money was raised. Peter forwarded two cheques to the poet, who was then living at Laugharne. Dylan wrote back in delight: 'I never thought I'd have so much, and was frightfully pleased: I'll be able to settle everything now.'[44] In a letter to Spender, he remarked that 'life's quite different now, and I'm beginning to work like a small, very slow horse.'[45] He declared to everyone who would listen that his and his family's lives were saved, and that he could go on living at Laugharne untroubled. But Dylan Thomas and money just couldn't stick together, and half a year later he was on the run from creditors again. 'After buying a few useless things,' he reported from London, 'the Watson money disappeared, quick as a sardine, and we've been cooped up here, in little, boiling rooms, for nearly three weeks, quite broke ... If I don't get a grant, the debtees will have to wait until my Watson comes in.'[46] His Watson did come in quite regularly – Dylan became a frequent visitor to the *Horizon* office; he would go straight to Peter if he was available, but Spender or Connolly would do at a pinch. Cyril recalled buying poems from him for cash 'as if they were packets of cocaine'.[47]

Dylan Thomas wasn't the only one. The *Horizon* 'Begging Bowl' was set up, which solicited donations from readers to help struggling artists. The readers responded, but it was Peter who met most of the costs.

In the early months of 1940, Peter – who was growing ever more involved with the running of the magazine – tried to combine charity with advertising, by approaching a friend in the Red Cross (for which he had long since stopped working) to discuss donating copies – initially he suggested selling them, but was told, 'as I suspected, the Red Cross does not buy – it only receives (*plutôt féminin*).'[48] Nevertheless, giving them surplus copies and asking readers to donate their read issues would be 'a good advertisement for us'.

Peter was becoming more involved in the editorial side of the magazine too – and beginning quietly to dominate it. There were frequent clashes between the strong personalities of Spender and Connolly, which Peter usually managed to defuse, bringing the day to a close with drinks, dinner and laughter.[49]

* * *

And so life went on for London's literary set. Then, quite suddenly, everything changed. On 10 May 1940 the Third Reich turned its attention towards its western enemies and launched a terrifying, lightning offensive against the Low Countries and France. By the end of the month the British Army was hanging on by its chinstraps at Dunkirk. Suddenly the war, which from Mayfair, Wales and Wiltshire had seemed such an unreal, distant thing, became a stark, staring reality. London – which Peter had always disliked – had become not just gloomy, not just blacked out, but also imminently dangerous.

Jean Connolly already had a ticket for America. She had heard that her mother was ill, and, guessing that the war would eventually make transatlantic travel difficult, decided to waste no time. With a sense of doom, she made out her will, leaving half her income to Cyril. He tried to persuade her not to go, but she was insistent. The next day, the German invasion of the Low Countries was announced, and Americans in Europe began streaming to the Atlantic ports. Sailings by all shipping lines were suspended, and the US State Department announced that just two ships would be available for refugees – the SS *Manhattan*, sailing from Genoa on 2 June, and the SS *Washington*, which would sail from Lisbon a week later, calling at Galway in neutral Ireland on 15 June to pick up additional passengers.[50]

That was where Jean would have to go. It was decided that Denham would go with her.[51] All the signs were that the *Washington* would be the very last chance to cross the Atlantic. The British Expeditionary Force had returned, draggled, weaponless and demoralised, to Britain, and the Wehrmacht was swarming towards Paris. If Jean and Denham didn't go now, they would be trapped, and so, in early June, they left for Ireland.

The SS *Washington* had been cruising in the Mediterranean when the captain received the order to divert and collect US citizens anxious to escape the German tide. On leaving Lisbon, the ship was already full to capacity, with hundreds more waiting to be picked up from Galway. Barely a day out from Lisbon, sailing at night, the *Washington* crossed the path of a German U-boat, which ordered it to heave to and signalled that it intended to launch torpedoes; they had ten minutes to abandon ship. The crew began loading passengers into lifeboats while the officers repeatedly signalled the U-boat that the *Washington* was an American ship. Eventually the German captain accepted the claim, and apologetically signalled the ship to sail on. It had been a tight scrape – liners had been sunk before, including the British *Athenia*, torpedoed on the first day of the war with three hundred Americans on board.

The *Washington* reached Galway without any further incident on 13 June, where Denham and Jean boarded, and reached New York a week later, horns blasting in celebration, to be greeted by reporters and a newsreel film crew. The ship was at almost double its thousand-passenger capacity, and the decks were piled with refugees' luggage.[52]

Those who had chosen to stay behind in Europe – like the indomitable Gertrude Stein and Alice B. Toklas – would see their adoptive countries overwhelmed by the Germans, while those left in Britain waited anxiously for the cross-Channel invasion that seemed likely to come soon.

To Peter Watson, London didn't look like a safe place to stay. It might be bombed flat at any moment. In June, with Denham and Jean only just departed for America, he moved *Horizon* – including Cyril, Stephen and Diana (recovered now from her injuries) – to the far end of Devon. Scouting ahead, he settled on a thatched cottage (named, with a literal-mindedness that was almost satirical, 'Thatched Cottage') overlooking the beach at Thurlestone Sands, between Plymouth and Salcombe. He had trouble finding a cook, and warned Cyril, 'we may have to live on scrambled eggs and gratin dauphinois for a time.'[53] Even so, the peace and quiet were a delight.

He eventually found a cook in Plymouth, which eased life at the cottage. But such was Peter's pleasure at being away from London that he didn't even mind cooking himself; he took lessons, and with local lobster at one shilling and sixpence each he could soon make a famous *homard au whisky*, as well as a delicious chocolate mousse. He began coming to life in a way he hadn't since the golden days of Paris. Discovering British art was a revelation, and he planned to go down to St Ives and explore the artists' colony, where he had heard 'there is war to the death between the realists and the abstractionists!'[54] He had begun buying Ben Nicholson's and Christopher Wood's work that year, and realised now how right they were about this part of England – the next step must be to see first-hand the place that had so inspired them.

'What this country needs,' Peter typed clumsily to Cecil Beaton (possibly a little the worse for wine), 'is *more and MORE* Art. Otherwise Life is not worth the trouble. These *are* my War Aims and I am trying my best to attain them ... Art must be put into EVERYTHING – not just into Writing, Painting etc; the whole World must swim with Art.'[55]

What some parts of the world were swimming in at that precise moment was blood and fire – and much of it was going on right over their heads, in the blue skies of a blissful English summer. It bolstered the spirits of Stephen, Peter and Cyril when they received appreciative letters from pilots who were flying in the Battle of Britain. Stephen recalled that a few even wrote that 'so long as *Horizon* continued they had a cause to fight for.'[56] The culture and free spirit represented by journals like *Horizon* and *New Writing* were, for the more artistic, literary-minded young men of the armed forces, an embodiment of the stand against Fascism. Two such pilots actually visited the *Horizon* staff; one of them, Gully Mason, the son of a mine owner, even contributed a short essay that was published in the June 1940 issue. The other, Timothy Corsellis, was a fighter pilot who wrote poetry and became a close friend of Stephen's; he later transferred to ferry piloting and was lost over the Atlantic.[57]

After a few months of Devonian idyll, Peter began to feel that it wasn't such a good idea after all. Cyril was moody and irritable, which caused friction between him and Diana. The once delightful atmosphere went gradually stale; what was more, Peter was paying for the whole household out of his own pocket, on top of the expense of running *Horizon*. He had all the bother of a seaside retreat but little of the pleasure. And after weeks of intense and spectacular fighting, the RAF seemed to be holding the Germans in check; an invasion seemed rather unlikely now, and it felt rather pointless to be sitting out the war down in Devon when London didn't seem likely to suffer any serious bombing.

Thatched Cottage was given up and the *Horizon* team headed back to the capital. They arrived in London in September, just in time for the beginning of the Blitz.

13

SPOILS OF WAR

1940

On the night of Sunday 8 December 1940 the bombers came again, as they did almost every night.

Droning dismally up the Thames estuary, the black-winged shapes crawled along the dark sky, among the pillars of searchlights and the flashes of anti-aircraft fire –relentlessly onward, over the homes and the docks and the offices. London had had three months of being slowly crushed and incinerated, and there seemed no end. Tonight's was a particularly heavy raid – four hundred black bombers came, raining incendiaries by the thousand, letting loose parachute mines to drift down, silent and lethal, bombs set to explode on impact, bombs set to tick for hours before blowing up among the rescue workers and firefighters, bombs to catch fire, bombs to break masonry, bombs to wear down the resistance of the city-dwellers. More than two hundred of them would die tonight, and almost two thousand buildings would be set alight.

As he did every night, Peter Watson sat out the raid in his flat at Athenaeum Court, the walls shaking, the sky beyond the blacked-out windows flickering with gunfire and flames. You could see the docks burning in the distance from the windows. 'I never go to a shelter,' he wrote to Cecil; 'I would rather die in my sleep.'[1]

Although the bombing was concentrated on industry and the docklands, the affluent West End wasn't immune. During a typical raid on the night of 17–18 September, Peter's former home in Berkeley Square was hit when two delayed-action bombs fell on the square. Number 40 was damaged by a delayed-action bomb,[2] while the building at number 30 was obliterated, just the steel frame of its lift shaft left standing amongst the rubble.[3]

On this December night, Westminster Abbey was damaged, a parachute mine fell near BBC Broadcasting House, and the *Horizon* office was hit – 'but we are carrying on,' Peter wrote. Bombs had fallen on Piccadilly too. 'There is a great jagged hole in the Ritz but so far this block has escaped.'[4]

At least Paris had been spared this kind of destruction. That, apparently, had been Peter's great fear. His art collection was unlikely now to be blown to bits or burned. Most of it was in the vault, and the rest should be safe from theft with Sherban Sidéry living in the flat. *Should* be safe ... but was it? There had been stories in the press and rumours on the grapevine about the Nazis in France looting art from Jews and museums.

* * *

The next morning, 9 December 1940, while the people of London were coming up out of the Tube stations and basements and back-garden shelters, or lifting the blackout blinds in their Mayfair apartments, blinking in the rising daylight, gazing on the new ruins, in Paris a small convoy of German military vehicles was speeding across the Pont Royal. A car, maybe two, and a couple of trucks, one containing a squad of soldiers.

They had hardly any distance to go – across the bridge and straight ahead down the rue du Bac. There, just beyond the bend, before the crossing with the Boulevard Saint-Germain, was their destination. The vehicles slammed to a halt outside the block at number 44. The small squad of soldiers in the field-grey and camouflage tunics of the Waffen-SS jumped out of the truck and took station on the pavement, while a gang of workmen in cloth caps opened the back doors of a lorry with *garde-meuble* (furniture warehouse) written on the side; a couple of officials in plainclothes got out of the car and hammered on the grey double door to summon the concierge.

Neighbours' curtains twitched and passers-by stopped and stared curiously – sights like this had become familiar, but not yet commonplace. What poor soul was going to be hauled away this time?

Boots clattered up the staircase to the first floor. The officials and soldiers made for the apartment at the rear, overlooking the courtyard. This was the address that had been given for the absent Englishman, Watson. There was no need to knock here – the officer in charge had the key, obtained from the Romanian custodian of the apartment.

The door swung open to reveal a luxurious residence – two bedrooms, bathroom and other appointments arranged around a large drawing room. All expensively furnished, carpeted and fitted. There were *objets d'art* here and there, a gramophone, cases full of books, and, filling much of the wall space in between, canvas after canvas of modern art. This was what they had come for. At a signal from the officer in charge, the cloth-capped workmen began taking down the pictures. A Picasso here, a nightmarish Dalí, a Paul Klee, a Tanguy, another Klee and another Picasso ... They were stacked in the hall, and then taken, one by one, down the stairs to the waiting furniture lorry. It was a calm, efficient business; these men had had a lot of practice.

These appropriations – normally from Jews – had begun within days of the Wehrmacht taking control of Paris. It was the same in every occupied country. At first the thefts of cultural property had been random raid-and-grab operations by *Einsatzgruppen* (task groups) of the SS – the death squads that operated in occupied zones. But by late summer of 1940, Reichsleiter Alfred Rosenberg had obtained authority from Hitler to form a dedicated organisation whose job would be to seize all antique manuscripts, books, artefacts, paintings, sculptures – in fact, any cultural property – from Jews and public institutions in the occupied zones. This body was called the Einsatzstab Reichsleiter Rosenberg – or ERR – and Paris, which until now had been the world's largest, most important centre for art dealing, was its richest source of booty.

In principle Rosenberg's seizure teams, with SS support and assistance from the collaborationist Sûreté (the French police) and the Wehrmacht secret police, were supposed to confine their operations to museums, libraries, Masonic premises, churches and the private collections of Jews. But in practice they took whatever seemed appropriate at the time.

Nobody's property was wholly safe – certainly not the departed citizens of enemy nations.

Exactly how the ERR had heard about Peter Watson's collection would never come to light. Everyone in the Paris art world knew of it. There were countless friends and acquaintances who had visited the rue du Bac apartment, and Parisian dealers like Paul Rosenberg and Pierre Colle who were Peter's close associates and friends knew about it ... and there was Sherban Sidéry, a critic and also a collector. The information might have been passed for personal gain by someone hoping to profit from it – a dealer, perhaps. Or it might have been extracted by pressure; the Nazis' intelligence-gathering system was hardly renowned for its politeness or subtlety. Some desperate *quid pro quo* negotiated by somebody trying to save himself, perhaps.

In all, twenty paintings were carried down from the apartment and stacked carefully in the waiting lorry. When the job was complete, the soldiers remounted, and the vehicles roared off the way they had come, across the Pont Royal, then along the embankment to the Place de la Concorde and the long, narrow edifice of the Jeu de Paume – the old tennis court in the Tuileries gardens – which had been commandeered and was the main sorting house for the ERR's pickings. The building was piled high with artworks and antiques in crates and stacked on pallets. It was alive with activity – SS officers, workmen, serious civilians – male and female – at desks, writing out reports, studying, identifying and cataloguing the items that came in. These were the ERR's Sonderstab Bildende Kunst (Special Staff, Fine Arts), and their task was to sort the material into categories. Artworks that were deemed suitable were to be shipped off to Germany, ostensibly for the Reich's museums, but many of the choicest items were actually being siphoned off into the private collections of leading Nazis – including Herman Goering and Alfred Rosenberg himself – while the rest went into secret underground storehouses. Art that was not suitable – the modern, the degenerate – was separated out and earmarked for sale abroad. The foreign currency raised would be channelled officially towards the building of the proposed *Führermuseum*. Much of the art would find its way into the hands of collaborators in the art world, who took a personal profit. Paintings that were not sold were burned.

Not all Germans supported the looting – General Otto von Stülpnagel, the military governor of France, objected to the despoliation of the nation's heritage; he protested to Hitler, and even dared to criticise Goering over it, but the Führer overruled him and eventually von Stülpnagel gave up.[5]

The twenty paintings seized from 44 rue du Bac were fed into the Nazi system, where they joined thirty-four of Peter Watson's other paintings that were already there – including two by Dalí, three each by Picasso, Braque and de Chirico, and over twenty more. These were the paintings that had been stored for safety in the vault of the Banque Nationale. The bank had been raided exactly a week earlier, on 2 December, by a parallel organisation, the Devisenschutzkommando (Foreign Exchange Protection Unit) of the SS. Like the ERR, the DSK was tasked with seizing valuables in occupied territories. The DSK – which was a much more militarised, forceful and ruthless organisation – specialised in ransacking banks for foreign currency, bullion, bonds and any other valuables, including art.

Along with Peter Watson's thirty-four paintings, the DSK took fifteen more that were listed as belonging to Sidéry. This might be taken as exculpating him from suspicion as the ERR's informer. Given the chronology of the raids, the DSK was probably the initial recipient of the intelligence about the Watson collection, and might well have tipped off its sister organisation, the ERR. The DSK, being entwined with the SS, was not averse to using coercion and torture to extract information. It might have been simple bad luck – the DSK scooping up the Watson collection during a routine bank raid. However it happened, most of the collection of over fifty immensely valuable paintings – meticulously selected and gathered and worth a fortune – vanished into the bureaucracy and from there proceeded either to the bonfires of insanity or into the huge underground black market.[6]

* * *

The news reached Peter very soon after the raid. 'I had an International Red Cross message from the Rumanian Sidéry,' he wrote to Cecil. 'The pictures I am afraid have gone.'[7]

He was astonishingly calm about the whole thing. It was a pity, he felt, 'because I had attempted to get the most interesting work of any painter I ever bought and it was all most deliberately chosen. But I don't care as it seems fatal to one's character to attach oneself too much to things.' He first wrote 'I don't care really', but then heavily crossed out 'really', as if to disclaim any care at all, slight or significant.

Peter had been at least half-expecting this to happen for a few months. In October there had been reports in the international press of a huge shipment of modern art being captured by the Royal Navy off Bermuda. The vessel, an American liner en route from Lisbon to the United States, contained hundreds of paintings – worth at least half a million dollars – by Cézanne, Degas, Renoir, Manet and others. The man in charge of the shipment, a Parisian dealer called Martin Fabiani, had claimed they were his property and that he was shipping them to America for safekeeping. But the authorities suspected he was selling them on behalf of the Nazis. The paintings were seized by the British and taken to Canada. Peter had almost convinced himself that his paintings were among the haul.[8] In fact at that time they were still in Paris, untouched.

His insouciance was temporary – he became more concerned about his art later, to a degree that would get him into trouble with the authorities, but for now Peter didn't care. He was caught up in a fleeting lightness of spirit – with Denham out of reach, he was a free agent, and had recently fallen in love. He never mentioned the name of this person (there had been so many brief dalliances in his life, and would be many more – Peter was suited to honeymoons, not for long-term relationships, as Stephen Spender once remarked) but he did let slip a reference to it in a letter to Cecil. 'It's all quite unsatisfactory of course but there it is. I just feel hopelessly susceptible that is all and it is no use trying to pretend it doesn't exist, is it? So I just burn away like a fuse, all day.'[9] (Meanwhile, Denham was in California, living off Peter's money and teasing the desires of Christopher Isherwood, who was writing movie scripts. Jean had joined him there, and was said to have taken a lover. It was an intense little triangle, inspiring Isherwood two decades later to fictionalise his brush with Denham Fouts in his novel, *Down There on a Visit*.)

A more fundamental change was coming over Peter at this time. The events of the past six months had altered his view of the world. The fortitude of the British had impressed him, while the behaviour of the French had made a deeply unfavourable impression. Their inclination to collaborate with Fascism was what stuck in his throat – whether it was those in Paris helping to ransack the nation's art treasures to satisfy the Nazis' greed and perverted ideas of culture, or the wealthy émigrés now living in London and New York who would be collaborators too if it weren't for their fear that France might end up at war with Britain and the United States. Peter wrote to Cecil:

> How I despise those super-rich (some of whom you and I have known very well) who sent all their money to England and America four years ago and are now living over here feeling very pro-Pétain, not daring to say so openly and afraid to return ... They seem to me a very dangerous leaven to be loose mixing with the English élite. Whereas other sincere anti-Hitler democrats are passing the war in camps where they are ill-treated by the real Nazis in the camp who sing 'Horst Wessel' all night long. But that is just part of the general hell of war, I suppose.[10]

France and the French were tainted, soiled. The place, the culture and the people had had too deep an effect on him for Peter to ever consider them dead to him, but they would never shine the way they had.

At the same time, he was impressed by his own bravery – or at least his carelessness – about the constant air raids. 'What a pity you have deserted London at a time like this,' he wrote to Cecil, who was at Ashcombe. 'Although if I had a nice country house like you have I would certainly go away.'[11] (It was a transparently lame concession – he could have had half a dozen country houses any time he liked.)

And so the war went on. The bombers came back nearly every night with their dismal droning, scattering fire and detonations through the streets of the city, and Peter stayed resolutely in his flat, never going to the shelter, preferring to die in his sleep.

14

THE WAR EFFORT

1940–1941

One by one, the war affected them all – drew them in or wore them down. The gay aesthetes of the thirties did their little bit in the big war. There was simply no escaping it; it had started as the great failure of European democracy, a rock on which to declaim the death of civilisation; but by and by it became a way of life, pervading everything. Cecil Beaton took up war photography for a while, and shot some of his most memorable images in Blitz hospitals and on the battlefields of Tunisia. Stephen Spender served as a fireman. Brian Howard got thrown out of MI5, later joined the RAF, and was thrown out of that as well (for general insubordination and referring to his superior officer as 'Colonel Cutie'). Oliver Messel designed camouflage, and spent his days dreaming up ways to disguise pillboxes as haystacks or cafés. Rex Whistler joined the Welsh Guards as soon as war broke out; he became a tank commander and was killed in the battle for Caen in 1944. A remarkable number of artists and their patrons were declared physically unfit for military service.

Some artists and writers signed up to do propaganda or take part in the official recording of the war. In 1939 the Ministry of Information had set up the War Artists' Advisory Committee, the result of hard lobbying by Sir Kenneth Clark, director of the National Gallery. The WAAC had the power to issue work permits and commissions to artists, and to purchase works from them. The official purpose was to create an artistic record of the war, but Clark later admitted that photography was better suited to that purpose, and that his real aim was 'simply to keep artists at work on any pretext, and, as far as possible, to prevent them from being killed'.[1] There was an acute awareness of how many gifted writers, artists and musicians must have died in the last war, and how much richer Europe's culture might now be if they had been preserved. Under the auspices of the committee, thousands of artworks were produced that might never have existed, and a whole generation of artists flocked to submit work for consideration.

Throughout the war, each man and woman in the art world did – or tried to do – his or her thing. But in general they took their time about it. For the first few years most of them tried to continue as they had before, and hated the new limitations on them. Peter Watson spent much of the war as he had spent the peace – travelling almost constantly. His movements now were confined to the British Isles, but he went to their very limits – the north of Scotland, the west of Wales, the furthest tip of Cornwall – as if pushing at the bounds that kept him in, and getting as far as he could from London, a city he had never loved, and which now had the added unattraction of being half in ruins and riddled with death and broken glass.

Besides travelling, he continued his one great purpose – collecting art and giving sustenance to artists. In his confinement, he discovered not only new insights into the British character but also a whole new generation of British artists who would otherwise have remained unknown to him. Since late 1939 he had been discovering his contemporaries – Ben Nicholson, Graham Sutherland and Christopher Wood – but now for the first time since Igor Markevitch he began to take on the patronage of a generation younger than himself. Four painters in particular became the principal foci of his life. One was English, two Scottish, and the fourth was from a distinguished family of Austrian Jewish immigrants.

In October 1940 Peter and Cyril Connolly had visited Edinburgh to experience the Scottish arts scene on behalf of *Horizon*. Encouraged by the magazine's success, Peter was taking a greater part in commissioning contributions – weekend visits to artists, lunches with critics, correspondence with writers. For the first time in his life he was helping to bring into existence something that hadn't been there before – the act of creation. And the same was true of his growing support for new artists.

In Edinburgh Peter and Cyril met with art critic John Tonge, who introduced them to a young and impecunious painter called Robert MacBryde. They took him to dinner at Edinburgh's Café Royal, and he and Peter liked each other immediately; almost on the spot Peter commissioned a portrait of himself.[2]

MacBryde was a memorable figure. After growing up in a rural village, he had studied at Glasgow School of Art; his work was heavily influenced by Cubism. Now, aged twenty-seven, he was living in a farmhouse outside Edinburgh and trying to make a name for himself. Tonge admired his work, but also fancied the young man, who was shortish and slightly built, with dark, heavy brows – he resembled an adolescent Neanderthal, but a rather sweet one.[3]

Robert was not available for seduction; he had already found his life partner, and they were inseparable. He had met Robert Colquhoun, a fellow artist from Kilmarnock, when they were students together at Glasgow. They became lovers and friends, and would stay together for life. They were known as the Two Roberts, and regarded as a double act even though they didn't work in collaboration; each followed his own artistic path. With the outbreak of war, Colquhoun had enlisted in the Royal Army Medical Corps, while MacBryde, who had hoped to join him, was rated unfit for service (he suffered from chronic ill health). Now, in late October 1940, Colquhoun – who also wasn't at all well – was in Edinburgh on leave, and MacBryde was trying everything he could to get him out of the army before his unit shipped out to India. Friends in the arts world were pulling strings and helping him make a case to the War Artists' Advisory Committee.

Peter visited MacBryde at home, where he bought some of his drawings and invited him to come with him to London to make a bid for recognition in the metropolitan art scene. It was a remarkable and irresistible offer, including access to Peter's contacts and full, almost unconditional, financial support. Not only would Peter pay MacBryde's keep and accommodate him, he would pay for him to further his education at an art school – perhaps the Ruskin at Oxford. Peter, getting carried away by the idea, suggested that he might take a country house in Devon and install MacBryde along with other young painters he was giving assistance to.

The young Scot – whose politics were strongly socialist – was unsure what to make of this 'young millionaire' so enthusiastically offering him the world. 'A strange crowd of fashionable squirts mill round him,' he wrote to his old art teacher in Glasgow, 'but he knows it and goes on with the production of *Horizon*.' With money and opportunity tempting him sorely, MacBryde reasoned that, with such support, 'I can be of special use to so many people and Peter's politics are quite left-wing'; moreover MacBryde believed he could 'bring to bear my Socialistic influence on him'.[4] He persuaded himself (apparently with some encouragement from Peter) that the 'young millionaire' was 'strangely caught up in this system and it occurred to him that he should get rid of his wealth' by giving it to poor deserving artists – the only question was 'who is to get it and what will they do with it'.[5] Wearied by his endless visits to Edinburgh labour exchange and excited by the thought of using Peter's money to promote his own political vision, MacBryde agreed. Besides, he had another motive for going to London – to get away from John Tonge's increasingly insistent attentions.[6]

There was just one problem – the other Robert. By late November Colquhoun had been posted to Leeds, and MacBryde had followed him there.[7] Efforts on his behalf continued, and by early 1941 Colquhoun had been discharged on medical grounds. He immediately joined MacBryde in London, and Peter supported both of them, introducing them to the writers and artists he knew and using his influence and their talent to get their work into London's commercial galleries.

For the first few months the Roberts lived in Peter's flat. This was a new place in Kensington. During *Horizon*'s period at Thatched Cottage, Peter had looked for an alternative to Athenaeum Court, but hadn't found one (wondering aloud if he could really 'go on collecting residences in Europe').[8] But by the beginning of 1941 he had settled on a new place. Number 10 Palace Gate was a brand-new apartment block. Aesthetically it was an ideal home for a man of Peter's contemporary artistic tastes. Constructed between 1937 and 1939, it was the work of Modernist architect Wells Coates, a follower of Le Corbusier and Gropius. It consisted of two conjoined split-level blocks of steel frame and concrete faced with *faux* white stone, the main block solidly rectilinear with seven storeys, fronted by a smaller six-storey block relieved by a gently curved front elevation, reminiscent of Le Corbusier's Pavillon Suisse in Paris. Inside were twenty-five flats ('ultra-modern', said the ads) of varying size, some split between floors due to the ingenious 'three-two' design of the building in which one floor in the six-storey side equalled one and a half on the seven-storey side.

The flats had become available for letting in 1940, but there were few takers. Aside from the depopulation of London due to evacuation, many of those who could afford to live in districts such as Mayfair and Kensington (including Cecil Beaton and Peter's mother) had opted to spend the war in their country homes. Landlords had to adapt, and the flats at 10 Palace Gate were advertised on wartime tenancies with rents slashed to between £150 and £225 per annum (down from £175 to £425). For that the tenants got porterage, central heating, constant hot water, lifts, and use of the building's own air-raid shelter (presumably this was the underground car park, repurposed for the duration).[9]

The apartment Peter took was surprisingly modest; flat 22 on the third floor had just one smallish bedroom, a fairly sizeable living room, a tiny kitchen and a spartan bathroom. At some point during the past few years he had apparently abandoned the longing for grandeur that had motivated him a decade earlier. Modern, warm and comfortable it might be, but compared to the rue du Bac apartment it was tiny and plain.

With two young artists living in it, the flat was even more cramped. On first arriving, Robert MacBryde described it as 'very very modern but of the first quality'. Peter told him about the loss of the art in his Paris flat, where there had been enough paintings to fill three apartments.[10] He had lots more art here – more than could be fitted into the small flat. MacBryde noted the good collection of British artists – 'two excellent Chris Woods … one of Ben Nicholson's latest landscapes … a good Henry Moore.'[11] There were two Graham Sutherlands – *Gorse on a Sea Wall* and *Entrance to a Lane* – but still dominating the British were works by Peter's favourite Europeans, including Max Ernst and Miró, and Picasso's nightmarish *Minotauromachy*.[12]

Not only were there paintings; Peter had also built up an invaluable library of modern and historic books on art and architecture, and complete runs of the art journals of the day: *Cahiers d'Art*, the organ founded by dealer Christian Zervos (a friend of Peter's), which styled itself the definitive catalogue of modern art since 1926; *Verve*, a Parisian journal rich in lithographs of contemporary works; *XXe Siècle*, which featured original engravings by artists such as Matisse, Miró and de

Chirico; and the Surrealist *Minotaure*, founded by Albert Skira, edited by André Breton and funded by Peter's close friend and Eton contemporary Edward James. Meanwhile, Peter's gramophone was supplied with jazz, neoclassical and avant-garde records – Stravinsky, Bartók, Françaix, and more. Small as it was, the flat was a powerful draw for enthusiastic young artists, somewhere they could study, meet their fellows and make contact with the influential figures in the art world whom Peter had at his fingertips.[13] At various times, dinner guests at the flat included Henry Moore, Augustus John (who at Peter's prompting was writing his autobiography for *Horizon*), Ben Nicholson, John Rothenstein (director of the Tate) and Graham Sutherland.

The Two Roberts settled in quickly, adapting well to the luxuries on offer. When MacBryde took ill with flu in March, he was served with China tea and scones in bed by Peter's Cockney charlady, while Colquhoun sat in the lounge, 'painting away at a still life of flowers removed from my bedside'.[14] Peter was away visiting E. M. Forster (another potential contributor to *Horizon* now that the previous year's spat was done with), and the flat was suddenly 'overcrowded with some of his less wealthy friends,' MacBryde recorded sardonically, 'who come to dispose of his well stocked tray of wines under the guise of visiting the "charming Scots boy with the bad flu"'.

* * *

When the Two Roberts first came down from Scotland in early 1941, they became part of the tiny, select group of Peter Watson's fledgling protégés. There was one already under his care who was even younger than they were but showed great promise; he was the grandson of Sigmund Freud, and quite a teenage prodigy.

He had come to Peter's attention through Stephen Spender. In 1939, Stephen and Inez – in the death throes of their marriage – were living in a house in Hampstead. The basement flat was occupied by the Austrian Jewish architect Ernst Freud and his family. Stephen got to know their rather eccentric sixteen-year-old son, Lucian, an intense youth whose mop of curly hair made him resemble Harpo Marx.[15] Stephen quickly recognised the talent in the boy – 'the most intelligent person I have met since I first knew Auden at Oxford'.[16] Lucian was an enthusiastic but largely self-taught painter; he needed proper tuition, and in April 1939 Stephen arranged for him to attend the new art school at Dedham in Suffolk run by the painters Cedric Morris and his partner Arthur Lett-Haines.

Through Stephen, Lucian came to the attention of Peter Watson, who was equally impressed by the boy's talent. In April 1940, the first published artwork by Lucian Freud – a self-portrait – appeared in *Horizon*; a simple and (*pace* the Morris school) untutored monochrome sketch, it was weirdly dysmorphic, skewed, quite unsettling, but also compelling. It would take an exceptionally perceptive eye to detect the potential in this quite crude drawing, but Peter Watson had that eye, and he saw what was in this boy.

By the end of 1940, Peter was giving Lucian his wholehearted support. In the autumn of that year, Ernst Freud, who had been unimpressed by the work his son was producing, had decreed that Lucian ought to give up painting and study for a proper profession; art was clearly not his vocation. Ernst would not go on paying for him to attend the Morris school; he regarded Morris's style, which Lucian was emulating, as 'revealing in a way which was almost improper'. Ernst wrote to Morris, 'I could not help but loathe the last picture he brought to London.'[17]

When Peter heard about this, he stepped in immediately, and on 2 November – about the same time as he was arranging to bring the Two Roberts down to London – he wrote to Cedric Morris:

> As there has been some question of Lucian's father urging him to discontinue his painting and take some other job, I decided that I would pay his expenses for the time being, to enable him to carry on with his work. I am doing this because I am very fond of him and believe in him. It would be disastrous for him to reorientate his whole existence at this moment unless it were absolutely inevitable.
>
> So perhaps you will send me an account for his expenses when convenient to you.[18]

Paying for Lucian's tuition at the Morris school was just the beginning – throughout the years that followed Lucian's progress would be entirely along a path built and smoothed for him by Peter Watson.

During 1941, Peter added a fourth painter to his list – another young boy whose acquaintance he had made the previous year. This time the connection was more personal. In April 1940 Peter had gone to the

London première of Shostakovich's Fifth Symphony at the Queen's Hall. There he met a bright and soulful young man called John Craxton.[19] He was seventeen years old, the son of a piano teacher at the Royal College of Music, and already an accomplished novice painter. As a fourteen-year-old Boy Scout he had visited the Paris Exposition of 1937 and seen Picasso's *Guernica*, and two years later had gone back to Paris to take life-drawing classes.[20]

John Craxton took to Peter Watson instantly, as if he were already an old friend (as people were inclined to do if Peter was in a mood to be congenial). After the concert they walked down Regent Street to Piccadilly together, talking all the way, and went into the Kardomah Café (part of a chain of tearooms noted for featuring live string quartets), where Peter had arranged to meet David Gascoyne; he was the first poet Craxton had ever met – 'a wonderfully handsome, romantic figure with a faraway look'.[21]

The young John Craxton was wholly entranced by Peter's charm and generosity, and by the sheer breadth and depth of his knowledge of art. But their friendship, and Peter's sponsorship of Craxton as an artist, didn't really get going until 1941, when he became part of the little group of enthusiasts who would come to the flat at 10 Palace Gate to experience the atmosphere, study the books and magazines, listen to records, and meet the other fascinating visitors. It was at Palace Gate that John Craxton first met Lucian Freud – an encounter that turned into a long and fruitful relationship.

Friendship was as important to Peter Watson as talent, and his choice of recipients for his patronage was partly based on whether he personally liked the artist – for a man with his sensibilities it could hardly be otherwise since their personality must be embodied in their work. Some artists he wouldn't support, no matter how gifted they were and however determinedly they lobbied him. One was the twenty-year-old Michael Ayrton; he'd had a good start, doing theatrical designs for a John Gielgud production, and had a remarkable, disturbing vision which in some respects was reminiscent of Tchelitchew, Ernst and Picasso; but Peter – who went to see his work in late 1940 – took a personal dislike to both the artist and his paintings that was so severe it was quite physical. He wasn't the only person who disliked Ayrton, but must have been among the most repelled; John Piper objected to the young painter's arrogance, and Peter concurred: 'I do agree with your advice to Ayrton,' he wrote to Piper. 'An "apprenticeship in humility" were my very words a year ago when I first went to see him. I was so horrified by the conceit of his pictures and of himself, I had to lie down upstairs, I felt so ill.'[22] After bumping into Ayrton again in the Redfern Gallery in early 1942 (and apparently being badgered by him for his support), Peter wrote to John Craxton: 'It is terrible how he really has a physical effect on me and how his persistence upsets me.'[23] It was rare for Peter to show this Tennant-ish effeteness, so Ayrton's effect upon him must have been quite atrocious.

* * *

London life went on and the bombs continued to fall. There were raids most nights through those early months of 1941. Robert Colquhoun observed, 'The destruction in the West End is incredible. Whole tracts of streets flattened out into a mass of rubble and bent iron. There is a miniature pyramid in Hyde Park not far from us built up of masonry and wreckage taken from bombed buildings. These heaps are all over London.'[24]

Living at Palace Gate, he and Robert MacBryde had acquired Peter's nonchalance – or fatalism – about the raids; 'it never worries us over much although bombs have fallen quite close.'[25] Despite the building proudly possessing its own private shelter, Peter still didn't go there, and the Roberts followed his example.

One night in April it got too close for comfort. West London experienced what Peter called 'a couple of the ripest blitzes yet – bombs falling everywhere'.[26] He was on the toilet when a parachute mine (possibly two) landed two hundred yards away from the building, blowing in the windows in the bedroom and sitting room. 'I don't know how we escaped yet,' MacBryde wrote. 'I had the back of my head cut a little, that was all. We drank a bottle of whisky and remained lying on the floor.'[27]

Even after that Peter wouldn't go to the shelter, still preferring to die in his bed (or on the toilet, as the case may be).

Despite the bombs and the rubble and the nightly terror, life in London continued – as it had in Shanghai in 1937 – whether in the clubs or the art galleries or simply boating on the Serpentine. 'Clumsy scarred London,' Robert Colquhoun wrote, 'can have delightful pleasures if looked for with a friend.'[28]

During early 1941, with the Roberts still living in his flat (which became decidedly chilly for a while until the windows were replaced), Peter considered taking a house in the country. He had spotted a six-bedroom place at Frome in Somerset: a medieval manor with an attached cottage and several acres of land, on the market for £3,300. The idea was that the Roberts – and perhaps Lucian Freud too – would live and work there, and it would be Peter's weekend getaway.[29] But the plan never came to anything. Eventually the Roberts took an apartment-studio of their own on the top floor of a big house in Cornwall Gardens, round the corner from Palace Gate.[30] There they had their own space and lived again among their own belongings – but it was all still paid for by Peter.

Taking advantage of the start Peter had given them, the Roberts largely went their own way, painting busily and integrating themselves into the arts scene. They became particularly friendly with Dylan Thomas and his wife Caitlin, to whom Peter had introduced them. Thomas had rented an old vicarage on the Thames at Kew and the four had an orgy weekend, in which the Roberts painted Dylan a mural (unpaid), 'to the accompaniment of lugubrious music played on an enormous piano by an equally lugubrious Welshman emaciated to a degree,' Robert C. reported. Afterwards they went outside by the water to listen to Dylan reading his poetry – 'and can he read. He read and we drank … all of us slightly in the other twilight world of hiccups.'[31] In this way Dylan's 'Watson money' was spent and the century's great literature was nurtured.

While the Roberts were well on their way, John Craxton and Lucian Freud were at an age where they still needed guidance, and Peter was keen to give it. Above all they needed tuition, and Peter set himself the task of arranging it.

The Craxton family's house had been damaged in the Blitz, and they had relocated to Cranborne Chase in Dorset, where they lived near the painter EQ Nicholson. She befriended young Johnnie, and he took up painting the local landscape.[32] But Peter felt that both Johnnie and Lucian needed proper, formal teaching, and of a better standard than that available at the Morris school. He was particularly concerned about Lucian's poor drawing skills. 'Lucian must learn to draw a hand before he distorts one,' he told Johnnie.[33] Peter wrote to Graham Sutherland for advice, and he recommended Goldsmiths College School of Art, which was one of the few London art schools still operating in wartime.

Sutherland wrote that 'Clive Gardiner the headmaster is sympathetic, progressive and erudite.'[34] He was a friend of Sutherland's, and was glad to take on the two students if they felt that the half-hour bus journey from Victoria wasn't excessive.

After they'd enrolled, it occurred to Peter that they also needed somewhere decent to live and work. This thought had struck him when he was reading about the life of Miró, a subject he'd studied closely; in August 1941, Peter's name had appeared for the first and only time in the pages of *Horizon*;[35] sandwiched between the fourth instalment of Augustus John's autobiography and an essay by George Orwell about H. G. Wells and the World State, was a short and oddly inconclusive piece by Peter Watson on Joan Miró, a painter he rated highly. Probably as part of his research for the article, he re-read Miró's essay in the May 1938 issue of *XXe Siècle*: 'Je rêve d'un grand atelier'. It occurred to Peter that this was exactly what both Johnnie Craxton and Lucian Freud needed – a proper space of their own. He phoned Craxton and asked him if he would like a studio. At the time he was living and working in 'a narrow room with just space for a bed'. Peter told him: 'Find yourself somewhere to work and send me the bill.'[36]

It was a move that was profoundly fortuitous for the future of British art. Peter followed up the phone call with a letter and an advance: 'How much do studios cost in this awful place?' he asked. 'Anyway here is £50 for a start. Look for something delicious.'[37] Craxton recalled:

> I found an upstairs maisonette in a Nash-style terrace [14 Abercorn Place] in St John's Wood. Lucian very quickly joined me, using the top floor as a studio. We lived and painted there for two years. We were inseparable at that point, like brothers. He was very unlike me and that's why we got on so well, because there was no clashing of styles ... I learnt from Lucian how to scrutinise, which I wasn't doing before, and Lucian learned how to plan pictures and use colour.[38]

All the expenses were picked up by Peter, as well as frequent handouts of £5 or £10 at a time. 'You could live on £2.10s a week then,' Craxton recalled, 'and £5 was just magical. He took you out for dinner in Soho ... and you'd say "thank you" and he'd turn around and say "Thank you, thank you!"'[39]

The story of how Miró had lived and suffered in 1918–19 was evidently on Peter's mind; as he wrote in his *Horizon* article: 'Much of his painting was done suffering the hunger caused by one uncertain meal each day. The apparently light-hearted and gay "Carneval d'Arlequin" is a composite of hallucinations caused by hunger from details scribbled each night on ends of paper.'[40] Despite such creative benefits, Peter was anxious that his protégés shouldn't suffer so. In September 1941 Lucian began a portrait in oils of Peter, who sent him 'ten little pounds to help keep alive all the little brush-strokes'.[41] Lucian worked at the portrait for a long time; Peter was delighted with the result, and kept it the rest of his life.

Peter became very attached to both Freud and Craxton, but it was the latter he was more fond of – perhaps because he was more genial, less intense. When the Craxton family lived in Dorset in 1941, Peter missed Johnnie terribly; he was 'one of the few I like to see and talk to a lot'.[42] The Blitz was still going on at this time, and Peter wrote that he felt like René Crevel, the Surrealist poet who had committed suicide in Switzerland in 1935, leaving a note saying 'Suis dégoûté de tout'. (Peter had known Crevel and visited him not long before his death, so must have had some insight into his state of mind.)[43] Peter's letter veered from longing to flirtation to exhortation and back again in a few sentences:

> But there again that is 'dangerous' Paris as Mrs Wood told you but I'm afraid I like that sort of danger. Paint a picture for me, will you and if I like it I'll buy it from you! You have such a talent if only you develop it. Yes you are indeed a real hope in all the Void. Oh but I shouldn't be indiscreet. But I always am. I have the sensation I ruin everything. One day I shall be found out and shot for it.[44]

Possibly Peter was a little the worse for drink when he wrote that letter, which revealed an attraction towards the eighteen-year-old that strayed beyond the bounds of patronage and friendship. Peter Watson was flesh and blood, and his desires must have been intermingled with his intellect, his personal emotions entangled with his aesthetic sensibilities.

It didn't go unnoticed. Both Peter and Stephen Spender – whose personal friendship with Lucian was as intense as Peter's with John Craxton – attracted some malicious gossip. The actor Michael Redgrave, who was bisexual and in a relationship at the time with Spender's ex-lover Tony Hyndman (who modelled at the Morris art school), noted in his diary the 'wild and amusing conversation' and the insinuations that went around, particularly about Spender's motives for helping Lucian.[45] (Stephen might have been a more attractive target for this kind of gossip as he was publicly heterosexual; after his divorce from Inez, in 1941 he married the concert pianist Natasha Litvin, with whom he remained for the rest of his life.)

In fact, Peter did occasionally take an interest in young artists that had more to do with sexual attraction than with artistic merit; whether sex was forthcoming or not, these relationships were short-lived. It was the art that fundamentally mattered to Peter; he might play the sugar daddy at times, but he never patronised anyone he didn't believe in with both his heart and his intellect.

If Peter sometimes let the boundaries blur, there is no evidence that he ever crossed them with John Craxton. For the rest of his life, Craxton would remember Peter only as a friend, a generous patron and an intellectual mentor. He imparted his ideas, cultivated through years of immersion in the European art world; Peter was troubled by the abstractions of contemporary aesthetics; he idealised modernity's rebellious freedom, but worried that young artists like Craxton and Freud (and the Roberts, for that matter) might be misled by them. Early in their friendship he wrote to Craxton:

> In such a time as this *everything* is permissible: the difficulty is to do anything successfully, i.e. it is impossible and absurd to turn out 3rd rate Paul Klees whereas it is not impossible or absurd to turn out 3rd rate Michelangelo, Degas or even Cézanne.
>
> To my mind it is a great mistake for painters to choose between prose and poetry or conscious and unconscious ... Great painting must have a synthesis of consciousness and unconsciousness, or prose as well as poetry. Also the poetry in a picture is not necessarily in the execution or in the subject, it is an essence which only the superior painter can impart. ...
>
> I tend to admire works by those who have great experience of life, Goya, Michelangelo, Delacroix, Picasso, it shows in their work.
>
> I agree that each new work must be a new adventure, a new discovery. Life renews itself every day and always comes back to strengthen the creator however much he may despair at moments.[46]

Peter himself sometimes despaired at the philistinism of the public, infuriated that they couldn't see what he could see in art. It depressed him to note the kind of stuff that would sell. When some of Jacob Epstein's 1933 Epping Forest watercolours ('dowdy', in Peter's view) were put up for sale at the Leicester Galleries, they sold £600 worth of them in one day; Peter wrote, 'Sometimes I just don't feel like lasting out this war ... I know now that I hate Modern Art. It is a menace and should be abolished. Far better for people to learn to make pots and pans and cakes.'[47]

But life would continue to strengthen him, for the time being; however, as the war progressed and the world changed in his eyes, the strength would be harder and harder to come by.

15

THE WORLD'S COLLAPSE

1941–1945

At the height of the Blitz in December 1940, Nancy Mitford, pouring a coulis of glee over a hard little crust of scorn, had written to a family friend that 'Cyril, Hog Watson and many another lefty are avoiding military service by dint of being editors of a magazine ... which is a reserved occupation, isn't it brilliant.'[1] Nancy, of course, did not think it was brilliant at all – as an avowed anti-Fascist, she was a supporter of the war; her husband was overseas serving with the Welsh Guards (the same regiment as Rex Whistler and A. J. Ayer), and Nancy spent time taking care of the Jewish refugees who were accommodated in the Mitford family home. Meanwhile, Diana and Oswald Mosley had been interned as Nazi sympathisers; Nancy had nothing but disdain for her Fascist sister, and had coolly informed on Diana to MI5. Her professed delight that Cyril Connolly and Peter Watson were 'avoiding military service' was ironic.

And if Nancy Mitford was privately gossiping about them, she was unlikely to be the only one among those tight, numerous, intersecting circles that made up British high society, and it must surely have come to Cyril and Peter's ears that some people regarded *Horizon* as an elaborate excuse for not being in uniform.

But they carried on with the magazine, and Peter travelled, bought art and cultivated the next generation of British painters. If they were consciously avoiding military service, it cannot have been for lack of physical courage. In sailing to China in 1937 and casually holidaying in Europe in September 1939, Peter had been blasé about remote danger; and his constant refusal to go to the air-raid shelters throughout the Blitz, even after near misses had damaged his home, argued a disregard for physical danger. Cyril showed the same kind of fatalistic courage during the Blitz. Caught out of doors during a raid, Cyril simply sheltered under a doorway, and said to Peter Quennell, who was with him at the time and utterly terrified, 'Be calm. Really, you know, we've all had interesting lives.'[2]

They must, therefore, have had their reasons. Fighting the war was not what they were made for; their talents and capacities lay elsewhere. And besides, in that first year or so of fighting, it still seemed that it was neither a fight for freedom nor a war on Fascism; merely a sign of the death of the Old World civilisation. But by 1941 that perception had started to change. In the August issue of *Horizon* (the same number in which Peter's essay on Miró appeared), George Orwell had published a withering, scornful attack on H. G. Wells – his boyhood hero – for his hackneyed, outdated and ineffectual promotion of the idea of a peaceful World State; Wells was 'too sane to understand the modern world', and against the demonic monster that had seized control of Germany, Orwell argued, there was nothing to do but fight for one's very survival.[3]

Peter had been immensely struck by Orwell's first article for *Horizon*, and must have been impressed by this one. He certainly disclaimed any ideological objection to war. He was not a pacifist, as he told his American acquaintance Parker Tyler – 'one must fight for anything worth having and rightly so.'[4]

According to those who knew him, Peter was deeply moved by the behaviour of the British people during the Blitz; although he might deplore their taste in art, their fortitude in weathering the bombing was a revelation to him. Across all classes he saw unity in the face of the threat of Nazi Germany, and it affected him profoundly and changed his view of Britain.[5]

So when his call-up came in late 1941 (his editorial role on the magazine was not in fact a reserved occupation) Peter made no attempt to get out of it; he simply sat back and waited to see what branch of the armed forces he would be assigned to. It turned out to be the RAF – possibly at his own request (most men of his class opted for either the air force or a guards regiment).[6] He wasn't exactly looking forward to his future but was at least resigned to it, and began telling people in the art world that he would be 'going into the Air Force soon now'.

It was just as well, perhaps, because aside from anything else, in July 1941 he and Cyril had been told by Harold Nicolson (who had a post in the Ministry of Information and had been a supporter of *Horizon*) that the magazine's paper allowance was likely to be axed.[7] Insofar as the magazine's value as a cultural morale-booster could be considered a contribution to the war effort, there would soon be nothing to contribute.

At about the same time as Peter was preparing for military service, Lucian Freud experienced a sudden rush of valour, ran off to Liverpool and enlisted in the Merchant Navy as an ordinary seaman. He managed one crossing in a North Atlantic convoy to Nova Scotia and back, under attack from U-boats and bombers, then fell ill with tonsillitis, was invalided out of the service and went back to being an art student. The only benefits he took away with him from his brief adventure were a chunky Navy sweater and the skill of cutting tattoos with a scalpel and Indian ink.[8] John Craxton, who had been terrified of being called up, was rejected as physically unfit.[9] If Sir Kenneth Clark's motive in creating the War Artists' Advisory Committee really was to preserve artists from the firing line, he need hardly have bothered – there seemed to be hardly a physically fit man among them.

Peter Watson was no different. At last he was summoned for his medical examination. He awaited the day with dread, too anxious even to reply to his friends' letters. He needn't have been; at thirty-two years old, his physique was exactly as spindly as it had been at twenty-two: arms and legs as thin as wands, with big hands and bony kneecaps that stood out like coal shovels; he was six feet two inches tall but weighed only nine stone. The doctors 'seemed genuinely distressed' by his condition (which was heightened by the intermittent jaundice that blighted him through much of his life). 'They were most polite,' Peter told John Craxton; 'I believe they will not take me for a fighting force ... I have been very gay indeed and have enjoyed everything hugely since.'[10] He had tried to do his duty, and it wasn't his fault if they wouldn't take him.

Horizon was also back on track. By the end of 1941, Kenneth Clark and Harold Nicolson's lobbying had succeeded in securing the paper supply, and the magazine's future – in the short term at least – was assured.

* * *

Not everything was sunny and gay in Peter's world. A few days after his medical, he went to stay with his mother at Sulhamstead. Lady Bessie only had a short time left to enjoy the manor, which was being snatched out from under her by the government. Although her favourite son would not be going into the RAF, her house would; Sulhamstead House, which had served as a convalescent home for officers during the First World War, was being pressed into service again; in 1940 part of it had been used briefly as the headquarters of the Special Service Brigade (the arm comprising Commando units), but now, in late 1941, it was being handed over entirely to the RAF as officers' accommodation for the Elementary Flying Training School at nearby RAF Theale.[11] Lady Bessie would be moving into one of the little gatehouse lodges for the duration.

Peter's elder brother, Sir Norman Watson, who had served in the RAF during the First World War and had now rejoined the Volunteer Reserve, had arranged the handover, apparently preferring that the house go to genteel RAF officers than to rowdy soldiers.

The two brothers had had little to do with each other for years now. Sir Norman's time was divided between developing a Canadian ski resort and his chairmanship of the Heston Aircraft Company, which he'd established in 1934 and which now had valuable Air Ministry contracts to provide modifications for special-purpose military aircraft. The last notice Peter had taken of his brother had been a fleeting encounter in Montreux in March 1936, when Peter met several young women who, according to a postcard he sent to Cecil Beaton, 'were proposed to by Sir Norman who ran away next day'. Despite the ambiguous wording, it was clearly Norman who had done the running away, not the women. 'He is le Don Juan des pâtisseries!' Peter wrote enigmatically;[12] he was acutely perspicacious about people – especially their emotional lives – and might have suspected that Sir Norman was secretly not a man for the ladies. And nothing had changed since – Norman was now forty-four years old, with a great estate, a fortune and several thriving commercial interests, but still showed not the slightest inclination to marry and produce an heir.

As for Peter's sister, Florence, he had no association with her at all. She continued to live for her own pursuits, which couldn't have been more different from Peter's. She still bred her great shaggy dogs, and had branched out into training and breeding racehorses – with some racing success. The rest of her energy was devoted to campaigning for the rights of women to become trainers and jockeys.

Lady Bessie Watson – or Dame Bessie, as she now was[13] – was not well, and hadn't been for some time. Peter started having to face the prospect of losing her. In early 1942 he wrote to Johnnie Craxton: 'I must have had flu rather badly as I am still feeling very weak although less depressed than a few days ago. Facing this world collapse needs all one's physical powers unimpaired. My mother is very ill again.'[14] The doctors diagnosed Hodgkin's lymphoma, a cancer of the white blood cells. It wasn't Peter's first encounter with the disease – his friend Desmond Parsons (brother of the Earl of Rosse and lover of Robert Byron) had died from it in Switzerland in 1937, aged only twenty-six. Peter was also aware that Humphrey Spender's wife, Margaret, seemed to have the disease. (She did, and died from it in 1945.)

Bessie, perhaps because of her age (she was now sixty-six) didn't endure the disease quite as long as Peter's young friends. She died on 25 June 1942. The funeral took place four days later; she was buried with Sir George. Bessie had come a long way from the back-terrace in Workington where she had grown up and been a teenage teacher, travelled an extraordinary road with her husband to the grandeur of Sulhamstead House and the quiet earth of a Berkshire country churchyard.[15]

Peter didn't record his feelings about her death – in fact he rarely mentioned her at all in his letters. There was one recent exception; the year before her death, Peter had been visiting her at Sulhamstead and happened to show her one of John Piper's paintings. He had recently taken young Craxton to spend a weekend with Piper, and was full of enthusiasm for him. She was delighted with it – 'It isn't like those garish modern pictures at all, is it?' It was unusual for them to share a liking for an artist; 'She considers Klee very childish!' Peter wrote to Myfanwy Piper. 'Not at all an adult mind.'[16] But Piper she liked. With anyone else, Peter might have been exasperated or even disgusted by such a contrary opinion, but his mother's verdict he regarded with indulgent amusement.

After all, it had been she who secured his future, encouraged him to follow the life of the aesthete and connoisseur in the face of his father's disapproval. Because of her he was a rich man in his own right rather than the impecunious outcast son of one. Cecil Beaton believed that Peter's relationship with his parents, including his mother, had been a bad one, and that she had even been cruel to him. However, Cecil had parental issues of his own that might have influenced him, and his notion of 'cruelty' included all manner of emotional slights, great and trivial. Other people who knew Peter closely came away with the impression that his mother had loved him, and that he had at least been fond of her in return.

That was over now; he was, in effect, alone; he had relations, but no longer any family. His family was the arts, and its practitioners were his surrogate progeny.

* * *

Peter was not only financing the new generation; he still took an interest in existing artists – during 1941, for example, he was funding Ben Nicholson, who had taken a house in the country in which to paint.[17] Having overlooked it for years, Peter had a lot to discover in contemporary British art. After his initial visit in 1940, he had become interested in the St Ives artists' colony, and in August 1942 he visited again.

The colony had been going since the 1880s, when, with the fishing industry in decline, artists began moving into the disused sail lofts and empty fishermen's cottages, and in the 1920s and 1930s the post-war generation settled in and made names for themselves – Ben Nicholson, Christopher Wood, Barbara Hepworth, among others – along with hordes of enthusiastic amateur painters and art lovers. When Peter Watson visited in 1942 it was carnival time, and the town was overcrowded – '*everyone* has gone quite mad,' he wrote to John Craxton.[18]

At the same time, Alfred Wallis, the melancholic St Ives rag-and-bone man who had become an influential painter, now aged eighty-six, was dying in the workhouse infirmary at Madron near Penzance. Although no evidence survives of Peter Watson having bought Wallis's paintings, he clearly took an interest in his work and probably contributed financially to his support; he certainly encountered the critic Adrian Stokes, who took a close personal interest in Wallis's welfare, and it was from him that Peter heard the news of the old man's death on 29 August.

The painter and writer Sven Berlin, who worked in Adrian Stokes's market garden, was a great admirer of Wallis, and wrote a long obituary, which he sent to Herbert Read, who in turn passed it on to Peter Watson. Peter accepted it for inclusion in the January 1943 number of *Horizon* and sent £10 in payment.[19] According to Berlin, Ben Nicholson, who with Christopher Wood had discovered Wallis in 1928, heard about the article 'and at once sent an article of his own to push in front of mine'.[20] As editor, Peter insisted on Berlin's article going first, and both duly appeared in the magazine, 'which left a splinter in Ben's finger', according to Berlin. (Despite the serenity of the place, the St Ives community had never been particularly harmonious – indeed it was the ongoing 'war to the death' amongst the realist and abstract painters that had drawn Peter to visit it the first time in 1940.)

Following publication of the obituaries there was further friction. A spiteful response came from Evelyn Waugh, who wrote a sarcastic letter to *Horizon*: 'Blue, decayed streaks of silliness are healthy in art as in cheese,' he declared, and offered to sponsor an 'Alfred Wallis Prize' to be awarded 'with preference for the old and famous rather than the young and contemporary. The work need not be complete in itself or in anything else.'[21] Cyril Connolly, as Waugh's friend, published the letter. Privately Peter called Waugh (who had once referred to him disdainfully as 'a pansy of means') a 'Catholic Fascist',[22] while Graham Greene wrote a public response suggesting that Waugh himself be awarded the first Alfred Wallis Prize 'for his little castrated letter ... As Alfred Wallis is dead and is unlikely, therefore, to notice Mr Waugh's generous offer, I suggest that the prize might more suitably bear the name of the donor.'[23]

Meanwhile, in St Ives the mortal remains of old Alfred Wallis himself, as oblivious in death as he had been in life to people's opinions of his painting, lay in peace under his tiled tomb on Barnoon Hill, overlooking the white sands of Porthmeor and the roiling green ocean.

* * *

Much as he liked Cornwall, it was the west coast of Wales that would become more significant for Peter, and he went there several times during the war years.

What appears to have drawn him in the first place was an acquaintance (probably a slight one) with Wogan Philipps, a failed artist from an ancient Welsh family who was married to novelist Rosamond Lehmann, the sister of *Horizon*'s rival John Lehmann. Wogan's father, Laurence Philipps, 1st Baron Milford, owned Picton Castle near Haverfordwest; Peter stayed at Picton, and wrote from there to John Craxton: 'Imagine my surprise when my host told me last night that he owned the castle I sent you the postcard of. He owns three castles in Wales.'[24]

Charmed by the white farmhouses of St David's ('rather like in Cornwall'), Peter was keen to go back, and to take young Craxton with him.[25] For one thing, he delighted in Johnnie's company, but he also felt that his art was missing something – he was overly drawn towards the pleasantly picturesque. Peter teased him sometimes about a cuteness he perceived in his choice of subjects – 'Are you painting many countryscapes or pussy-cats,' he inquired in one letter,[26] and in postcard of one of St Ives' quaint alleys: 'I have done my best for you. Here is your house, a shaft of sunlight and *zwei Katze*.'[27]

Craxton visited South Wales in March 1942 with EQ Nicholson, and found it stimulating;[28] he produced an eloquent, elemental ink study of Llanthony Abbey framed in tentacle-like tree roots, which marked a significant departure from sunlight and cats.

In the summer of 1943 Peter took him to stay with Graham and Kathleen Sutherland, who were living in one of those charming white farmhouses in the wild prehistoric landscape of St David's Head. It was a formative experience for the young painter. He learned some crucial and surprisingly basic lessons from Sutherland, including the importance of invention. One day Sutherland showed him the place that had inspired his *Entrance to a Lane*, which Craxton had studied and admired so often in Peter's flat. 'But there are no trees overhanging it!' he objected. Of course not, Sutherland said; he'd taken them from somewhere else. 'You must invent,' he told the young man. It was what Picasso did all the time – 'taking natural forms and reinventing them'.[29]

That holiday at St David's planted an even more important seed: the whole experience of its light and landscape. 'There were cloudless days,' Craxton recalled, 'and the land was reduced to basic elements of life; rocks, fig trees, gorse, the nearness of sea on all sides, a brilliantly clear light. Everything was stripped away – all the verbiage, that is – to the essential sources of existence.'[30] He and Peter went for walks, and took a rain-sodden bicycle hike to Haverfordwest. On one of the cloudless days they sat and talked together about this glorious setting, and Peter recalled his travels through Greece with Igor Markevitch in 1935. The rocky, gorsey landscape and light of Pembrokeshire were just like those in Greece, he said. For Craxton, this conversation was 'the crystallisation of my desire to travel to Greece'. Eventually, once the war ended and he became free to travel, this desire would change his life and his direction as a painter. But for now he contented himself with Pembrokeshire, returning in July 1944 to stay with the Sutherlands.[31]

In that year John Craxton transitioned from his student phase and could at last call himself an artist – and a prominent one – with his first solo exhibition at the Leicester Galleries, where he sold paintings to (among others) John Lehmann and the poet Geoffrey Grigson. The latter commissioned him to illustrate his next book of poetry – the beginning of a partnership that Peter Watson helped finance.[32]

By this time, Peter, who was growing ever more weary with the war and with London, had finally taken a house in the country. Tickerage Mill was a rambling, higgledy-piggledy agglomeration of honeyed brick lazing by a lakeside near Uckfield in Sussex. It belonged to the painter and journalist Dick Wyndham, and Peter and Cyril Connolly had both been to the notoriously wild parties Wyndham had held there during the 1930s. Cyril described a version of it in his book *The Unquiet Grave*, eulogising the womb-like setting amidst a chestnut wood, 'the black sunlit marsh marigolds, the wood-fire crackling in the low bedroom, the creak of the cellar-door'.

Peter rented Tickerage for a year from early 1944, and spent all the time he could there. Dick Wyndham's old-fashioned, cluttered, ramshackle furnishings weren't at all Peter's style, so he changed everything to meet his own refined modern tastes. Not wanting to inconvenience his friend, he brought John Craxton down first to make drawings of every room, so that Wyndham's furniture – which Peter placed in storage for the duration – could all be put back exactly as it had been. (The fact that he didn't simply photograph the rooms says much about Peter's aesthetic values.) With the furnishings settled to his satisfaction, Tickerage's rickety walls began to be arrayed with his constantly growing collection of new paintings.

Tickerage became a social oasis again during Peter's residence. Among the guests was the South African composer Priaulx Rainier, whom Peter knew through the musical circle that included Michael Tippett. She described Peter, dressed in an immaculate white suit, presiding over a dinner table that was unusually replete; he had supplemented his rations by gathering produce from local farmers, including duck eggs and other off-ration items. The only thing lacking from an otherwise splendid dinner was good wine; by way of explanation, Peter showed Priaulx the wine cellar: 'he beckoned to me secretly … Descending a staircase to the cellar below, he switched on a light. There, securely engaged within a fine steel grill could be seen dozens of bottles of vintage wine!' This was Dick Wyndham's celebrated collection, which was not part of the letting arrangement. 'Which shall we choose for dinner?' Peter asked Priaulx with a smile. 'Let us enjoy in imagination at least!'[33]

Peter would travel down to Tickerage from London whenever the bombs became too much for him. The German V-1 flying bombs and V-2 rockets – which began to hit London in June and September 1944 – frayed the nerves of Londoners in a way the Blitz hadn't. They were random, unpredictable; they could come any time; the V-1s, or doodlebugs, sometimes came in waves, sometimes singly. Peter, having lived so calmly through the worst nights of the Blitz, found that 'the doodles are so bad for the stomach.' When he heard the drone, all he could do was lie biting the carpet in a state of terror, sometimes for hours.[34]

During 1944, apparently in the lead-up to D-Day, Peter was mysteriously – and very briefly – drawn into military activities. Longing to travel with John Craxton, he had to decline: 'I am afraid I will not be able to go to Wales or anywhere else … now that His Majesty claims my attention [and] my time is not my own – stern duty calls.'[35] Whatever this stern duty was, it involved night manoeuvres and parades, interspersed with gatherings at Tickerage with friends, including a weekend with artist Gerald Wilde and David Gascoyne.[36]

Gascoyne, unchanged since his angst-ridden days in Paris before the war, had remained a gloomy presence in Peter's life. He and Wilde didn't get on at Tickerage, which amused Peter and frayed his nerves at the same time. 'I am getting used to that sort of discord,' he wrote, 'as most

Above left: Sir George Watson.

Above right: Lady Bessie Watson by Sir John Lavery.

Below: R. A. Young's House at Eton in 1926, after he had taken over from Goodhart. Peter Watson is standing, slightly left of centre, with his hands in his pockets.

Victor William 'Peter' Watson, a drawing by Cecil Beaton, early 1930s.

Peter with Oliver Messel.

Above: Cecil Beaton in the circus room at Ashcombe. The murals were by Pavel Tchelitchew, Rex Whistler, Oliver Messel and others.

Below: John Craxton at work on *Pastoral for P.W.* in 1948.

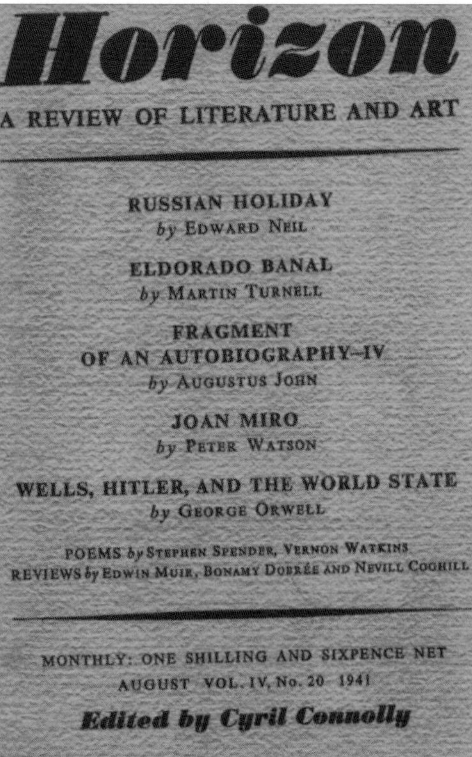

Horizon

A REVIEW OF LITERATURE AND ART

RUSSIAN HOLIDAY
by EDWARD NEIL

ELDORADO BANAL
by MARTIN TURNELL

FRAGMENT
OF AN AUTOBIOGRAPHY–IV
by AUGUSTUS JOHN

JOAN MIRO
by PETER WATSON

WELLS, HITLER, AND THE WORLD STATE
by GEORGE ORWELL

POEMS *by* STEPHEN SPENDER, VERNON WATKINS
REVIEWS *by* EDWIN MUIR, BONAMY DOBRÉE AND NEVILL COGHILL

MONTHLY: ONE SHILLING AND SIXPENCE NET
AUGUST VOL. IV, No. 20 1941

Edited by Cyril Connolly

Above left: Peter (standing, left), Salvador Dalí (reclining) and a friend sunbathing.

Above right: Igor Markevitch in about 1929.

Below left: The front cover of the August 1941 edition of *Horizon*, which featured Peter's piece on Joan Miró.

Below right: Cyril Connolly in the early 1950s.

Above: Waldemar Hansen (right) with Lucian Freud caught by a street photographer outside the National Gallery in 1947.

Below: Peter Watson, Zette and Michel Leiris and Sonia Orwell at Farley Farm House in East Sussex.

Above: 'The best-kept boy in the world', the beautiful Denham Fouts, Watson's American lover, photographed by George Platt Lynes in 1935.

Below: Norman Fowler (left) with his sailing companion Edward Allcard and yachtswoman Ann Davison at Torpoint, Cornwall, May 1952.

Above: Peter Watson outside the home of Lee Miller and Roland Penrose in 1951.

Below: Stephen Spender and his wife Natasha at a party, c. 1950.

of my friends always seem to hate each other and all attempts to bring them together result in disharmony.'[37] Gascoyne had worked himself into a crisis worthy of Denham Fouts, and when they were due to leave for London, Peter 'went up to find him lying fully dressed on his bed with the black out up complaining of *angoisse* and saying he was unable to travel.' This came on top of an incident a few days earlier when Gascoyne claimed to have experienced a premonition that his father had committed suicide. Too scared to do anything about it, he asked Peter to phone and inquire. He did, and found the Gascoyne family all alive and well – 'Oh the egotism of romantics!'[38]

* * *

While Peter pursued his course as a patron during the war years, *Horizon* had expanded its output; they began publishing books, including Cyril Connolly's *The Unquiet Grave* – a continuation of the self-negation of *Enemies of Promise* – which he dedicated to Peter. It was enormously popular.

Cyril's personal life had moved on since Jean's departure in 1940. Although he still imagined that she might come back to him, he had taken up with yet another woman; Diana had left him, and he had fallen in love with Lys Lubbock, the bored wife of a schoolteacher. Like all Cyril's women, Lys was intelligent, strong, and startlingly good-looking; she was also American-born and fifteen years his junior. He had a gift for attracting beautiful young women, despite his porcine shape and unfortunate features; possibly it was the combination of his powerful intellect and personal charm, together with an underlying vulnerability – the air of needing to be looked after.

Lys obliged his needs in every respect – she left her husband to live with Cyril, and took over the management of his finances, as well as becoming, in effect, the manager of *Horizon*. By the summer of 1945, Cyril and Lys had been dislodged from several flats by the London County Council (they were required for emergency housing), and had finally settled in a house in Sussex Place in Regent's Park (near where *Horizon* had been born). John Craxton moved in temporarily to design the décor, and set about making it a neo-Georgian palace.

Peter's love life during the war was subdued. In a sense, he remained faithful to Denham, and took no serious lover. He missed Denny and was feeling the approach of middle age, as men will in their mid-thirties. But the casual sex life that had always been a part of his existence – whether he was with a regular partner or not – continued.

Sometimes it overlapped with his patronage; he certainly flirted with John Craxton and was clearly a little in love with him for a while. (Nothing physical appears to have happened; although Craxton was bisexual, no evidence survives of any consummation.) John Craxton's art was strong enough that the relationship survived. Likewise Eduardo Paolozzi: 'I was an erotic image for Peter Watson,' he recalled. 'He always fell for foreign boys who were talented.' Peter bought Paolozzi's work, introduced him to other young artists, and after the war took him to dine with Giacometti;[39] Peter might have fancied the young Scottish-Italian, but it was the work that counted.

Some other artists caught Peter's interest primarily for sexual reasons; in 1942 he had a fleeting brush with Keith Vaughan, a young artist whose work he went to see on the possibility of supporting him. Vaughan, who was terribly anxious to have Peter Watson's patronage, worked hard to secure it, but Peter was apparently mainly interested in his personal attractions. Vaughan found himself being dined expensively, followed by an evening at Peter's flat. He felt himself terribly gauche and inexperienced in the presence of the cosmopolitan and sophisticated Peter, in a flat that had 'every refinement and luxury of comfort and cultured living'. Peter sat curled up, translating aloud from Gide while Vaughan put Mahler's *Das Lied von der Erde* on the gramophone. The unsophisticated young artist 'felt shabby and awkward with someone who has such easy command over life'.[40] In his diary, Vaughan agonised over the obvious undercurrent of Peter's interest:

> … at midnight I went, Peter insisting that I stay, but I fear he wants an affair and awkwardness and shyness made me afraid … Peter is not unattractive, but his easy superiority warps my style. Stupidly and gauchely I insisted on going. As we opened the outer door there stood on the threshold the most delightful New Zealand sailor. Peter must have wished me elsewhere at that moment.[41]

Feeling that he had made a mistake, Vaughan returned the next evening to the flat, uninvited, and found himself intruding upon a scene similar to the one he had enjoyed the previous evening. This time David Gascoyne was the guest. They all chatted happily together and listened to records, particularly Brahms' Second Piano Concerto (with Peter insisting for some reason on omitting one particular movement). But Peter made no overtures towards Vaughan this time; he had missed his chance. Without a sexual relationship, Peter was not sufficiently interested in his art to take notice of him, and he faded away from the Watson orbit.

* * *

As the end of the war approached, Peter's moods became unstable. He started to swing between a whimsical gaiety and the most abject, pessimistic gloom.

His whimsy came out in letters to John Craxton, Lucian Freud and Cyril Connolly. With the same playfulness he had shared with Cecil Beaton, he toyed with their names. Craxton was occasionally Johnnnnnnie, Lucian was Lucio or Looooocian, and Cyril was usually either Squirrel or Squiggles; Tickerage was variously Tick, Tix, or Tick Tock. He made light of his everyday life and affected to scorn the bombs.

But underneath it all a deep sense of darkness and doom was starting to build; it would grow over the coming years until it shadowed all his thoughts. He yearned for a united, culturally sophisticated Europe, but could see only conflict and moral cowardice. In the closing days of the war he wrote to John Craxton:

> I am going to try to be as little as possible in London this summer. The closing scene of this real Götterdämmerung is unbearably long and tedious. It seems wicked to complain when hundreds are losing their lives every day but why can't the Germans decide to surrender; let us make a United Europe from Lisbon to Danzig to Athens which with *all* the colonies concerned would make the richest, most exciting possible combination –culturally and economically stimulating.[42]

His vision was less rosily optimistic than it first seemed – his culturally stimulating union would 'give everyone something to fight the next war about'. He was becoming convinced that the world was destined for a future riven by perpetual Armageddon:

> The world is today much too small to stick to a system which died with Napoleon in 1815. And why won't they? Because people have no vision, are afraid of being daring and imaginative, therefore all the big changes are made by the wrong people, such as the Communists or the Fascists, for the wrong reasons. And if we don't make them, they will be made again for the wrong reasons.
>
> ... I feel so strongly about this, more strongly than I feel about ART and you know how I *love* that. Altho' there is nothing quite like ART is there.
>
> But the claustrophobia is increasing and I can't stand it. *Je n'en peux plus*.[43]

This last cry was the frustration of a man confined too long to his home islands. Peter longed to escape, to travel again, to visit the lands he had loved. 'I feel I shall die if I don't get away from this country soon. The atmosphere has completely clogged up my mind.'[44] Nancy Cunard (who had spent the war working in London as a translator for the French Resistance) had written him 'a very gay letter' from Paris – 'she says conditions are appalling but much mental stimulus.'

Even more intriguingly, he had heard news of his looted paintings from his acquaintance Douglas Cooper.

Cooper was an art historian and collector with strong connections to the Parisian art world. In 1939 he had served briefly as a medic in an improvised civilian unit commanded by Étienne de Beaumont, and later worked in RAF intelligence. He was now working for the Monuments, Fine Arts and Archives programme run by the Allied occupying forces in Europe – the so-called Monuments Men. Peter met Cooper in London and was told that some of his paintings had been discovered stored in the Musée du Jeu de Paume. They had been rescued from a train transporting looted artworks to Germany; it had been caught sitting in a siding in a Paris railway station when the city was liberated in August 1944, and the cargo of paintings had been returned to the building where the ERR had stored them nearly five years earlier.[45]

Peter was both eager and anxious to get to Paris, but it was easier said than done – Britain and Europe were still heavily militarised, and cross-border movements were restricted. Eventually, in early July 1945, Peter and Cyril acquired the necessary exit permits allowing them to travel to France on *Horizon* business. What should have been a journey of rediscovery turned into one of the most dispiriting and painful periods of Peter Watson's life. He anticipated being away six weeks;[46] in fact it would be closer to six months before he saw England again.

16

EVERY KIND OF DISASTER

1945–1946

Paris was haunted: full of the ghosts of the missing, of old friends and long-gone happiness, and, if you looked in the wrong places, the lingering spectres of Nazism.

Peter Watson and Cyril Connolly flew in from London in early July 1945, at the height of a European heatwave. Ostensibly they were here to solicit articles for *Horizon*, and would be travelling on to Switzerland for more of the same, but really their motives were more complicated.

Cyril in particular was looking forward to sampling the pleasures of European travel again. He'd been to Paris in January, in the midst of a bitter winter, while heavy fighting was still going on all along the German borderlands. It hadn't been a happy visit; he'd been taken to see a cellar where the Gestapo had executed people, and it had shaken him badly. His stay had been productive, though; he'd met Simone de Beauvoir and secured a scoop on Jean-Paul Sartre's manifesto for a new literary magazine, *Les Temps Modernes*,[1] which would eventually launch in October that year; de Beauvoir gave Cyril a copy of Sartre's keynote essay, which appeared in English translation as 'The Case for Responsible Literature' in the May 1945 issue of *Horizon*. Throughout the war the magazine had promoted the literature of the Resistance, and in the immediate post-war years gave intensive coverage to the new era in French writing.

For Peter, this trip to Paris was dominated by his need to discover what had been going on at his apartment while it was in the care of Sherban Sidéry, and what exactly had happened to his paintings. After his initial fatalism, Peter had become more concerned, and apparently tried to contact Sidéry in 1942 – this resulted in Peter being investigated by Special Branch and cautioned for 'attempting to communicate with a person in enemy territory'.[2] He had been in touch with Sidéry since the war's end, but the Romanian was evasive and hadn't given Peter a satisfactory account.

Landing in Paris in a blaze of summer heat, Peter and Cyril went straight from the airport to the rue du Bac, where they were intending to stay. From the outside, number 44 had the same shabby-genteel look as when Peter had left during that hectic first week of September 1939. But inside, the familiar apartment on the first floor was as different as it could possibly be.

The place that had been a byword for comfort, elegance and conviviality was now a hollow shell – deserted, bleak, and all but empty. The walls, which had been laid out with the choicest modern paintings, were bare, and most of the furniture was gone. There were some chests of drawers, a sofa in the dining room, and one of the beds was still there, but much of the rest had vanished, as had virtually all the moveable belongings. There was no sign of Sidéry, but there were the traces of his five-year occupancy. Searching through drawers, Peter came across pawn tickets for some of the missing items – including a set of gold-plated cutlery.[3] Everywhere was filthy and in disarray.

Peter was heartbroken, and Cyril was depressed, unsettled by memories of the times he'd spent here before the war. He found a photograph of Jean taken by Man Ray, which Denham had liked and had pinned to the bathroom wall; it was still there, dusty and curling at the edges. In the drawing room there was a sprig of mistletoe, dry and shrivelled now, still hanging from the ceiling where Jean had pinned it during that dramatic Christmas in 1938.[4] It had been a turbulent time, the apartment crowded with guests and visitors, and Denham – fit to burst with energy and frustration – reclining on the sofa by the fire nursing his injured foot. Visitors had come and gone at all hours, including the workmen and decorators Peter had hired, as well as disreputable friends of Denham's from the Parisian underworld. There had been a robbery on Christmas Eve – some person wandering in with the crowd – in which several valuables were filched and David Gascoyne had lost his new overcoat ...[5]

All life had gone from the apartment now, and the decorators' labours were masked by dirt and dust. There was no clean bed linen and no hot water, and Cyril had to sleep on the sofa in the dining room. His January visit to Paris might have been disturbing, but at least his accommodation at the British Embassy had been first-rate. (Duff Cooper was now British Ambassador, and he and Diana had put Cyril up and entertained him lavishly.) The rue du Bac no longer offered the comfort that had attracted Cyril to Peter Watson. 'It is so strange,' Cyril wrote to Lys, 'that Peter, who once had a genius for "gracious living" now comes to symbolise morbid discomfort to me.'[6]

Over the next few days, Peter tried to tidy up the flat, but little could be done about its dilapidated state – as far as Peter could discover, there were no paints or materials to be had in Paris.[7] (It was the same with artists' materials; John Craxton had asked Peter to get him some conté crayon, but they couldn't be had; Peter asked in several shops, but even the French artists couldn't get it.[8])

For the time being, there was also nothing to be done about the missing paintings; the authorities were overwhelmed with the volume of recovered artworks and flooded with requests for information. Peter decided to set that matter aside for the time being, and did his best to enjoy Paris. It wasn't easy. There were no buses or taxis, so he was forced to venture for the first time into the Métro, which he found amazing.[9] Re-establishing some of his contacts in the art world, he visited the gallery owner Christian Zervos at his home, and saw for the first time Picasso's *Night Fishing at Antibes*, painted in the last weeks of peace in 1939. 'I was breathstruck,' he wrote to Lucian Freud; 'surely one of his greatest pictures.'[10]

But Peter wasn't buying. Art prices in Paris had rocketed. Works by new painters now cost between £300 and £500 – which was ridiculous – while pictures by established names such as Braque, Picasso or Matisse were going for between £1,200 and £4,000. 'It's all crazy,' Peter wrote to Craxton, 'and god knows who buys them, because I don't know the people rich enough.'[11]

Everything in Paris was horrifyingly expensive; even a packet of

Chesterfield cigarettes (Peter's favoured brand) cost 120 francs – equivalent to 12 shillings, or about four times the normal price in Britain. When Peter and Cyril lunched at Maxim's with the critic Raymond Mortimer and André Gide (now in his seventy-sixth year), the bill came to nearly 4,000 francs (about £20), a shocking amount.[12]

Peter and Cyril also dined with Marie-Laure de Noailles at her home, and Peter found himself 'very much out of sympathy' with her.[13] The last time he had seen her in 1939 they had quarrelled bitterly; Peter didn't disclose the cause of the argument, merely stating that she had 'driven me from her house ... by saying how much she despised me'. (She was known for her volatile emotions, and perhaps their falling-out had had some connection with his involvement in Igor and Kyra's wedding, and might have been further fuelled by the fact – as some believed – that Marie-Laure was in love with Peter.[14]) Now, with the war over, she made a gushing fuss of him that embarrassed and irritated him. There was gossip going about that she had taken a German lover during the occupation. 'What was the war about anyway?' Peter wondered scornfully. 'She cheats on every score and like all people who want everything ends up with nothing except a court of hangers-on.' Cyril, Peter claimed, also thought that she 'behaved in a thoroughly bitchy, artificial way' that evening. 'I am getting too old now to be impressed by cleverness,' Peter wrote. 'I hate it ... Intelligence yes but cleverness no.'[15]

And yet, in spite of everything – the situation with the flat, art prices flying through the roof, the depressing, lingering atmosphere of the war, and the ruin of some of his French friendships – in Peter's mind Paris was still '*far* more agreeable than London, *much* cleaner, lighter, gayer, better food.'[16]

Also, in spite of its desperate condition, his apartment had already begun to regain a little of its pre-war life. Peter and Cyril were in Paris only a week, but by the end of it there were six friends staying with them in the flat. On the evening of their departure for Switzerland, they gave a cocktail party ('white wine, ice and peaches floating all over the place') for sixty friends and acquaintances.[17]

That evening, Peter and Cyril boarded the train for Berne. They both hoped that Switzerland, which hadn't been touched by fighting, might still offer some of the atmosphere and physical delights of Europe before the war. 'Paris was lovely and *tragic*,' in Peter's eyes,[18] while to Cyril the glorious city was 'all the same and all so changed ... like a beautiful woman who has had a stroke'.[19] Switzerland, they anticipated, would be as lovely as ever, and unmarred.

It was. Cyril celebrated the difference in a delirious, breathless wall of prose in his editorial in the special Swiss number of *Horizon*, which appeared in February 1946:

> The journey from Paris, in the July heat-wave, was a nightmare of discomfort. The train, leaving at nine in the evening, did not reach the Swiss frontier till noon the next day; foodless, waterless, seatless, the occupants stood ... while the train passed the long hours of tropical night panting and blowing beside some dried-up waterhole. ... Then suddenly Canaan ... the Val de Travers! ... whose chalets and trout-streams and widening pastures ... unfurl themselves far below. Such intoxication, to those deprived of it since 1939, that every sleeper on the track, every cable and pylon, every newly born aroma of mountain sunlight and fir-forest and the name of every station seemed the last unbearable saturation-point in the rebirth of feeling.[20]

And the hotel! The Bellevue Palace in Berne lived up to its name, the rooms (with balconies!) overlooking soul-quenching vistas of forest and mountain. And the shops! 'The town of Berne is, after five years of England, sheer hallucination,' Cyril wrote. He and Peter wandered through the streets goggling like children in a Christmas toyshop. Glittering windows were decked with the best of everything in the world: jewellers, tobacconists, boutiques, wine shops, antiquarian booksellers ... They suffered none of the shortages that plagued London and Paris. Peter marvelled at the new architecture that had gone up since 1939 – 'so well-made, the silver doors look as if they came from Cartier'.[21]

While they luxuriated in all that was on offer, Peter and Cyril were acutely conscious of the true cost of it: 'A certain price in guilt and smugness ... the hall-mark of the neutral; not to have been bombed, not to have been invaded, not to have been ruined in the cause of freedom.'[22] And at the same time, while luxuries were plentiful for the rich, the bare essentials of life were rationed, and the poor suffered as they did everywhere in Europe.

As well as the pleasures of shopping and dining, Peter and Cyril travelled out into the countryside. They took the train to Interlaken and stayed in a lakeside hotel, where they swam in the mild blue waters. Cyril, spellbound by the setting, described swimming in the river Aar: 'You undress and change and then walk up the riverside path for as long as you like, then plunge in and are carried down by the current to where you undressed – a wonderful feeling.'[23]

But Peter wasn't only here for pleasure and *Horizon*; he was also working on behalf of his protégés. In Paris he had shown photos of works by Lucian Freud and John Craxton to *galeristes* Christian Zervos and Pierre Loeb, and both were interested. In Berne he lunched with Lady Noel Norton, wife of the British Minister; before the war she had owned and run the London Gallery in Cork Street (of which Peter was a director) and was 'art *MAD* – much more than I'.[24] The following year, when John Craxton went to Greece, Lady Norton (whose husband had by then become ambassador in Athens) would be an invaluable supporter.

At the beginning of August, Peter and Cyril travelled to the Alpine resort of Gstaad ('delicious here – blazing sun and *lots* of butter'[25]), where they were royally entertained; at dinner Peter sat sandwiched between the niece of the (recently defunct) king of Italy and the daughter of the (deceased) king of Spain. They talked about the recent socialist victory in Britain's general election; like many intellectuals his age, Peter had voted Labour. 'Everyone is horrorstruck,' he wrote to Brian Howard. 'They give it one year. I am amazed, delighted but apprehensive.'[26] After Gstaad Peter and Cyril travelled on to Basel.

That was where things changed, suddenly and dramatically.

In Basel Peter visited the Kunstmuseum, Switzerland's principal museum of art, and got the shock of his life. On prominent display was a particularly interesting painting by Salvador Dalí – a medium-sized square canvas from 1936 titled *Perspectives*. This was one of the artist's many compositions of eerie figures arranged in beach or desert landscapes – in this case an endless plain of sand under a stormy sky, filled with tortured, cavorting and frolicking people. It was a painting that Peter was intimately familiar with; indeed, the last time he had contemplated it had been in 1939, on the wall of his rue du Bac apartment.

It was scarcely believable. *Here*, in a supposedly respectable public gallery, they were exhibiting looted treasures – *his* looted treasures. Bewildered, incensed and indignant, Peter confronted the gallery management. They too were indignant – more so even than Peter himself.[27] Douglas Cooper, who was in Switzerland conducting his investigations into Nazi looting, looked into the case. It was discovered that the Kunstmuseum had bought *Perspectives* from the Galerie Hans Ulrich Gasser in Zurich, and that Gasser had bought it in 1941 from Swiss art collector and publisher Albert Skira, who was a friend of Peter's and the founder (with Edward James, another friend) of the art journal *Minotaure*. From Skira, the paper trail led back inevitably to Paris and the gallery of Renou and Colle.[28] This was another shocking blow – Pierre Colle had also been a friend; he and Peter had travelled to America together, done business together, and socialised together, and it was absolutely certain that Colle – who had visited the flat – would have recognised this painting as Peter's. Peter believed that Skira too must have recognised the picture. The feeling of betrayal was breathtaking – far worse than the actual loss of any paintings. Cooper's investigation proved that *Perspectives* had been among the items taken by the Nazis, so there could have been no doubt in Colle's mind that he was handling looted property.

Coming on top of Sidéry's betrayal, it was hard to bear. And under the circumstances it was all too easy to suspect that Sidéry himself had perhaps had a hand in leading the ERR and the DSK to Peter's treasures. After all, he had pawned nearly everything of value in the flat. As the weeks passed, Sidéry – far more than either Skira or Colle – became the focus of Peter's rage: 'I think Sidéry a revolting sort of person,' he wrote; 'preserve me from aesthetic Roman Catholic homosexual snobs.'[29]

As if he hadn't had misfortune enough, by the time he had a chance to do anything about the discovery, Peter was struck down by a recurrence of the jaundice that had dogged him periodically through his life. And this time it came in force.

Initially the onset wasn't severe, but was sufficient to put him off travelling. He and Cyril had intended to journey back to England together in August, but when Peter started feeling unwell, he let Cyril go home alone while he travelled to Vulpera-Tarasp, a spa region in the mountains near St Moritz, to 'do a cure' by consuming the local mineral waters – the favoured panacea of his mother's generation. He wrote to Lucian Freud: 'Every morning and evening I drink large glasses of *Bonifazius Quelle* and (can you believe it) *Luzius Quelle*.'[30] (Both of these were sold commercially in the nineteenth and twentieth centuries, and Luzius-Quelle was particularly advertised for its 'powerfully laxative' effect.)

Peter wasn't particularly sorry about being parted from Cyril. Ever since Paris he had been finding his company increasingly trying; the discomforts of the rue du Bac and the journey to Switzerland had made him moody; what was more, he had been unable (or just didn't bother) to conceal his disappointment that Peter didn't seem as richly generous as he had once been. Peter wrote to Cecil Beaton complaining about Cyril's 'greed and snobbery'.[31] 'He is so vain, so touchy, so anxious all at the same time. I am quite the wrong person to deal with such a mixture over a long period.' (Cecil Beaton knew this very well, from personal experience.) Even worse than being grumpy, Cyril had started to lose his temper with Peter in front of other people. It all seemed to come down to money and comfort. 'He can never get over the fact,' Peter wrote, 'that I *won't* behave like a conventional rich man, always go to the best restaurant, hotel, travel first class etc. I suppose the rich reassure him but it is horrifying to watch him making up to them and his contempt for people with different standards.' With sickbed humour, Peter added: 'This must sound very jaundiced but it really isn't. He just makes me feel deeply unhappy after a time, all that welter of unsatisfied desires and jealousies.'

Even at a distance Cyril's neediness was draining; he had arrived back in England to find that Jean had sent him divorce papers from Reno, Nevada. Although he was with Lys now and there wasn't a hope of Jean coming back to him, he was upset, and complained to Peter about it. Peter tried to be encouraging, exhorting him to get in touch with Jeannie ('I am *sure* the case is not one of those hopeless ones')[32] but it was no go.

Despite his consuming the waters of Vulpera in quantity, they failed to effect a cure; on the contrary, Peter's jaundice got rapidly worse. On his doctor's advice he moved to the Clinic San Rocco at Lugano, down near the Italian border. By the time he arrived there, his skin was turning from yellow to green and beginning to peel.[33]

He spent most of the next two months in bed in his room in the clinic. It was a marvel of Swiss cleanliness and efficiency, and he was thankful he'd fallen ill here rather than in England. He was put on a diet of spaghetti and rice with mashed turnip or carrot, and three glasses of grape juice a day. His condition continued to deteriorate, and by early October he was suffering from constant nausea and depressive neurasthenia, and his physical symptoms had turned biblical: 'Pee the colour of black coffee and boils on the legs are the latest delights.'[34] The doctors began subjecting him to 'the most undignified treatments. I have to swallow a tube which I can only do with the greatest amount of horror and retching, wait *4–5 hours* until I digest the nozzle and the bile pours out.'[35] They gave him a gastric lavage with magnesium, 'which leaves one completely washed out for 3 days'. All this was followed by a blood transfusion. Gradually, after several weeks, the nausea abated, but he was left so physically weak he couldn't stand.

His friends back in England, reading the series of letters in which he documented his condition, grew severely worried. Cecil Beaton in particular took fright and showered him with telegrams promising to come out to Switzerland immediately to see him. Peter strenuously dissuaded him; his nerves couldn't stand the fuss, and he didn't want Cecil wasting a valuable exit visa (not to mention the money). As Peter wrote to Cyril, 'It isn't as if I were dying and wished to communicate the Secret of Life.'[36]

The secret of life might be beyond his ken, but Peter certainly communicated a great deal else. Despite his weakness and sickness, he spent most of his weeks in the Lugano clinic writing letters and working tirelessly on behalf of *Horizon*. Cyril had left without properly attending to the contributors they'd arranged for the Swiss issue of the magazine (despite this being the very reason they'd come to Switzerland in the first place), and so Peter took on the correspondence himself, as well as seeing to the translation of the German-language contributions. At the same time, he drew up detailed instructions for Cyril to deal with the art content of upcoming issues. Where he got the energy from was a mystery.

By the end of October, Peter was well enough to leave the clinic, although he wasn't yet fit for the journey home. Instead he went to Basel, where he stayed with his old friend Christophe Bernoulli, another art dealer.[37]

On top of all his other troubles, Peter had continued to pursue the matter of his stolen paintings. He'd been visited at the clinic by Douglas Cooper and they continued to inquire into how his Dalí had reached the Kunstmuseum. When Peter and Cooper had confronted Albert Skira, he initially denied ever handling it (and 'went through a pantomime of showing us a list of his pictures in which it was not included'). But eventually he admitted he'd bought it in Paris from Colle.[38]

Peter was seething with indignation, but he was in a dilemma; prior to this discovery, he and Cyril had been hoping that Skira would act as *Horizon*'s publisher in Europe. Peter had understandably gone off the idea, but Cyril was still insistent. Eventually Peter was forced to climb down; he wrote an abject letter to Skira, assuring him that he was certain that he had acted in good faith and been ignorant of the Dalí's provenance: 'You never came to my flat in Paris and so could have no idea that this painting belonged to me. ... I am very anxious to do all I can to help you and to prevent you incurring any difficulty or blame.'[39]

Skira passed this letter to the investigators as proof of his innocence; they were instantly suspicious, as it flatly contradicted the information Peter had given to Douglas Cooper. The Economic Warfare Department of the Foreign Office circulated a memo about it: 'We intended to question Watson about this complete bouleversement on his part, but he had already left Switzerland for England.' The writer was wary of 'nourishing unworthy suspicions about Mr Watson', but was fairly convinced that it was because of his need for a European publisher for his magazine. It was suggested that Mr Watson should be interviewed, to establish 'that there is nothing "phoney" about this sudden change of mind'. (If this interview ever took place, no record of it has been found.) It was further noted: 'For what it is worth, we may add that rumours still persist that Skira worked with the Germans in the early part of the war.'[40]

The saga of the paintings would drag on for years. Meanwhile, Peter was reluctantly on his way home.

Before returning to England, he stopped off in Paris, arriving in the middle of November. Despite the state it was in, he was delighted to be back in his flat ('which I find more sympathetic in the winter') and he began making headway getting it habitable again. Almost everything had to be bought on the black market, but he managed to employ two servants and get the household running again. He also found a new apartment-sitter – this time a person he had known longer than Sherban Sidéry, and whom he trusted entirely. Felix Rollo was a British-Egyptian gentleman of leisure who had long been a member of the Parisian arts and fashion scene; how Peter knew Felix is lost to history, but he was a friend of Coco Chanel, Christian Bérard and *Vogue* photographer Horst P. Horst, and Peter probably knew him through Cecil Beaton or Marie-Laure, or both. Felix was convalescing from an accident in which he'd been badly burned, so Peter put him up in the apartment and hired two nurses (in addition to the servants) to look after him. He spent most of his time in bed. 'He really has ghastly burns,' Peter wrote, 'which he shows me every time I go in.'[41]

Meanwhile, Peter finally had the opportunity to look into the matter of his other missing paintings. He made contact with the Commission de Récuperation Artistique and visited the Musée du Jeu de Paume, where Douglas Cooper claimed to have found some paintings of his. He had a harrowing time, searching through the 'massacred and scratched pictures, covering myself with the dust and filth of six years.'[42] He managed to identify several of his pictures; none were of any great value, aside from a Klee and an oil by Juan Gris titled *Le Lad*. It was a dispiriting outcome. He wrote to the Commission, providing them with a list in quadruplicate of all the pictures missing from his apartment, together with a list of those he had recognised at the Jeu de Paume. He stated that Felix Rollo would be living in the apartment until the spring and that he had full powers to act in Peter's name while he was in England, and would be able to receive the pictures whenever the Commission was able to release them.[43]

As if there weren't already enough things making Paris uncongenial, Peter's very home suddenly came under threat. The flat's owner, Étienne de Beaumont, whom Peter had imagined was a friend, now began threatening to turf him out. Under a new French law, properties could only be let to tenants who were in residence for ten months of every year, and they were not allowed to sublet. De Beaumont confronted Peter with this law, and pointed out that it also gave him the power to evict with only two weeks' notice.

For Peter, the very idea of staying permanently in one place for almost the entire year was unthinkable, even if it was Paris. He had dark suspicious of Étienne, just as he had of several of his wealthy French friends, including Marie-Laure. De Beaumont, Peter learned, had been photographed in 1942 welcoming Reichsmarschall Goering and General von Stülpnagel (the military governor of occupied France) into his Paris home.[44] What was more, Peter was sure Étienne's motive for threatening him with eviction had little to do with obeying the law and plenty to do with money; with all the improvements Peter had made during his tenancy in 1938 and 1939 – bathroom fittings, central heating, wood panelling – de Beaumont could easily get 100,000 francs a year for it, compared to the 28,000 Peter paid. 'But that is Anglo Français amitié for you,' Peter wrote bitterly. 'Every kind of disaster seems to rain on me.'[45]

Perhaps because of his long illness, he was full of bitter feelings towards Europeans who hadn't suffered in the war. While in the clinic at Lugano, he'd heard from Gala Dalí – 'a rather disgusting suck-up letter', he called it. Gala and Salvador had spent the war in America, staying at the Del Monte Lodge in Pebble Beach, California, and Peter – whose views had changed radically since he'd agreed so vehemently with Cyril's defence of Isherwood and Auden in 1939 – wasn't in the mood to be sympathetic with Europeans who'd decamped to the States. Gala's letter gushed about how hard Salvador had worked all through the war; it was a 'revolting letter ... just like an old business firm's letter making contact with old clients'.[46] For the time being, the Dalís joined Marie-Laure and Étienne de Beaumont on the debit side of Peter's moral ledger. Some of these friendships would be repaired, but it would take time.

It wasn't all gloom in Paris. Peter met up with Nancy Cunard, which raised his spirits, and he got to know Albert Camus, whom he liked very much; he went to see Camus's *Caligula* – 'an extraordinary play and am bringing back a copy for Laurence Olivier. Perhaps he would play it – it would be magnificent if he did.'[47] On the other hand, being back in Parisian high society was not so congenial. Peter was invited to the British Embassy by the scandalous French novelist Louise Lévêque de Vilmori, who was the mistress of ambassador Duff Cooper. Peter found this kind of social stratum as wearying as ever – 'decidedly I am still not made for High Life,' he wrote to Cecil Beaton. 'I never feel all those people mean a thing they say when together in a bunch. However if there is Low life there must be High life, I suppose!'[48]

There certainly was low life in France just then. 'Existence is tragic here in so many ways,' Peter wrote, touched by the plight of ordinary citizens, 'and I cannot think quite what France is going to do.'[49] When confronted with such endemic misery, Peter's love of art faltered. He wrote to John Craxton that 'when material difficulties become too great an interest in art becomes for me almost something morbid – maybe because I don't prefer art to life, I don't know. My greatest wish now is to get right away out of this completely wrecked Western Europe [to] where *life* still functions.'[50]

Counteracting the gloom, there was one bright spot on the horizon. Peter had heard some thrilling news from California: 'There is a chance Denham comes here for Christmas,' he told Cyril. Indeed, by the time Peter received Denny's letter, the long-gone lover had already left California for New York, intending to sail for Europe. 'He seems to think he could get a visa for a few weeks visit. I hope he can but think it rather optimistic.'[51]

It was. The whole idea was overly optimistic in every possible way.

* * *

Denham didn't make it to Europe that Christmas. Another half a year would go by before he and Peter would be reunited.

He had spent most of the war in California. Having registered with the draft board as a conscientious objector, he lived off Peter's money, toyed with organic farming for a while, worked briefly as a cook in a conscientious objectors' camp, and got into a long and complicated affair with Christopher Isherwood. Denham was a source of sexual torment to the Englishman, as he was to all those who got entangled with him. True to form, Denham became financially indebted to Isherwood, who unlike Peter Watson didn't have the means or the inclination to be forbearing about it.

By summer 1945 Denham was renting a canyon-side apartment at 137 Entrada Drive in Santa Monica, close to the beach. Intending to leave soon for New York and Europe, he offered to sublet it to Isherwood, who had been writing screenplays for Warner Bros and was temporarily flush with cash.[52] For a while they shared the apartment, Isherwood sleeping in the living room beneath the huge Picasso canvas, *Reading at a Table*, the one Peter had given to Denham before the war – its immense artistic and monetary value a measure of how powerfully he loved him. In 1939 Peter had lent the painting to the Museum of Modern Art in New York for an exhibition celebrating forty years of Picasso's art; unable to ship it back they had stored it in their vault through much of the war, until Denham came to reclaim it and take it out to California, where it dominated the Entrada Drive apartment, sharing wall space with army posters depicting the risks of gonorrhoea.

Isherwood detested the painting; he claimed that sleeping beneath it gave him a dreadful nightmare about Nazi Germany, and later Stephen

Spender claimed (probably apocryphally) that Isherwood had thrown darts at it.[53]

When Denham was preparing to leave for New York that September, Isherwood reminded him that he owed him money. The size of Denham's debt wasn't recorded, but must have been substantial, and Isherwood knew him well enough to guess that the chances of him dying or disappearing before it was paid were far from slim. Since Denham didn't have the means, there was only one way to settle it. On 20 September 1945, he sat down and wrote out a short bequest:

> To whom it may concern:
>
> The picture 'Girl Reading' [the alternate title of *Reading at a Table*] by Picasso which is my property, having been given to me by Peter Watson, is to be the property of Christopher Isherwood in the event of my dying or disappearing before it is sold in consideration of debts I owe to him and because he is my best friend.[54]

Leaving the declaration in Isherwood's hands, Denham left for New York, transporting the painting with him. In November, he met a couple from Chicago at a cocktail party. Samuel and Florene Marx were interested in the painting, and in late November they bought it for $12,500.[55] One of Peter's most treasured artworks, given in love to the person he was devoted to, was let go without qualms, traded for cash to pay off debts incurred to a casual boyfriend – and other debts too, no doubt, some of them probably much less salubrious.

Denham returned to California, paid Isherwood, then headed east again. Eventually, in the early summer of 1946, while Peter was still trying to refurbish his apartment to the standard of 1939 (at the same time fending off Étienne de Beaumont's continuing threats to repossess it), Denham Fouts finally returned to the rue du Bac in all his dissipated splendour.

Peter was excited, nervous, and relieved. In spite of everything, he still loved Denham, and had missed him sorely. He hoped – with truly superhuman optimism – that years of deprivation during the war would have cured Denham of his drug addictions. The world had moved on a long way since they'd last been in the rue du Bac together, and Peter had changed – growing more mature but also developing new cracks in his personality – but Denham Fouts had barely altered at all; even physically he looked exactly as he had, still like a youth despite being over thirty. He had brought all his old character traits with him from California and left a trail of detritus in his wake; his cocaine and opium habits were as much a part of him as ever. It wasn't for nothing that Jean Cocteau – himself a byword for disreputable, decadent hedonism – considered Denham Fouts 'a bad influence'.

Blinded by his own joy, Peter threw a party to welcome the beloved wanderer home. Among the invited guests was the latest recipient of Peter's patronage, a young painter called Michael Wishart, who had just turned eighteen and was a precocious talent; like Lucian Freud he had been a student of Cedric Morris and had taken Peter's fancy. Unlike either Freud or Craxton, Wishart was worldly; he had been familiar with the sexual underbelly of England from adolescence. He'd had a fling with a German prisoner of war, and had danced at the Gargoyle Club – the Soho venue owned by Stephen Tennant's brother David – when he was only twelve.

But even Michael Wishart felt quite out of his depth at that party: 'Very shy, I arrived to find a large salon filling up with men and their expensive-looking toy-friends.'[56] Among them he recognised Baron Alexis de Rédé – the darling of Marie-Laure de Noailles and Étienne de Beaumont's *saloniste* circle – and his keeper Arturo López-Willshaw, the art-collecting son of an Argentinean guano tycoon; also present were the nineteen-year-old poet Olivier Larronde, protégé of Cocteau and Jean Genet, with his inseparable partner Jean-Pierre Lacloche, offspring of the Lacloche jewellery family; Michael Wishart also recognised the artist Maurice van Moppès and actor Jean Marais, among others ... Peter was there too, dressed in an unusually casual fashion in a white suit and plimsolls. The relaxed manner of his dress did not, on this occasion, match his state of mind.

> Usually so poised, he seemed on that evening very distracted. There was no sign of Denham. More and more tinted men arrived. Champagne bottles were exploding, punctuating the familiar shrill chatter of the parrot house. It was becoming a fun party, which is to say a claustrophobic nightmare. No one dared ask where the guest of honour was.[57]

Michael wandered from room to room, marvelling at the people and the décor. There were beautiful lampstands and chairs made by Diego Giacometti (brother of Alberto), and the walls had been partly repopulated with Peter's collection of paintings. In the bathroom, which was decorated in mauve marble with gold-plated taps in the shape of swans' heads, he found Jean Marais, 'surrounded by a claque of pretty youths who were taking it in turns with a powder puff' in front of an ornate mirror.

But still there was no sign of Denham. Peter's nerves and his mood deteriorated as the evening passed; he went from anxiety to embarrassment and finally to anger. At one point Michael heard Peter shouting through a locked bedroom door.

As dusk fell and the atmosphere grew awkward, guests began to drift away. Eventually, Peter himself left and didn't return. Apparently unable to drag himself away, Michael found himself alone in the apartment. For a while he stood there in melancholy silence. Suddenly the locked bedroom door flung open, and Michael was confronted by a muscular young man.

> He wore nothing but cream-coloured flannel trousers and had the torso of an athlete. Along his beautiful shoulders and golden forearms ran snow-white mice with startled pink eyes, which he stroked gently with the backs of his hands. He had the air of a sleepwalker and for some time stood silently in the doorway, as though accustoming himself to the light. He seemed unaware of my presence. Then he said 'Trotsky'. I thought he must be dreaming awake ... until an enormous black dog appeared, answering to his name. He rubbed a dark head against Denham's pale, flannel thighs.[58]

When Denham turned back into the dimly lit, panelled bedroom, Michael – already falling in love – followed him. They spent the night together, overlooked by the startlingly erotic Tchelitchew *Bathers*, which had been restored to its position above the bed, listening to LPs of American musicals and sharing an opium pipe, Michael stroking Denham's beautiful limbs while he dozed in the haze. Denham had no idea who Michael was, but pressed him to stay – 'I don't want to be alone tonight.' In between blackouts he leafed through an American newspaper and showed Michael a birthday telegram he'd received from King Paul of Greece ('We had some great times together on a yacht before the war,' Denham said). They dropped off to sleep and didn't wake until the next evening, when the maid brought Denham's breakfast of cereal, coffee, calvados and a copy of the *Herald Tribune*. When Michael got up to leave, Denham didn't reply to his goodbye – he was engrossed in the financial market reports in the paper.[59]

It was the beginning of a fitful relationship that lasted through that summer. Peter never appeared in the apartment, and delirious hours were spent in that bedroom, with Denny's Tchelitchew, his de Chirico still life and the Toulon view by Francis Rose. Sometimes he and Michael travelled down to Toulon, where they bought opium. Denham claimed he was the model for the drug addict Sophie in Somerset Maugham's *The Razor's Edge*, who also bought drugs in Toulon. 'Certainly Maugham had been fascinated by Denham,' Michael recalled, 'and there was a great resemblance, of which Denham was strangely proud.' At weekends Denham's other boyfriend joined them in the flat – Gérard, a sixteen-year-old Denny had picked up on a Brittany beach. Gérard and Denham dressed in fabulously expensive suits made by the Duke of Windsor's tailor – paid for by Peter – and smoked cigarettes from a Fabergé case.

Fine clothes, limitless drugs, boys, and a maid at his call ... Denham Fouts was back in his element, and it would take a titanic will to lever him out of it.

* * *

Peter – hurt, angry, ashamed of his inability to cure Denham's problems, and conscious that his money was helping to sustain his drugged existence – kept his distance during this period. He believed he had done everything he could for this hopeless, helpless, feckless and destructive love, and would carrying on doing so for a long time; but by the end of that year he had reached the end of his willingness to keep the love alive.

With the lingering sensations of war and the abject misery that attached to Denham, Peter was growing almost as sick of Paris and Europe as he was of London. 'Ne me parle pas d'Albion,' he wrote to John Craxton, who was then in Greece with Lucian Freud. 'It's had it! I have finally decided I *can't* cope. Why if one is on the winning side of a war life should be greyer, dingier and more despairing I simply cannot understand. It's the worst standard of life west of the Iron Curtain.'[60] Paris, meanwhile was 'full of *Nazis*'. He had taken to calling the rue du Bac 'Bachstrasse' – the man who had once adored Germany now used its language to denigrate the city he still couldn't help but love.

'Blackest, deepest depression has settled on me here,' he wrote. 'Civilisation is just simply stopping in front of one's eyes ... with a coming winter of mass destitution and starvation. All optimistic and positive opinions seem a mockery. And the problems of art pure anachronisms ... Paris is very depressing ... there is such a feeling of impending disaster and prices soar and dishonesty is the general rule.'[61]

Peter Watson was never inclined to scrutinise and pick apart his own feelings; undoubtedly the situation in Europe – including the plight of the deprived classes – affected him emotionally. But equally undoubtedly his perception of a crisis in society was partly a projection of his disillusion and disgust over Denham and himself. And whatever the root cause, his pessimism was affecting his other, deepest love: art. It was the same problem he'd experienced the previous year, struggling to sustain his passion in the face of endemic suffering. 'I think I've lost my interest in art,' he wrote to Craxton. 'I am only interested in life ... Cubism is certainly dead. Existentialism is dying and Lettrism is being born.'[62] He no longer seemed sure where art was coming from or going to; he was bewildered by Graham Sutherland's new *Crucifixion*: 'I simply *can't* understand modern religious art. It all seems too impure and of mixed motives to me.'[63]

The sullying of the Christ myth and the concept of self-sacrifice would come to preoccupy Peter in the years to come; for now it just bewildered him.

He had to get away. In November 1946, Peter and Cyril Connolly departed England for another of their *Horizon* missions. Having put together the Swiss number, which had appeared in February (not very dazzlingly, it had to be said – the quality of contributions wasn't stellar), they had decided to do an American one – a much more promising idea.

When Peter and Cyril sailed from Liverpool for New York on 19 November,[64] Peter was looking forward to a rerun of his earlier visits – a few weeks in New York, 'and then vamoose to Cuba or Mexico'; he saw himself in Havana, where 'there is more colour in January with a fragrant green Partagas [a brand of cigar] between the teeth'.[65]

It was now more than eight years since he'd last set foot in America

– and what changes those years had wrought. He'd sailed from these shores in April 1938, exhausted and disenchanted by Hollywood and New York, but anticipating a new life in Paris with Denham. Now all that had gone up in a blaze of war and a haze of opium smoke. Peter's hopes, such as they were, were pinned on a Cuban cigar, a balmy winter in the Caribbean, and little else. He hadn't the slightest idea of the surprise New York held in store for him.

17

THE NEW WORLD

1946–1947

In the early spring of 1946, while Peter Watson was still looking forward to Denham Fouts' return to Europe, two young men met for the first time on a street in New York. It was a chance encounter that would have long-term repercussions for Peter Watson – repercussions that would ultimately be fatal. Appropriately, the cause of the encounter was a sold-out performance of *Swan Lake*.

Waldemar Hansen was a poet and a playwright – at least in his dreams – and by day worked in the offices of New Jersey Zinc. He was twenty-three years old, from Buffalo on the chilly shores of Lake Erie; life had prepared him to be the clean-cut, square-jawed college boy, but nature hadn't made him that way. After a short stint at college in Buffalo, in 1944 he'd come to New York City to follow his dream of being a writer. His jaw was strong but a little too thin, his underlip was plump, giving him the appearance of being on the verge of a sulk, and his crew cut was thick and unruly, never quite standing up straight. He was eager, talkative, and had made himself learned in art and literature.

On that spring evening in early 1946 he arrived at the theatre to find that the performance of *Swan Lake* was sold out. Turning away in disappointment, Waldemar met a man on the sidewalk who had two unwanted tickets – he was just giving them away. 'I'll take one,' said Waldemar.[1]

'I'll take the other,' said a voice beside him.

The voice belonged to a tall, slender, good-looking young man in a white sailor's uniform. A sailor going to *Swan Lake*? Waldemar struck up a conversation with him as they went in. They sat together through the performance, and continued their conversation afterwards. The sailor's name was Norman Fowler; he was nineteen and a motor machinist aboard a US Navy destroyer.[2] Like Waldemar he dreamed of a creative life – as a man of his hands, Norman wanted to be a sculptor.

They both came from blue-collar backgrounds. Waldemar's parents were immigrants – his father was a Danish housepainter (who died when Waldemar was very young) and his Jewish mother was the daughter of an English rabbi. Norman had been born in Kansas City, Missouri, the third child of a machinist; during the Depression his father lost his business and they migrated to California, and by 1940 they were living in a working-class district of Los Angeles, between East San Gabriel and Temple City.[3]

That first meeting in New York formed a bond. Norman had to return to his ship in New York Harbour the next day, but they stayed in touch, and the next time Norman came to New York he and Waldemar slept together for the first time. It was an intense – and for Waldemar slightly unnerving – sexual affair, conducted in the interludes provided by Norman's passes.

Waldemar was a bright, ambitious and capable young man; he knew what he wanted in life, and understood how to go about getting it. He had joined a poetry group, and was making headway in the New York literary world. He shared an apartment at 201 East 38th Street with John Myers, a writer who also came from Buffalo and was quite well plugged into the New York scene; he was a friend of the writer Parker Tyler, who was close to Charles Henri Ford and Pavel Tchelitchew. Myers had worked as managing editor on Tyler and Ford's arts magazine, *View*, and through him Waldemar was making his way into the periphery of their world and becoming known for his poetry.

Norman was different; although he was ambitious too, he wasn't clear-sighted; in fact he showed distinct signs of being a little unstable. He was prone to mystical daydreaming, and sometimes slipped into near-catatonic states, so spaced-out that on at least one occasion Waldemar had to slap him to bring him round. His letters could sometimes be barely coherent, and his behaviour was often peculiar. On one occasion he arrived at the 38th Street apartment unannounced, to find that Waldemar was away at his sister's wedding. He accused Waldemar of playing hide-and-seek: 'I had forgotten your sister's wedding,' he wrote, 'simply because I did not want to remember it.'[4]

Possibly the war had had an effect on Norman. He'd enlisted in the Navy very young, and by March 1945 was serving as a fireman aboard an LCI – a small assault ship designed for landing troops on beaches[5] – which had taken part in the invasion of Okinawa and later ferried Allied prisoners of war out of Japan. Shortly after that, Norman had switched trades to motor machinist (his father's metier) and transferred to a different ship in home waters.[6]

Whatever the cause, Norman Fowler had an unsettling air about him. But he was attractive – nervy, sexy, and with the lean, supple body of an athlete. If he didn't get a break as a sculptor, he had thoughts of being a dancer.

By the summer of 1946, Norman was in New York more frequently. He'd transferred again to a transport ship based at Norfolk, Virginia, which periodically visited the city.[7] Waldemar had by now introduced Norman to John Myers, Charles Henri Ford and Pavel Tchelitchew, whom Norman presumptuously began referring to as 'Pavlik' before he'd even met him. ('Please not play Hide and Seek when we see Pavlik,' he'd written to Waldemar; 'I want to meet him very much.')[8]

On New Year's Eve 1946, Waldemar, Norman and John Myers went out together to celebrate; they ended up at a party given by the actress and socialite Ruth Ford, who was the sister of Charles Henri.[9] By the time they reached the party, Waldemar had had more booze than he could cope with, and he went home early, feeling ill. After he'd gone, Norman mingled with the guests, and was introduced to an Englishman who was a close friend of both Charles Henri and Pavlik; he was almost two decades older than Norman, but slim, attractive, beautifully dressed, and utterly charming. His name was Peter Watson. The attraction between them was instantaneous, intense and – for Peter – alluringly dangerous.

* * *

After their arrival in New York on the Monday after Thanksgiving, Peter and Cyril hadn't spent much time together. While Peter quietly went about catching up with his old friends, some of whom he hadn't seen since before the war, Cyril found himself lionised everywhere. At the age of forty-three he had found celebrity at last; his reputation as a fashionable literary heavyweight had preceded him, and New York publishers were falling over themselves to sign him up. He was interviewed on the radio and in the *New Yorker*, and dined out with E. E. Cummings (whom he admired to a worshipful degree) as well as old friends like Wystan Auden.

'Cyril's triumphant progress here must be seen to be believed,' Peter wrote to Brian Howard. He and Cyril had lunched with the director of the Metropolitan Museum of Art, who, in honour of Cyril, gave them a personal guided tour of the museum galleries – 'everything else is rather on that level. It's much too much for me.'[10] Clement Greenberg called Cyril Connolly's visit the most successful since Oscar Wilde's.[11]

By late December Cyril had had three weeks of this treatment and was exhausted by it; he flew west to spend Christmas in California. Peter stayed on in New York, making up for lost time with Charley Ford, Parker Tyler and Pavlik. When he went to Ruth Ford's New Year's Eve party, he had no idea what he was letting himself in for.

Whatever happened inside him when he was introduced to Norman Fowler, it was instant – a heart tremor, a lightning bolt, a rush of blood to the extremities. Norman was fresh, twenty years old, lithe-limbed, a sailor (titillating) and an aspiring artist (intriguing), and he had an abstracted, reckless air. Given the desperate state of Peter's relationship with Denham, he was unusually susceptible. Looking back on this episode a few months later, he would recognise that his life had become 'a pathetic echo of a past existence. I had quite lost hope of finding real happiness in an outside relationship – I was willing to fall in love with … anyone.'[12]

Perhaps he didn't quite fall in love with Norman that evening, but he was smitten. He must have responded to the palpable element of instability in the young man – reminiscent of Denham; a spectre from the dark, dangerous side. 'I'm afraid I like that sort of danger,' he'd once confessed to John Craxton. Whether or not there was any trace of love at first sight, there was certainly a powerful erotic charge. Peter and Norman had sex that night.

It was another fleeting encounter. Norman had to be back aboard his ship the next day, and Peter didn't see him again for a long time. Norman hoped that a relationship would develop; he was working towards his discharge from the Navy, and must have been conscious of the help that the lovely, charming, well-connected Peter Watson could give him in realising his ambitions. But by the time Norman next came ashore in New York, Peter had already moved on – physically and romantically.[13]

By the middle of January Cyril had had enough of America, and sailed back to England, straight into the unwelcoming arms of the bitterest winter Britain had suffered in living memory. For weeks everything was under thick snow or frozen solid, fuel was short, and coats and gloves had to be worn indoors. Peter stayed behind in New York; perhaps it was his long wartime absence, or perhaps it was sexual exhilaration, but for once America had failed to weary him. He booked to sail home in March, and carried on enjoying himself.

In late February, Peter was invited to dinner by John Myers, the friend of Parker Tyler and Charley Ford, at his apartment on East 38th Street. Myers was a writer, a critic and an art connoisseur. He was a neat man, with tidily parted hair and cherubic features; he favoured preppy bow ties, had an overtly camp manner that clashed with his huge, lumbering physique, and he could be witheringly, scathingly opinionated – a towering, full-on bitch. Joining them for dinner was Myers' much quieter room-mate, Waldemar Hansen.

Again there were lightning bolts. Despite the slight physical resemblance, Waldemar was absolutely different from Norman: intelligent and knowledgeable, but diffident and with genteel manners. Having failed to meet Peter Watson on New Year's Eve, Waldemar was bowled over now:

> Peter had a wonderfully engaging way about him, a winsome way of smiling, a way of making people feel that he was absolutely on their wavelength. Early in our first evening together it was quite clear that something was transpiring between us. In the course of dinner we had both fallen quite silent, with John Myers doing all the talking, and Peter was simply looking at me mutely, and I was looking back at him. It really was love at first sight.[14]

The attraction burst into flames immediately. Peter stayed that night in Waldemar's bed.

Unlike Norman, Waldemar didn't have to rush off. But with only ten days left before Peter was due to sail for England, time was pressing and they spent almost every hour together. They dined at the romantic Russian Tea Room near Central Park. They passed days in Peter's hotel suite at the St Regis, where they lay in bed and Peter fed Waldemar kadota figs. They invented pet names for each other – Waldemar was Brown Bear, and Peter was Pumpkin. They took the ferry to Staten Island, where they talked about their feelings for one another. Waldemar reminded Peter of the lovelorn Jay Gatsby's observation that Daisy Buchanan's marriage to Tom was 'just personal' – that it was not a grand, romantic, all-dominating passion. *The Great Gatsby* was 'an extraordinary book', Peter thought, 'but what a fantastically perspicacious remark that is'. He assured Waldemar later that 'my feelings for you "are not only personal".'[15]

As soon as Peter sailed away from New York on the *Queen Elizabeth*, he began to perceive those ten days as 'a strange episode isolated from my life'.[16] On a cloud, he enjoyed the 'tasteless comfort' and the celebrity company on the ship – movie stars Burgess Meredith and Paulette Goddard were aboard, along with fashion designers Edward Molyneux and Elsa Schiaparelli (Coco Chanel's deadly rival at the time). The Labour government's erratic food minister John Strachey was there too, and film director Gabriel Pascal, who won £1,600 in a gambling pool and threw an all-night party on the proceeds.[17]

But when he reached London, Peter felt overwhelmed by the gloom he always felt in that city – loneliness and dreadful, debilitating ennui. A flurry of letters from Waldemar – which must have flown the Atlantic and overtaken him – came through the door, but Peter couldn't bring himself to reply for several days. When he replied to Waldemar, he told him, 'You do not know about the English problem and what a hell each return to this dying country means.'[18] He suffered from 'a terrible psychological jam which gets me every time I get back to England. It goes back to the times when I used to race abroad to get away from my family I think.'[19]

This was a remarkable revelation. Peter almost never referred to his family in writing, and then only when he was speaking to those closest to him, like Cecil Beaton or John Craxton. When he did refer to 'my family' (distinct from 'my mamma' or 'my brother'), he was conceiving them as a bloc – brother, sister, parents, all suffused with the awful, stressful tensions of a family composed of individuals with strong temperaments who had little in common with each other. His love for his mother – which was also sometimes fraught and troubled – seems to have been something that stood apart from the concept of 'family' in his mind. Her death had seemed like the world's collapse to him, but the notion of family was still bound up with the blackest depression.

By Monday he had conquered it. With the memory of his days with Waldemar running in his nerve-ends, he came soaring out of his depression, buzzing with an energy he hadn't experienced for a long time. He sat down immediately and wrote Waldemar a letter; the next day he wrote another. It wasn't enough to write; he needed to hear Waldemar's voice, and he spent two days trying to arrange a telephone call to New York. There was no direct line – a chain of operators had to be involved to link up the two callers at an appointed time. Peter waited for hours, 'seething with anxiety', scared that Waldemar would miss the connection. When at last it came together, it was a joy to hear Waldemar's 'real American voice sound like a succulent slice of fruit cake over all those waves'.[20]

At last Peter was able to see his future course clearly. The very next day, he set out for Paris, intending to finish it once and for all with Denham and pack up the rue du Bac apartment. It didn't quite work out that way. He had overestimated the brief flame of his infatuation with Waldemar and forgotten how potent Denny's hold on him was. He told Denham everything, but the reaction cowed him into silence – 'I cannot mention it often to him as I know it would upset him,' Peter wrote lamely to Waldemar.[21] Although he claimed to have a 'monstrous obsession' with Waldemar, it was a green, young, incipient love that seemed to stand little chance against the potent, soul-deep obsession with Denham. Even with Étienne de Beaumont now threatening legal action to get his apartment back and lodging complaints about the noise and antisocial behaviour of its occupant, Peter couldn't evict Denham yet, much less cut him off. What was more, Denham knew it and played on Peter's weakness with the skill of a musician. Peter could only dimly understand the effect Denham had. Recalling his return to Paris the previous summer, Peter wrote:

> I knew my feelings for him were dead altho' I will always feel affection for him, in his way. He lapsed into a sort of prewar cocktail haute pederastic life which still goes on in Paris. In fact he is now trying to imitate me as I was in 1933 ... I have implored him to do something, appealed to his conscience, my wishes, everything, have done everything except stop him having money as my god I do really believe in freedom and free decision. I am racked by wondering what I could have done that I didn't do ... He is stuck at 16 years old and resists any attempt to grow. And yet I feel it must be my fault somehow.[22]

Over the next few weeks, Peter's emotions caromed from one place to another: frustration, misery, joy, guilt, self-doubt, sexual desire ... All he knew was that he wanted Waldemar with him. He wanted to hold him, talk to him, teach him, guide him, show him Europe, and conduct him into the world of the arts. His feelings about Waldemar were fraternal, patrician, sexual and childlike all at once – he adored Waldemar's youth, his vulnerability, and his 'sulky sensual lips', and imagined that eventually he might be the solution to Peter's ills, the trail of thread that would lead out of the labyrinth haunted by the beast-man Denham. Peter regained some of the giggling delight that had charmed and perplexed Cecil Beaton in their youth, but it was all interspersed with periods of bleakness.

When Waldemar received the invitation to come to London and live with Peter, it was still barely a month since they'd first met. In the meantime he'd learned a little about Peter Watson – the truth about just how rich his Pumpkin was, for one thing. In later life, he would describe himself agonising over whether he should accept – whether it would be right to be kept by a rich man.[23] But his doubts – if they were real – were overcome in a matter of days. By 24 March it had been firmly settled that Waldemar would come to England in April.

Peter began making plans. He had decided that Waldemar must come by air – above all, it would be quicker, but it would also be much cheaper, and Peter needed to watch his spending abroad, where he was no longer such a man of means.

This was another aftershock of the war; the British government, overseeing the impoverished ruins of the nation and faced with the task of hauling it out of the financial pit the war had left it in, had imposed severe controls on the flow of money out of the country. In industry and commerce, exports were encouraged (or enforced by making the supply of materials dependent on meeting export targets) and imports were all but banned. For individuals, strict limits were placed on the amount of currency that could be taken abroad. Since November 1945, the personal allowance had been £100 a year;[24] for a man like Peter, that was a piffling, petty sum. When he and Cyril went to New York, they'd wangled a business allowance on top of their personal amounts, but Peter thought it unlikely he'd ever get another one. He had deposited a lump in his New York bank and had authorised his banker to give money to Waldemar, but although Peter told him to spend whatever he needed to for his journey, he exhorted him to be careful, and to bring no more than $200 – 'if I am ever to come to America again I must keep all the money there I can.'[25] It preyed on Peter's mind, and in almost every one of the string of letters he sent Waldemar over the next few weeks, he reminded him again and again not to spend the money – Peter would buy him anything he needed after he arrived.

In the meantime Peter amused himself as best he could in Paris and tried to get along with Denham. Neither pursuit was successful. A lot of new '*boîtes* for boys' had opened in Paris, but Peter found they no longer amused him at all. 'Everyone seems so polite and gentle after New York – it's quite a shock.'[26]

Even though the decision had already been made, Peter intermittently laid a bait trail to encourage Waldemar to come across the ocean – he referred casually to his literary acquaintances ('got quite a few things done and been to see Camus') and alluded to the Parisian nightlife, hinted at the patronage he could give, described his vulnerability to Brown Bear's charm ('this puppet is sad and he's slumped against the wall with his eyes crossed') and planned the elegant transformation he would instigate in Waldemar's wardrobe.

As the time drew nearer, Peter's desires began to get the better of him, and by the beginning of April he was positively simmering. He had two photographs of Waldemar: a butch passport photo he called 'Waldemar *sauvage*' and another of 'the charming waif' to whom he'd fed figs in his suite at the St Regis – 'tame and affectionate and tender' – and he wondered which was the real Waldemar, and 'which will get off the aeroplane':

> I would have eaten both photographs by now if it hadn't meant losing them. But I consult them most evenings for answers to my questions and I tell them how *deadly* bored I am without you.
>
> I have got quite a cockstand thinking about you now that I must stop. Silly isn't it? And I thought my feeling for you was so spiritual! But it is I swear and emotional and intellectual. Brain, guts, prick – everything.[27]

And then, perhaps encouraged by this ardour, Waldemar made a mistake. Exactly what he did, what he said, what he wrote, has been lost – but he apparently tried to test his hold on Peter, attempted to try a little of Denham's style (or what he imagined Denham's style to be). With only a week to go before he was due to set out for Europe, he wrote Peter a letter (subsequently lost) which hinted that he was having second thoughts, that he doubted Peter's feelings, that their sexual relationship wasn't all it might be, that Waldemar himself might be attracted to others – now and in Europe – and that he might indeed turn out to be 'Waldemar *sauvage*'. He knew about Peter's fling with Norman in New York, and apparently alluded to his own satisfying sexual relationship with him, and that he would have to sacrifice that for Peter.

Although Peter didn't yet know Waldemar very well, he sensed that the boy was showing off, toying with him. (John Myers noted that Waldemar had a strong streak of the drama queen in him – 'You'll camp it up on your death bed so help me.')[28] Hurt and indignant, Peter sent a tidal wave of stern reproof back across the Atlantic – a declaration whose strength was entirely at odds with his feeble failure to confront Denham. The letter swung disorientatingly between wounded feelings and portentous threats. Waldemar's letter had 'stuck swords' in him, 'and has gone on twisting them since'.

> I hate cruelty and I know it is part of us all ... What is significant is that you *know* I am vulnerable to cruelty at the same time that you are only vulnerable to kindness ... I will find out soon but I will not necessarily fight with the weapons you choose for me.
>
> I can tell that you resent me and yourself for your not indulging your own sexual whims.
>
> And if I said go ahead, pick up anyone that attracts you – the more the better, or if I said 'what the hell', you are going to make

my life so deeply miserable that when you arrive we shall just be on polite and formal terms, you shall have your culture trip thro' Europe, go back to NY and we will part with stiff upper lips.

... If you hurt me it will have certain results and I will be forced into some form of self-defence. ... No – you will not get weak kindness from me – you may very well get violence such as you never bargained for. ... There will be no hearts on plates for cruel, self-obsessed, parvenue egomaniacs. What are you prepared to give anyway?

... You are playing with all that is most dangerous and profound in life. You can cause wreckage to yourself as well as to me, damage which would last many years in your case because your interior life is so vivid ... I don't think you will ever despise me, unless it were for having suffered (horrible word) in life. And as a poet if you do that you are a worthless shit, and a fake. Yes, I can muster the great unspecific against you until I find the chinks. I am not unobservant so it won't take long.

Well – are you still willing to say yes to life, or would you rather cancel your passage and regard me as an unfortunate and inconvenient mistake?

You are perfectly free to disappear. Or come over if you like and you shall go where you want with whom you want without me and you can be one of the people I have 'helped' ...

Waldemar, don't torture yourself and me. I am mad to see you. If it is all a mistake we will know. If it is not, you will not regret it.[29]

Having delivered this stern rebuke, and having said he wouldn't do so, Peter laid his heart on a plate, concluding the letter: 'Right now I do love you with agony' and signing himself 'Peter Pumpkin Pants'.

Waldemar came.

18

TWO AMERICANS IN PARIS

1947

The eastern Atlantic sunrise glittered on the silver wings and propellers of an American Overseas Airlines Lockheed Constellation as it dipped over the green coast of Ireland, curving down towards Shannon Airport.

It was two in the morning by Waldemar Hansen's watch, still on New York time, and yet 'here we were, flying in bright sunlight over Spenser's Ireland.'[1] It had been a long journey; even the most modern airliners still didn't have the range to cross the Atlantic in one hop; they flew from New York to Newfoundland, and then a second leg to Ireland. Waldemar had spent this longest part of the trip sandwiched between a British member of parliament and a Chicago millionaire ('We had a discussion on politics, and I was appalled to discover that they were dumber than I was.')[2]

Waldemar believed he was ready for whatever lay ahead of him. He had weathered Peter's emotions and prepared himself psychologically for the opportunities that were being offered to him. Crucially, he had settled things with Norman. Waldemar knew about Peter's fling with Norman at New Year's, and Norman knew about Waldemar's more involved relationship. When it came to it, with no obvious signs of regret, Waldemar chose Peter over Norman, and flew off to meet his destiny. Meanwhile, at the very moment Waldemar's plane was coming in to land at Shannon – on the morning of Saturday 19 April 1947 – Norman was going through his discharge from the Navy and looking forward to an uncertain future, with only vague and rather hopeless ideas of being either a sculptor or a dancer.

After landing, Waldemar went through customs, spending almost the last pennies of Peter's money on cigarette duty. He had expected to find Peter waiting for him, but instead he found a note:

> I will wait for you in the Ardhu Hotel ... Take a car, taxi or mule if you can ... I await you, more or less a wodge of wine jelly.
> I had the most *appalling* journey getting here but gee what determination.
> Hop in quick – I'll feed you kadota figs à la St Regis.
> Welcome – Welcome – Welcome
> A penny for each thought,
> weakly pumping Pumpkin.[3]

Waldemar boarded a worn green bus bound for Limerick and, after struggling with the shillings and pence, settled down to watch the Irish countryside, the mule carts and the flame-haired boys flit by, 'grinning like a child from ear to ear'. He got off at Ardhu House – a Victorian pile just outside Limerick – and hauled his own luggage up the drive. Discovering that Peter was at breakfast, Waldemar went upstairs.

While he was washing and shaving, the door opened and Peter appeared. 'We were both scared stiff,' Waldemar recalled, 'and I kept talking a mile a minute, and then we began to laugh. We laughed and laughed and I knew then that everything was all right, and that this was no stranger.'[4]

They went into Limerick, where Waldemar was charmed by the Georgian architecture, disorientated by the familiar, out-of-place sight of a Woolworths store and a movie poster for *The Blue Dahlia*, and shocked by the poverty. They passed a line of people with buckets queuing for coal, and in the post office they were approached by 'three little girls with bare feet, matted hair and sores on their legs', begging for pennies. Waldemar gave them some coins, and they trailed after him for streets.[5]

It moved him, but not enough to put him off his lunch. The only half-decent restaurant in Limerick was the Savoy, where they had a meal Waldemar judged 'dreadful and tasteless', and that evening they sat in one of the parlours of the Ardhu and held hands. In many ways Peter was a gentle soul, and some boyfriends were surprised at how content he was to spend an evening sitting and just holding hands. Later, though, despite the freezing bedroom, Waldemar and Peter burrowed into the hot-water-bottled bed and 'carried on like mad'.[6]

Waldemar's 'culture tour' and induction into Peter Watson's world of influence began immediately. Hiring a Chrysler (probably pre-war) and an Irish chauffeur, they motored down to visit the novelist Elizabeth Bowen, who was in residence at Bowen's Court, the family seat between Limerick and Cork. The housepainter's son from Buffalo was both delighted and dismayed to find himself admitted by a maid into a grand dining hall with a long table draped in white linen and walls hung with ancestral Bowen portraits, with a bowl of daffodils on the table and a small electric heater battling ineffectually against the icy cold. From there Peter and Waldemar were taken to the library, a den of antique comfort with a fire blazing in the grate. Eventually their hostess appeared, and Waldemar's heart paused in excitement; she was heavily done up in tweeds – 'a handsome woman,' Waldemar thought, 'almost masculine but not a dyke, I'm told ... A very British accent, with a strong tendency to stuttering.' Waldemar liked her immediately; he gave her American cigarettes, and showed a keen interest in her restoration schemes for the crumbling old house, while she gave her visitors a guided tour and an excellent lunch. Waldemar promised to write a poem on Bowen's Court and send it to her.[7]

He made a start in the car that afternoon, sketching out verses while he and Peter dozed in the back seat with a rug over their knees as the car rolled on to Dublin.

They stayed at the Shelbourne Hotel on St Stephen's Green, where they drank dreadful sidecars (cognac and orange) in the bar and ate a 'not-so-hot' dinner served by tail-coated waiters. Peter told Waldemar that it was the best food he was likely to get in a long time, so he ate all he could. Dublin was a rerun of Limerick – all delightful eighteenth-century architecture and shocking poverty ('I won't soon forget the old Irish woman who fell on her knees and crossed herself and blessed me with tears in her eyes when I gave her half a crown').[8] They hired bikes and scooted all over the city, and saw *Gilda*, which Peter loved, although they were both annoyed that the Irish censors had cut out Rita Hayworth's celebrated striptease scene. Every night they shared one bed warmed with a stone hot-water bottle and mussed up the other to avoid scandalising the chambermaids.

After a week in Ireland they flew to London. Probably taking his cue from Peter, Waldemar hated the city on sight – 'ugly and monstrously Victorian' – and found the food '*simply dreadful*' even in the best restaurants. Peter's flat was an island of tasteful modernity, furnished in the Watson manner with a mixture of contemporary and eighteenth-century pieces. Within a couple of days, Waldemar had made himself master of the tiny kitchen, and was already referring to the place as 'our apartment'. After a triumphant debut dinner cooked by Waldemar, he and Peter 'fell into paroxysms of lust, and carried on all over the apartment for hours! La!'[9]

Peter proposed taking Waldemar to Paris in a few weeks, and in the meantime began introducing him to his London circle – a thing he could never have done with Denham, even if he'd wanted to.

In the first few days Waldemar met Douglas Cooper (who completely won him over), A. J. Ayer, Brian Howard and Lucian Freud (still being billed socially as 'grandson of Sigmund' despite his own growing profile as a painter). Visiting his studio – which had a zebra's head on the wall and a live falcon flying loose around the room – Waldemar found Lucian's art 'schizophrenic and rather compelling' and Lucian himself 'very charming, rather wistful with mad, schizoid eyes, and a very shrewd perceptive ability'. Lucian offered to do Waldemar's portrait, and he was 'rather intrigued to see what I'll look like after going through that strange personal prism'.[10]

Waldemar was also introduced to *Horizon* – in particular to its talented and tireless editorial assistant, twenty-nine-year-old Sonia Brownell. She was a decidedly attractive young woman whose good nature matched her good looks (although professionally she could be assertive and even callous). She and Waldemar hit it off right away. He gave her one of his poems for consideration, and she loved it. This was unusual – Sonia didn't normally like American poetry; in her literary-critical lexicon the phrase 'very American' meant 'not real poetry'.[11]

Sonia was probably inclined to like Waldemar for Peter's sake. Since starting work for *Horizon* during the war, she had grown deeply attached to Peter, and although he'd been cool towards her at first, he had become as fond of her as she was of him. She had little money, and he often treated her to dinners and outings to the cinema (she loved movies, especially if they had Humphrey Bogart in them), or even European holidays. Some believed that if Peter had been heterosexual, he and Sonia might have married. But Cyril Connolly, who saw Sonia's adoration of Peter at close quarters (and whose own sexual vanity was apparently irritated by it), knew it to be more nuanced – for Sonia, Peter's sexuality was part of the draw. In an unpublished story, 'Happy Deathbeds', Cyril fictionalised the relationship, portraying Sonia's infatuation as the worship of an ideal. She could truly love Peter because, 'being homosexual, he inspired no sexual ambivalence, she could not hate him for desiring her or for desiring another woman. In the sex-war he was a kind of angel of man's who was on her side.'[12]

She told Waldemar his poem was the best thing they had available in the office, and he was vain and charmed enough not to notice that this might be slightly back-handed praise. He was given work to do, sifting the poetry submissions, and earned a guinea for it. His poem went into the magazine, and Cyril asked him for more; later he would be given the opportunity to write review articles too, exercising his poetic erudition at great length. Waldemar's letters to John Myers were infested with his opinions – of literature, of plays, of food, people, and British men (who were mostly pompous and dull). Almost everything he said was so perfectly compatible with Peter's thinking on every subject that one could wonder how much of it was Waldemar's own.

Waldemar didn't always realise the significance of the people he was introduced to. In late May he and Peter lunched with 'a boy called Michael Nelson' who had some vague kind of association with *Horizon*.[13] What Waldemar didn't know was that Nelson, a young journalist, was – or had been – one of Peter's boy-toys, enticed to London with the promise of literary glamour and expensive presents; he apparently hadn't played ball, and would soon be on his way out. (Even at this moment, Nelson was busy writing a savage novel satirising Peter and his whole world, and doing it with so much unconcealed factual detail that it could not be published in Peter's lifetime.)[14]

There was only one of Peter's friends whom Waldemar was prepared to dislike – even before he met him. 'Everybody dishes Stephen Spender,' he wrote to Myers. 'Apparently he is quite dishonest, to himself and everybody else ... I hope to meet him when he comes back from France, and get more dirt on him.'[15] This prejudice was a mystery, and perhaps indicated a degree of jealousy – personal and literary. Or it might give a taste of Peter's own attitude to Stephen, which was complex – he was attached to him as a friend, but occasionally treated him with a disdain that was close to bullying (as with the episode of the pinstripe suit).

Meanwhile, Waldemar waited for poetic inspiration to come, but there were many distractions. He became a regular at the Gargoyle Club, either with Peter or Sonia, visited galleries with Lucian, and spent every day in the constant social round, in which he gathered 'tons and tons of dishery about the international set, dear', which he saved up for John Myers, his dishing partner of choice. 'Nothing to dish about Pete and I,' he wrote, 'since we get along as well as you and I do. He's so divine my dear, and am I lucky.'[16] Peter opened a bank account for him, and Waldemar began taking French lessons in preparation for their visit to Paris in June.

* * *

'Paris is the next best thing to Paradise!' Waldemar wrote to John Myers. 'Love those people! And the food!! You haven't eaten until you've been to Paris.'[17]

Not everything was wonderful, though. One feature of Paris that Waldemar hated on sight was Denham Fouts. Having enjoyed only the briefest peek at Peter's divine apartment, Waldemar was taken to stay instead at the Pont Royal Hotel, which stood on a branch of the rue du Bac, opposite number 44. This would become Peter's regular Paris home from now on – he couldn't bear to live in the apartment with Denham, but neither could he stand to be far away. As if to prove to Waldemar that it was over with Denham, and to Denham that his new love was real, Peter brought them together for lunch one day – 'and that was really quelque chose!' Waldemar wrote.

> Denham has a southern accent, is madly neurotic and stupid. He was very anti-Semitic at lunch, and I let him have both barrels ... He's the kind of person you want to smack, dear. I know definitely that Peter is not the slightest bit in love with D. anymore – but

> Peter's soft heart will go on doling out the moolah for years. D. is totally ungrateful.[18]

Waldemar was offended by Denham referring to Peter's apartment as 'my house' (apparently this was different from Waldemar referring to the Palace Gate flat as 'our apartment'). 'It burns my ass, but I'm not interfering. P. asks my advice, and I say – "It's your problem, sweetie."'[19] Étienne de Beaumont wanted Denham out of the apartment, and had given Peter until October to see to it. It preyed on his mind, but there seemed to be nothing he could do about it.

Denham aside, Waldemar took to Paris with shivers of joy; no young man had ever been so romantically entertained, and no aspiring poet had ever been plugged so quickly and so precisely into the literary elite. There was a new Genet play to take in, and a new Surrealist opera by Francis Poulenc, *Les mamelles de Tirésias* at the Opéra Comique. (Peter, who was a friend of Poulenc, had been anticipating this new work for over a year, but was disappointed by it; he and Waldemar felt that its surreal elements were hackneyed now.) They joined up with Elizabeth Bowen (who'd enjoyed Waldemar's poem about Bowen's Court) and Sonia ('so sweet and I wish we could find a lovely man for her').[20] There were new Picassos to see, which were inevitably wonderful. Peter introduced Waldemar to Olivier Larronde and Alberto Giacometti, and conducted him to a cocktail party at the house of publisher Gaston Gallimard, where the guest of honour was John Steinbeck.

There were also nocturnal pleasures. Peter took Waldemar to the nightclubs and the *boîtes*, and he was enthralled:

> It's like Berlin, 1941 ... the queens go round and round in those weird polkas or whatever they are. The Paris boys are a well-behaved lot, no rowdyism, very little painting up. Many of them are very masculine. There is also a barge on the Seine called the Bain Deligny, a most ingenious place. It has a wonderful swimming pool ... Apparently it was a royal barge at one time, and the inside is all moorish influence, so that you feel you're in a harem.[21]

Waldemar took careful note of the men posing 'with muscles rippling like the waves of the Mediterranean' and felt embarrassed in his old-style swimming trunks; 'The men (every single one of them, straight and gay) wear a teeny-tiny loin cloth, for which the word obscene would be an understatement.'[22] (Although his costume was old-fashioned, Waldemar's slang wasn't – his generation was the first to bring the fashionable new usage of the word 'gay' across the Atlantic, but it hadn't caught on yet.) Waldemar was astonished at the amount of dope-smoking and opium-eating that went on – among the artistic and bourgeois classes as well as the underworlders – and was amazed that Peter had remained clean.

From Paris, Peter and Waldemar travelled down to the Côte d'Azur and stopped at Hyères, where Peter hoped to call on Marie-Laure. Two years on from the war, he had begun to thaw towards those French friends whose behaviour during the war had been, in his mind, shameful – Marie-Laure and Jean Cocteau among them. (During the occupation, Cocteau had been persuaded to admire Hitler, and privately criticised the French for disrespecting him.) 'Peter says the war is over,' Waldemar wrote, 'and what can one do about it, so the truth has just been dropped.'[23] Unfortunately, Marie-Laure was away. Peter chatted to her gardener, who still remembered him after nearly a decade's absence. The house wasn't used so much now by the family, and the servants' quarters had been turned into a hospital for children with tuberculosis.

From Hyères, they took a boat to the Île de Porquerolles, where they stayed at a little hotel and spent their time swimming, then travelled on to Monte Carlo, where they met up with Francis Bacon. Peter had visited him there the year before, and been amazed by the reckless energy with which he pursued both his painting and his gambling.

Bacon had first come to Monte Carlo in 1946 with £200 he'd made from the sale of his canvas titled *Painting*, a typically disturbing work that resembled an Existentialist Bosch nightmare. Peter, visiting him that year, had written to John Craxton: 'I saw quite a bit of Francis Bacon in Monte Carlo. What an extraordinary character he is – gambling away all night and then retiring to some secret hideaway to continue his 12 x 10!' Peter hadn't been able to stay long; he couldn't stand the pace – 'it takes all sorts of stimulants to stimulate!'[24] To Waldemar and most of the world, Bacon was still just 'a young English painter ... who is a descendant of *the* Francis Bacon'; he was more interested in 'the old ladies with their lorgnettes and hard makeup' gambling away doggedly.[25]

By the time he and Waldemar had spent a few days in Cannes, Peter was beginning to feel the squeeze of the currency restrictions.

In Paris he had arranged a number of private exchanges – mainly with Americans – whereby they would transfer money to him in their home country and he transferred money to them in London. It would provide a buffer against the British government's restrictions, but such arrangements were complex and tiresome to negotiate; it was no substitute for being able to simply spend one's own money wherever one chose. So, leaving Cannes behind, they went to Switzerland and checked into the Palace Hotel in St Moritz – even this was cheaper than Cannes, where the usual super-expense of living had been multiplied by France's runaway inflation. Waldemar was pleased to be back in a country that was even more 'anal-erotic' than America, in which everything was spotlessly clean.

Inspired by the fresh air, Peter and Waldemar took packed lunches and hiked high into the mountains to Fuorcla Surlej, where cows grazed beside a mountain lake and yodellers could be heard echoing across the slopes. After eating their picnic on the mountaintop, they hiked on towards a nearby glacier. Waldemar recalled the scene:

> We found two little blue enzians [gentians] growing in the shadow of a rock. They make a liqueur from these flowers, called gebirge enzian ... The path was littered with harebells, lovely blue, bell-like flowers right out of Wuthering Heights. There are also little pink flowers, and edelweiss ... Peter was so adventurous that he took me off the path, and there we were, sliding down slate and getting deeper and deeper into the forests. When we got thirsty we stopped at little mountain streams, for the water is crystal clear and bubbling.[26]

Their course took them westward down the mountain, and eventually they found themselves on the shore of the Silsersee and traced their way back to St Moritz. It was Swiss National Day, so in spite of their aching bones, they went out into the village of Sils Maria and mingled with locals celebrating, listening faithfully to all fifty-five verses of the national anthem, watching the fireworks and joining in with sparklers. 'The children were carrying lanterns on sticks, and their faces were lovely in the glow ... The mountain paths were alive at regular intervals with bonfires. It was all very homey and gemutlich.'[27]

In St Moritz Waldemar noticed how many wealthy women there were holidaying with their teenage sons: 'Lots of mother and son love: that certainly takes care of their future neurosis. The boys are very "Death in Venice" lovely.'[28] If Peter noticed it too, it must have reminded him of a previous visit, fourteen years earlier, when he'd met Blanche Oelrichs and fallen in love with her beautiful son Robin. Poor Robin was long gone now – he'd committed suicide in 1944, aged twenty-eight, and Blanche would never get over it.

Waldemar was surer now than ever that he truly loved Peter, and had no doubts about their future together. He would write poetry and plays, and they would travel and live in bliss. The European tour continued – from Switzerland to Italy, which was still under an American military government. Waldemar noted the art (the Sistine Chapel ceiling, he decided, was 'simply boy after boy after boy, in various muscular positions') and cast a critical eye on the homosexual trade in Rome and Capri:

> Rome is quite gay on the Via Veneto, where American soldier-queens sit in bars and camp with the local belles. I am told that everyone in Italy is gay, for money. It's like pre-Hitler Berlin. Some little fellow named Adrian has been my guide to Capri ... Adrian speaks pidgin English, and told me that *all* the Americans were gay during the war. One day he showed me his photos – picture after picture of handsome marines, sailors and soldiers: 'love to Adrian', etc.[29]

In Capri Peter and Waldemar met up with Norman Douglas, the elderly, disgraced novelist whose sexual tastes, like those of Denham Fouts, ran to post-pubescent boys. He'd fled from England in 1916, skipping bail after being arrested and charged with sexual assault on a sixteen-year-old boy. One later writer attempted to exculpate him: 'Norman Douglas of Capri, and of Naples and Florence, was formerly of England, which he fled during the war to avoid persecution for kissing a boy and giving him some cakes and a shilling.'[30] Waldemar was charmed by him; he found him witty and loveably acerbic about the world, and seemed to think nothing odd in the fact that when Douglas dined with him and Peter he brought with him 'a little Neapolitan boy whom he is taking care of. He found the child starving in Naples ... The child has lovely long eyelashes, and is called Ettore.'[31]

The poverty in Italy struck Waldemar even more forcefully than that in Ireland. 'Yet it is a monstrous truth that poverty is as picturesque as it is appalling.'[32]

* * *

Gradually the tour wound its way back across the Continent, and by the end of the summer the couple were back in the Palace Gate flat and settling into a regular domestic life. Peter, who had been conducting *Horizon* business throughout their travels, was hoping to focus on a new venture; alongside Waldemar, it was his hope for the future.

As far back as late 1945, Peter had begun discussing the possibility of founding a museum of modern art in London with a select group of friends and colleagues – including Surrealist painter E. L. T. Mesens, critic Herbert Read and artist Roland Penrose. Other capital cities had such museums, but not London. On 22 January 1946 Penrose, Read and Mesens sent letters formally inviting Peter Watson, the film producer George Hoellering, art critic Robert Melville, Jacques Brunius and the publisher of Lund Humphries, Peter Gregory, to meet to discuss the creation in London of a centre 'from which a Museum of Modern Art could ultimately be planned'.[33]

The core of this group originated in the London Gallery, a commercial enterprise that had been founded at 28 Cork Street in 1936 by Mrs (later Lady) Norton (who later assisted John Craxton in Greece). Roland Penrose had taken control of it by 1938, at a similar time to Mesens getting involved, and Peter Watson was later brought in as a director. The gallery had formed the epicentre of London's Surrealist exhibitions in the late 1930s; it also published the *London Gallery Bulletin* and there was even a publishing division, called London Gallery Editions.

By November 1946 Peter was writing to John Craxton that 'the modern museum looks like getting under way.'[34] But there was still a lot to do. During 1947 more people were brought into the project – including ballet choreographer Frederick Ashton, conductor and producer Edward Clark (who had put on Igor Markevitch's *Le Paradis perdu*, and had been brought in at Peter's suggestion), poet Geoffrey Grigson, and several others. A committee had been formed under Herbert Read's chairmanship, and the 'modern museum' had evolved and been given a name. In the September 1947 number of *Horizon*, Peter placed a full-page announcement:

> THE INSTITUTE OF
> CONTEMPORARY ARTS
>
> A committee of all the arts (painting, sculpture, architecture, literature, music, theatre, film, ballet, and broadcasting) has been at work for some months, making plans for the creation of an
>
> INSTITUTE OF CONTEMPORARY ARTS
>
> The committee is convinced that an institute which will bring the arts together under one roof and provide a permanent co-operative and educational centre is urgently needed.

The Institute, besides being a co-operative, would be progressive and have an experimental ethos not driven by profit; it would be creative, in that it would commission new works 'courageous in character' and would 'enable artists of all kinds to join in the search for new forms of social expression'. But there was a problem – although it had a policy and a mission and a committee, the Institute of Contemporary Arts still only existed on paper. Before it could actually *do* anything, it needed premises. The announcement set a target of £50,000, and asked for donations. Peter Watson himself made an initial donation of £500, and the public response was good.

For the time being, the ICA's committee meetings were held at the London Gallery at 23 Brook Street, and its exhibition space was in basement rooms beneath the Academy Cinema in Oxford Street; it was here that its first art shows would be held the following year.

It was as well that Peter had a new large-scale project to devote himself to, because by 1947 it looked as if *Horizon* might not last much longer. Aside from the personal irritations that had grown between Peter and Cyril Connolly since the early years of the war, their editorial relationship was becoming disputatious.

There was a flare-up in October 1947 over the inclusion of two pieces of writing. One was an essay by Herbert Read on 'The Fate of Modern Painting'. It was a contentious article, in which Read pointed his finger at the 'vast organization of exhibitionism, salesmanship and propaganda' that had built up in the art world; artists were being artificially sustained by an expensive public system rather than commercialising their art, as writers, photographers, film-makers, and every other creative person had to.[35] Cyril apparently didn't like the article, but Peter defended it strongly. Read, he argued, was delving deep into a profound problem that caused 'all the disagreeableness and horrors of the time we live in'. The article was courageous, Peter felt, and would make Read 'unpopular with painters, art galleries, and all the nonsense which backs up the racket'.[36] The article was already slated for inclusion, and duly appeared in the November issue.

Peter and Cyril then had a dispute over a long story – really a novella – by Evelyn Waugh; it was a satirical piece called 'The Loved One', based on Waugh's visit to the Forest Lawn cemetery in Hollywood. Waugh had offered *Horizon* the opportunity to publish it, and Cyril wanted to do it as an entire issue. Peter disliked the story intensely. He had a personal antipathy to Waugh anyway (the 'Catholic Fascist') and liked him even less on the evidence of the satire in 'The Loved One'. Peter thought it well written, but it was 'neither farce nor tragedy' and lacked human feeling. 'How he hates everyone! I should not wish to be him. I just don't understand how he can be religious in any way.'[37] Pressed to justify himself, Peter went on: 'I don't much like satire because I think it is all too often used as a mask to cover an inner emptiness.'[38]

Peter had also reacted negatively to an article about William Beckford, the eighteenth-century art and furniture collector.[39] In both cases, Cyril infuriated Peter by treating his objections as if they were a bar to publication, and was indignant about his editorship being interfered with. 'It is nothing to do with any prohibition of mine,' Peter wrote, 'as you well know ... My opinion about something is *not* a prohibition and I really resent it being taken as one.' The whole dispute was 'all too silly' and all Peter wanted Cyril to do was 'put in exactly what you like as you know I think your judgment is better than anyone else's, you silly thing.'[40] He also accepted that Waugh should be paid extra 'just because he is Evelyn Waugh'. And so 'The Loved One' was published in the February 1948 number of *Horizon*, taking up the entire magazine and prefaced by an approving introduction from Cyril.

As the next few years passed, the frictions between Peter and Cyril over *Horizon* would continue and slowly escalate. There was more to it than mere difference of opinion; for although Peter was still dedicated to the magazine, Cyril, perhaps only unconsciously at this stage, was looking for a way out.

19

THIEVES, DOPE-PEDDLERS AND PURVEYORS OF LOVE

1947–1948

While the frictions with Cyril rumbled on, Peter went to Paris for yet another attempt to sort out Denham, leaving Waldemar alone in the Palace Gate flat. This would be Peter's last chance to deal with Denham before next year: as of 1 October 1947 the currency allowance was being withdrawn completely, and travel would be impossible for a while.[1]

Denham, perhaps because he knew Peter's weakness so well, had overdosed and been taken to the American Hospital at Neuilly-sur-Seine to be 'disintoxicated'. So when Peter went to see him, he felt it impossible to berate or argue with him – he had 'been through hell', even if it was a hell entirely of his own making. At the merest hint of rebuke, he accused Peter of sadism.[2] 'I think D. is really going quite mad now and I can hardly speak to him without exploding with rage.' Therefore Peter kept silent.[3]

Denham was still refusing to move out of the rue du Bac apartment, so Peter – who was receiving letters from Étienne de Beaumont threatening legal action if the flat wasn't vacated by 15 October – told Denham and Étienne that it was between them. In the meantime, he began removing his more valuable belongings – including half a dozen paintings.

Étienne – who had been away from Paris – came back especially to see that M. Fouts was ejected on the appointed day, and also tried to prevent Peter from removing his possessions. But when de Beaumont arrived at 44 rue du Bac, he found that Denham had discharged himself from the hospital, had struggled back to the apartment with the help of two nurses, and was waiting for him with a lawyer on hand. It was explained to the astonished count that M. Fouts, as a long-time resident, was legally entitled to stay in the apartment until alternative accommodation was found for him. De Beaumont, thwarted and seething impotently, stormed out and wrote to Peter threatening (again) to bring a lawsuit against him.[4]

Denham instantly dropped back into his habitual lifestyle. His neuroses had intensified and he had alienated virtually all his Parisian friends. The only one who stuck around was Mopsa Sternheim, the middle-aged, heroin-addicted daughter of the art collector Thea Sternheim and dramatist Carl. Back in the 1920s Mopsa had been a sensation, noted for her dark, weirdly masculine looks; René Crevel had been in love with her, and hoped to marry her until his suicide in 1935. Life had ruined her; after surviving Ravensbrück concentration camp, Mopsa had returned to Paris and now spent her days in Denham's company, putting up with his anti-Semitic ramblings for the sake of the needle.[5]

Peter was beset on all sides. David Gascoyne was in Paris, depending on Peter for support, and Francis Bacon had written from Monte Carlo appealing for money. Peter, whose allowance of francs was running out fast, could do nothing for him. On top of that, the agents who managed 10 Palace Gate had written to him 'complaining in a general way' about loud music coming from the flat during his absence.[6]

He'd also heard from Norman Fowler – an 'unexpected and strange' communication (Norman never wrote any other kind). He'd been nurturing a hope of becoming a dancer, and Peter had tried to help him by putting him in touch with his friend Lincoln Kirstein. Perhaps this was aiming a little high; Kirstein was the founder of the School of American Ballet in New York and of the Ballet Society (which in 1948 became the New York City Ballet). Norman had now given up the idea, Peter heard, 'as he didn't like to approach Kirstein! Strange indeed.'[7] Referring to Denham but probably thinking of others too, Peter complained, 'How dreadfully feeble weak characters are and how they make the strong pay for their weakness.'[8]

At the same time, Peter was caught up in a dispute over another of his looted paintings. Back in April, he'd been walking along the rue de l'Abbaye, not far from the rue du Bac, and passed the Galerie Zak, which was owned by his acquaintance Victor Raykis. Glancing in the window, as he inevitably did whenever he passed, Peter's eye had been caught by a familiar image. It was *Les Faubourgs* by Georges Rouault, one of the artist's many heavily lined paintings depicting streets of black-windowed buildings. The shock was dramatic – the same sensation he'd experienced in the Kunstmuseum in Basel in 1945. This painting was his, bought in 1936 from the dealer Joseph Hersel, and among those taken by the Nazis. Immediately after spotting the painting Peter had written to the French authorities, but now, six months later, he still hadn't got his painting back. In fact, the dispute would drag on for a while yet. Brian Howard, who owed Raykis money, was outraged, especially as he'd been made to feel ashamed for not paying his debt – 'I shall pay that snivelling old receiver of stolen goods when and if P. gets his Rouault, and not one second before ... All that talk about gentlemanliness, forsooth! I never heard of such hypocritical bosh.'[9] (Peter did eventually get his Rouault back, but it isn't recorded whether Brian paid his debt.)

Despite all these headaches – Cyril, Denham, Norman, Bacon, Gascoyne and Raykis – Peter managed to lift his spirits. Apart from being still freshly in love with Waldemar, he had Sonia's company in Paris, and they always loved being with each other. She wrote to Waldemar and he gained the impression that she was carrying a torch for someone in Paris; this 'someone', it would turn out, was Maurice Merleau-Ponty, philosopher and political editor of Sartre's *Les Temps Modernes*; Sonia had just met and fallen in love with him. She was melancholy when she returned alone, which saddened Waldemar. 'She's such a sweetie: unselfish, and practically the brains and motion of *Horizon* as far as I can make out.'[10]

Alone in London (aside from his regular socialising with the likes of Douglas Cooper and Brian Howard, who was becoming more and more of an ordeal to everyone who knew him – 'the promise that never fulfils itself'), Waldemar was 'desperately lonely' and had 'suffered from all sorts of fears' while Peter was away. 'As time goes by, it is driven home to me more and more how absolutely ravingly in love with P. I am.' Waldemar, who had been accustomed to quick sexual thrills and 'chasing around 42nd Street', had never expected to be so in love, so content just to have his intimate relationship with Peter. 'And now I have terribly morbid and ungrounded fears of losing him, which is of course silly because (a) he loves me dearly, and (b) he would never do anything like that.'[11]

Peter returned in late October, laden with love and gifts, including Jean Genet's scandalous new novel, *Querelle de Brest*, a sort of erotic picaresque about a criminal sailor. It was so hot that even in Paris it had had to be published privately (a printing limited to 460 numbered copies). It was filled with pornographic illustrations by Jean Cocteau – 'pages and pages of naked matelots with you-know-what hanging down to the knees, and standing up inside of handkerchiefs,' wrote Waldemar.[12]

He was ecstatic with Peter but unhappy in London. Aside from having made a handful of good friends, he was oppressed by the atmosphere of gloom, the rationing, the bad food, and the general Englishness of it all. In Waldemar's mind, everything came down to this. One word of American slang summed it up for him – Englishmen were *pills*: bores. He didn't think of himself as 'rabidly anti-English', but still: 'The English are so reserved, so cold, so priggish, so snobbish, so pilly.'[13] England's autumnal melancholy was getting him down. On the other hand, he had high hopes of a new exhibition of Lucian Freud and John Craxton, which promised to feature Lucian's portrait of him. 'Lucian's talent is impressive,' Waldemar wrote; 'very profoundly neurotic with a Germanic realism, and sort of half-primitive. It isn't fully developed yet, but he seems to have *something* very definite.'

At the same time, Waldemar was trying hard to push forward his own career. Back in New York he had co-authored a play, *Inherit the Wind* (which he sarcastically referred to as *Inherit the Royalties*), and there were tantalising glimpses of it being given a New York production, but nothing ever seemed settled. Eventually, in March 1948, the play would get a London production at the Playhouse in Charing Cross, featuring Michael Hordern, a rising star in British films. This aside, Waldemar Hansen's literary career would always be a struggle without any clear payoff.

* * *

As the melancholy English autumn faded to gloomy winter, Peter and Waldemar's relationship – still only eight months old – began to show signs of wearing thin. They were still in love, but had become prone to quarrelling. However, Waldemar had learned a new trick: he had discovered that Peter loved him better after a quarrel, and was 'absolutely adoring when I am cruel to him ... I couldn't ever be a Denham, but I can do a fair apache dance in a pinch!' Waldemar might not quite be Denham, but he had learned another of his traits – how to blame his own cruelty on Peter himself: 'that girl's unconscious works over-time to figure out ways of making me hurt her. La, la!'[14]

During this period, Waldemar wrote a short poem in which he tried to peer into Peter's private thoughts. 'Avez-Vous Quelque Chose à Déclarer?' was written in two acrostic stanzas, and cast Peter in the guise of a tightly controlled country, fearful of allowing emotions to be smuggled across his borders:

Passage is doubtful through this winter landscape.
Enter: the stranger with continental baggage,
The smile for inspectors with a flare for drama.
Escape? But all are searched for smuggled goods:
Reformers have been known to carry love.

Wishing the customs not-so-strict, I watch
All thieves, dope-peddlers and purveyors of love
Taken aside for further questioning.
Sir, I am lonely here. The sentries bar
Only the personal that I could love:
None of the other passengers are bothered.[15]

The sentries barring the 'personal' was perhaps a suggestion that Peter's love didn't measure up to Daisy Buchanan's after all, let alone Jay Gatsby's. The poem was published in the American magazine *Poetry* in May 1948.

Conditions in London grew ever more bleak. Peter and his friends were now dependent for luxuries on food parcels from America; *Horizon* had instituted a new Begging Bowl for its impoverished contributors, and American readers provided a wealth of stuff that was rationed or just unobtainable in Britain. Waldemar reckoned Cyril Connolly siphoned off a lot of it for himself. Peter never got any, but John Myers sent parcels privately to Waldemar and they lived on those, supplemented with pheasant, which wasn't rationed.

As winter fell, Waldemar travelled to Cardiff to pay a duty visit to his uncle and maternal grandmother. 'Granny recognizes no-one,' he wrote; 'sits by the fire and chants in Yiddish all day long.' The uncle was 'a rather chipper little man of 59, who keeps a little draper's shop from which he makes no money, and is a book-maker at the dog-track on Saturday nights'. The whole weekend was drenched in Welsh rain, and was 'ineffably melancholy'.[16]

All Waldemar had to cheer him was the prospect of Christmas in Paris and the happy news that Denham had finally been kicked out of the flat. What Waldemar probably didn't know was that he had moved into another apartment in a different building in the rue du Bac, still at Peter's expense.

* * *

January 1948 saw the publication of *Other Voices, Other Rooms*, the autobiographical debut novel by Truman Capote. By April it was a sensation everywhere, and in May Capote arrived in London and found his way – probably through Christopher Isherwood and Cecil Beaton, as well as a prior acquaintance with Peter Watson – to Waldemar. They became friends almost immediately. Waldemar needed a confidant; his relationship with Peter was not going well.

He was alone again in the Palace Gate flat; the currency allowance had been reinstated, and Peter had gone off to Switzerland on business, leaving Waldemar in a state of suspense and sadness. Their relationship had entered a dry, uncomfortable patch. Peter had started to become uncommunicative – even secretive; Waldemar found him 'really quite strange and moody, and I never know half the time what is going on in his *tête*. I am madly affectionate, but sometimes I do despair.' Peter had taken to sleeping on the sitting-room sofa; Waldemar was a restless sleeper, he said, but their sexual relationship was almost dead, and Waldemar had all but given up 'trying to make magic'.[17] Peter had started to think that Waldemar ought to live more independently and have friends of his own age. He was socialising with the *Horizon* crowd, as well as Christopher Isherwood (who was back in England now), Auden and others, but they were all primarily Peter's friends. Word reached Waldemar's ears that Peter had been complaining to people about being tied to him. The source was John Myers, Waldemar's former room-mate and constant confidant, who wrote to Waldemar that he knew from a reliable source that Peter had been saying to people in Paris and London that he had 'brought this boy over from America' and felt 'stuck' with him and 'didn't know what to do with him'; moreover 'the boy' was impossible to deal with and 'nobody could stand him'.[18]

Given that Peter had never been inclined to be indiscreet about his romantic relationships, it is virtually certain that, if these allegations were not wholly fabricated, he had more likely been talking about Denham, but by the time his words had been Chinese-whispered across the Atlantic to East 38th Street, it seemed to John Myers (who had been receiving a constant flow of commentary on the relationship) that Peter had been 'dishing' about Waldemar. Alluding to Ibsen's *A Doll's House*, Myers had urged Waldemar to 'do a Nora' and leave this suffocating relationship.[19]

Meanwhile, Peter was writing cheerful letters from Ascona in Switzerland about visiting the Italian sculptor Marino Marini and lunching with the illegitimate son of Edward VII,[20] and updating Waldemar on the gossip from Paris about Sartre and Poulenc and the avant-garde composer René Leibowitz, who had taken up playing jazz piano in a bar-restaurant, and about Gore Vidal, who was staying at the Pont Royal and had been introduced to Denham by Christopher Isherwood. (Vidal was slightly perplexed by Peter; like Capote he seemed to want to disdain him but couldn't help liking him: 'Watson was a charming man, tall, thin, perverse. One of those intricate English queer types who usually end up as field marshals, but because he was so rich he never had to do anything.'[21])

In Zurich Peter noted the new fashions: 'The bright young men wear new look coats which come half-way down between the ass and the knees and are really rather fetching.'[22] Although he was titillated by the sight, he was also becoming acutely conscious that he had once been – and was no longer – one of the bright young men. This year he would turn forty, and he had developed 'an acute and painful sense of the passage of time'.[23]

But his letters were breezy, and after a year with Waldemar he felt both comfortable and affectionate enough to begin addressing him as

'Dear Ugly Face' as well as 'Waldy'. It seemed he was quite capable of being affectionate when he was at a distance, and quite unconscious of the problems that Waldemar perceived in their relationship.

Peter was intending to stop in Paris on his way back to London. He wrote to Waldemar asking that, if he happened to meet Truman Capote, 'send him to see me in Paris.' But as for Waldemar himself, it would not be worth his coming over.[24] Peter simply hated to have his friends rush needlessly to greet him, putting themselves to unwarranted trouble, but the way he worded it, it must have felt like a snub, and Waldemar was hurt; he consulted Capote himself for counsel and solace.

They had been together in London a couple of weeks and were firm friends already – Waldemar thought Truman was 'an absolute angel', which on short acquaintance he must have seemed (angelic Capote might well be in some ways to some people, but he was far from absolutely so).[25]

Capote was already planning to go to Paris. He had been summoned. The story behind it became a minor legend. It was said that Denham Fouts, still taking occasional notice of the outside world through his fog of opium smoke, had seen *Other Voices, Other Rooms*, and been intrigued by the provocative dust-jacket photo of Capote by Harold Halma (some versions of the story say it was a publicity photo by Cecil Beaton that Denham saw). The photo was provocative, sullen, and, to a man with Denham's tastes, alluring; Truman Capote at the age of twenty-four had the look of adolescence; he was a sulky-eyed, blond bundle of teen sexuality. Denham was captivated, and sent Capote a blank cheque with a note saying simply: 'Come.'

And Capote came.

But not without some caution. He already knew of Denham – everybody in the gay literary world knew about Denny and Isherwood (or 'Issyvoo', as Capote called him) and about Denny and Peter Watson; 'Denny, long before he surfaced in my cove, was a legend,' Capote wrote.[26]

He had learned the details of Denham and Peter's relationship from gossip, and learned a few more intimate details from Cecil Beaton and Waldemar. Capote was fascinated. His view of Peter was complicated; there seemed to be a part of Truman Capote that wanted to dislike Peter Watson but couldn't. He described him as 'not just another rich queen, but – in a stooped, intellectual, bitter-lipped style – one of the most personable men in England.'[27] Capote believed there was a dark side; Cecil Beaton had confided to him the story of his and Peter's voyage to America in 1931, and Capote, with the instincts of a born bitch, interpreted Peter's behaviour towards Cecil as deliberate sadism; he had knowingly set forth with the 'love-besotted' Cecil, 'whom he punished by never permitting a kiss or caress, though night after night they slept in the same narrow bed – that is, Mr Watson slept while his perfectly decent but disintegrating friend twitched with insomnia and an aching scrotum'.[28]

Cecil also told Capote his own feelings about Denham. Cecil had heard about the 'appalling dogfights' between him and Peter and thought vengefully that it was 'just what Peter needed'. Cecil hated Denham with – in Capote's words – 'an unconsumed passion'.[29] Capote came away with an impression of Peter and Denham that was filtered by Cecil's memory of the pain he had experienced with Peter. Capote summed it up:

> Of course, as is true of most men sadistically streaked, Watson had paralleling masochistic impulses; but it took Denny, with his *púttána*'s [prostitute's] instinct for an ashamed client's unspoken needs, to divine this and act accordingly. Once the tables are turned, only a humiliator can appreciate humiliation's sweeter edges: Watson was in love with Denny's cruelty, for Watson was an artist recognizing the work of a superior artist, labors that left the quinine-elegant Mr. W. stretched in stark-awake comas of jealousy and delicious despair. The Beloved even used his drug addiction to sado-romantic advantage, for Watson, while forced to supply the money that supported a habit he deplored, was convinced that only his love and attention could rescue The Beloved from a heroin grave. When The Beloved truly desired a turn of the screw, he had merely to turn to his medicine chest.[30]

With this picture in his mind, how could a man with Truman Capote's instinct for dangerous stimulation ignore Denham's summons?

When Waldemar told him that Peter was in Paris, and that his own relations with him were at a low ebb, Capote pressed him to come too. They despatched a telegram to Peter: 'Changing voices, changing rooms. Two dancing daughters arriving Pont Royal Sunday evening. Perhaps they can fit you in for a tango.'[31]

In Paris, Waldemar showed Capote the night-world of the jazz clubs and *boîtes*. They were both politely friendly to Peter, but Waldemar – on Capote's advice – kept him at a distance, refused to dance attendance on him (let alone tango with him) or show any affection; the two dancing daughters entertained themselves and let Mr Watson stew.

What really interested Capote, of course, was Denham, and he found his way to the rue du Bac, where Denny, having been ejected by Étienne de Beaumont, lived in an apartment at number 33, described by Gore Vidal as furnished 'with only a bed and six Venetian chairs'.[32] When Capote went to the apartment, 'the Denham Fouts I encountered there, though paler than his favourite ivory opium pipe, was not much changed from Herr Issyvoo's California friend: he still looked vulnerably young, as though youth were a chemical solution in which Fouts was permanently incarcerated.'[33]

Once he was through the door, Capote was drawn into a relationship similar to the one Michael Wishart had sleepwalked into two years earlier:

> ... although he wanted us to share the same bed, his interest in me was romantic but not sexual; nor was he disposed toward anyone else; he said he hadn't had his circle squared in two years, for opium and cocaine had castrated him. We often went to Champs Elysées movies in the afternoon, and at some juncture he always, having begun slightly to sweat, hurried to the men's room and dosed himself with drugs; in the evening he inhaled opium or sipped opium tea, a concoction he brewed by boiling in water the crusts of opium that had accumulated inside his pipe.[34]

While Truman was inhaling the essence of Denham, Waldemar had made a breakthrough with Peter. A few days of cool treatment brought Mr W to simmering point. One afternoon he seized Waldemar and took him back to his room in the Pont Royal, where they 'carried on madly', with a passion reminiscent of their tour through Ireland a year earlier. Waldemar was reassured that Peter really loved him, that 'my worries were foolish and ill-founded' and that this reunion 'was all I needed to know'.[35]

They talked over their relationship and made plans for the future. They would tour Europe through the summer and then in the autumn sail for New York. They would stay in the Americas for several months and holiday in the Caribbean.

It didn't quite work out that way.

* * *

In September, Waldemar wrote to John Myers, letting him know that he would be arriving in New York in a few weeks. He and Peter were having a few days in Paris before Waldemar's departure. He would be going to America alone.

The currency export regulations were as tight as ever, and now the US had introduced a new rule in response: to get a visitor's visa, a foreign national had to have an endorsement from a wealthy American citizen – a kind of financial guarantor, who had to give evidence of his or her own finances. Peter was working on it. But there was more to the situation than money.

Waldemar reported to Myers that things were 'going well' with Peter, although there was gossip going around that the relationship was all but over, and in the picture Waldemar drew it was hard to see any sign of anything going well. Peter had gone back to being 'moody and strange a lot of the time, so depressed', sometimes to a degree that he wouldn't eat.[36] His depression seemed to be about the state of the world – the same pessimism about the future that had first set in as the war was ending. Waldemar believed it was caused by the gulf between Peter's pre-war life as 'one of the richest young men in England' and the existence he had now, confined to London much of the time, unable to take money abroad, barred by government regulations from importing any art. He lived in a comfortable modern flat, but it was tiny – Waldemar couldn't get over the fact that Cyril Connolly lived in splendour in Regent's Park, and wondered sourly where the money came from.

In his own way, Waldemar was developing the same feeling about Peter that Cyril had in 1945 – unable to understand or tolerate Peter's refusal to behave 'like a conventional rich man' (as Peter had put it). It depressed Waldemar just as it had depressed Cyril. There were no Rolls-Royces, no Bentleys – Peter no longer even kept a car. And this was by choice, for within Britain he was about as wealthy as he had ever been; he was never short of ready cash from his trust fund. Having lived the rich man's life to its fullest extent in the thirties, he had moved towards a kind of asceticism that he made no attempt to rationalise, other than to hint that it was connected in some way with his gloomy prognostications about civilisation's doomed future. In truth, Peter hardly knew himself what it was all about.

He did know one thing, however: he knew that he wanted Waldemar to be independent of him. He still believed that he had caused Denham's problems, or at least that he had failed to cure them, and he didn't want the same thing to happen to Waldemar:

> The only way for you to find out who you are is through your own work, and it is now time for you to devote yourself seriously to it. Through it you will exist on your own, and that I sense is terribly important to you. Denham and what happened to him is the perfect example of someone evading every issue through someone else, and when he does have to stand on his own legs, they just aren't there ... Such people are diabolical in pinning the blame on to others (mothers, money, this and that). Also money isn't the slightest help for the real problems.[37]

'I'm terribly, terribly, terribly fond of him,' Waldemar wrote. 'Which is as much as the heart can ask at times.'[38]

Waldemar sailed for New York on the *Queen Elizabeth* on 1 October 1948. Meanwhile, Peter worked away at getting some rich American friend to give him the endorsement he needed to get his visa so that he could follow him; he had hopes of George Cukor, who was visiting London.

Then, in the middle of December, just a couple of weeks before he was hoping to travel, Peter received a telegram that almost knocked him off his feet. Denham Fouts was dead.

20

EUPHORIA AND DREAD

1948–1949

Denham had finally left Paris after his short, castrato relationship with Truman Capote. He drifted to Italy, where he took up with another lover, Anthony Watson-Gandy, a young Englishman who had been an RAF officer during the war. They lived in Rome at the Pensione Foggetti at 84 Via Marche – an old stone apartment block not dissimilar to 44 rue du Bac. Young Anthony took what care he could of Denham, who was as helpless and perpetually fogged as ever.

On Thursday 16 December 1948, Denham and Anthony were apparently intending to go out for the evening; that afternoon, at about quarter past five, Denham went to the bathroom. He was gone for a while, and when his friend went in to look for him, he found him collapsed on the toilet, quite dead.

Whichever way you looked at it, it was hardly surprising that Denham should die so young (he was thirty-four, although he'd continued knocking two years off his age, and the death report said thirty-two). What *was* surprising, though, was that it turned out to be neither the cocaine nor the heroin nor the alcohol that had killed him. An autopsy was carried out, which discovered that he had suffered from hypoplastic left heart syndrome, a congenital condition in which the aorta and left ventricle of the heart are underdeveloped; it was remarkable that he had survived to adulthood, let alone lived as long as he had.[1] Denham was buried in Rome's Cimitero Acattolico, the non-Catholic foreigners' cemetery, where many dissipated expatriates – including both Keats and Shelley – had been laid to rest. The scrapings of cash and personal effects Denham had left behind weren't enough to pay his debts in Rome; his father, Edwin Fouts, had to send $230.45 to cover the shortfall.[2]

Most people who had known him and weren't privy to the autopsy report naturally assumed that Denny had died from drugs; had they known the truth, some of them – especially Peter Watson – might have thought it morbidly appropriate that in fact Denham Fouts had died from a malformed heart.

If Peter had known this, he might have been a little less ready to accuse himself of responsibility. As it was, it would take him a long time to get over the shock of Denham's death.

* * *

On New Year's Day 1949, Peter boarded the *Queen Mary* at Southampton. It was eighteen years almost to the day since he'd set out on his first voyage to America, on New Year's Eve 1930, arriving late at the dockside giggling and laden with parcels, while Cecil Beaton paced the decks in anxiety. How much had changed since then.

One thing that had survived the years between was his friendship with Cecil, which had settled into a reliable amity. Part of Cecil still loved Peter as longingly as ever, but he had learned how to keep it down. In the first year after the war, when Cecil resumed his journeys to New York, Peter had revived the practice of ordering items that couldn't be obtained in Britain – new recordings by Bartók, Stravinsky, Schoenberg, Milhaud and Hindemith. He'd also requested Frances Fox Hair Ointment, which he'd used since before the war but could no longer get in London.[3] Cecil, who earned much of his income in America and was less affected by the currency restrictions, had obliged.

If the departure date hadn't reminded Peter of that first voyage, the shipboard company might. Several of his and Cecil's mutual friends from before the war were on board, such as Olga Lynn and Catherine d'Erlanger. Mostly, though, the ship was 'full of flabby Hollywood queens', whom Peter found irritating to talk to.[4] Charles Laughton was aboard, but whether he was included in the flabby anathema, Peter didn't say. He was stuck with them for a long time. The ship ran aground at Cherbourg and had to return to Southampton for makeshift repairs ('stuffing the bottom of the boat with concrete', according to Peter[5]), then sailed again three days later.

Throughout the voyage Peter dwelt on his memories and feelings about Denham. Before leaving London he had written to Waldemar, warning him that 'Denham's death has affected me rather deeply ... Please be very patient with me because I shall arrive in a very depressed condition.'[6] In fact it had changed everything. He'd been transfixed by it ever since receiving the telegram, but during the Atlantic crossing he withdrew into himself, brooding over the past and growing ever more depressed and restless. By the time Waldemar met him at the Cunard dock in New York, Peter was in a miserable, twitchy state.

Waldemar had taken time to readjust to life in America; he felt like a foreigner, and for all the disdain he'd felt for London and the English, he had become adapted to it. And he missed his friends. They had missed him too. At Halloween Sonia had sent him a postcard, recalling the party he had given at Palace Gate the previous year – 'Peter and Lys and I are sitting here in tears in the gloaming ... We miss you and wish we could have another party.'[7] He was again living with John Myers in their old apartment. But that wouldn't do for the big reunion. From the dock, he and Peter went to the Weylin Hotel on Madison Avenue and East 54th Street, where they had a double room reserved.

The reunion wasn't what Waldemar had hoped for – on the contrary, Peter was more withdrawn and gloomy than ever. They'd been at the hotel for hardly any time when Peter suddenly revealed that he wanted a separation. He felt that the relationship was wrong, uncomfortable, and he wanted to spend his time in America on his own, so that he could work out his feelings.[8]

Shocked and grieved, Waldemar pushed Peter to explain, and made an upsetting discovery. Peter confessed that he had never entirely got over his fleeting, exciting encounter with Norman Fowler two years earlier. Waldemar knew that Peter and Norman had written to each other since, but that had been to do with Norman's absurd notions of becoming a dancer or a sculptor. But Peter revealed that he had feelings for Norman. He didn't actually break up with Waldemar, and wasn't definitely intending to seek Norman out; he simply wanted to be left to his own devices.

Peter had people to see – mostly on business to do with the ICA and *Horizon*. The former was still struggling to come into existence, hosting some well-received poetry recitals but also failing to earn money with its avant-garde film screenings and art exhibitions; meanwhile the latter was struggling to stay alive, so there was much to do.

They made their arrangements and parted. With money from Peter, Waldemar set off for Jamaica, where he hoped to focus on his writing; Peter would join him there as soon as he had finished his business and thought things through.

Peter spent most of the next few weeks in New York, Montreal and Boston, having a 'fairly profitable' time.[9] He secured some articles for the magazine and spent time with Mary McCarthy, the author, critic and political activist, who had just been awarded the *Horizon* Prize; like Evelyn Waugh before her (but without the conflict) she was having a whole issue devoted to her new novella, *The Oasis*, a story about a doomed intellectual utopia.[10] She had the distinction of being the first and last recipient of the prize. Peter had liked her story, and now enjoyed her company. He also had a meeting with the editor of *Fortune* and met up with Greta Garbo.

His relationship with Garbo was an odd and awkward one. Nobody had easy relations with this lady, but Peter's were especially tricky. She was Cecil Beaton's other obsession; after his brief encounter with her in 1932, he had managed to make contact again after the war, and a rather strange courtship had grown up between them. Knowing the intensity of Cecil's feelings for Peter, she was jealous, while Peter was gently amused by the romance.[11] (Later that year, Peter would stay for the first time at Reddish House – Cecil's new country home, which he'd taken after being forced out of Ashcombe in 1945 – and Cecil would find the old feelings reignited: 'I feel all the same emotions and now he has left I feel quite a void in my life,'[12] he wrote in his diary, although he claimed that he no longer suffered the pain of his unrequited love.[13] There really seemed to be no peace for Cecil, even with marriage to Greta Garbo in prospect.)

By the time Peter was back in his suite at the Weylin in New York in early February, his depression had been replaced by a mood of euphoria, and he dreaded slumping back into the pit. He put off joining

Waldemar; instead he wrote to him saying that he would probably go out to California for a week, then fly down to New Orleans and come to Jamaica.[14] He left unspoken the crucial detail – of which they were both acutely conscious – that Norman lived in California.

* * *

By the end of February, Waldemar had been alone in Jamaica for nearly two months, and hadn't heard a word from Peter for three weeks. Then a four-page letter came from Hollywood, where Peter was staying at the Montecito Apartments – a Mayan/Art Deco block popular with movie stars.

The letter threw Waldemar into a sleepless, painful despair. He wrote to John Myers: 'I'm very unhappy today ... It seems that the ax has finally fallen.'[15]

Peter's letter was apologetic but blunt. After leaving New York he had stopped off in Chicago and San Francisco, but had eventually made his way to Los Angeles. 'Norman met me,' he wrote. 'How to explain what has happened? We just seemed to take up where we left off. I don't know what to say as there's no rational way of explaining such a thing.'[16]

It seemed that Peter had been harbouring a longing for Norman for a considerable time now – it explained his silences, his moodiness with Waldemar. He'd done nothing about it until now because he didn't think there was any hope of ever meeting Norman again:

> I could not talk to you about it. I felt far too vulnerable.
>
> In a way this cannot be too much of a shock to you. You had always told me that there was no *ecstasy* between us. This was in its way quite true and was no fault of yours or mine. Not that I expect to live in ecstasy or would ever hope for it but it expressed what you want.
>
> Of course I feel guilty although I know I have not really done harm to you. I am most attached to you and will always be, I think. I am grateful for the consideration you have always shown me.
>
> ... I must tell you that my deepest emotions are involved and that this is really important to me.[17]

It certainly looked like a severing axe-blow; and yet Peter still intended to come to Jamaica in a few days and meet up with Waldemar, if Waldemar wanted to – but from now on it would have to be 'a very different relationship'.

Waldemar was hurt, desperate and indignant. He wrote to John Myers telling him all about it, and denying that he had ever complained about a lack of 'ecstasy' in the relationship (in fact he had made such complaints several times in letters to Myers). He described how he had written Peter a long letter, 'and then tore it up. Then I sent instead a very short note ... I didn't rant and rave ... though I did say that I hoped his trip to the moon was worth his incredibly bad behaviour towards me.'[18]

He was jealous; his vanity was wounded. Peter's choice of lover was as irksome as the infidelity itself. 'Norman Fowler!' Waldemar wrote in swirling pen-strokes (too emotional to manage his usual typewriter). 'How many cups of breakfast coffee will that last? ... But to think I've been a stop-gap for his loneliness from the beginning! What kind of behaviour is it when you fall in love with one person and then invite another to live with you ...?'[19]

Despite the sudden flowering of a love he'd thought hopeless, Peter was depressed and listless in California. His friends couldn't cheer him up. He'd been spending time in Hollywood with George Cukor, Christopher Isherwood and Max Ernst as well as having his ecstatic physical reunion with Norman, but everything seemed gloomy to him. 'Hollywood is awful and I hate it,' he wrote to Waldemar, in the same letter in which he had delivered the axe-blow. 'It has the kiss of death on it and I wouldn't like to live here.' He was still convinced that another world war was coming – 'Am more and more depressed by the approaching war.'[20]

A week later, Peter wrote to Waldemar again, announcing his imminent arrival in Jamaica. Waldemar was still there – he couldn't resist meeting Peter, and he nervously took heart from the fact that this second letter made no mention of Norman. 'I certainly don't intend to allow myself to seize upon it as a shred of hope,' he wrote to Myers (although that was exactly what he did). Figuring out Peter's feelings was 'worse than trying to analyze Soviet foreign policy ... He leaves so many loose ends because he's a *moral coward*. But what does it serve me to be bitter now?'[21]

From Jamaica, Peter and Waldemar travelled back to New York. At the end of April Peter sailed home. They'd had a kind of reconciliation.

After two months in Jamaica and New York, Peter couldn't make up his mind what to do with the future, and when he left for England, Waldemar went with him.

* * *

The last year of the 1940s brought many changes in Peter's world. Through those middle months of 1949 he vacillated over Waldemar. They resumed their life together in London, but there was no improvement; Waldemar, acting on the advice of Brian Howard (a doubtful source of wisdom), was standing back and letting Peter come to his own decision.

Peter wasn't devoting much time to *Horizon* nowadays, preferring to give his energy to the Institute of Contemporary Arts. It had held its first exhibition in the hall beneath the Academy Cinema in early 1948. Titled '40 Years of Modern Art', it was huge – embracing artists from Bacon and Arp to Tchelitchew and Wood; Craxton, Freud, MacBryde and Colquhoun were exhibited alongside Hepworth, Moore, Gris, Magritte, Matisse, Mondrian, Man Ray, Picasso, Paul Klee, Miró, Giacometti ... the list went on and on. Later that year, it was followed by '40,000 Years of Modern Art', which included many of the same, plus Brancusi, Gaudier Breszka, de Chirico, and more, alongside prehistoric and primitive works.[22]

More ICA exhibitions followed one after another, and brought in tens of thousands of visitors, but little money. But fundraising was going well, and the Arts Council was offering a grant. There had been well-attended poetry readings by T. S. Eliot, Dylan Thomas, Cecil Day Lewis and W. H. Auden. Despite the difficulty of getting pictures for exhibitions (due to the import ban and Douglas Cooper's obstinate refusal to lend anything from his unrivalled collection)[23] Peter and the committee were looking for proper exhibition premises.

It wasn't only Peter who was turning away from *Horizon*. Cyril wasn't putting much effort into the magazine either. His commitment to it had dwindled. Most of the interesting new writing was coming from America now, and the notion of a British literary magazine seemed redundant. Peter disagreed; he found this attitude reprehensible, and, knowing Cyril as he did, he attributed it to laziness and a failure of character. By the end of July, the situation was verging on open hostility. 'A rather terrible showdown with Cyril is about to happen,' Peter wrote.

'Either the magazine will end in November or continue under very different auspices.' Cyril had 'behaved with shattering cynicism and it has upset me so much'.[24] Peter began looking into the possibility of selling *Horizon*, but that would only be viable with an editor in place. So began an intermittent and ultimately hopeless search for a replacement for Cyril.

There was even some friction with one of Peter's dearest protégés. Lucian Freud was suing *TIME* magazine over a May 1947 profile that had singled him out as 'the standout of a not-too-brilliant show of "New Generation" art in London'. The contentious part was *TIME*'s claim that he had used the occasion 'to blast at what was wrong with British painting'; he had allegedly said that everything in Britain was 'so foul and filthy' that artists either went crazy or became Surrealists.[25] In his lawsuit, Lucian claimed that, as he was foreign-born, this profile had damaged his reputation in the art world, making him seem disloyal to his adoptive country. Cyril Connolly – who was a fan and had just bought Lucian's portrait of Anne Dunn – agreed to give evidence in support. However, Peter refused. 'I will *not* get up with such nonsense,' he wrote. 'Nor will I speak for the art world.'[26]

Peter was right – for a man who claimed to be in such bad odour, young Lucian was doing awfully well. By the following year, his shows were selling out, and Peter declared that Lucian had the opportunity to 'become *the* chic portrait painter if he wants'. But critical acclaim, lucrative sales and successful exhibitions couldn't prevent him being so broke that his telephone was cut off.[27] He told Peter he had spent all his income for the next eighteen months; moreover, he was in trouble with the police, having wrecked a car belonging to Viscountess Rothermere (whose portrait he was painting) while driving without a licence.[28]

John Craxton, meanwhile, was spending most of his time in Crete, living off the ceaseless inspiration of the Greek islands. In 1948 he had completed his masterpiece, *Pastoral for P.W.*, which was intended as a homage and gift to Peter (although Peter, who didn't like being in the spotlight, insisted on its title being reduced to just *Pastoral*). It was a vast canvas, more than two metres by two and a half. The size was a sly joke about the minuscule size of Peter's flat, which had 'hardly room to swing a mouse'. It was 'an act of joie de vivre', Craxton recalled later, and 'a gesture against confined space'; 'I bought the largest piece of canvas available and nailed it to the largest wall of my room.'[29] The painting

– which showed a pronounced Cubist influence – depicted Craxton himself as a white-clad piper on a Cretan mountainside, surrounded by spindly trees and demonic goats. The painting was in part a celebration of music, while the goats were originally intended to be 'capricious' symbols of Craxton's friends – a large one on the right of the canvas representing Peter Watson, and one below Lady Norton (the 'art *MAD*' wife of the British ambassador to Greece). Peter approved the painting (he liked its 'dislocated rhythms') and reproduced it, but could never house it, and never owned it.

Meanwhile, for Waldemar, life in that minuscule Palace Gate flat was tense and unhappy. London was even more miserable than it had been a year earlier. Even though rationing had been relaxed (milk and sweets were off the ration now), little else had changed. All Waldemar's friends seemed to be in decline. Peter had fallen out with Douglas Cooper, Sonia was depressed and gaining weight 'as a defense against her raging unhappiness', Cyril Connolly was fatter than ever and spent whole days in bed, Brian Howard was drinking heavily and doing 'the same old Apache dance' with his boyfriend, Sam (an Irishman he'd met in the RAF during the war).

What was more, many in London's literary community were tight-lipped with anger against young Waldemar Hansen – during his last stay he had written a 'London Letter' that had now been published in the Chicago-based *Poetry* magazine; in it he dragged contemporary British literature – and its personalities – through a shredder and dumped the remains in a mud puddle. 'Spender and Day Lewis', the article went, 'and *all* the younger poets are dressing up in the old clothes found in the attic of a hampering and outdated and unrenewed romanticism.' There was no invigorating proletarian art, Waldemar argued, and the poetry of the older generation – especially Edith Sitwell – was just plain bad. Waldemar condemned the mass of the English people as 'law-abiding and unindividualistic, hypocritical, witless and insensitive', and referred the reader to George Orwell for a corresponding English view.[30]

'Everyone is furious with me,' Waldemar wrote to John Myers.[31] One person had said to a friend of Waldemar's, 'He comes and lives here and eats our food, then betrays us.' Not everyone shared this opinion, but enough did to make Waldemar's life uncomfortable. 'I can't tell you how *awful* the ambience is here,' Waldemar wrote. 'Everything is dead or dying, magazines going out of existence left and right, the same awful food, the same ugly, pasty faces, the same overwhelming lack of life.'[32]

Between Waldemar and Peter there was a continuous force that seemed to hold them together and yet keep them at a distance. They'd had a few blow-ups shortly after returning to London, but had settled into a civil yet tense companionship. Peter valued Waldemar as a confidant and friend. Peter was 'crotchety and grouchy, and loathes England, and has nothing but glowing praise for America',[33] yet Waldemar was conscious that this praise was at least partly motivated by the thought of a certain person back in Los Angeles. Waldemar had caught Peter studying airline timetables to California when they were on the ship back to England, and there had briefly been talk of his making a trip out there in August. But that had stopped when they reached London, and Waldemar was fairly sure that Peter hadn't heard from Norman since his return; 'Frankly, I think that will all end gradually.' Brian Howard believed that Peter must settle down, and Waldemar agreed – and, 'when he makes up his mind to do so, he will realize that *I* am the one he must settle down with.'[34] In the meantime, Waldemar thought he might go alone to France for the summer, and leave Peter to his own devices: 'I think it best to let the hawk fly high until he decides to do what he wants to do.'

It didn't take long to discover that the hawk had been flying in skies that Waldemar knew nothing about. On 8 June Waldemar returned to London from a holiday in Edinburgh. Alone in the flat, he found a letter that had been left lying on Peter's bed. It was postmarked in California.

Waldemar looked at the envelope with dismay, 'and after a negligible struggle with my conscience, I read it.'[35] It was from Norman.

Immediately Waldemar understood what had been going on since that time in the Weylin Hotel in New York in January. They had been in communication all along. Peter's apparent indecisiveness, his willingness to keep Waldemar around, was not because of any inability to choose between him and Norman – it was simply that *Norman was uncertain about coming to Europe*. He'd felt bound to his family, so he said, but now he felt ready. He was scraping together the money for a passage to Rio de Janeiro, where he hoped to get a job, and was asking Peter to pay the rest of his fare to Europe.

Now Waldemar understood it all, including why there had been an airline timetable to South American countries on Peter's desk.

Seething, Waldemar could no longer endure Peter's company – they bickered all that day and then, in the course of a blazing row that night, it became obvious to Peter that Waldemar had seen Norman's letter. Waldemar raged at Peter, who – even more maddeningly – 'took it like water off a duck's back'. Waldemar said he didn't intend to stick around – he would go to Paris and then 'spend the summer in some quiet corner of France, writing'.[36]

* * *

And that was what he did. From the moment he departed Palace Gate, Waldemar finally ceased to be Peter's partner in life. They continued – bizarrely – corresponding with each other, and transitioned into a strange, frostily civil friendship, but love was dead, and Waldemar was still in terrible, chronic pain.

Truman Capote was in Paris, about to travel down to Tunisia via Spain, where Cecil Beaton would be joining him later. He met up with Waldemar, and heard the whole story. Fizzing with excitement, Capote wrote to a friend: '[D]o you remember Waldemar Hansen? I saw him in Paris, and he is a wreck: the poor thing has been ousted by Peter Watson, and it is one of the most fabulous stories you've ever heard.'[37] The story, à la Capote, was that 'Peter Watson ran off with someone else, a brickhead from California who had been Waldemar's lover before he met Peter and who W had rejected in favor of Mr Watson! How's that for irony?'[38]

John Myers, who'd received a detailed commentary from Waldemar throughout the relationship (and had talked to Peter himself during the period in New York after they came back from Jamaica) also noted the irony, but he was also conscious of a lot more. He wrote Waldemar a long letter full of indignation on Waldemar's behalf but also laden with *I-told-you-so*. Myers suspected that the erratic, selfish Norman was an exact replacement for Denham – not as a person to love but as a kind of victim to be manipulated. (Myers believed, with remarkable spite and ignorance, that Peter had made Denham the way he was.) Norman was 'a perfect type for P.'s purpose, deliciously half-psychoanalysed, young, stupid, and pretty. La!'[39]

Perhaps there was guilt involved in Myers' uncharitable analysis. Charles Henri Ford, who'd been there at the beginning, believed that Myers, who was keen to see Waldemar get on in his career, had deliberately thrust him in Peter's path. ('John Myers was always trying to push Waldemar in this direction,' Ford wrote tartly, many years later; 'the chief attraction, I understood, being P's large appendage.'[40])

According to Myers, Peter had originally mistaken Waldemar's 'Day to Day Jitter as the real thing, the thing which Denham had to such a gorgeous extent: that overall Here-We-Come-Lucifer-On-the-Damnation-Train.' As for Norman:

> Do you think for one moment that that little bitch hasn't been scheming and planning to land P. ever since the day he met him and got a taste of the High Life at Ruth Ford's party? What queen wouldn't sell her ass and cock and soul for a European fling?? In case you've forgotten (*I* haven't) N. is frightfully mediocre, the most average faggot that ever came down the turnpike but with a certain instinctive shrewdness in getting what he wants. It is the triumph of his life that he is fully revenged for the rejection he got from you.[41]

Waldemar wasn't exempt from blame; Myers believed Peter had been right to take issue with Waldemar becoming so dependent on him running his life. At the same time Myers warned Waldemar to dial down the melodramatic tone of his account of the relationship – he was risking 'making your experience into the mediocre camp of a thousand rejected queens ... you should protect your memory of Peter from yourself.'

He reminded Waldemar that 'Peter was never your dish of sexual tea.' According to Myers, Waldemar had complained of a previous lover that 'he is one of those people who has such a hard time coming'; Waldemar had always preferred a 'quick sexual rapport, and intense sexual imagination'. In fact, Waldemar *had* had those things with Peter – that first time in New York and again in Ireland, and during the first weeks in London. The problem was, as Stephen Spender (who knew and understood Peter Watson better than John Myers did) would later put it: Peter was 'essentially made for honeymoons and not for marriages':

> I mean that the best possible relationship to have with Peter was to be taken up by him very intensely for a few weeks, and then simply to remain on his visiting list for the rest of one's time ... Peter dropped people ... I think that for some people the honeymoon

> is an ideal kind of relationship. All that matters is that it should end with understanding and mutual respect. With Peter's friends, who were more or less his equals, this happened. What was really unfortunate was when ... a friend really fell in love with him or became completely dependent on him.[42]

The example Spender chose to illustrate this was Denham – he might more accurately have picked Cecil Beaton or Waldemar. Denham was different; Denham needed Peter for safety and support, but Peter needed him at an altogether deeper, more inexplicable level, and he would never recover entirely from his death.

According to John Myers: 'Who but a man clutching at straws could ever otherwise have chosen Norman?????? Peter speaks about the "peace" that he experiences with N. What "peace"? ... Even the most normal heterosexuals don't go in for such a "peace" and it's absurd of Peter to pull that out of his shrinking hat.'[43]

The real reason why things had turned out like this had been under Waldemar's nose all along – right there in one of Peter's earliest letters to him, back in the exhilarating days before they met up in Ireland. Peter had said that his 'greatest need is to love rather than to be loved'.[44] He'd said this in reference to Waldemar, but it was quite clear that it applied more accurately to Denham. 'I have plenty of guilt about him,' he wrote in the same letter, 'although it is not justified.' Peter had built a lot of his own sense of self-worth into loving Denham and trying to fix him; this was what triggered Peter's deepest, most instinctive, uncontrollable feelings – someone bad or broken who needed him.

Decades later, Waldemar would come to the conclusion that Peter was, 'on one level, a very involved masochist, and he really wanted to be tormented'.[45] Perhaps this was so, but it failed to account for how deeply unhappy Peter was made by Denham's treatment of him. From a sufficiently cynical and embittered viewpoint, any desire to help a cruel beloved will look like masochism.

Peter had once written to Waldemar: 'I know two facts about life. Everything has to be paid for in some way or other and it is so easy to spoil things and having done so one still has to go on living. And yet love is one of the ways of redemption, perhaps the only way if only it can take over the intensity and powers of one's bad feelings.'[46] Peter needed to guide and help people, but only up to a point. Waldemar had become dependent on him, and Peter was irritated by it, but only because Waldemar didn't *need* to be dependent; he was quite capable of going his own way. They'd had their honeymoon; Peter had given him the advantages he needed to get on in life; now it was time to part.

* * *

They spent that summer in Europe – but separately this time. In July Peter took Sonia to Paris, by which time Waldemar had moved on to Duingt, a little lakeside town in the French Alps.

Peter hoped a spell in Paris would cheer Sonia up. In fact it pushed her towards a critical juncture in her life. In the spring she had become close to George Orwell, who had taken a fancy to her some years earlier; they'd had a brief affair back then and he'd proposed to her, but she'd refused him. Now Orwell was severely ill with tuberculosis; Sonia had visited him, and he'd proposed to her again. She was still in a relationship with Maurice Merleau-Ponty, and she couldn't decide what to do. It had been during a visit to Paris with Peter two years ago that she'd first met Merleau-Ponty, and now, on this visit, she went to see him; there was an acrimonious row, which brought the affair to an end. When Sonia returned to London, she agreed to marry George Orwell.

People gossiped about her; some said it was a 'Florence Nightingale gesture', and some even suspected her of mercenary motives. *Nineteen Eighty-Four* had just been published, and was a huge bestseller; after years of struggling, Orwell was rich. But even those close to her – including Waldemar and Peter – couldn't understand her motives. Peter was shocked and suspected there wasn't much love there, and Waldemar thought that, since she no longer loved Merleau-Ponty, 'any choice she makes would not really matter.'[47] Both Waldemar and Peter were perhaps reading their own situation into Sonia's.

For them, the crucial moment came at the end of July, when, after months of separation, indecision and secret correspondence, Norman Fowler arrived in London.

He was still intending to take a job in Brazil, but had decided to visit Europe en route. It wasn't yet clear how long he would stay – it could be weeks or months. Having topped up Waldemar's bank account with £300 so that he'd be secure when he returned to London,[48] Peter whisked Norman off on a tour of Europe.

This was what he enjoyed doing best – taking a beloved person (friend, lover, *ingénu* protégé) around his favourite places, showing them the sights, the cultural highlights, the architecture, the galleries; he'd done it with Cecil Beaton nearly twenty years ago, and with Igor Markevitch, Stephen Spender, and Waldemar. Now it was the turn of Norman Fowler. There is no evidence to suggest that Norman was particularly appreciative of it; he loved to travel, but tended to be inward-looking, dwelling in the world of his own strange mind. But Peter was delighted by the experience. They went to Rome, Switzerland and Paris, and in late September began wending their way back towards London, where Waldemar, having returned from France a few weeks earlier, had taken up residence in the Palace Gate flat.

Waldemar had tried to cope with the death of his dream in several ways. In Paris he had begun an affair with a 'young painter' – he let slip just once that this boy's name was Phillip, but was otherwise discreet. He'd ended the affair when he realised that he was re-enacting his relationship with Peter, creating a situation in which Waldemar became Peter and Phillip was Waldemar.[49]

He also attempted to work out his feelings by writing a new play – a self-consciously nihilistic drama set in Jamaica called *The Quadroon*, in which the characters would destroy their own inner selves through hypocrisy. For one character – who just happened to be called Norman – the self-destruction would be literal. Later Waldemar sent a draft to Peter, who understandably didn't like it, even allowing for 'all the subjective content which might prejudice me'. He thought the piece 'agonised and distorted – you seem to indulge *all* the characters in more than their fair share of unpleasantness'. The characters were all 'cynical and wordy', and as for 'Norman', he was 'somehow unreal and his suicide is far less convincing than the end of your last play'. Peter also took exception to the philosophy expressed in the play – that 'man is a useless passion' and that 'humanism is a dead end'. Peter 'violently disagreed' with the former, and insisted that humanism 'isn't and can never be' dead. 'What else is valid? Even art without humanism is minor.'[50]

Peter and Norman arrived in London on 2 October. Waldemar had packed his things and moved out of Palace Gate a few days earlier and was staying with friends, artist and writer Toni del Renzio and illustrator Enid Furlonger, who lived together in a platonic, sibling-like relationship. It had been heartbreaking to leave the flat, knowing that Norman would soon be installed in his place.

To Waldemar's surprise, Norman travelled on to Brazil after only a few days in London, still intending to take up his job (working in a book store, apparently). When Waldemar and Peter met up again, after a brief phase of awkwardness, a new friendship blossomed. Waldemar was elated, but not enough to get up false hopes of Peter choosing him over Norman.[51] It was difficult to tell what Peter's feelings were about Norman – he didn't talk about them to anyone – but all their friends who had seen them together were convinced that the relationship was a settled, lasting thing. Peter would shortly be going to Rio to join up with him, while Waldemar would be returning home to New York alone.

Waldemar found comfort in the prospect of going back to America. His view of Europe, and particularly of London, had become morbid, and now he saw Peter as part of it:

> His melancholy is *fatal*, of that I am convinced. In some remarkable way ... just the ambience of being in Europe was a fine thing. But I can't be here any longer ... Europe is old, old, and it makes you feel old. If the world is collapsing, let me at least go back to America where there is still a semblance of youth ... I see death everywhere in this city ... I've been tied to a corpse, and I want to get away.[52]

* * *

In October Sonia married George Orwell in his hospital room; he had dressed smartly but he was so weak he had to remain confined to his bed throughout the ceremony. His health rallied a little during the weeks after the wedding, but it was brief; in January 1950 the tuberculosis won and Sonia became a widow only three months after being a bride.

The day before the wedding, Peter, preoccupied by the cynicism that caused people to read selfish motives into selfless gestures, wrote enigmatically:

> All counted, one can *do* so little for someone – for anyone. Even history compromises and corrupts those who die for others. How on earth did Jesus Christ manage alone to preserve his death as an

> uncorrupt gesture. After all there have been thousands of Christs throughout history and no one makes a religion of *them*.[53]

He might well have been thinking of Sonia; more likely he was thinking of himself, and of the constructions people placed upon his relationships with Denham, Waldemar and Norman. But why he should choose to express it as *dying* for others is a mystery. He seems to have imagined himself a martyr to hopeless love, but until now he had expressed no notion of death being a part of the deal.

At the end of October, Waldemar Hansen left England aboard the *Queen Elizabeth*. His luggage consisted of two suitcases, one box and a typewriter,[54] plus enough heartache and self-pity to fill the ship twice over. Just over a month later, Peter Watson also left England; he travelled down through Spain to Portugal, and at Lisbon he boarded the SS *Alcantara* bound for Rio de Janeiro.

21

THE GARDENS OF THE WEST

1950–1953

On a grey day in the middle of March, Norman Fowler looked out of the window of the Palace Gate flat and saw London under its habitual miasma of coal smoke and damp. He had been in the city just four days, displaced from his natural environment, healthy, tanned by a Brazilian sun and braced by ocean breezes, and he wondered what the world meant by it all.

Puzzled, he sat down and began a rather odd letter to his dear friend Waldemar. 'Dear Mother,' he wrote. '(This attitude will not please you).'

> As Jesu was stripped of his majic when confronted by the *familiar*, so I am.
> And as the *stranger* Jesu appeared, his majic was manifold, so I am not.
> It is strange when we turn upon ourselves and discover a faceless clock (the new turned penny of *your* dream).[1]

How very strange life was. Waldemar had sat on this very spot with his typewriter and chattered out thousands of words to John Myers in New York, detailing his life, his loathing of London, his love for Peter and all their problems. Now Waldemar had gone back over there and Norman was here. 'God how complicated is our tangram,' he wrote; 'we were born under the sign of abstraction.'[2]

At the end of two months in the Americas – Rio, Trinidad, Haiti and beyond – Peter and Norman had stopped off in New York, then sailed for England on the *Queen Mary*.[3] Once Peter had got over his usual reaction to being back in London, he felt fairly positive (by his standards). He settled Norman into the flat and started planning their shared life, in which Norman would pursue his dream of being a sculptor. 'Norman is well,' Peter wrote to Waldemar; 'loves England and is going to start work as soon as he finds the room.'[4]

On that March day, Norman concluded his short, peculiar letter:

Thanks for the telegram
the voyage was without interest
London is mordantly gloomy[5]

Then he added a hasty postscript: 'We are going to look for a place in the country this week, I think it for the best?'

Peter acknowledged that he was looking out for a 'Renaissance manoir' somewhere. 'I long to get away from the buzz and schmuzz and the telephone and should have no difficulty in organising a rest-home for breakdown cases.'[6] It wasn't the first time he'd considered a house in the country, and as usual (with the exception of Thatched Cottage and Tickerage, neither of which had lasted long), the plan was enthusiastically pursued for a while before being abandoned. He still had in mind a Beaton-style place, just as he had imagined back in the early 1930s; he wrote to Brian Howard: 'I am very choosy and want something small but terribly grand and aristocratic. No cottages please – however cunningly converted. When the hydrogen bomb bursts I want to disintegrate in ... dust made up of Renaissance plaster-work, William Kent tables, Picassos, brandy and Alban Berg records.'[7] But although he made an offer on a sixteenth-century farmhouse in Wiltshire,[8] the plan fizzled out. Peter complained that it was 'infernally complicated to find a house', but this seems like the protest of a man who couldn't find the motivation to try very hard.

It wasn't long before he was writing to Waldemar again: 'London is indescribable,' he complained. 'I see few enough people and Norman sees literally no one. I could not feel more demoralised, discouraged and empty of hope.'[9]

The initial buzz of his new life with Norman had survived precisely two months of London. Naturally Peter laid the blame on the city itself, and on England and the state of the world. He appeared not to notice that Norman staying indoors and seeing nobody was Norman's own choice; he had been bored at first, but as the months passed, he withdrew into himself, and claimed to find peace there.[10] Eventually, Peter would begin to find this vaguely disturbing.

* * *

Although the Institute of Contemporary Arts was progressing, Peter had less to occupy his days now; at the end of 1949, *Horizon* had finally come to an end.

In the November issue, Cyril's editorial announced that the next number would be the last. He cited several reasons. The magazine was increasingly expensive to produce and declining constantly in popularity; it was difficult to find really fresh, interesting contributions from British writers, and the most vital content – especially in the field of short fiction – was now coming from America. In 1949 there had been contributions from Truman Capote, George Santayana, Mary McCarthy and James Lord (with whom Peter had a close friendship, Lord being a friend, and later biographer, of Picasso and Giacometti); there had also been pieces by Auden, Simone de Beauvoir, Lawrence Durrell and others, but the growing transatlantic flavour was difficult to miss. 'Many of our considerable literary talents', Cyril wrote, 'have grown unwilling to write except for dollars, or have become psychologically impotent.'[11]

The magazine's political will had gone, too; looking back later, Cyril would describe it as having become 'as powerless as a fly waving and buzzing among its silent comrades on the poisoned paper'.[12] To cap it all, the magazine's staff were being ejected from their pleasant offices in Bedford Square, which had been furnished from Peter's surplus possessions and adorned with his art.

Many critics, Cyril said, felt that *Horizon* had enjoyed its moment and served its purpose when Europe was at war. It had been a cultural rallying point and a repository for energetic, imaginative and opinionated writing. The magazine still sold passably well in America, but its time in

Britain was about done. Cyril left the door ajar, suggesting that *Horizon* might return at the end of 1950, but in truth there was no hope. Cyril recalled later:

> We closed the long windows over Bedford Square, the telephone was taken, the furniture stored, the back numbers went to their cellar, the files rotted in the dust. Only contributions continued inexorably to be delivered, like a suicide's milk, and keep on coming.[13]

Peter had read Cyril's penultimate editorial and been both saddened and angered by it; he called it 'the most dishonest series of reasons for stopping'.[14] He knew all the unspoken causes of the magazine's demise: Cyril no longer wanted to edit it; he saw himself as a writer, not a magazine editor. And yet his writing career wasn't going well, entirely due to the same lassitude and lack of dedication that caused him to neglect *Horizon*. He'd promised his publisher, Hamish Hamilton, a travel book about France, but never got beyond note-taking. Rather than demanding the advance back, Hamilton began withholding royalties on *The Unquiet Grave*.[15] (Some years later, the American publisher Cass Canfield described Cyril Connolly as 'one of the most charmingly devious literary gentlemen not actually behind bars'.)[16]

Cyril's private life blotted out much of the time that might have been used for creative effort. He constantly socialised and womanised, and his relationship with Lys was in its last throes. In 1946 she had changed her name by deed poll to Connolly, which was as close as she could get to a legal marriage to him, but now he was drifting away from her, falling in love with other women (though he still expected her to be loyal to him). The latest was the novelist Barbara Skelton – another brilliant and beautiful woman drawn to the Connolly magnet. They were married in 1950. Peter and Cyril would remain friends, but in most respects Cyril Connolly would continue on his way, charmed and cursed professionally and personally, while Peter Watson went in a direction of his own.

Peter had made some effort to keep *Horizon* going. He'd searched for a replacement editor, and had tried to get Stephen Spender to return (he'd drifted away from running *Horizon* during the war, although he had continued to contribute articles and poems), but nobody wanted to do it. Peter put the magazine up for sale, asking a modest price – just enough to cover the overdraft on its account – and although he had some nibbles from Britain and America, they came to nothing. He claimed that 'after ten years I will be thoroughly glad not to feel the responsibility of it',[17] but there was a lingering bitterness that would re-emerge from time to time when he saw other magazines either fail or succeed. In 1950 Peter watched despondently as Penguin closed down John Lehmann's *New Writing*. At the same time, Hulton's *World Review* and *Cornhill Magazine* were both in crisis.[18] Peter was disgusted by the appearance of a new organ founded by John Davenport; *Circus* was intended as an 'irreverent, unserious' arts magazine ('Join *Circus* and see life on stilts', its advertising said); Peter thought it 'a ghastly 3rd rate *Lilliput*'.[19] It launched on April Fools' Day 1950, and Peter must have experienced some satisfaction when, despite an impressive list of contributors (including Dylan Thomas, Augustus John and several others who had written for *Horizon*), it folded after a few issues, its backer having withdrawn his support after discovering that his magazine was being edited by Communists.[20]

For Peter, the crisis in publishing was yet another sign of civilisation's end times. Culture and politics were in terminal decline. He felt that the Western world was 'hellbent towards another war which as far as I can see will hasten not check the ever increasing neo-barbarism':

> It is monstrous to go chucking atom bombs around but it might quite possibly be true that they are the last hope to preserve civilised values. Unless one pins faith into the lapel of the next world, which I personally don't, we can but shudder at what awaits one 'in the gardens of the West'.[21]

Peter was quoting from Cyril Connolly's last editorial for *Horizon*, in which he had called time on the modern movement, arguing that there could be no improvements in the world and no end to dreadful things: 'It is closing time in the gardens of the West and from now on an artist will be judged only by the resonance of his solitude or the quality of his despair.'[22]

The eternally confusing problem for Peter was that he could not reconcile his humanist sympathies, which were gentle, with his cultural values, which were all about vitality and violent revolutionary energy.

It seemed that a society could not have both. In December 1949, when he was travelling down through Spain en route to meet Norman in Brazil, he had been appalled by the divisions under Franco's regime: 'I never thought the duality of staggering luxury and abject poverty could be so nauseating.' And yet Portugal, he found, was like a 'Catholic Switzerland, prosperous-seeming, picturesque and dead, dead'.[23] Britain itself was an example *par excellence*: 'The truth is that England is the *only* country to have achieved a gradual, reasonable and peaceful revolution and yet life here is stiflingly dull and second-rate.'[24] And Brazil, which was bursting with vitality, had virtually no literary life at all, and their one brilliant architect, Oscar Niemeyer, was a Communist and received no commissions.[25]

In May Peter sent Waldemar a piece cut from the *Spectator*, an article by a Cambridge undergraduate: 'One of the most dangerous, and yet most attractive, characteristics of young British people in the years before the war was their insatiable desire for the overthrow of governments, the success of new movements in art and the eclipse of all that was conventional ... Today this youthful idealism is hard to find.' Young people had accepted 'the uselessness of ideals' and the human race seemed bent on self-destruction; in consequence people were retreating into banality and conservatism. 'This want of pioneering fervour is evident in most of the arts and particularly in modern society', the article went on.[26] It was a state of affairs that would persist for years yet; more than a decade would pass before youth would rediscover its violently subversive bent, and by then Peter Watson would not be around to witness it.

There were other ways in which Peter was hankering after the pre-war days – not least the carelessness of his own youth. During his recent eye-opening train journey through Spain to Lisbon, he had shared his *wagon-lit* with 'two pre-war types' called Bill Finlay and Leslie Eggleton, with whom he drank champagne (a bon voyage gift from the American writer James Lord) and flirted; he met them again in Lisbon 'and had to struggle for my virtue – at my age!'[27] He was forty now, but somehow seemed to feel older.

The post-war world was a tough place for the rich who were old enough to remember the pre-war years. The working class in Britain complained about rationing and were subjected to smog and the lingering presence of bombsites, but life had improved for them – the grinding unemployment of the 1930s was gone, they had a National Health Service, free secondary schooling for their children, rapidly improving housing conditions, and some hope for the future. For the rich who had dined and partied lavishly in St Moritz, Cannes and New York through the Great Depression, and who had built their lives around art and sensual pleasures, the world had shrunk and shrivelled. And for those like Peter Watson who lacked the reactionary tendency to take refuge in conservatism, it seemed to have become a desperate world with a desperate future. Peter was shocked and saddened by poverty, but life hadn't equipped him to empathise with it, nor given him a political doctrine to advocate against it. So he voted Labour and despaired.

* * *

As 1950 passed, Peter's relationship with Norman continued on a steady but strangely uneasy course. There were no quarrels, but apparently not much passion of any kind. Peter settled into the state that seemed to be his natural one: he worried about his beloved.

There were no drugs, no wild behaviour, no boys, no disreputable friends. Indeed, Norman had no friends at all. By July he was refusing to go out or see anyone. 'I tried to press him to do so,' Peter wrote to Waldemar, 'but I soon realised it was no good.'[28] (Had Peter thought about the matter, it might have struck him as significant that Waldemar was still his favoured confidant.) Norman was supposed to be finding himself a studio and getting on with work, but all he did was stay in the flat all day, reading every book he could find on mysticism, and was upset that Peter couldn't take the subject seriously. He'd been kind to Peter when he was ill with an infected foot, and 'most forbearing' with Peter's 'jaundiced irritability', but he never *did* anything. According to Peter, Norman was longing to go and live in the country, but of course Peter had lost his enthusiasm for it. His trustees had agreed to buy a property for him 'almost anywhere', and he thought he might fancy Bermuda.[29] That fancy never came to anything either.

By the end of that summer, Norman had retreated even deeper within himself. Through Peter's contacts, he had been given a sculpture commission, despite having no body of work and no studio. The experimental Group Theatre company was putting on a production of Sartre's *The Flies*, an Existentialist take on Euripides' *Electra*; it would be the first ever production of a Sartre play in English.[30] Francis Bacon was doing the sets, and the Group invited Norman to provide a statue of Zeus.[31] But there is no evidence that a studio was ever found or the commission executed.

Instead, Norman went on researching mysticism, listening to Bach and exploring his relationship with himself. He described his inner life in a letter to Waldemar, summed up in a quotation from Giacomo Leopardi's 'Dialogue Between Torquato Tasso and his Familiar Spirit', in which the poet Tasso says, when asked by the spirit how he feels about his isolation from society:

> I am sure that I felt more boredom at first: but little by little my mind, not being occupied with anything else, and with nothing to distract it, is becoming accustomed to converse with itself far more often and with greater satisfaction than before, and is acquiring a habit and a faculty of discoursing, nay of chattering within itself so that sometimes it seems as though I had as it were a whole company of persons within my head talking together; and every subject, however trivial, that comes into my thoughts, is enough to give rise to a great discussion between me and myself.[32]

Norman was fascinated by Leopardi's dream of solitude and idleness, and was content to emulate it. In September Peter had taken Norman to Paris, but he had returned early to London; he preferred it here. 'London gives me such a feeling of relief, a profound sense of quiet – I think it so close to my concept of death.'[33]

* * *

If Norman ever discussed these thoughts with Peter, no trace of it remains. He probably didn't, since Peter simply assumed that Norman must find London as depressing as he did – he wrote to James Lord in November that Norman was 'very run-down and pale, poor thing, after too long in this city'.[34] Perhaps Peter didn't notice because he had his own preoccupations of the spirit (the doom of civilisation and the impending outbreak of the Third World War) and the demands of culture.

By December 1950, the London Gallery had been shut down, after losing £5,000 over the preceding four years through its gallery and book divisions.[35] Peter had been the only director who went to all the London Gallery's shows, recalled jazz singer George Melly, who worked in the gallery; Peter would walk around the exhibitions muttering 'No tension, no tension' – 'a sweet man, but an utter depressive'.[36] Melly nicknamed him 'Pat Pat' (due to his patting Melly's assistant affectionately on the head). When the gallery closed down, its stock was auctioned off. Melly recalled: 'My task was to remove the works one by one from the stacks and show them to the reluctant punters.' But whereas the other directors (Mesens, Penrose, Zwemmer) bought a few things, 'Pat Pat bid for nothing, contributing only a few despairing groans when one of those inexplicably dreadful pictures which lurk in every gallery's stock was placed before him.'[37]

But while the London Gallery was dying, the ICA was coming into its own. Permanent premises had been secured in May, and on 13 December 1950 the Institute of Contemporary Arts officially opened its doors in Dover Street, Mayfair.

The opening was conducted by the young Earl of Harewood (the king's nephew), whose artistic credentials included editing *Opera* magazine (the following year he became director of the Royal Opera House); Peter thought him 'ever so nice'.[38] The opening exhibition was a mixed one, titled '1950: Aspects of British Art'. All handpicked by Peter, the selection included, *inter alia*, Barbara Hepworth, Patrick Heron, Henry Moore, Richard Hamilton, Eduardo Paolozzi, John Piper, Julian Trevelyan, and Michael Ayrton (presumably Peter had got over his antipathy to this young man in the past eight years).[39] 'And are they dull!' Peter wrote; 'but I have done my best ... It's not that they are dull but I wasn't allowed to choose amongst the more interesting because we've had them before.'[40]

It was also still impossible to borrow paintings from Douglas Cooper; Peter had fallen out with him once and for all earlier that year, after Cooper wrote a review in which he called the directors of the ICA (in Peter's words) 'irresponsible dilettantes' and declared it a crime that public money was given to them by the Arts Council. After that, Peter felt it was 'impossible for me to see him'.[41]

Nonetheless, by the following year Peter was able to report that the ICA was 'thriving, in spite of a hopeless budget'.[42] Things were looking up; there had been personal breakthrough too – Norman had at last been levered out of the flat and out of London, and indeed out of England. He was still searching for solitude, but at least he was getting out of the city of doom, and Peter couldn't have been more pleased.

He couldn't have foreseen that the trip would ultimately lead to notoriety, acute embarrassment, and attention from MI5.

* * *

John Craxton was inadvertently the cause of Norman's precipitate departure. After several years in Greece, Craxton had returned to London in 1950, where he was working with Frederick Ashton on a ballet for the Royal Opera House. (This was the beginning of a friendship between Craxton and Ashton and a short-lived romance with ballerina Margot Fonteyn.)[43]

Peter introduced him to Norman and, remarkably, Craxton liked him immensely. Norman could be very winning – despite his introversion, he had a warm side to him, expressed through a huge, handsome, reassuring smile. Johnnie happened to mention that Greece was 'the best place to be', and shortly afterwards Norman packed up and took a ship for Athens. Johnnie wrote ahead to Lady Norton that 'a young American sculptor' called Norman Fowler, who was 'a very good friend of mine and of Peter Watson', would be arriving soon; he was 'the nicest and the best company'. He hoped Norman would visit Lady Norton, and promised that if he did, she would find that he had in him 'more than you can imagine an American has'.[44] It did slightly puzzle him that Norman had talked of living in a monastery, which wasn't quite what John Craxton regarded as the best use of one's time in Greece.

Norman apparently enjoyed himself, but it didn't all go well. At some point, he spent a while at a small hotel in Nice, living a monk-like life. Francis Bacon, who was staying nearby in the Hotel Victoria, had been losing heavily at the tables in Monte Carlo and desperately needed money. One of his companions pointed out that Norman 'lived on baked beans but was stinking rich'. Some unnamed person suggested 'a little burglary' while Norman was out. Bacon himself shinned up the drainpipe ('he had tremendous strength and vitality'), infiltrated Norman's room and got away with £300 in cash. Bacon went straight to the casino, where he gambled while his friends drank champagne.[45] (If Peter ever learned of this theft, he either never discovered that Francis Bacon was the culprit or didn't hold it against him for long.)

Soon after Norman had left England, Peter decided to follow him. Conditions in London were inhuman; winter was clinging on, with freezing rain and snow in late March, and coal supplies had run out. 'Everyone is bankrupt here,' Peter wrote to James Lord, who was in Capri, 'which doesn't add to the joy of life – and at last they see what the future is likely to bring – damn-all. However I guess I'll feel gayer when I come south.'[46]

In the meantime, he had to deal with the still-twitching remains of the dead *Horizon*, in the form of stacks of unsold books. A lot of titles had been put out under the Horizon imprint through publisher Chatto & Windus, including translations of Sartre's critique *Baudelaire* and Gide's novel *Theseus*; then there were *Tea With Mr Goodman* by Philip Toynbee, *1 x 1* by E. E. Cummings, and the first edition of Cyril Connolly's *The Unquiet Grave*, along with books on the art of John Craxton, André Masson, and an expensive 'continental style' (soft-backed) edition of Goya priced at two guineas. Peter was dragged into depressing negotiations with Chatto over what to do with the remaining copies, which the publisher was keen to get rid of.[47] Over the next two years, some would be sold off through Zwemmer, the art bookshop in Charing Cross Road, but hundreds of copies of Cummings and the Craxton book ended up pulped.

By late May, Peter was keener than ever to get away from it all and head south for the Mediterranean. He caught up with Norman, who was roaming around Greece, and they set off together for Italy, where Peter had arranged to visit Wystan Auden, who had a villa in the coastal village of Forio on the tiny volcanic island of Ischia in the Gulf of Naples. Auden lived there with his life partner and collaborator, the American poet and librettist Chester Kallman; the two had recently been working together on a libretto for Stravinsky's *The Rake's Progress*, which was due to be premiered in Venice in September. When Peter and Norman arrived at Forio d'Ischia at the beginning of June, Auden himself had only just arrived, having been staying in London with Stephen Spender. None of them had the faintest idea that their holiday arrangements were about to land them in the middle of one of the most infamous espionage dramas of the century. Some investigators believed that Auden knew ahead of time what was about to happen, but he denied it.

Exactly a week before Peter and Norman's arrival, on 25 May 1951, two Foreign Office diplomatic officials had disappeared from their homes in England. One was Donald Duart Maclean, a high-flyer who was head of the FO's American Department in Whitehall; the other was Guy Francis de Moncy Burgess, a dissolute Old Etonian who was second secretary at the British Embassy in Washington, who had returned to London for a visit earlier that month. Both men left the country and vanished simultaneously, and the inference was that they had gone off (or been taken) together. At first the investigation was low-key. Special Branch believed initially that they might have gone on holiday, but the Security Service, MI5, had graver suspicions.

Both Maclean and Burgess had been under observation by MI5 for some time. Burgess was not under direct suspicion, but he mingled with people who were deeply suspect – such as Baroness Moura Budberg, the celebrated Russian *saloniste*, spy and double agent – and he had a reputation for heavy drinking, indiscretion and homosexuality, but until his disappearance he was not believed to be a spy himself.[48] Donald Maclean, however, *was* under suspicion. The atmosphere within the intelligence and diplomatic communities at the time was bordering on paranoia, compounded by incompetence, double-dealing and the hampering effect of school-tie loyalties. Many innocents were investigated, and several traitors (such as Burgess) were overlooked. Donald Maclean was one of those who were suspected – rightly, in his case – of being Soviet spies. He was under surveillance by MI5, and his KGB masters believed that if he were interrogated he would crack and give away the identities of his fellow agents. They instructed him to flee the country. To be on the safe side, they ordered him to bring Burgess too.

On 25 May, just three days before MI5 were intending to bring Maclean in for interrogation, the two men set off. Taking Burgess's car, they travelled down to Southampton and took a ferry to Saint-Malo. At that point they vanished without trace.

Both Special Branch and MI5 worked frantically and fruitlessly to pick up their trail. Although the public were not informed yet, rumours ran around London society among those who had known the two men. Moura Budberg kept her MI5 investigator (who also happened to be a personal friend) informed of the gossip – some said Burgess and Maclean had been kidnapped, some that they were spies, and some suggested that they were homosexual lovers and had gone for a secret holiday aboard a yacht in the Mediterranean.[49] This last idea seemed to tally – at least in part – with information picked up from interviews with

Burgess's other acquaintances and friends, including W. H. Auden and Stephen Spender, both of whom had been known Communists and on MI5's files for many years. Cyril Connolly, who wasn't a Communist, was also being watched by MI5, and happened to be a friend of Donald Maclean.[50] A tap was placed on Cyril's telephone,[51] and several people were interviewed.

Interrogation of Spender revealed that on 24 May, the day before the disappearance, Guy Burgess had telephoned Spender's house in St John's Wood, asking for Auden (who was staying with him). Auden was out, and Spender took a message. There was confusion about what the message was, but it was believed that Burgess had asked if he could come and stay with Auden at his villa. (Further information indicated that Auden and Burgess had met in New York in March and talked about such a visit.) Almost immediately after this phone call, Auden had departed for Forio d'Ischia, where he arrived on 28 May, while Stephen and Natasha Spender set off for their Italian holiday home on Lake Garda.

MI5 expected Burgess and Maclean to show up in Forio at any moment. Armed Italian police were posted on the island's landing stage, provided with photos of the missing men. And then it was discovered that two men had *already* arrived and were staying at the villa; they had come on 1 June, and one of them appeared to match the description of Burgess – dark, slightly built, elegant and English. Upon investigation the man gave his name as Peter Watson, and his companion was an American called Norman Fowler; both gave the same address: 10 Palace Gate, London.

Auden was interviewed by Italian police and by an MI5 operative; he initially claimed that he'd never received Burgess's message, but upon being interrogated again he admitted that he 'probably' had received it.[52] It was the MI5 agent's opinion that Auden was drinking heavily and had deliberately lied in his first interview. Meanwhile, because of the missing diplomats' American connections, the FBI were taking an interest and asking for details,[53] and questions were even being asked in the US Senate.[54] The American connection grew even more intriguing when a second young American – one William Weaver – arrived on 7 June.[55] He was a translator of Italian literature and a friend of both Auden and Spender.

On the same day, the story of the 'missing diplomatists' exploded in the British press, which until now had held back. The Foreign Office issued a statement, and the *Daily Express* was the first to break the story – they had sent a correspondent to Ischia, and he reported that close watch was being kept on everyone at Auden's villa. He secured an interview with the man himself, who gave his opinion that Burgess and Maclean had known about Britain's nuclear secrets and must have been kidnapped in France (when interviewed by MI5 again, he denied that he'd said this to the reporter).[56]

Both Peter and Norman – as well as Weaver – were kept under intense scrutiny by police and MI5 during their stay, which lasted until 9 June.

It must have transpired in his interviews that Peter had known Guy Burgess, although he'd never been a close friend; they had lunched together at the Reform Club,[57] and had shared pick-up boyfriends during the war; one young man later described how Peter drew him in with gifts and attention, outfitting him at his extremely fashionable and smart tailors, Lesley & Roberts at 16 St George Street, Hanover Square; through Peter the young man met Guy Burgess at a nightclub (Burgess indiscreetly told the young man that he was in intelligence and could get him a job).[58] In addition, both Burgess and Maclean had visited Peter's Palace Gate flat.[59]

An urgent message was sent from the MI5 agent in Italy to his headquarters: 'Please can you identify for me a certain Peter WATSON who is apparently well known in literary circles and a friend of AUDEN.'[60] The files were searched, and 'PF. 147,223' was written above Peter's name on the agent's message – this was the reference number of an MI5 personal surveillance file. Peter Watson, apparently, was already under scrutiny, and had been for some time – probably more than a decade.[61]

The fact that he was close to Stephen Spender, René Crevel and several other Communists (despite having no sympathy with Communism himself) might have been enough; at the time when Stephen and Inez Spender stayed at the rue du Bac apartment in 1938, Stephen was under investigation and suspected of being under Comintern influence.[62] Peter's visits to Nazi Germany and his two arrests there might also have been a factor. The question is impossible to answer because the relevant facts – the date when the file began, together with the reason why Peter Watson was deemed to be of interest, and what information was gathered – were later lost when the file was destroyed by MI5.[63] The only surviving traces of its existence would be the cross-references in other people's files.

When Peter and Norman went back to London, MI5 continued to keep an eye on them, as well as on Burgess and Maclean's other friends and acquaintances. Cyril's phone continued to be monitored, and Stephen Spender's mail was intercepted. The hunt for the missing diplomats would go on for months to come, and the suspicions would linger for years.

In fact, while MI5 and Europe's police forces scoured the Continent in June 1951, Burgess and Maclean were already being debriefed in Moscow, having travelled across Europe from Saint-Malo on false passports provided by the KGB. The story would run in the British media for several years. Speculation was boosted again in 1953 when Maclean's wife disappeared; then in 1954 the suspicions of a Russian connection were confirmed when Vladimir Petrov, a diplomat at the Soviet Embassy in Australia, defected; he told the press that Burgess and Maclean had been 'long-term Soviet agents', and in 1955 the Foreign Office finally confirmed this rumour.[64]

After this episode a faint odour of espionage would linger in the vicinity of Peter Watson for the rest of his life and beyond; the questions of why MI5 had first taken an interest and why they later destroyed the file would remain unanswered.

* * *

Norman's travels in the Mediterranean that year had another consequence; he still hankered after a solitary life of contemplation, but he had also rediscovered a liking for the sea. As a Navy fireman and machinist, he had never been a particularly nautical sort of sailor, but he had spent a couple of years at sea and must have got salt water in his veins. He conceived the idea of combining the two pursuits – by sailing the world alone in his own small boat.

In fact it wasn't quite so small. Peter, who would do anything, spend any amount, to satisfy the whims of a beloved, financed the purchase and fitting out of a yacht – a forty-one-foot twelve-tonner, cutter-rigged, called the *Catania*.[65] She was bought and laid up on the hard at Mashfords boat yard at Torpoint in Cornwall from late 1951 until May 1952, being fitted out for a voyage across the Atlantic; Norman's intention was to sail single-handed to the Caribbean, through the Panama Canal and on to California.

Peter had no intention of going with him – 'I of course wouldn't go to sea, as I hate the movement,' he wrote to Waldemar,[66] who had been asking whether Norman was happy in his new life. Peter replied:

> Heaven knows, are you? Am I? Happiness doesn't seem very real any more. It is very difficult to be happy unless you have a place in life and it isn't going to be easy to find out what his is. This is the reason he hankers after isolation, monasteries etc. which gives you a ready-made situation and takes away the need to create one oneself. Like all romantically spiritual people he is basically afraid of people and life and mentally rather selfish, but so are artists, and it is a form of self-protection in the young. He is anyway unlikely to ever develop into a worldly person who copes easily with life.[67]

Yearning to find his place in life and excited by the thought that he was about to find it, Norman lived at Torpoint, overseeing the work on *Catania*. 'The people are not beautiful', he wrote, 'in any sense of that word', but *Catania* was 'something to fall hopelessly in love with'.[68] His strange, quixotic behaviour made a strong impression on the unbeautiful people at Mashfords boat yard. They included the celebrated yachtswoman Ann Davison, who was having a boat fitted out for her own transatlantic crossing (she hoped to become the first woman to cross single-handed), which was scheduled for May 1952. She found the young American astonishing and fascinating:

> Norman was highly strung, temperamental, spontaneous and unpredictable. He would be executing a ballet dance in the sheds one minute, with giant leaps and entrechats – to the utter stupefaction of the yard hands – and talking sombrely of retiring to a monastery the next. He would discuss any subject that occurred with an impatient fluency and utter disregard of interruption that completely threw the stolid British reserve with which he was surrounded. The stolid British reserve took him very seriously and was frightened silly both by him and for him.[69]

They had good reason to be frightened for him. Despite his service in the US Navy, of course he knew little about sailing boats. (Neither did Ann; together they presented 'a united front of ignorance'[70] to the experts around them.) Therefore, when it came time for him to set out on his voyage, he was joined by an experienced yachtsman, Edward Allcard, a thirty-five-year-old Englishman who had sailed the Atlantic single-handed twice in 1949 and 1951 and was looking for passage to the States. Slight, bearded and bespectacled, Allcard was another Old Etonian and altogether unlike his American companion.

They set off in May 1952, 'to the usual accompaniment of press, cameras, and cheers'; Norman called out to Ann: 'Hurry up, and we'll celebrate in Madeira.'[71]

It was not a happy voyage. Relations between Norman and Allcard were strained, and by the time they reached the West Indies (having stopped off at Brest and Madeira), they had reached breaking point. Allcard disliked Norman with a passion that grew with every degree westward; despite having little experience, Norman was a know-all and would denigrate Allcard's seamanship – for instance, by suggesting that their skipper/assistant relationship resulted not from Allcard's superior knowledge but from a fear of performing physical tasks himself. 'His most infuriating habit', Allcard would recall, '(which made me want to hit him) was to criticise every job I did or comment I made. He was a jeerer.'[72] Allcard set *Catania* up with an automatic steering system, and thereafter kept as far apart from Norman as was possible on a forty-one-foot yacht.

Ann Davison, who embarked on her voyage shortly after Norman, reached St Thomas in the US Virgin Islands in January 1953 (thus succeeding in her record attempt despite her inexperience), where she caught up with Norman: 'He came to meet me at the dock and started talking as soon as he was within shouting distance. He'd had a *wonderful* trip across to Bermuda.'[73] He'd been abandoned by the exasperated Allcard, who had gone on to New York; instead Norman had taken on a Bermudan boy to help handle the yacht.

This was what Norman had wanted all along; he was, in effect, alone at last on the sea, with the journey to Panama and California (or back to England, or to Africa – he just couldn't decide) still ahead of him. Before leaving England, he had written a last letter to Waldemar, in which he tried (in his own semi-coherent manner) to capture his feelings about the world and his life. At the time, things with Peter were 'not a little mad',[74] and it was as if Norman was viewing the voyage ahead as a passage from one life to another.

> I know 'a little bit about a lot of things' as concerns the human spirit. It has taken more than the three years that I've been here but it has helped, Soho clubs, movies, fog, English apathy, a stupid dogged passion for early musics, a million cigarettes and seemingly as many books. All about bridges and the water that flows under them.[75]

He had been looking forward to 'the monastic and the open sea' and the spiritual enlightenment they would bring; he quoted from Hilaire Belloc's *The Cruise of the Nona*: 'All that which concerns the sea is profound and final. The sea provides visions, darknesses, revelations ... It is the common sacrament of this world.'[76] ('But is there a choice Mr Belloc?' he added.) Dream visions had come to Norman in the days when the *Catania* was in the boat yard – violent ones. 'Dreams are like death,' he wrote, and he described in detail a horrifically violent dream in which he battled with a figure representing himself on the edge of the sea: 'The sea the sky me and me all blood.'[77]

All the rest of his life Norman would look for solace and peace, but it would always remain out of his grasp – perhaps because there was no peace within his turbulent mind.

22

DANGEROUS PURSUITS

1953–1956

In 1953, Alberto Giacometti began work on his portrait of Peter Watson. The painting was done in his studio in the narrow, crowded rue Hippolyte-Maindron in Montparnasse. Each day Peter dressed in his habitual suit – always exquisitely tailor-cut by either Lesley & Roberts in George Street, Hanover Square, or in Savile Row – and took a taxi to Giacometti's studio, where he sat with the natural light from the studio window full on him. The portrait was apparently done by request of the artist rather than on a commission from Peter. They had known each other for years; Peter had owned Giacometti's works, and had commissioned décor from his brother Diego – the sculpted lamp standards in the rue du Bac apartment, and a chandelier that had once hung in the *Horizon* office (rediscovered many years later by John Craxton in an antiques shop).

Giacometti had picked his subject well, and of the several portraits made of Peter Watson in this period of his life, his was perhaps the most telling. Lucian Freud's 1945 charcoal-and-chalk drawing captured his melancholy beauty. Cecil Beaton had photographed Peter around 1950 – an unusually simple, formal headshot with the same spirit of beauty as Freud's drawing. Time and care had chiselled Peter's boyish features into sharp lines and had pouched his eyes, which gazed into Cecil's lens with a penetrating, hypnotic drowsiness. But it was Giacometti who saw past the sculpted lines of the face and into the spirit within. His Peter Watson – elongated, sitting stiffly upright, blank-eyed – was a man paralysed and hollowed out by life. A man washed up and left stranded by love, human nature and the state of civilisation.

He was a man still capable of pleasure – Cecil's photograph caught a whisper of a smile in the eyes – but he was a man dominated by a sadness that sometimes edged close to despair.

* * *

After sailing away in spring 1952, Norman spent much of his time travelling the oceans, although from time to time the currents (probably the currents of financial necessity) carried him back to London. Peter missed him painfully when he was away,[1] but as time went on he grew accustomed to Norman's absences, yet worried intensely about his state of mind and his future.

Peter was kept occupied by the ICA, which was doing well, with a constant run of exhibitions and events. By 1954 Peter would be reporting that it had 'settled down into an English institution',[2] but even as early as 1952 it was clear that it would be a success; it had evolved from the original conception that it would be a London equivalent of New York's Museum of Modern Art – it would be livelier and more diverse than that.

During those early years of the 1950s Peter's life evolved too. He was becoming less and less like the rich, indulged young man of the 1930s. His life had lost most of its opulence, and he no longer seemed to care. He had voted Labour in the 1945 general election, and when the next election came around in October 1951 he had mixed feelings. 'What to vote?' he wrote. 'I really can't know. I know I am not a Conservative.' His only political concerns were Fascism, which was dead now, and Communism, which was still a threat that had to be defeated. The only recourse was the Labour Party. 'However it also means I vote myself into liquidation with the sort of taxes and levies they propose, yet what does that really matter.'[3] Perhaps Robert MacBryde had been close to the mark in 1940 when he surmised that Peter was a natural left-winger who secretly desired to get rid of his wealth.

But Labour voters seemed to be thin on the ground these days. Peter's long-serving charlady, Mrs Mitchell, had declared her intention to vote Tory, as had the building's porters.[4] Riding along on this kind of popular vote, Winston Churchill was returned to power and Peter remained politically unhappy but safe from liquidation for the time being.

He was still irked by the limit on taking currency abroad. During 1952 the allowance was reduced from £100 to £25;[5] this was insupportable and the £100 limit had to be restored. These restrictions would remain in place until 1959, but nonetheless Peter continued to travel as much as he could – mostly in Europe. During the 1950s he ranged farther afield than before, taking in Scandinavia and Denmark. This was possibly a financial consideration; in 1950 Scandinavia had joined the sterling area – the group of nations that pegged their currencies to the pound; free exchange was allowed within the sterling area and there were no personal travel limits. Many rich Britons had considered buying flats in Stockholm and Oslo.[6]

There may have been another, much more subtle, reason for Peter's altered travel habits in this period. The intelligence services in Britain and the United States were becoming interested in culture as a weapon for the campaign against Communism, and cultural figures who had the right kind of anti-Communist leanings were being subtly recruited.

In 1953, Stephen Spender, who had once been a member of the British Communist Party, founded the British-based Anglo-American literary magazine *Encounter* with American writer Irving Kristol. In some ways *Encounter* was similar to *Horizon*, with many of the same contributors, but it had a much simpler, anti-Communist political agenda and a secret backer – the CIA. Spender had lost his sympathy for Communism during the war, and was now firmly opposed to it. He had become involved with the anti-Communist Congress for Cultural Freedom, and *Encounter* was, in effect, the organisation's house magazine.[7] People working for it were vetted by the CIA and MI6, using information provided by MI5.

By 1955, MI5 had reluctantly accepted that Stephen Spender was 'no longer a communist' and yet he remained 'active in the field of civil and cultural liberties', which meant he continued to be of interest to the Security Service,[8] but also useful to the Secret Intelligence Service and the CIA.[9] (There seems to have been a strange conflict of interests here – 'cultural freedom' was held to be one of the cornerstones of Western democracy in CIA and MI6 propaganda activities, but individuals who campaigned for it were regarded by MI5 as potential subversives. If they were conscious of this irony, they did not comment on it.)

Peter Watson had never had any sympathy with Communism, and now regarded it as a menace to civilisation. He attended at least one Congress for Cultural Freedom conference, and thought *Encounter* 'quite good' (he was always a one for faint praise), but regretted that there was a 'very strong English hostility' against its ethos. 'Many people here hate *active* anti-communism,' he wrote.[10] He ranked cultural and personal freedoms above almost all else, and his pattern of travel – subtly altering during the 1950s towards the nations bordering the Soviet bloc – and the contacts he had with the rich and influential through art dealing and arranging exhibitions for the ICA would have made him attractive to those elements in MI6 and the CIA that were encouraging projects like *Encounter*. But if Peter Watson was being used as a source of intelligence, it is now impossible to be sure – any traces would have been destroyed along with the other contents of his MI5 dossier.

He had other concerns about the security of Western freedom. By 1952 Peter was losing his certainty that there would be another war, but was alarmed in 1952 when West Germany was allowed to rearm and become part of the European Defence Community. 'It's like 1932 again,' he wrote.[11]

The only hope was art – and Peter was no longer sure that it could be a force for good. In response to an outburst of idealism from Waldemar, Peter wrote: 'Ethics unfortunately have very little to do with artistic production and achievement. I don't consider Picasso ethically luminous, being a communist with 4 houses in France, riding around in a white Cadillac, giving out inches of nonsense at 3000 dollars a time – but I still consider him the genius of painting.'[12]

Peter had a tendency nowadays to stick with the geniuses he knew. After 1945 he had got over his disgust with Salvador and Gala Dalí and made friends again – Salvador had given him an inscribed copy of his autobiography in 1946 and in 1950 executed a painting especially for him – *Plage Erotique* ('Erotic Beach'), a minuscule oil-on-panel picture just 17 by 15 centimetres but meticulously detailed; it was similar in concept to the lost *Perspectives* of 1936 – a surreal landscape of green fields and sea populated by eerie, grotesque figures brandishing ominously huge erections.

The geniuses of the past were repeating themselves, and there was too little new genius in the world nowadays – or so it seemed to the forty-five-year-old Peter. 'The young here are interested in either the neo-constructivists or the new form of academic art-school realism, both of which bore me excessively.'[13] In a letter to Nicolas Calas, who seemed bemused by Francis Bacon, Peter wrote: 'Yes, I do think Bacon an interesting painter. If you lived here, you would see he is one of the only people – there are not more than two or three in any case. His hallucinations are expressed by a real painter – perhaps a kind of contemporary Fuseli.'[14] As for contemporary American art, he disliked it entirely – 'I can't take American painting seriously ... and I am not going to pretend. In fact I am sick of pretending so much as it is.'[15]

The despair Peter had felt when Epstein's 'dowdy' watercolours proved so popular in 1942 came back to him with the ICA's constant inability to sell much work. (Although the Institute was thriving, it was doing so largely on public money.) In 1955 Peter complained to Pavel Tchelitchew that, although there was 'an immense picture buying boom in London', it 'never touches us, or anything we show'.[16] A few months later, he was dismayed when an exhibition of Leonardo Cremonini at the Hanover Gallery (for which Stephen Spender wrote the catalogue) sold half the paintings on offer. Peter appreciated Cremonini's talent, but 'his impersonal sculptural vision of human beings is too close to a certain attitude in England [of] Henry Moore, Robert Colquhoun and others which I have resisted for some time.'[17]

It ultimately came down to humanity for Peter Watson – to love, personal devotion and sacrifice, and finding one's place in the world. It tormented him to think of the people he loved – particularly Norman, who spent most of his time at sea or on remote island retreats – being unable to find their place and the peace of mind they needed. He wrote to Waldemar in summer 1955:

> Norman is on a rock in the sea where there are no whites. He must go mad if he insists on this withdrawal. There can be no satisfaction in living for oneself. Maybe he'll work it out but in the meantime he will go through terrible suffering. "We need one another" as Lawrence said. But one can tell people nothing, they must find [out] on their own.[18]

In spite of this piece of wisdom, Peter never seemed able to remove the suffering from his own life – he needed to love more than be loved, but it seemed to make him unhappy. In 1952 Cecil Beaton had described to Peter how 'neurotic and difficult' Greta Garbo had become. 'What did he expect?' Peter wrote. 'How could that work out? The emotions have so little to do with what is suitable.'[19] This was true – in Peter's case as much as in Cecil's.

In both cases, the emotions involved seem in retrospect to have been on a course towards terrible conflict.

* * *

Norman returned to England from the Caribbean in March 1954, arriving by ship from Grenada.[20] Apparently he was daunted by crossing the Atlantic without a skilled companion, and seems to have left *Catania* in the Americas somewhere. He stayed quietly in London for four months, but then the questing spirit took him again, and in July he set off on a ship bound for Los Angeles;[21] a year later he was living in isolation on his 'rock in the sea'.

During Norman's absences, Peter didn't succumb to loneliness. He sought consolation and titillation in the same way he had done – almost without interruption – for more than a quarter of a century. From the cabarets and hot, stifling 'queer places' of Berlin and Munich in the early 1930s, where the young men sported their toned torsos in unbuttoned shirts, to the *boîtes* of Paris and the nightclubs of wartime London, Peter had been an avid seeker of quick and dangerous thrills. He'd always had a fetish for good-looking young sailors – which had perhaps influenced his attraction to Norman Fowler – and also for beautiful but rough and uncultured young men; again, this applied to Norman and also to Denham Fouts, but not to the unfortunate Waldemar.

In gloomy London in the 1950s, there were several places where well-off men could cruise for gritty action with their working-class counterparts. One was the public lavatory at Piccadilly Circus underground station; a much more popular (and salubrious) one was Bermondsey swimming baths, where East End boys could be picked up. The comedian Kenneth Williams went to Bermondsey baths in the late 1950s and thought it 'quite fabulous', and the novelist Rodney Garland featured it in his 1953 crime thriller *The Heart in Exile* – a landmark of gay fiction.[22]

Yet another venue was the down-at-heel Victorian Turkish baths in Harrow Road – a modern-day bagnio of distinctly ill repute. The baths were popular with gay men partly because they were open twenty-four hours a day, and much of the sexual activity took place in the night watches. They could be risky places to go; complaints had been made to the London County Council, and various undercover investigations had been carried out, but the trade went on – it was unstoppable.[23]

Peter Watson went to all these venues. Aside from the risk of being caught in a clean-up operation, there were other dangers: many of the men who scored pick-ups in these places ended up suffering for it, robbed or burgled or worse by the men they took home, and unable to do anything about it for fear of the police.[24] Peter was no exception. The American writer Stuart Preston, who knew him during the war (when Preston was in London as part of Eisenhower's intelligence staff), wrote that Peter 'liked to find rough boys in bars who stole his gold cigarette case. Well he was lucky. He found them.'[25] His addiction to dangerous thrills contributed to Peter's reputation for masochism.

Sometimes a pick-up could lead to a relationship. It had with Denham in Berlin in 1933, and it did again in early 1952 – this time more casually and with none of the heartache.

Norman was away in Cornwall when it began, overseeing the work on *Catania* and impressing the locals with his repertoire of eccentric tics. One day in January, Peter went with his old school friend Alan Pryce-Jones to the Harrow Road Turkish baths. They had apparently seen little of each other since their time at Eton thirty years earlier, but the gay cruising scene brought them back together. On this particular visit, Peter took home a young man called Alex.

'Good-looking and thick' (his own description), Alex Leslie was in his early twenties, a male nurse from Plymouth who was working in a London hospital.[26] He went with Peter from Harrow Road to Palace Gate – dropping Pryce-Jones at his flat in the Albany building in Piccadilly on the way. They travelled in Peter's car. He had given up his carless state, but had no intention of reverting to his pre-war splendour; he now drove a decidedly modest Riley saloon – a touch more stylish and expensive than a Rover, perhaps (and more old-fashioned, with flared front wings and narrow bonnet), but otherwise a solid middle-class motor. From the garage beneath 10 Palace Gate, Peter took Alex up in the lift to flat 22, and into a life of luxury that would last several bewildering years.

The flat made a lasting impression on Alex. The furniture was mostly antique now, with few modern pieces – apparently a reversion to the style in which Peter had furnished his mother's house in South Street and his own in Shepherd's Close (sofa table, breakfront bookcase and large desk, sabre-leg dining chairs, marble-topped Regency side cabinet). Besides the paintings, Peter had a Barbara Hepworth sculpture on a stand and a small Henry Moore bronze of three figures on the windowsill. One wall was entirely filled with books and the well-thumbed runs of *Cahiers d'Art*, *Minotaure Horizon* and all the rest.

Alex found himself in a peculiar relationship. Like Waldemar before him, he thought Peter's sexual personality odd – the fact that he could be satisfied by an evening spent sitting and holding hands was extraordinary; for a man so keen on cruising, most of the time he was sexually almost inert. They slept together – Peter's night attire consisting of a bed jacket and drawstring trousers – but it wasn't a tumultuous affair.

Other contemporaries noticed that Peter's sexual persona was quirky, and like his social manner it could change with his environment. The artist Richard Hamilton, who worked at the ICA in its early days and was exhibited there several times, recalled how Peter's usually elegant, subdued and formal manner could switch in an instant to audacious camp. One day he and Hamilton were hanging an exhibition at the ICA when Philip Johnson, the famously gay American architect, made an appearance; Peter transformed instantly into a flamboyant queen, mincing across the room, kissing Johnson and talking in an affectedly camp manner that was quite unlike his usual speech. The moment Johnson left, Peter reverted to his usual persona and the hanging continued.[27]

The greater part of Peter's erotic drive seems to have been visual – perhaps related at some level to his passion for art. He was drawn to good-looking men and could fall in love, but there was rarely much of a physical need in him. He liked to look at pictures, and had magazines sent over from the United States. In the 1950s America was a rich source of soft-core magazines thinly disguised as 'physique' publications, such as *Vim*, *Adonis* and *Grecian Guild Pictorial*, all featuring photos of beautiful, muscular, oiled young men – ostensibly intended as 'art' or 'fitness' studies but mainly of interest to gay men. Gay lifestyle magazines were available from America as well – like *One* ('The Homosexual Magazine'), which ran articles ranging from studies of homosexual psychology to fun, Cocteauesque ruminations on the appeal of sailors. Besides the magazines, Peter also had a collection of explicit pornographic photos locked away in the filing cabinet in his bedroom where he also kept his cash.

Alex was channelled – again like Waldemar and apparently without thought – into a kind of public-school fagging role; he cooked in the tiny kitchen on the same electric stove that had irritated Waldemar, and was expected to make Peter's coffee. Entirely *unlike* Waldemar, Alex was not taken out and was never introduced to Peter's friends. If any of them visited the flat while he was there, Alex would be hastily shepherded into the bedroom.

During 1953, while London was preparing itself for the coronation of the new Queen Elizabeth, Peter had an awkward reminder of how picking up young men could go wrong – and not necessarily for the man doing the picking up.

Over Easter in 1953, Stephen Spender's former boyfriend, Tony Hyndman – lover of Michael Redgrave, artists' model and long-term hanger-on – wangled his way into the flat while Peter was away in Paris. He told the porter that Peter had said he was to have the keys, and installed himself there for the week with a sixteen-year-old boy – apparently a pick-up from one of the cruising venues. It was a rerun of Denham Fouts and Sherban Sidéry combined. Tony pawned a typewriter, a camera and some suits, sold off twenty books (including valuable first editions), ordered brandy, champagne and whisky on Peter's wine merchant account, and let the boy take away a selection of Peter's clothes. Tony even had the cheek to phone Peter in Paris a couple of times to ask if he wanted his mail forwarded (claiming that he'd merely been passing the flat and wanted to be helpful).[28]

When Peter returned and discovered what had been going on, he was exasperated rather than angry. He managed to buy back a few of the pawned items, but the rest was lost. He'd been giving handouts to Tony for as long as he'd known him – fifteen years now, ever since Stephen had brought him into Peter's orbit during the rue du Bac days before the war. Perhaps Peter felt a degree of responsibility for him – after all, Denham had helped complete the ruination of Tony by introducing him to opium.[29] But this was the limit.

The incident didn't end there. The weekend after his return to Palace Gate, Peter went away to Stratford (apparently with Alex) and came back to find the flat burgled. The cashbox had been opened and £300 taken. Peter had reason to believe that the burglar was the father of Tony's sixteen-year-old boyfriend.[30]

To cap it all, a few weeks afterwards Tony had the amazing gall to ask Peter for a loan, on the understanding that Stephen Spender would repay it. Peter wrote to Stephen in protest, and got an apologetic letter back. Peter didn't tell Stephen the reason he suspected that the boy's father had been the burglar – there'd been an element of malice in the robbery. The thief had got into the filing cabinet in the bedroom and found Peter's collection of pornographic photos, which he then left spread out on the bed. Coming in to clean the next day, Mrs Mitchell found them; appalled, she told the porter.[31] Fortunately, the matter was hushed up (apparently with the help of a pay-off[32]), but it had become even more unthinkable to report any of the thefts to the police, and Peter chose to draw a veil over it. 'Of course you are not in any way implicated,' he wrote to Stephen, refusing to accept any compensation. 'Fortunately in my case such events are irritating but not tragic as they could be to others.'[33] Still more worried than angry at Tony, Peter wondered if he might benefit from some kind of treatment – not only did he never do any work, he also didn't even bother to draw his unemployment money.

Tony was far from the only person Peter propped up financially year after year and got little in return from except exasperation and pain: Brian Howard was a constant recipient, as was the writer Gerald Hamilton – the so-called 'wickedest man in Europe'.[34] In 1942 he had been arrested in connection with bankruptcy, and persuaded Peter to stand bail. He also had countless lavish dinners at Peter's expense; eventually Peter was driven to remark that Gerald was getting too expensive for him: 'When one dines with him it is no longer a question of caviar or foie gras, but of caviar *and* foie gras. And he will order the most expensive brandy on the wine list.'[35] At least that was preferable to being burgled.

Perhaps Peter was afflicted with masochism, as some people said; or perhaps those people were overlooking a deeper motivation. It was the same impulse that had made him endure years of pain at Denham's hands in the hope that he could cure him, and had drawn him to Norman Fowler with all his problems, and the same thing that still kept him urging Waldemar to work at his writing and make the best of his talents, and made him angry when he didn't. Peter's place in the world, as he saw it, was to help.

* * *

During this time, Peter began to mellow towards London, and even felt a little stirring of the patriotic sentiment that had briefly uplifted him in the Blitz. The coronation, which took place on 2 June 1953, delighted him. With four days to go, the capital had gone 'quite, quite mad ... you can't move an inch in the centre with all the charabancs from the provinces touring the decorations.'[36] The day itself was 'a really fantastic historical pageant'.[37] The weather was horrible – as cold as November and pouring with rain – but the event still managed to be a triumph.[38] Peter stood with the damp crowds in Hyde Park to see the procession go up the East Carriage Drive, and felt that 'it all had a kind of Byzantine magnificence which no other country could even attempt.' His enthusiasm was tempered by his political conscience: 'It is sad, though, that all our magnificence seems to have to be historical and to accentuate the feudal.'[39] By the following year Peter was describing London as 'quiet, homely, rather smug',[40] which was mild criticism from the man who had quite recently thought it the worst place in the world.

Peter went on seeing Alex, although they were both still visiting the pick-up places, and would bump into each other from time to time. Peter was intrigued and attracted by the new fashion among young men, which came from the working-class areas and spread into the West End. 'The men's Edwardian clothes have to be seen to be believed,' he wrote to Nicolas Calas in early 1954. 'I suppose they'll get to 3rd Avenue eventually.'[41] They didn't – the papers were already scandalised by the violent behaviour of these young men; the term 'Teddy boy' had been coined, and by the end of the year, prim, grim notices began appearing outside dance halls and hotel ballrooms all over the country – 'No Edwardian clothing or crepe soles!', 'Youths in Edwardian dress will not be admitted.'

If Peter saw in these boys a return of the vitalising pre-war spirit of youthful rebellion, he must have been disappointed. There was no art or literary movement associated with it – although there was a new and vital form of music that frightened the middle-aged generation as much as the violence. It was a working-class and suburban phenomenon, and the urbane Peter Watson apparently didn't understand it, much less sympathise with it.

Growing increasingly attached to Alex, Peter asked him to move into the flat. But the young Devonian had had enough of London, and had decided to move back to his native Plymouth. Peter travelled down to visit him several times. (He'd sold his Riley and now drove an equally old-fashioned grey Sunbeam-Talbot.) They stayed in hotels together, and went out on the town. There were a few gay spots in Plymouth and Torquay, and Alex was utterly bewildered by the realisation that Peter seemed to know all of them already.[42] He wasn't aware of Peter's long association with this part of the world – the time at Thatched Cottage (which presumably hadn't all been spent cooking lobster and editing *Horizon*) and his many visits to Cornwall. Peter had also passed through Plymouth going to and from New York in the 1930s, and must have explored the town. More recently, he must have visited the Plymouth area when Norman was having the *Catania* fitted out at Torpoint. But apparently he didn't talk to Alex about any of this – he just let him wonder.

In fact, Alex was so puzzled that it even crossed his mind that Peter might have some ulterior purpose in Plymouth. He knew that Peter had had a connection to the Russian spies, Burgess and Maclean; the story still flared up from time to time in the press, and still made Peter feel uneasy. He admitted that he'd known them, and mentioned that he believed Special Branch was still watching him. (He was probably right – MI5 and Special Branch retained their interest in Stephen Spender until 1959, even though he was working for *Encounter* on behalf of the CIA and MI6, and probably maintained their watch on Peter.)

Moreover, Alex had the same feeling about Peter that everyone else close to him, from Cecil Beaton to Waldemar Hansen, had felt at one time or another – his secretiveness, the sense that there was a whole side to his life that he didn't talk about. Usually it was the existence of a lover, and in this case it might have been the same; not a new lover but the persistence and impending return of an existing one.

In early 1956, Norman left his rock in the sea and reappeared in London.

* * *

Peter had spent much of the summer and winter of 1955 touring Europe – just as he had before the war. There were new places on his itinerary

– such as Copenhagen, where the summer light was wonderful and the American Navy was in (the sailors disappointingly 'drunk and awful').[43] But most of his destinations were the old places; he went to Vienna again – the city where he'd captured the heart of Cecil Beaton a quarter of a century earlier, and Berlin, where he'd met Denham in 1933; and he visited Baden-Baden, where he'd kept his mother company when she was taking a cure.

His travelling that year was solitary, and he seemed to be haunting Europe as much as touring it. Early one September morning in Milan, the American composer Ned Rorem was taking a taxi to the airport when he spotted Peter walking the streets alone:

> So I shouted, and we had breakfast. Now it's never strange to see Peter in any city you accidentally happen to be in because he travels (despite his money complaints) into places where intelligent natures would expect consolation, and does it alone, hating train company and suspicious of love.[44]

Some company Peter found congenial; he spent Christmas in Switzerland with his old friends Christophe and Alice Bernoulli, and managed to enjoy it; afterwards he travelled on through France. En route he visited Le Corbusier's chapel of Notre Dame du Haut at Ronchamp, which had opened in June 1955; he found the brilliant white, pueblo-like structure 'absolutely *sensational*' and 'probably the most important building of the 20th century ... I had not expected such a surprise.'[45]

After a stopover in Paris, Peter had to hurry back to London for Sunday 8 January. He had an important appointment; after fifteen years in residence, he was leaving 10 Palace Gate and seeking new accommodation.

He never recorded his reasons for leaving. (If Mrs Mitchell was blackmailing him, that could be sufficient, but given the date, it could more likely have been the expiry of a fifteen-year lease. Moreover, he seems to have carried on employing Mrs Mitchell after leaving Palace Gate.[46]) He seemed quite content about the move, even though he initially had little idea where he was going and feared that it would take at least a month to move because of all his paintings.[47] In the event, he moved a little further towards the Buckingham Palace end of Kensington, to a flat in a house on the edge of Knightsbridge – a radical change of architectural scene from the Le Corbusier-influenced modernity of 10 Palace Gate.

Number 53 Rutland Gate was a mid-Victorian townhouse in a terrace of identical edifices – elegant and pleasant, but barely distinguishable from hundreds of others in Kensington, Knightsbridge and Mayfair. Its ambience must have seemed reminiscent of 36 South Street and 1 Shepherd's Close, and according to his friends he was happy with it.[48] But this time Peter only had a small slice of the house; flat 3 was on the first floor front, and rather larger than the Palace Gate flat; it had two bedrooms and a bigger living room and kitchen. The move did take a long time, and by the end of it Peter was exhausted; he wrote to Alex complaining that it had brought on a bout of his chronic jaundice.[49]

The rents in Rutland Gate might well have been cheaper than in 10 Palace Gate, and perhaps Peter no longer cared much what kind of building he lived in. His enthusiasm for Notre Dame du Haut notwithstanding, he was having trouble maintaining his passion for modern art in a world that was dominated by abstraction and expressionism, both of which he abhorred: 'I really can't sustain interest in this sort of personality expression in paint, however lively or modern. It is only decoration and a kind of narcissistic display. The visible world is so much more interesting.'[50] He wrote to Pavel Tchelitchew in January 1956 that nowadays it was all 'international "tachisme" in every country or a kind of social-political vulgar realism. What a choice. One goes on looking and hoping but my interest is becoming very strained and forced.'[51] A few years earlier, at a screening of Chaplin's *Limelight*, Peter had wept when the disenchanted old clown delivered the line: 'Life isn't a gag anymore; I can't see the joke ... I hate the theatre.'[52]

And yet Peter went on giving his time, energy and expertise to the ICA – there were committee meetings, exhibitions to arrange and hang, catalogues to be written or overseen, and Peter was taking charge of most of it. A high point had come at the beginning of 1955, when he collaborated with Francis Bacon to put together a show of his work at the ICA. It was opened by Sir Colin Anderson – shipping magnate, art patron and fan of Bacon – on the evening of 19 January 1955. The catalogue had an essay by Max Clarac-Sérou of the Galerie du Dragon in Paris, which Peter had translated. Thirteen paintings were exhibited, chosen to convey a fairly unsubtle message: arranged opposite each other were Bacon's 'screaming popes' and his similarly styled businessmen, and between them a picture of two men wrestling – a recognisably homoerotic symbol. The exhibition was controversial, attracting a visit from the police to verify that there were no obscene pictures, and ran for a month. Although only thirteen paintings were shown, it had the huge significance of being Francis Bacon's first retrospective; he had ceased to be merely a brilliant young painter and was becoming, like Lucian Freud, a vital link in the art history of Britain and the world.[53]

Wherever Peter was getting the energy or drive from, neither he nor his friends could tell; not only art but also life itself was slipping out of his grasp. In summer 1955, he had written to Waldemar: 'How awful the passage of time becomes as one advances through life. Everything goes out of focus so disconcertingly and so quickly.'[54]

This would be Peter's last surviving letter to Waldemar. Time was slipping by more rapidly than he realised.

* * *

Norman returned to London in February – apparently at Peter's request – after a vague and mysterious period spent in the Virgin Islands;[55] from the tropical swelter he came back to a particularly nasty and persistent winter that seemed intent on dragging on until it had choked spring out of existence.

Peter's reunion with his wandering American love was scarcely recorded by him. He didn't even make very much of it with Norman himself; Norman later said that if Peter's friends (apparently going largely by intuition) hadn't assured him that Peter was pleased to have him back, he wouldn't have guessed it.[56] Peculiar behaviour given that Peter had *asked* him to come back. The attraction was waning, and had possibly even blinked out altogether; for although Norman had some of the same unsettling 'Damnation-Train' charisma that had made Denham Fouts so compelling for Peter, he was a mere shadow of Denny in almost every way – his upstairs room might not be entirely or reliably occupied, but he wasn't a heavy drinker, he took no drugs, he lived a healthy outdoor life, and his appeal to Peter's need to love and mend (or to his masochism, if that was what it was) must have been far less powerful.

Whether Norman intended to stay for long this time is also unknown; but they resumed their life together, and the atmosphere in the Rutland

Gate flat seems to have acquired a new element of tension. They no longer shared a bed – Norman now had his own room.[57]

His monk-like island life had not made Norman any saner, more stable or more at ease with himself or the world. And yet even he was alert enough to see that Peter wasn't quite the same. Like every other person before him, Norman began to perceive Peter's secretive side. Whether he was still seeing Alex, or was in some new affair, or was simply following his instinct to keep a part of his life entirely to himself, Peter did not necessarily take Norman with him when he went away, and didn't necessarily tell him where he had been when he got back.

This must have worried Norman; aside from the personal jealousy of a lover, he was dependent on Peter for his entire existence – the yacht, financial support, a home to come back to – but also for his future; in 1950, at the height of their relationship, Peter had made Norman the main beneficiary of his will, and he had a great deal to lose if Peter were to move on to somebody else.

Peter wasn't the only person whose relationship was strained. Cecil Beaton returned to England in April[58] after a stressful visit to New York. His relationship with Greta Garbo had been troubled recently – they'd quarrelled during his previous visit, and during this one they had been reduced to communicating via Truman Capote; but they'd had a reconciliation eventually, and Cecil had hopes that 'it was not too late, after all, to try and recapture the past.'[59]

In this frame of mind, he lunched with Peter at a Wheeler's fish restaurant near the ICA in Dover Street; Peter was busy hanging an exhibition of garden designs by the Brazilian landscape architect Roberto Burle Marx (due to open on 21 April),[60] and couldn't spare the time to come to Cecil's house in Pelham Place. They had a lively conversation, as they always did, but Cecil was dismayed by Peter's appearance: 'terribly thin – skin taut over his cheekbones and chin very pointed'.[61] He had lived through a miserable winter and had been ill with jaundice; but Cecil's physician, Dr Gottfried, had been treating him and he seemed full of life. (Christopher Isherwood had noticed an improvement too – after he and Peter had dined together in February, Christopher had noted what 'a strangely charming wry-smiling creature' Peter was, 'with an almost coquettish air of despair about him'.[62] Less perceptive friends could see only the depression.)

In Cecil's eyes, Peter seemed also to have achieved a new maturity. 'I thought he was a completely fulfilled, integrated person,' Cecil wrote later; 'someone who has been through many vicissitudes and has now discovered himself.'[63] That evening he recorded in his diary: 'When I am with Peter I am somewhat self conscious of the fact that I love him so very much that it puts me at an unfair disadvantage. But today he talked with such gusto and intelligence that I was very happy to sit and admire his point of view, his ever sensitive appreciation for so many aspects of art and life.'[64]

But his appearance bothered Cecil. Aside from his physical condition, he was poorly dressed in an ugly mackintosh that would have unthinkable for the Peter Watson of old, and 'his hair, once so sexily lotioned, was on end.' He looked bohemian – thinner and gaunt, and his complexion was yellowed by jaundice. When he talked animatedly, he looked 'like a ruffled old chicken'; his face was badly shaved and had cuts here and there. 'But however awful he looked,' Cecil thought, 'he had a quality of beauty.'[65]

It seemed to Cecil that 'it had taken him until middle age to discover what life was about for him and now with his knowledge and appreciation he was a most distinguished and noble civilized human being.'[66]

Peter and Cecil arranged to meet again the following Monday evening; the illustrator Richard 'Dickie' Chopping was giving a dinner to celebrate his joint exhibition with Francis Bacon at the Hanover Gallery. (The exhibition was another significant one, leading to Dickie being commissioned by Ian Fleming to design covers for the James Bond novels.) But when Monday came, Cecil, Dickie, Francis Bacon and Rosamond Lehmann were there but Peter wasn't; he was in bed with a cold.[67] Cecil thought perhaps he should invite Peter down to Reddish for a weekend's rest; Cecil's aunt Cada, who had been struck blind, would be staying, and Cecil knew Peter would be a sympathetic fellow guest. But Cecil was busy with work (he'd recently designed the costumes for *My Fair Lady*, and was now catching up with work on his next book, *Face of the World*), and by the time he got around to phoning Peter, there was no answer – just a constant engaged signal.[68] During the last days of April he rang repeatedly (it later transpired that Peter's telephone had been out of order for some days) and when he finally got through, he was told by a woman with a foreign accent, whom he took to be the maid or cleaner, that Mr Watson was away, and would be back in a couple of days.[69] Cecil would always regret that he hadn't phoned earlier in the week and fixed for Peter to come to Reddish for that weekend.

Another person who had expected to see Peter but missed him was George Harris, who had been a sales manager for *Horizon* and now worked for *Encounter*; Peter was the only person from either magazine who had ever befriended George, and had invited him to come up to the flat sometime and hear his new gramophone. George never got the chance.[70]

Peter had gone away on Friday 27 April, intending to come back on Thursday 3 May. Nobody seemed to know quite where he went; Peter often travelled without telling anyone where he was going. It was mentioned, though, that he would spend the weekend with his sister in Newmarket. This was extraordinary; if it was true, it would be the only recorded instance of his ever visiting either of his siblings. He rarely talked about them, aside from occasional disparaging references to his brother. (He had described to Christopher Isherwood in February 'how crazy his brother and his nephew are getting. "They always treated me as the abnormal one, and now I'm beginning to see that I am far saner than they are."')[71] Also, even if true, it would not account for the five nights he was away. Florence did not live in Newmarket, but she would be there for Tuesday 1 May (one of her horses, Fire Cross, was running in the 4 o'clock May Maiden Two-Year-Old Stakes)[72] and might well stay there during the preceding weekend; presumably Peter had arranged to meet up with her rather than stay with her.

Aside from that, no clear idea of where Peter spent those five days and nights would ever be discovered.

Wherever he went, it apparently didn't go quite as expected. Norman received a postcard from Peter on Tuesday saying that he would be back on Thursday. (Where the card was sent from, Norman didn't say, and it was not preserved.) In the event, Peter came back from his travels a day earlier than intended, arriving late in the evening of Wednesday 2 May.

He was tired, and told Norman that he had driven all the way from Warwickshire. This was another oddity – seeing Florence *and* visiting the county of his Watson ancestors. But apparently not; when pressed, Peter admitted that he hadn't seen Florence after all, although he wouldn't tell Norman where he *had* been or with whom. 'With friends,' he said evasively. Norman, whose jealous suspicions were now fully aroused, demanded names, but Peter refused to give them. He had always been this way; the thing he valued above all others was his personal freedom – this was a compulsion that was rooted deep in his character, and for Peter his personal freedom included the freedom not to let anyone, no matter who they were, intrude into parts of his life where they weren't welcome. Anybody – friend, family, lover – who demanded private information from Peter Watson was asking for a cold, angry refusal.

Like every other person before him, Norman began to perceive Peter's secretive side, and experienced it with particularly shocking force. It must have been deeply wounding to discover that he was excluded from a whole sector of Peter's life. And although Norman wasn't the most astute person in the world, he must have been conscious that Peter had been fairly seriously involved with at least one other young man while he'd been on his oceanic travels.

A furious quarrel developed. Peter, already overtired, became 'extremely agitated'. In an effort to calm him, Norman offered him a glass of wine. Peter didn't normally drink these days, but he accepted; in his present state, he said, a drink was exactly what he needed.[73] It didn't have the desired effect; the row carried on for hours – a bitter exchange of recrimination, interrogation and ice-cold spite; Norman recalled afterwards that Peter had been as nasty to him as possible for six long hours.[74] No account would ever be given, of course, of how Norman had behaved towards Peter during that time.

Finally, Peter ordered Norman to go to bed, and he obeyed. A few minutes later, when Norman was settling down, Peter came in with a suitcase; he emptied it, then announced that he was going for a bath. This was another unusual act – Peter normally bathed in the morning, not at bedtime.[75]

Norman apparently said nothing; he merely stayed in bed and settled down to sleep. With hot water thundering into the bath and steam drifting into the hallway, Peter disappeared into the bathroom. The door snapped shut behind him.

23

THE REALM OF ECSTASY

1956

The street door of 53 Rutland Gate flew open, and a half-dressed young man came leaping down the steps to the pavement. Without pausing to consider his direction, he took off running along the dark street, looking for a policeman.

It was never recorded how far he had to search or how long he was gone, but by the time Norman returned to the flat with the constable and the front door and the bathroom door had been broken down, it was too late.

* * *

Cecil Beaton was having his evening tea in his house in Pelham Place – just a few streets away from Rutland Gate – when the telephone rang.[1]

He picked it up and was surprised to hear the voice of Toni del Renzio, whom Cecil had last seen a week or so earlier at the ICA. He said he had bad news about Peter. Cecil braced himself to hear that Peter was seriously ill again or in some kind of trouble, and wasn't at all prepared for the blow that came. Peter was dead.

Listening to the details, Cecil felt faint. He couldn't believe it, it wasn't possible – Peter couldn't die before him; he'd been so sure of this, he'd made Peter executor of his will. And he wasn't even supposed to be at home last night – let alone drowned in his bath ... so Cecil reasoned, retreating in panic in the face of a truth he couldn't accept.

After putting the phone down, Cecil went back to his sitting room and his half-eaten boiled egg and toast. In a daze, he sat and finished them, tears running down his cheeks and Toni's words tumbling through his mind. As he finished eating, the truth finally sank in and overwhelmed him; he began to weep and howl, losing control of himself ...

> ... and suddenly saw myself in the looking glass – the shock was enough to make me want to die as well – my face was contorted and swollen, mauve, my hair white, untidy and almost bald – I looked like the most terrible old man – and it was appalling that this terrible old man was grieving for the love of his life.[2]

* * *

Stephen Spender was in the offices of *Encounter* when he heard the news. The assistant editor, John Hall, came into Stephen's office and, with a grin, asked, 'Do you know this fellow Peter Watson who's been found dead in his bath? It was announced in the stop press of the *News Chronicle* this morning.'

In this cruelly abrupt manner, 'I heard of the death of one of my greatest friends. I can hardly imagine any death that could leave his friends sadder.'[3]

Like everyone else, it would take Stephen some days – and a lot of talk with other friends – to take in the news and realise the enormity of the loss. Stephen's thoughts went to Norman and the dreadful grief he must be going through. He found out that Norman was staying with Toni del Renzio and Enid Furlonger, and on the following Monday he went round to pay a visit.

The house was at 43 Paultons Square, Chelsea – the same place Waldemar had stayed seven years earlier when he'd been forced out of the Palace Gate flat so that Peter could bring Norman to live there. Norman was asleep when Stephen arrived. He'd been in a bad way since the fatal night – he'd been in a hysterical state when Peter's body was taken away; he'd collapsed and was taken to hospital. Geoffrey Lawson of the ICA collected him the next day and took him to Toni and Enid's place.[4]

When Norman woke he was willing to talk to Stephen about what had happened. He described those last hours with Peter – but said nothing about what had occurred after the bathroom door shut.

> He spoke about the terrible guilt he felt on account of Peter, and about what he called his responsibility. He said Peter had so many friends – by which I suppose he meant there were many people to hold him, Norman, responsible. I said that on the contrary Peter's friends would feel only grateful to Norman for having come back to be with him. There was no idea of responsibility in anyone's mind.[5]

Their conversation was repeatedly interrupted by Norman breaking down. Stephen thought it good that Norman evidently had 'a capacity to sleep which he accepts and does not question at all'.[6] There was apparently no insomnia, no troubling dreams.

The same couldn't be said for Stephen himself – Peter's death would trouble his dreams as well as his waking thoughts for some time to come.

* * *

The inquest took place the next day, Tuesday 8 May, in the grim brick edifice of the coroner's court in Horseferry Road, Westminster.

Of all Peter's friends and acquaintances, Stephen Spender was the only one whose curiosity moved him to attend.[7] Only that morning, Sonia Orwell had phoned him from Paris and told him that everyone there was saying Peter had committed suicide. Everyone had been able to see how depressed and pessimistic he had been since the war. Lucian Freud, for instance, believed that Peter had become disenchanted with humanity and with art.[8] The notion of suicide had originated with Toni del Renzio – and presumably he must have been influenced by talking to Norman.

That, however, was not the verdict reached by the inquest.

Stephen Spender was powerfully struck by much of what he saw that day; the intense, astonishing consultation beforehand between Sir Norman Watson (so remarkable in his resemblance to Peter, the same stooping height, the same little wrinkles at the angle of the jaw), Norman Fowler and Peter's doctor, all agreeing that Peter must have fallen asleep in his bath and drowned accidentally; and the coroner's air of a man who'd come to fix a problem rather than adjudicate a peculiar death.

When Norman was put in the witness box, he described his last evening with Peter – the argument, the wine, the order to go to bed, and Peter going for his bath. What happened after that was puzzling, to say the least:

> Norman went to sleep. He woke up in the middle of the night, feeling extremely worried. He started looking around the flat for Peter. He found the bathroom door locked. He called to Peter and got no answer. Finally, terrified, he went into the street and summoned a policeman.[9]

Peter's doctor gave evidence that Peter had died by drowning – not from a heart attack or any other natural cause, and not by suicide. He had clearly intended to take a normal bath, and had soaped himself (the evidence being that soap was found in the stomach).[10]

On these grounds, the verdict was accidental death; Stephen Spender noted that the coroner 'was extremely emphatic that any possibility of suicide was quite ruled out'.[11] The death certificate was signed on 10 May, with the cause of death given as 'asphyxia due to drowning in a domestic bath when overcome by heat and fatigue – Accidental'.

The inquest left unanswered one or two questions that occurred to Stephen. He was puzzled by the way both Norman and Sir Norman affirmed that Peter was a very heavy sleeper, and might easily have drowned once under the water; and yet this contradicted Norman's statement that Peter had not been sleeping at all well lately.

There were other questions that either didn't occur to Stephen Spender or which he didn't write about in his diary. How likely would it be that a man in a tense, strung-out state after a flaming row would drop off to sleep? The effect of an overly hot bath made him faint? But according to Alex, one of Peter's foibles was meanness with the hot water.

The most glaring, bewildering questions were over Norman's actions after Peter went to the bathroom, and the chronology in which they occurred. After going to sleep, what caused Norman to wake up 'terribly worried' and why did he then search the flat for Peter? The taps were still running, he said, when he knocked on the bathroom door, and the bath was overflowing when the policeman arrived; in a small flat, the noise of a filling bath would be audible everywhere, so why search? And if he had slept for any length of time, would the bath not be overflowing and flooding the flat by this time?

And the most puzzling question of all – which nobody seems to have asked openly: why did an athletic, strong young man like Norman, believing he had cause for alarm about what had happened to Peter in the bathroom, not simply break down the locked door himself? Why did he run out of the house and seek a policeman, rather than telephoning for a more useful ambulance? (The telephone had been out of order, but was working again by Monday or Tuesday.) And having served several years in the US Navy, Norman would have been trained in first aid, lifesaving and artificial respiration.[12] Whatever he believed was going on in that locked bathroom, he was more equipped to deal with it himself than the average London bobby.

Then there was the other question – which nobody asked because the only man who knew about it was Robert Jolliff, Sir Norman Watson's personal assistant, who inspected the flat immediately after the incident: the bathroom key on the floor inside the room. It might have shot out when the door was barged by the policeman – but having been turned in the lock, the probability of its being in line with the keyhole would be remote. It was as if the door had been locked from the outside and the key pushed underneath it.

There were no signs of violence – but as the infamous 'Brides in the Bath' case had proved decades earlier, it is quite easy for a victim to be drowned by a person they trust without leaving any trace of a struggle.[13]

Stephen Spender thought of none of these things – he appeared to have no suspicion of Norman at all – but nevertheless his close interest in the case offended Norman deeply. Toni del Renzio told Stephen that Norman was 'very annoyed' that he had come to the inquest and that 'no friend of Peter except himself had the right to attend.' Ever charitable, Stephen attributed this hostility to grief and to Norman's need to possess Peter's death because he'd been 'so little involved in his life'.[14]

Five days after the inquest, Norman wrote to Waldemar, expressing his feelings in his usual disjointed, peculiar manner. One thing was clear, though: that while Cecil had been 'beautifully kind by his understanding', 'Stephen has been too morbid and unkind ever to forgive.'[15]

As for himself, Norman wrote that he had 'somewhat recovered to a dull and distant feeling of removal'. Then, in a line that might have been addressed either to Waldemar or to Peter's spirit, he wrote: 'You knew us both as we perhaps never knew ourselves and that special understanding remains. The real mirror has passed – plunged.'[16]

So had the truth. Re-evaluation of the evidence would be impossible because, as with Peter Watson's MI5 file, the records of the inquest were later destroyed. In later years, an uncomfortable theory would arise among some of Peter's relatives that he had in fact been liquidated by some branch of the security or intelligence services.[17] If so, this might explain Norman's peculiar actions on that night, the holes in his story, the state of terror he claimed he was in, his belief that he was under surveillance, and his odd, paranoid reaction to Stephen Spender having attended the inquest. That might also explain the disappearance of the MI5 file and the inquest records.

The truth about what went on behind that bathroom door would always remain elusive.

* * *

Cecil Beaton couldn't have borne attending the inquest. He went down to Reddish the weekend after Peter's death. The first morning after hearing the news, he had woken sobbing. 'Mrs Cartwright the nice cleaning woman tried to comfort me,'[18] he wrote, but he was inconsolable.

If anything, being at Reddish made it worse. Even though Peter hadn't come here as often as he'd been to Ashcombe, his visits had been happy ones. The last one had been the previous summer; Cecil reread the postcard Peter had sent to thank him for 'a glorious weekend. I enjoyed every moment of it. You have infused your domain with a very special kind of lyricism and atmosphere.'[19] It was also infused with memories of Peter; all his letters were here – Cecil had kept every one – and a set of silver-backed hairbrushes Peter had given him, with Cecil's name engraved in Peter's handwriting … 'Here a painting of Ashcombe we had found together – so many books – so many memories – snap shots taken in every part of the world – America – Mexico – Austria – Germany – France.'

> And every memory – even the sad ones of our troubles and complications, were fragrant – for they were all to do with someone who, though difficult, and sometimes cruel, and always provocative – was really a rare enough person to have had the quality of quickening me to a fuller appreciation of life than anyone else I have ever known.[20]

Cecil wrote to Garbo, hoping to share the loss of the first of his two great loves with the second. He tried to explain his vision of what Peter had become. Whereas most others had seen him as depressed and pessimistic,[21] Cecil had perceived something else emerging – a maturity, a loss of selfishness.

> I must tell you of something that has made me feel so upset, so abysmally sad that I have been crying like a hysterical child most of the day and night. My lifelong friend Peter – died yesterday … [It] is a terrible accident to have happen to anyone but that it should have been Peter who is no longer with us is very hard to bear. He had been through so many vicissitudes – and at last had come through as such a fulfilled and integrated person on terms with everyone – and his own terms. He had developed enormously as a person – and had become a sort of queer saint.[22]

Possibly Cecil was using the word *queer* in both its senses, but there was little ambiguity in the word *saint*. Although nearly everyone was conscious of Peter's goodness (and his faults), Cecil saw it all differently, and seemed to think that Peter had become a sort of martyr. In a sense it was true; Peter had suffered for other people's sins – their greed, their sloth, and their lust – more than he had for his own, as he himself recognised. ('All counted, one can *do* so little for someone – for anyone. Even history compromises and corrupts those who die for others … After all there have been thousands of Christs throughout history and no one makes a religion of them.'[23]).

Cecil went on:

> No one has really made such an impression on me and I can't bear to think there's no further link – I don't even have the consolation that other bereaved people have that there is an afterlife – The void is utter. Of course I shall continue tomorrow morning with my active life ... but I shall always feel an emptiness sometimes – when I get back from America and want to telephone him, or in America when I feel it would be nice to send him a postcard.[24]

Despite his own grief, one of the first things Cecil had done the day after Peter's death was to cable Waldemar in New York. 'I feel such a terrible void,' Waldemar wrote back, 'and haven't been able to cry at all, but just go around feeling sick to my stomach.'[25] Even John Myers, who had been so angry and scathing about Peter's treatment of Waldemar, had made peace with him since, and wept on the phone when Waldemar told him the news.

As for Cecil himself:

> I gave myself up to mourning Peter – I looked at an album of photographs of him that had been taken in New York one winter – they still haunted me with the allure that I have never been able to overcome. I read letters and postcards from him and was so tremendously grateful to find a few of them that did show that he had been very fond of me – 'I do need you as a friend' – 'I miss you so much and think of all our other trips' – for someone so uncommunicative as he, and to someone as tiresome and possessive as I have been to him these letters showed tolerance and sweetness.[26]

* * *

The funeral was held at Golders Green Crematorium on Thursday 10 May. It was a brief, perfunctory business, and, to some of the friends attending, an affront to Peter's person and memory.

There were about thirty people there – Cyril Connolly and Stephen and Natasha Spender went together. Cecil Beaton arrived alone. Roland Penrose came with his wife, Lee Miller, the American photojournalist (yet another of MI5's suspects). Toni del Renzio was there, along with Graham Sutherland and Alex Reid of the Reid and Lefevre Gallery. Peter's brother and sister were both in attendance – probably the first time most of Peter's friends had ever seen any member of his family. There were various trustees, lawyers and business associates of the family. And then there was Norman – 'staring very hard and white faced'.[27]

Cecil Beaton was upset by the whole affair:

> The coffin was totally against his taste; the red brick chapel and all the details of the service were the sort of things Peter would have no patience for.
>
> ... The service was meaningless to me in my hollow state of mind. I noticed that Cyril Connolly was weeping and I loved him for that; but from my seat in the back of the church I could not see or feel anything but anonymity.
>
> It was a cold, horrid afternoon. The chapel door was open and gusts of gritty wind gushed from the asphalt outside. The clergyman hurried through the service in double-quick time, and the appalling moment came when the metal doors opened on their mechanical hinges and the coffin slowly moved forth on a conveyor belt to the other world.[28]

Cecil was 'strangely unmoved' by the sight – but then:

> Suddenly a ray of brilliant sunshine came down onto the flowers. It was a most dramatic and beautiful effect – the lilies became incandescent in this drab, horrible surrounding. I almost believed that this symbol meant that Peter had attained a happiness that was denied him on this earth, and it helped me to think that he might be in a state of serenity after his turbulent years.[29]

Outside afterwards, as people stood about looking at the wreaths and flowers, Lee Miller cried, while Stephen Spender thought 'Cecil looked as if he did not want anyone to speak to him.'[30] But Peter's brother and sister both engaged him in conversation. Sir Norman asked a few questions about Peter's recent health and spirits, but seemed to have no idea of his life in recent years. Florence (whom Cecil thought 'strangely hideous') was 'very matter of fact and straightforward'; she appeared to have read Stephen Spender's surprisingly trite obituary in Saturday's *Times* and been impressed by it; she remarked that Peter 'was interested in furthering the creation of works of art'. Cecil noted sourly: 'Her interests are in one activity – in the breeding of animals.'[31]

(Cecil was doing Florence Nagle an injustice; besides breeding dogs and training racehorses, she was a feminist campaigner; at this time she was leading and financing a long-running legal campaign to force the Jockey Club to drop its ban on female jockeys and its refusal to license female trainers; she would eventually succeed in 1966.)

In the car on the way home, Cyril Connolly remarked to Stephen what an 'inhuman' service it had been, 'dominated by the idea of the cremation itself'. Suddenly Cyril remarked: 'This shows how strange life is. Two weeks ago, and none of us would have realized that Peter Watson, this elegant and intelligent young man, was going to be drowned within a few days and then burned.'[32]

'Of course,' Stephen wrote, 'every time someone dies, the whole light in which the universe has all met at one's point of consciousness, is put out. People never seem conscious enough of the fact that if the human race disappeared, the universe would have no centre.'[33]

Stephen tried twice more to express his feelings about Peter in obituaries in the *New Statesman* and *Art* magazine. He fixated on the difference between the 'rich, generous and handsome young man' of the pre-war years and the dreadful, desperate pessimism of his later life. Privately he had admitted that Peter's pessimism and depression had made it hard for him to stand his company.[34] Stephen seemed unaware of the positive change that Cecil could see – the new maturity and energy. Also writing in *Art* magazine, Herbert Read described Peter's work for the ICA: '[F]or several years he had been virtually in charge of the exhibition policy of the Institute and he never shirked the dull administrative work which such a position involved.'[35]

Read also noted what he called the 'rare combination' of Peter Watson's encouragement to young artists on the one hand and his sensibility and enthusiasm on the other. Henry Moore had said something similar to Stephen when he visited him at Hoglands, his home and studio in the Hertfordshire countryside; Moore 'spoke very sympathetically of Peter Watson, and said how many people now whom he had helped would be without assistance'. Stephen remarked that Peter's patronage was different from that of people like Sir Kenneth Clark; Peter's help was personal, helping people 'first because he thought they had talent, and afterwards because he remembered that they were human beings who simply needed help'. Moore agreed: 'Yes,' he said, 'being helped by the Clarks was rather like being helped by the Ford Foundation.'[36]

Stephen admitted that Peter Watson 'had a certain vanity or pride about his own expertise which made him sometimes rather contemptuous of the opinions of other people who talked about painting without, in his view, their knowing about it'. And yet Stephen thought him 'one of the most consistently good people, in the part that he played in other people's lives, that I have known. His faults can all be put down either to the fact that he was self-educated, so that he had the self-educated person's mistrust of other people's knowledge, or simply that he tired easily, was not very strong, and had many people making more demands on him than he could possibly fulfil.'[37]

Although he occasionally supported people in expectation of a sexual return, more often he did so out of pure friendship. He became close to the novelist Anna Kavan, who worked for *Horizon* and was one of several women with whom he had platonic friendships. Although his relationship with her was perhaps less emotionally charged than with Sonia Orwell, it was more intense. Kavan, like Denham Fouts, was hopelessly addicted to heroin. She and Peter were patients of the eccentric German psychiatrist Dr Karl Theodore Bluth, who both treated and supplied her heroin habit.[38] Peter brightened her life, tried hard to help her with her personal problems, and published her work many times in *Horizon*.

Not everyone thought fondly of Peter Watson; Waldemar had once told him that some (unidentified) friends had called him a 'monster'. Peter was taken aback; it was a mystery to him why anyone would say such a thing:

> Looking back over my life I fail to see whom I have harmed deliberately or by accident. By now I know that with the best intentions in the world one can never do anyone any good ... My only asset has been a certain amount of money and enthusiasm. Since the War both have considerably decreased but I cannot

> see that I have used either to other people's disadvantage. I have been most conscientious in *not* trying to influence the young (and therefore the influenceable) according to my own ideas.[39]

Cyril Connolly told Stephen that, for some days after Peter's death, 'he found himself all the time thinking very sweetly of Peter, as though all the affection that Peter felt for his friends was present in his mind and he was haunted by it. He said this gave him the feeling of Peter being near to him, and one could not at all explain it.'[40] Stephen believed that death does something to one's perception of the deceased because 'we are denied knowing what we feel about certain of our friends until they are dead', because 'they are always attached to a future ... Death cuts them off at an instant from this idea ... and thus we are able to enter into them as it were outside the stream of our personal history, and to experience them for a few days of intense feeling as though they are entirely in a present which has neither past nor future.'[41]

This kind of abstraction was of no use to Cecil Beaton. Having known and loved Peter longer, more closely and more intensely than any person living, he was torn by a grief from which he would never entirely recover. A world without Peter was a broken, incomplete one.

Of all Cecil's friends, it was Truman Capote who perceived most clearly what Peter and Cecil had meant to each other. For once, he set aside his acerbic humour and wrote Cecil a letter of simple compassion:

> I didn't know about Peter's death until your letter came, and it touched and grieved me very much. I know what a tragedy it has been for you to lose a friend, and a friendship, that has meant all he has meant in your life. Especially in the spring, when one is so longing for beginnings, continuations; not endings. Your letter made me inexpressibly sad; for you, for Peter. He loved you, Cecil: you were his youth, as much as he was yours. The last time I saw him, in Rome, 1954, he told me you were more marked by 'tender honesty' than anyone he'd ever known. I remember because I liked the phrase 'tender honesty,' and knew what it meant.[42]

Cecil wrote in his diary that above and beyond all the anguish, 'I am deeply glad that there has been someone like Peter who has been able to bring out my tenderest feelings and has lifted me into the realms of ecstasy.'[43]

EPILOGUE

1956–1971

For man walketh in a vain shadow, and disquieteth himself in vain: he heapeth up riches, and cannot tell who shall gather them.
'Order for the Burial of the Dead', *Book of Common Prayer*

On the eastern boundary of the Caribbean Sea, within the long chain of the Leeward Islands, which arc out from Puerto Rico like the tail of a whip, lies the little cluster of the British Virgin Islands. In their midst, just a handful of miles long by a mile wide, is the idyllic little nail-paring of green hills, white sand and azure coves called Tortola Island.

Tortola and all its neighbouring isles had once been the haunt of pirates. Nowadays – in the second half of the twentieth century – it was home to an odd assortment of characters. Distinct among them was a young American. He was rich, and a bit of a patron in his way – he sponsored many community projects, including the founding of a cinema in Road Town (Tortola's little port) and the establishment of the *Tortola Times*. He was a popular figure, pleasant and well liked in the British Virgin Islands' various communities; he visited them all, sailing from island to island in his yacht.

Not very much was known about the American's origins. His name was Norman Fowler, and he had first arrived around 1955 or 1956, moving here – so he said – from his home in the United States. He told people he'd been born about 1933 and was the son of a wealthy and prominent American family. At first he'd settled on the outlying Anegada Island, where he'd involved himself in the shark-hunting trade, but after while he'd moved to Tortola. Perhaps he was attracted here by the community, or perhaps by the fact that from Tortola's shores you could see in the near distance a little privately owned island that was his namesake – Norman Island (apparently named after some eighteenth-century pirate). Norman was a tiny, rocky place, and its eastern end was partly embraced by the outstretched arms of a larger, lusher island of white beaches and blue harbours, which through the ineffable workings of fate, happened to be named Peter.

* * *

Norman hadn't hung around long in London after Peter died.

At the end of May 1956, John Myers and his partner Herbert Machiz flew into London. It had been arranged weeks before that Peter would put them up in his new flat before they set off on their tour of Europe.[1] Instead they were met at the airport by Norman, alone. Still in an emotional state after nearly four weeks, Norman told them what had happened (they already knew, of course, from Cecil via Waldemar). 'Peter is dead,' he told them. 'He had some kind of attack while he was in the bathtub and fainted; the water came up over his nose.' And then, remarkably, he added: 'The whole thing is so grotesque and to complete the nightmare, I'm under police surveillance.'[2]

If this was true, it was unlikely to be the regular Metropolitan Police – after all, the inquest had ruled out any question of foul play. But Special Branch might well have taken an interest, along with MI5; Peter was still on their files, as were several of the people at his funeral.

Norman had decided, within days of Peter's death, that he could not stay in London, and had told Enid Furlonger during that first weekend that he meant to leave for California 'in four or five weeks'.[3]

He could afford to go wherever he wanted now, wherever he felt safe from watching eyes. Peter's will, which had been created in 1950, was proved on 13 July 1956 by Sir Norman and the executors. His trust fund – which had formed the foundation of his wealth since 1930 – was not his own to dispose of, so it reverted to the Watson family. The will disposed only of his ready money and possessions, which were substantial: the net amount was £120,004, after payment of just over £79,000 in estate duty.[4]

Several of Peter's friends were given bequests. David Gascoyne and Brian Howard were left £2,000 each; Cyril Connolly and Sonia Orwell got £1,000 each. Stephen Spender – who was contacted by the solicitors seeking Cyril's and Sonia's addresses – was hurt to learn that there was nothing for him, and 'all day I had a quite childish feeling of being very hurt, and feeling left out ... I was left feeling that I did not want a bequest at all, but would just like to have a line in his will mentioning my name.'[5]

On top of these bequests, there were four annuities, all of them to women, and all reaching back into the early days of Peter's life. One was for Olga 'Oggie' Lynn, the American soprano who had been a close friend since the early 1930s. Two more were for two elderly ladies living in Brewery Cottages, Sulhamstead – presumably former servants of his parents, perhaps governesses or nursemaids. The fourth annuity was for Miss Mary Alice Atkinson – Bessie's older sister, eighty-three years old and still living in 5 Bank Street, Workington, the same little Cumbrian backstreet terrace in which she and Bessie had spent their childhood.

Everything else went to Norman Fowler. Once probate was published, it became known to everyone that he was the principal beneficiary, which gave rise to suspicions among some people that the most likely cause of death might not have been an unfortunate accident after all.[6] (Until now, nobody had had any notion that Norman could have any motive.)

Besides the money, Norman inherited all Peter's belongings, including his paintings, sculptures and rare books. Despite his pretensions to be an artist and aesthete, Norman immediately began selling them off – every single piece.

A small flurry of letters between art dealers erupted, speculating about what items might be in the collection and what might be available to buy. At the first meeting of the ICA management committee since Peter's death, Dorothy Morland, the Institute's director, reported on the possibility of a memorial exhibition of pictures from Peter's collection, but Mr Fowler had told her that he intended shipping the pictures to the United States, although he *might* be prepared to delay. Roland Penrose arranged a meeting with Norman to discuss this; he later reported that the meeting had taken place and that there would be no such exhibition. Norman was keen to get out of the country with the pictures without delay.

Instead the ICA decided to organise a memorial concert later in the year. It was held at the Wigmore Hall in London on Tuesday 16 October 1956, and consisted of music that Peter was known to have liked: Stravinsky's Concerto for Two Pianos, Schoenberg's Serenade Op. 24 and Bartók's Sonata for Two Pianos and Percussion. The ensemble was conducted by his friend René Leibowitz, the pianos were played by Janine Reding and Henri Piette – a Belgian couple who were popular duettists – and among the soloists was Julian Bream on guitar. The Serenade was particularly well received – with 'shouts of joy' from the audience, who demanded an encore.[7]

Meanwhile, Norman got on with the business of selling. He had more than just the contents of the flat to dispose of; Peter had been a generous lender of artworks and other belongings, so now they all had to be rounded up, accounted for and sold. The solicitors placed an advertisement in *The Times*: 'Will anyone having anything (pictures, sculptures, books, etc.) on loan from the late Mr Watson ... please communicate with Messrs Maddisons and Lambs of 2 Clement's Inn, Strand.'[8]

Later that year – around the time of the ICA memorial concert – Sotheby's auctioned much of Peter's collection of books and manuscripts. They included an edition of Balzac's *Le Chef-d'oeuvre inconnu* with woodcuts by Picasso; a presentation copy of Picasso's *Le Désir attrapé*, inscribed 'pour Peter Watson' by Picasso with a pen-and-ink self-portrait above; Dalí's *The Secret Life of Salvador Dalí*, with a drawing and the inscription 'Pour Peter amicablement Salvador Dalí 1946'; a signed fair manuscript of Stephen Spender's poems (specially written out for Peter in July 1939); an unpublished short story by R. L. Stevenson; personally inscribed works by Cyril Connolly, Max Ernst, Wifredo Lam, John Piper, and more.[9]

Everything had to go – all the care and love and personal friendship that had gone into building the collection counted for nothing under the auctioneer's hammer. The lots sold for between £130 and £145 each. The Balzac edition was bought by Dorothy Morland, and the Stevenson manuscript by Ian Fleming.[10] Further items kept coming to light – including more rare art books – and the selling-off of Peter's library was still going on two years after his death.[11]

The Spender manuscript was possibly the most personal – not merely inscribed but written out by hand as a gift to Peter after their pre-war tour of Switzerland. Norman had gone to see Stephen (despite the animosity he felt towards him for attending the inquest) to tell him that this manuscript was included in Peter's estate. He mentioned that he had sold 'nearly everything' of Peter's already, and seemed doubtful what to do with the manuscript. At first Stephen thought he was being offered his gift back as a memento – but no, Norman was just seeking approval for including it in the sale.[12]

Very little happiness came out of the dispersal of Peter Watson's estate. In typical spirit, Evelyn Waugh remarked that Cyril Connolly had been consorting with his stockbroker ever since getting his legacy.[13] In an eerie echo of Peter's own life, Brian Howard spent part of his bequest on commissioning a new yacht for his long-term boyfriend, while the rest was spent on a fur coat for his mother, which she didn't want.[14] It all ended with grim, tragic resonance for Brian in January 1958 when his boyfriend was found dead in his bath, asphyxiated by a faulty gas pipe in the hot water geyser. A few days after receiving the news, Brian committed suicide.

Brian had been deeply upset when he heard of Peter's death. He wrote to his old friend, John Banting: 'Of Peter I can't yet speak. He was my greatest friend, and *The Times* obituary, splendid and full of praise as it was, didn't do him justice. He was an angel, and never said or did a mean or ignoble thing his whole life long. His criticisms of me, lately, were earned, alas. I could make a list of present-day, celebrated painters and writers who owe their all to him.'[15]

* * *

Within months of Peter's death, Norman had reached the British Virgin Islands, where he settled at first on Anegada, a large, barely inhabited island some distance away from the main group. It seemed that he was trying to get as far away from humanity as he could.

He invested in the shark-hunting business, and in May 1957 wrote to Waldemar that business was 'sound'.[16] He spoke as if Waldemar were a bosom friend, but Waldemar seemed not to see it that way. A few months later he had a dream about Norman that was so disturbing he wrote it down in detail – a violent vision with sexual overtones, in which two versions of Norman, wild with rage, attempted to strangle him.[17]

Waldemar wasn't the only one who dreamed. Stephen Spender was haunted by the memory of Peter for many years, and dreamed about him occasionally – dreams that he wished could go on, so that he could have more time with him. In 1966 he published a poem in *Encounter* – 'Isé: Voice from a Skull (remembering Peter Watson)'. After it was published he continued reworking it and it was republished in a revised form. It described a journey in Japan and a sudden surprising memory of Peter:

… IV
Suddenly I hear your voice
Inside my skull, peal – like the tongue
Inside a pilgrim's bell – peal out
In those gay sneering tones I knew:
'You were
Once my companion on a journey
The far side of the world, the Alps,
Rock-leaded windows of Europe
You saw fields diamonded as harlequin
Reflect upon my laughing eyes, who now
Am dragged under the soil in a net
That tangles smile and eyeballs with
Their visions rainbowed still.
But you,
Lacking my eyes through which you looked,
Turn like a shadow round the sunlit dial.'[18]

In another poem – 'On the Photograph of a Friend, Dead' – which was possibly about both Virginia Woolf and Peter Watson, Stephen reflected on the tragedy of memory:

Dead friend, this picture proves there was an instant
That with a place – a leaf-dazzling garden – crossed
When – mirror of midday – you sent
Shadow and light from living flesh into
The sensitive dark instrument

... Reverse of that reverse, your photograph
Now positively scans me with
Your quizzical ironic framed half-laugh.
Your gaze oblique under sun-sculpted lids
Endlessly asks me: 'Is this all we have?'[19]

It was. Just as there was no memorial service to Peter Watson, there was no memorial of any permanent kind. His parents, later joined by Florence, rest together in the graveyard at St Michael's, Sulhamstead Bannister, but there is no stone to the younger son nor any plaque to him among the many thousands at Golders Green Crematorium. All that remained was the photographs, the letters and the memories, all of which diminished as the people who knew and loved him died in their turn.

John Craxton was one of the last. He was in Greece when he heard about Peter's death and was deeply distraught. He honoured his patron's memory by speaking well of him at every possible opportunity throughout the remainder of his life. In many ways John Craxton became the keeper of Peter Watson's memory in the long years of neglect that followed.

* * *

After the failure of Norman's shark-hunting business (he'd tried to create a cooperative on Anegada, but the local fishermen didn't trust him or his idea, even after he'd sunk $16,000 into it),[20] he moved to Tortola and became a popular member of the community, with a long string of charitable and business ventures (mostly failed) to his name. For unknown reasons, he knocked seven years off his age, while for easily guessable reasons he claimed to have inherited his money from his wealthy parents.

He became a bit of a local landmark and mascot for the people of the British Virgin Islands. Visitors who met him invariably remembered him. One who was there in 1966 came away with the impression that Norman Fowler was a jigsaw obsessive. By that time he had a house in Tortola plus an apartment in St Thomas in the US Virgin Islands; he was in the habit of buying three 1,000-piece jigsaws at a time, mixing up all the pieces and doing all three puzzles at once.[21] Presumably he had a problem finding things to do to pass the time; perhaps his conscience made him sleepless as the years rolled by.

In 1968, Norman moved on again, this time to St Kitts and Nevis, farther east in the Leeward Islands, where he was one of the few white people among the mostly black population. He settled on the island of Nevis, where he purchased the Bath Hotel, an elegant eighteenth-century pile in Charlestown with a two-storey bathhouse attached to it (from which it took its name). He set about restoring the hotel, and lived in one of its suites.

His residency there lasted just over two years. On 23 March 1971, at the age of forty-four, Norman Fowler was found dead. He had lost consciousness while bathing in the hot bathhouse and drowned.

It was front-page news in his local paper back on Tortola: 'There is profound sympathy here over the sad news of his death.'[22] The coroner's inquest returned an open verdict – simply 'death by drowning in hot water bath'. There was suspicion locally that he had been murdered, and the case was investigated, but no evidence was ever found and the case was dropped.[23]

The only person who had known the truth of what had really happened in the bathroom at 53 Rutland Gate fifteen years earlier was now beyond recall, and the remnants of his memory and his fortune – a fortune created in the grey shopping streets of England and enhanced by years of devotion in the galleries of Paris, Vienna and London – dissipated like scraps of sailcloth on the ocean winds.

APPENDIX

A ROOM IN CHELSEA SQUARE

At some point around 1940, a young man who had been working as a journalist on a provincial newspaper entered the orbit of *Horizon*. Michael Nelson, judging by the book he subsequently wrote, found the extreme cultural sophistication of Cyril Connolly and Peter Watson difficult to comprehend. There is always a danger in treating a work of fiction as fact and Michael Nelson's *A Room in Chelsea Square* is no exception. In many ways it resembles *The Girls of Radcliff Hall*, but with the 'girls' a decade older and the pen writing about them dipped in a darker ink.

Like Berners, Nelson hardly troubled to disguise the main characters. The principal character is a self-portrait named Nicholas, a young, attractive journalist who is lured up to London by Patrick, a rich man who runs a literary magazine with his friends Ronnie and Christopher (Cyril Connolly and Stephen Spender respectively). None of them are likeable characters; Patrick, in some ways, is a detestable one, but is inescapably an accurate portrait of Peter Watson.

Not much is known about Michael Nelson. Born in 1921, he was at Bryanston School at about the same time as Lucian Freud, until he was expelled for drunkenness. After working as a journalist he came to London in 1940 and had some work published in *Horizon* before moving on to become John Lehmann's secretary and then being called up into the army. His book, which was written in the late 1940s and eventually published anonymously in 1958, describes the creation of a magazine, which is clearly a skit on the creation of *Horizon*.

The storyline is light, but the portrayal of the characters is not. Christopher (Spender) gets off comparatively lightly as he is just made to seem foolish; Ronnie (Connolly) is depicted as a grotesque specimen with many vices – particularly sloth and gluttony – who persistently maltreats his lady companion. Patrick is rich, vapid, emotionally manipulative and happy to use his wealth to buy the sexual favours he wants from gullible – or simply greedy – young men. On the surface his character is fey and camp, but beneath there is moral wickedness, as he develops his sexual position like a chess player.

Patrick has come across the narrator, Nicholas, in Kent, and has lured him up to London with the prospect of a job in the literary world. When the young man arrives, Patrick, who has already bought him a gold cigarette case and a Picasso engraving, takes him to stay in a suite at the 'Rialto' (the Ritz). Nicholas either fails to grasp the terms of the bargain that he has struck or realises them and resists them; either way, he does not succumb to Patrick's charms physically, although he happily enjoys expensive meals, gifts and cash handouts. Eventually Patrick realises that Nicholas is not for him and abruptly and ruthlessly terminates their connection, promptly replacing him with another similar young man – who happens to be the assistant in the jewellers' shop where Patrick bought the gold cigarette case. (This transition may be based loosely on the start of Peter's relationship with Waldemar Hansen, since we know that Michael Nelson and Waldemar met at least once shortly after the latter's first arrival in London.[1] Since Waldemar was an innocent party, the embittered author perhaps felt inclined to disguise him more thoroughly than the other characters.)

Described as being bored by politics, Patrick comes out with a remark that is pure Watson: 'Boredom terrifies me more than anything else.' In a similar vein Patrick becomes bored with Ronnie as he does with everybody.

Patrick is said to 'hate practical people'. He turns up late for dinner dates and vanishes to Paris with little warning when it happens to suit him. He uses his money as a means to a sexual end. The porter at his block of flats bemoans the fact that Patrick is always losing keys to the flat as a result of lending them to visiting young men. Indeed, Waldemar Hansen took the flat keys away with him when he was ejected, and Peter had to ask for them back. The truth was that, certainly when he was without the regular presence of a constant partner such as Waldemar or Norman, and even while they were around, Peter was openly promiscuous; men came and went. And yet according to men who knew him intimately – such as Waldemar and Alex Leslie – he didn't have a very intense physical sex drive.

In *A Room in Chelsea Square* Nelson writes of Patrick:

> By accepting what Patrick gave he entered into a contract. There was nothing legally binding about it, but the terms were implied. It might be an unwritten law. The fact remained that one always had to pay for what one had.

This closely echoes one of Peter's letters to Waldemar:

> I know two facts about life. Everything has to be paid for in some way or other and it is so easy to spoil things and having done so one still has to go on living. And yet love is one of the ways of redemption, perhaps the only way if only it can take over the intensity and powers of one's bad feelings.[2]

Note that Patrick only represents the first half of Peter's statement. On close examination, Michael Nelson's understanding of Peter Watson's psychology appears relatively skin-deep; he saw the transaction but didn't really understand either it or the person thrusting it upon him.

The Spender character attempts to sum up Patrick's personality; his words are trite, a complete misfire that bears no resemblance to what the real Stephen Spender actually thought of Peter Watson. 'Christopher' says of Patrick:

> I'm sorry for him. I can see the loneliness behind his rich exterior. The rich are the loneliest people in the world. They can never know the meaning of friendship. They think their friends only love them for their money.

Peter Watson did not think like this, and Stephen Spender did not think this of him. It is a hackneyed and unfortunately quite cheap shot at a cartoon version of a rich man that lets down an otherwise precise portrayal of Peter.

A Room in Chelsea Square could not possibly have been published during Peter Watson's lifetime. Whereas the teasing he had suffered at the hands of Gerald Berners was cruel and no doubt hurtful to the young Peter in the mid-1930s, that book had been privately printed and circulated only among the cognoscenti as a private joke. Whereas Berners was, and crucially remained, a friend of Peter's, and had come from the same world, Michael Nelson was merely a brief acquaintance, a visitor to the Watson world, and clearly an embittered one. The extreme manipulation he describes his character experiencing at the hands of Patrick is probably an exaggeration of what had actually happened, but in its core features is undoubtedly accurate.

When *A Room in Chelsea Square* finally appeared in 1958, it was published anonymously – even though Peter's death had removed the risk of libel, the homosexual themes were extremely controversial. The book received good reviews from Malcolm Bradbury, John Betjeman and several others. It wasn't hugely popular, though, and sank without trace for a while. In later years it was revived and republished as part of the efflorescence of gay fiction. It still excites mixed responses. In the introduction to a recent edition, critic Gregory Woods writes that, on the one hand, 'it is a parade of negative representations of homosexual men, following many of the imposed, homophobic stereotypes of the age' and 'has not a single attractive and sympathetic character with whom the gay reader can identify'; but, on the other hand, 'Its main virtue is that it takes homosexuality completely for granted. There is anguish aplenty, but not about being gay.'[3]

In a way, that last sentence neatly encapsulates the life of Peter Watson himself.

NOTES

1 – A VIOLENT QUARREL

[1] This was told to Sir Rodney Touche (Sir Norman Watson's biographer) by Robert Jolliff.

[2] Spender, diary entry, 9 May 1956, *New Selected Journals*, p. 229.

[3] Beaton, diary entry, 6 May 1956, *Restless Years*, pp. 44–5. (Beaton did not write his diary daily; he wrote up days and weeks at a time in retrospect.)

[4] Beaton, letter to Garbo, 4 May 1956, PCB A2/14a/127.

[5] Spender, diary entry, 7 May 1956, PSS.

[6] Spender, diary entry, 9 May 1956, *New Selected Journals*, pp. 229–31. (The inquest was held on 8 May; Spender described it in his journal the following day.)

[7] Spender, diary entry, 9 May 1956, *New Selected Journals*, pp. 229–31.

2 – BETWEEN THE PRINCE AND THE FROG

[1] Pryce-Jones, *The Bonus of Laughter*, pp. 28–9. Each house at Eton was known by the name of its housemaster (such as Goodhart's, after housemaster A. M. Goodhart) but also, confusingly, by the permanent name of the house itself.

[2] Description based on Green, *Pack My Bag*, pp. 69–70. The novelist Henry Green (whose real name was Yorke) was a contemporary at Eton, and was in the same house as Alan Pryce-Jones.

[3] Pryce-Jones, *Private Opinion*, pp. 20–21. Despite his sophistication, Peter had not

yet acquired a taste for art, so his walls were probably decorated with the same stock prints as every other boy's.

[4] Pryce-Jones, *The Bonus of Laughter*, p. 29. *Quelques Fleurs* was introduced by French perfumer Houbigant in 1912, and was the first perfume to use a bouquet of floral scents (hence the name). During the 1920s René Lalique designed a range of Art Deco bottles for it.

[5] Eton's admission records from this period do not name the boys' prep schools; instead they give the name of each boy's former headmaster. In Peter Watson's case this was Mr Godfrey Worsley, head of Evelyn's at Colham Green, Hillingdon, which was founded in 1872. It struggled in the post-war period, eventually closing in 1931.

[6] Grimond, *Memoirs*, p. 41.

[7] The relationship between Waugh and the Lygon family, and the connection with *Brideshead*, is documented by Paula Byrne in *Mad World*. See also Alexander Waugh's review in the *Literary Review*, August 2009, pp. 26–7, available online at www.literaryreview.co.uk/waugh_08_09.html (retrieved 30 July 2014).

[8] David Herbert, cited in Vickers, *Cecil Beaton*, p. 147.

[9] Sulhamstead House was constructed around 1800 by modifying an earlier manor house. It had been in the hands of the Thoyts family since the mid-eighteenth century, and was sold to George Watson after the death of the last Lord of the Manor, Major William Richard Mortimer Thoyts.

[10] Certain bequests in his will to former Sulhamstead servants and to his mother's sister indicate that he remained in touch with people whom a man in his position might reasonably have been expected to ignore or forget.

[11] The portraits were painted in 1913. The portrait of Sir George has since disappeared, but the one of Lady Watson was until recently in the possession of the family.

[12] Although Peter wrote almost nothing about his family, he did apparently talk to some close friends about them. The portrayal here is partly derived from the summary given by Michael Shelden in *Friends of Promise* (p. 26), which was based on interviews with some of Peter's intimate friends.

[13] *The Times*, 12 March 1920, p. 8.

[14] England & Wales census records, 1861–91. The Watsons appear to have moved several times in the area around Foleshill and Walsgrave-on-Sowe (northeast of Coventry), but their household remained fairly consistent. William Watson farmed 416 acres and employed about a dozen labourers.

[15] The whole story of the Maypole Dairy Company is told in Mathias, *Retailing Revolution*, pp. 165–91.

[16] *The Times*, 15 February 1910, p. 14.

[17] England & Wales census records, 1881–91. Birth and christening records indicate that 'Bessie' was her given name, not a diminutive.

[18] *The Times*, 9 May 1908, p. 20; Neild & Neild, *Financial History of Trinity College*, p. 93. £82,000 in 1908 equates to approximately £8.6 million now. The estate was bought from George Watson by the Hon. John Ward, son-in-law of the US Ambassador and friend of King Edward VII.

[19] The address on his birth certificate is Kaylis House, Chauntry Road. Although the road is still there, there are few old houses surviving, and none with that name.

[20] England & Wales census, 1911. Louise Stewart was twenty-six years old and came from Glasgow.

[21] Sale notices in *The Times*, 3 August 1910, p. 9; 12 November 1910, p. 20; will of Major William Thoyts reported in *The Times*, 30 April 1910, p. 13.

[22] The 1st Earl (5th Baron) Sondes changed the family name from Watson to Milles in the late nineteenth century. But there were many (presumably related) Watsons who shared the same coat of arms and motto (seven are listed in *Fairbairn's Book of Crests* for 1905, pp. 579–80).

[23] Sulhamstead estate records, Berkshire Record office D/EX 975.

[24] Description by Emma Elizabeth Thoyts (daughter of the previous owner), 1890, available online at www.mayfamilyhistory.co.uk/places/sulhse_eet.html (retrieved 12 July 2014).

[25] Lavery painted both George and Bessie; the Herkomer portrait was made at the expense of the Maypole Dairy Company and presented to Sir George at the company's annual dinner in 1913 (*The Times*, 4 February 1913, p. 9).

[26] Leading articles were also carried by *The Times* (5 December 1919) and the *Observer* (7 December 1919), included with the associated letters and lecture in Bryce, *The Study of American History*. The chair was titular, not attached to any university, and was intended to be held by eminent academics for short periods. The Sir George Watson chair still exists, still hosted by the American Society in London (formerly the Anglo-American Society).

[27] The organ – or at least its pipe ranks – still survives as the organ of the Abbey Church, Ballasalla, Isle of Man. See Kewley, *Churches of Mann*; Kewley's entry on the Sulhamstead organ is available online at www.culturevannin.im/special/church_organ/Abbey_Church_Ballasalla.pdf (retrieved 18 July 2014).

[28] This was less of a departure than it might sound. The agricultural shows featured entries on behalf of the King and many members of the more rustic nobility.

3 – 'NOTHING IS MORE AWFUL THAN TOO MUCH REALITY'

[1] Anthony Wagner (*Herald's World*, pp. 17–19), who was an exact contemporary of Peter Watson, was a King's Scholar. In his first year Wagner fagged for George Orwell, who was a sixth-form Colleger. Wagner recalled Orwell as a 'gentle and kind' fagmaster. (See also Lehmann, *Whispering Gallery*, pp. 95–6; Connolly, *Enemies of Promise*, p. 173ff. on the position of King's Scholars at Eton.)

[2] The term 'Oppidan' hints at the higher prestige of the Collegers; historically, an oppidan was an inhabitant of a university town who was not a member of the university – a townsman, an outsider. The King's Scholars were the historic core of Eton College, and the Oppidans were, in a sense, the cash supply that kept the institution running.

[3] All pupils had to have achieved a pass mark in the Common Entrance exam which was shared by all public schools. Different schools had different pass marks; Eton's standards at this time were not very exacting (other than for King's Scholars, who had to pass a special, much more challenging, exam).

[4] See Joyce (*State of Freedom*, pp. 267–9) for a summary of the Eton system in the nineteenth and early twentieth centuries. In the 1940s, Eton began to reform itself, introducing a new system whereby fees and admissions were regulated centrally by the school.

[5] Nonetheless, the building names were also used, and, even more confusingly, had often acquired their names from the masters who had founded them.

[6] Venn & Venn, *Alumni Cantabrigienses*, p. 83.

[7] Powell, *To Keep the Ball Rolling*, pp. 29–30.

[8] Reminiscences of literary historian and academic Lord David Cecil, according to his son (Cecil, 'My Father at Eton', in Cranborne, *David Cecil*, pp. 20–23). Cecil was the youngest child of the Marquess of Salisbury; he went on to be professor of English literature at Oxford.

[9] Powell, *To Keep the Ball Rolling*, pp. 29–30; see also Powell, 'An Early Friendship', in Cranborne, *David Cecil*, pp. 28–31 and Cecil, 'My Father at Eton'. Anthony Powell, who arrived at Eton in summer 1919, fagged for David Cecil.

[10] Keith Vaughan, journal entry for 16 May 1942, TGA 200817/1/10.

[11] Routine described by Robert Byron, broadly contemporary with Peter Watson, quoted by Knox, *Robert Byron*, p. 22.

[12] Peter told this to Cecil Beaton in 1931 – writing about how cruel and callous Peter could be, Beaton wrote that 'we gossiped until very late one night and he told me about his life at Oxford and at school – He was head of the house and beat the bad boys and I was very impressed – so commendable' (Beaton, diary entry for 2 February 1931, PCB).

[13] Herbert, *Second Son*, p. 27.

[14] Lowe, *Edward James*, pp. 21–42.

[15] Lehmann, *Whispering Gallery*, pp. 100–101.

[16] Pryce-Jones, *Private Opinion*, p. 19.

[17] The pre-war attitude was exemplified by Henry Newboldt's 1892 poem 'Vitaï Lambada', which links public-school sporting spirit with martial courage, linked together by the rallying cry 'Play up! play up! and play the game!'.

[18] Connolly describes the revolution in *Enemies of Promise*, pp. 181–96, and John Lehmann describes its effect in *Whispering Gallery*, pp. 96–7.

[19] Waugh acknowledged the source: 'There is an aesthetic bugger who sometimes turns up in my novels under various names – that was Brian and Harold Acton. People think it was all Harold, who is a much sweeter and saner man.' Waugh added, 'I used to know Brian Howard well – a dazzling young man to my innocent eyes. In later life he became very dangerous – constantly attacking people with his fists in public places – so I kept clear of him. He was consumptive but the immediate cause of his death was a broken heart' (Waugh, *The Letters of Evelyn Waugh*, p. 505).

[20] Powell, *Keep the Ball Rolling*, pp. 46–8.

[21] Pryce-Jones, *Private Opinion*, p. 20.

[22] Knox, *Robert Byron*, p. 28.

[23] Herbert, *Second Son*, pp. 27–8; Lees-Milne, *Another Self*, pp. 47–52. The otherwise sensible James Lees-Milne was one of the 'Dolly Sisters', the adventure being his one and only 'alignment with the wrong, raffish set' at Eton.

[24] Powell, *Keep the Ball Rolling*, p. 48.

[25] Lehmann, *Whispering Gallery*, p. 102.

[26] Green, *Pack My Bag*, p. 72.

[27] Pearson, *Life of Ian Fleming*, pp. 25–7. There is no evidence that Peter Watson and Fleming knew each other, but they were certainly part of the same Eton subculture, identified as a 'set' by another contemporary, the writer James Lees-Milne (*Another Self*, pp. 45–7).

[28] Powell, *Keep the Ball Rolling*, p. 58.

[29] Lehmann, *Whispering Gallery*, pp. 97–8.

[30] Powell, *Keep the Ball Rolling*, p. 60.

[31] Lees-Milne, *Another Self*, p. 45.

[32] Alan Pryce-Jones in *ADAM International Review* nos. 385–90 (1974/5).

[33] Alan Pryce-Jones in *ADAM International Review* nos. 385–90 (1974/5).

[34] Powell, *Keep the Ball Rolling*, pp. 30-31.

[35] Herbert, *Second Son*, p. 28.

[36] Powell, *Keep the Ball Rolling*, p. 31.

[37] Pryce-Jones, *Bonus of Laughter*, p. 4.

[38] Bankhead, *Tallulah*, p. 156.

[39] As usually happened at Eton, the identity of the house was continued; it became Young's house, but was regarded as a continuation of Goodhart's. This is reflected in the lineage of the A. M. Goodhart Dining Club, which was founded in 1912 for old boys of Goodhart's house. The club still exists, and is open to all later members of the successor houses, from Young's down to the present day.

[40] Lees-Milne, *Another Self*, p. 61.

4 – THE FREEDOM OF THE WORLD

[1] Watson, postcard to Connolly, postmarked London, 17 January 1945, CCP. The words could alternatively be translated, 'In this house I found myself.' Belying his apparently poor performance at school, Peter wrote the message in perfect and correctly accented Greek.

[2] Connolly, *Enemies of Promise*, p. 253.

[3] Archive information from Michael Riordan, St John's College, Oxford.

[4] Archive information from Michael Riordan, St John's College, Oxford.

[5] Beaton, diary entries for October 1922, *Wandering Years*.

[6] Lees-Milne, *Another Self*, p. 63.

[7] Connolly, *Enemies of Promise*, p. 252.

[8] Pryce-Jones, *Bonus of Laughter*, p. 49.

[9] Pryce-Jones, *Bonus of Laughter*, p. 51.

[10] Pryce-Jones, *Bonus of Laughter*, p. 50.

[11] Pryce-Jones, *Bonus of Laughter*, p. 53.

[12] Oxford University Undergraduate Registers, via Emma Harrold, Oxford University Archives, Bodleian Library, Oxford.

[13] St John's College List, via Michael Riordan, Archivist, St John's and The Queen's Colleges, Oxford.

[14] Cross, *Evan Frederic Morgan*, p. 65.

[15] Isherwood, *Christopher and His Kind*, p. 30.

[16] Isherwood, *Christopher and His Kind*, pp. 31–2.

[17] Nancy Mitford, letter to Mark Ogilvie-Grant, 23 January 1930, in Mitford, *Love from Nancy*, p. 35. There is no record of Peter's sending-down in the university or college archives; for the period in question, the registers only record successes in examinations.

[18] One million pounds in 1930 would be equivalent to about £55m today. Peter's annual income of £50,000 would be equivalent to about £2.75m. These figures

are approximate; changes in actual spending power and relative wealth since 1930 mean that inflation-based comparisons are not entirely reliable. Since the original trust documents are unobtainable, the figure of £1 million is an estimate based on the amounts later willed to Norman and Florence.

[19] Sulhamstead estate records, Berkshire Record office D/EX 975.

[20] The arrangement of trust funds was (and is) secretive. We know of the existence and date of Peter's fund from several sources, including his own will, which refers to it. The trust would have been set up so that it reverted to the family on his death. His sister Florence's will mentions a trust called '"H" Fund', which had been created by Sir George on 6 January 1930 and is presumably Peter's.

[21] William George Watson, death certificate, 12 July 1930, St Marylebone district, St Mary sub-district. Cause of death was 'cardiac failure following operation' and 'cancer of lower pelvic colon of 10 months history & chronic obstruction'. There is evidence that Sir George had been optimistic about his illness and did not expect to die so soon. Just over a week earlier he had advertised in *The Times* (1 July 1930, p. 3) for a new head chauffeur ('Rolls school: personal references indispensable: cottage provided – Address full particulars Sir George Watson').

[22] Funeral reported in *The Times*, 16 July 1930, p. 17.

[23] Will of Sir William George Watson, signed 9 July 1930, proved 20 August 1930 (see also report in the *Manchester Guardian*, 23 August 1930, p. 8). The exact value of the estate was returned at £2,019,841.

[24] The actual percentage placed into trusts is unknown, and the atmosphere of discretion surrounding trusts is such that any modern tax lawyer would be unwilling to make even an approximate estimate.

[25] The company found itself pilloried during the war for profiteering – unfairly, because prices were regulated by the government. Sir George was stung by the accusations, and wrote twice to *The Times* describing Maypole's difficult situation (*The Times*, 14 May 1918, p. 8; 21 February 1919, p. 2). See also Mathias, *Retailing Revolution*, pp. 216–36.

[26] The Honours (Prevention of Abuses) Act 1925 made it a misdemeanour to 'obtain from any person, for himself or for any other person, or for any purpose, any gift, money or valuable consideration as an inducement or reward for procuring or assisting or endeavouring to procure the grant of a dignity or title of honour'; see www.legislation.gov.uk/ukpga/Geo5/15-16/72/section/1 (retrieved 6 August 2014).

[27] The case was summarised in the Law Reports in *The Times*, 12 June 1934, p. 5, and 7 July 1934, p. 4. The arrest and imprisonment of Maundy Gregory was reported in *The Times* of 17 February 1933, p. 9; 22 February 1933, p. 11. The Watson name was kept quiet during the scandal, evidence being given in court by

Mr W. T. Norton (the executor) on behalf of an unnamed deceased testator. The fact that Sir George hoped to purchase a barony prompts the question of whether he also purchased his baronetcy. He probably did not. At the time, in 1910, he had been quite involved in influencing government policy on trade, as well as a vital link in Britain's food supply at a time when war and revolution were looming in Europe, and a baronetcy would not be an inappropriate reward; moreover, his naivety in giving such a huge sum to the defunct Maundy Gregory suggests that he wasn't accustomed to such shady dealings.

[28] The story of Lake Louise is told by Touche, *Brown Cows, Sacred Cows*. The resort still exists: see www.posthotel.com/about/history.html (retrieved 7 August 2014).

[29] The Heston Aircraft Company made light aircraft for private and commercial use. Founded in 1929 by the early 1930s it was struggling. Sir Norman Watson took it over; the original board of directors resigned en masse, leaving only Norman (*Flight International*, vol. 26 [1934], p. 886). During the Second World War, the company did Air Ministry work, modifying military aircraft for alternative purposes (such as the adapting Spitfires for photo-reconnaissance).

[30] Florence Nagle's story is told in Somerfield, *Mission Accomplished*.

[31] Florence's grandson, Alasdair Nagle, believes that she might have had lesbian relationships with two women who were her partners in owning and breeding dogs and racehorses, and who lived with her (Nagle, personal communication to Adrian Clark, 22 July 2014). Sir Norman Watson's biographer, Sir Rodney Touche, interviewing Norman's 'girlfriends' (of whom he had several) 'gained the impression that he had covert homosexual leanings' (Touche, personal communication to Adrian Clark, 21 July 2014).

[32] By contrast, his Eton and Oxford contemporary Edward James, who was similarly wealthy, had inherited young due to his father's premature death, and when he came of age he found himself encumbered by a Sussex estate even larger and more burdensome than Sulhamstead, as well as a house in Wimpole Street.

5 – A SWOON OF ROMANTIC LOVE

[1] See Vickers, *Cecil Beaton*, p. 122ff.

[2] Beaton, *The Wandering Years*, pp. 219–22. While at the Duckworth offices, he met a young 'black-clad assistant' who was friendly but 'pervaded a Dickensian misery'; this assistant was none other than Anthony Powell, former Goodhartian Etonian and future novelist. His air of gloom was caused not, as Cecil thought, by being 'caught in the trap of a publishing firm' but by a severe bout of unrequited love for an unattainable girl (Powell, *Keep the Ball Rolling*, p. 195). Beaton wasn't yet equipped to recognise the symptoms.

[3] Beaton, *The Wandering Years*, pp. 220–21. Edith Olivier (b. 1872) was a cousin (once removed) of Laurence Olivier. Rex Whistler was *not* related to the painter James McNeill Whistler, although people often assumed that he was.

[4] Beaton, *The Wandering Years*, p. 221.

[5] Beaton, diary, 21 December 1926, PCB, quoted in Vickers, *Cecil Beaton*, p. 84. Oliver Messel and Cecil Beaton were born on, respectively, 13 and 14 January 1904. They appear to have first met in the mid-1920s, having gone to different schools and colleges (Cecil, Harrow and Cambridge; Oliver, Eton and the Slade School of Art).

[6] Beaton, *The Wandering Years*, p. 222. Peter and Oliver had been briefly contemporary with each other at Eton, but probably not acquainted. They were likely introduced later through mutual acquaintances – possibly Brian Howard, Harold Acton or Robert Byron (Thomas Messel, personal communication to Adrian Clark, 8 July 2014).

[7] Beaton, diary, 6 May 1956, PCB (recollections written down in the days after Peter's death).

[8] Fragments of this conversation are recorded in Beaton, *The Wandering Years*, p. 222, and diary, 6 May 1956, PCB.

[9] Beaton, *The Wandering Years*, p. 222; diary, 6 May 1956, PCB.

[10] Loos, quoted by Vickers, *Cecil Beaton*, p. 123.

[11] Beaton, diary, 10 January 1924, quoted in Vickers, *Cecil Beaton*, p. 123. The performance would have been the musical comedy *Stop Flirting*, which had a long run at the Shaftesbury Theatre and on tour (*The Times*, 10 March 1924, p. 10). In 1932 Adèle retired and married the son of the Duke of Devonshire.

[12] Vickers, *Cecil Beaton*, pp. 3–7. Cecil was deeply upset when he learned about his ancestry from his father.

[13] Beaton, diary, 6 May 1956, PCB.

[14] Beaton, diary, 6 May 1956, PCB. Cecil didn't note down the title of this song, although he did later refer to it as 'the sex appeal record' (Beaton, letter to Watson, undated, PCB A2/38).

[15] Beaton, letter to Watson, undated (probably May 1933), PCB A2/38.

[16] Beaton, diary, 6 May 1956, PCB; Vickers, *Cecil Beaton*, pp. 73–5.

[17] Beaton mentions the planned visit to Mrs Keppel in his recollections (diary, 6 May 1956, PCB); the connection might have come through Oliver Messel, as there is no evidence of Cecil ever being acquainted with the former royal mistress. Alternatively, the connection could have been through Mrs Keppel's equally sensational daughter, Violet Trefusis, who was popular with the young men of Peter and Cecil's circles despite being a generation older (as were several much older women, such as Sybil Colefax and Edith Olivier). Cecil and Violet were certainly acquainted.

[18] Beaton, diary, 6 May 1956, PCB.

[19] Beaton, diary, 6 May 1956, PCB.

[20] Beaton, *The Wandering Years*, p. 222.

[21] Beaton, diary, 6 May 1956, PCB. In 1930, colourful cars were becoming more fashionable – at the Paris Motor Show it was noted that British exhibitors 'add to their well-known mechanical excellency a gayer and more daring taste in coachwork' (*The Times*, 3 October 1930, p. 10). Prices varied; at the Olympia Motor Show in London, it was reported that Rolls-Royce exhibited: ''four models on their own stand – three 40 h.p. "Phantoms" at about £3,000 each, and a 20 h.p. "Windover enclosed limousine body", seating six, at £2,141' (*The Spectator*, 18 October 1930, p. 558).

[22] Nancy Mitford, letter to Tom Mitford, 1 November 1930, in *Love from Nancy*, pp. 35–6n. Enigmatically, Nancy went on, '– I won't go into the reason why because the matron might read this during your moments of delirium & it would be awkward for you' (Tom was in hospital at the time).

[23] Beaton, *The Wandering Years*, p. 223.

[24] Beaton, diary, 6 May 1956, PCB.

[25] Middleboe, *Edith Olivier*, p. 115.

[26] Beaton, diary, 6 May 1956, PCB.

[27] Beaton, diary, 6 May 1956, PCB.

[28] Edith Olivier, letter to Beaton, 3 November 1930, PCB A1/398/31.

[29] Peter's mother would soon be departing for Cannes. During Sir George's lifetime, the couple had frequently followed the fashionable set to either Cannes or St Moritz in the winter season. Now that Bessie was a widow, it had become the unmarried Sir Norman's job to accompany his mother on her holidays; this year they stayed at the Beau-Site hotel in Cannes (*The Times* court circular, 19 January 1931).

[30] According to Beaton's diary account (written some years after the event) and Vickers' biography (*Cecil Beaton*, p. 150), this voyage took place in January 1931 aboard the Cunard liner RMS *Aquitania* (which sailed from Southampton on 7 January). According to passenger lists, however, Cecil and Peter sailed aboard the *Majestic* on 31 December 1930 (BTP outwards, 31 December 1930, Southampton–New York). The *Majestic*, which at the time was the largest ship of any kind in the world, was less fashionable than the *Aquitania*, but every bit as opulent. Beaton's account of this trip to America is spread over many different entries in his diary, including notes written in January 1931, October 1931, February 1933 and on 6 May 1956 (unpublished diaries, PCB).

[31] John McCormack was very popular in Europe and America at this time. Byron

Haskin, who had directed one silent comedy, was virtually unknown; in the post-war period he became a TV producer and director, partly responsible for shows including *The Outer Limits* and *Star Trek*.

[32] Beaton, diary, 6 May 1956, PCB.

[33] Watson, letter to Beaton, undated (probably February 1932), PCB A1/553/20).

[34] Beaton, diary, January 1931, PCB.

[35] Fred and Adèle had finished the run of *Smiles* on 10 January 1931, and would not be starring again until the opening of musical revue *The Band Wagon* in June (see Internet Broadway Database, ibdb.com/person.php?id=30282, retrieved 19 August 2014). Soon after their encounter with Cecil and Peter, the Astaires sailed for Europe (sailing reported in *The Brooklyn Daily Eagle*, 21 January 1931, p. 17).

[36] Bankhead, *Tallulah*, p. 155. The story was suppressed in the major British and American newspapers (perhaps through fear of Miss Bankhead's lawyers), but the *Pittsburgh Post-Gazette* (17 January 1931) reported that the Home Office had asked her to leave in connection with the incident some years earlier in which 'two Eton students, belonging to prominent families, were expelled for attending a party with Miss Bankhead'. In fact the boys had not been expelled, thanks to the intervention of Tallulah's lawyers.

[37] Beaton, *Book of Beauty*, p. 41. What she thought of this description he didn't note. He did observe, though, that the book had 'ignited perhaps less of a blaze than I had hoped'. He heard that Lady Maud Cunard 'added to the conflagration by throwing her copy into the fire. Her luncheon guests were astonished to watch her thrusting a poker through the burning covers as she exclaimed in a high canary squeak, "He calls me a hostess, that shows he's a low fellow!"' (Beaton, *The Wandering Years*, p. 224).

[38] The *Manchester Guardian*, 14 January 1931, p. 4. The film was *Tarnished Lady*, directed by George Cukor and co-starring Clive Brook. She told the newspapers that if the film was unsuccessful, she intended to return to London.

[39] Beaton, diary, January 1931, end October 1931, PCB.

[40] Beaton, diary, January 1931, PCB.

[41] Beaton, diary, 2 February 1931, PCB.

[42] Beaton, diary, end October 1931, PCB.

[43] Watson, letter to Beaton, undated (probably March 1931), PCB A1/553/16.

[44] Watson, undated postcard to Beaton, PCB A1/553/3. The postcard was marked for 'Water Post' and addressed to 'K. Beaton esq., Stateroom 17', and signed 'Pete Pitt Peter'. At this time Peter was calling Cecil 'Kell'.

[45] Beaton, diary, recollection written at the end of October 1931, PCB. Cecil's account of this incident is quite elliptical, but there is a clear implication that in not paying

for Cecil's journey, Peter was departing from the arrangement that had brought them this far. The evidence shows that *both* men travelled by land, setting out two days apart. Cecil crossed the border at El Paso, Texas, on 17 February 1931, and Peter on 19 February (Port of El Paso Manifest, National Archives and Records Administration, Washington, DC; Record Group: 85, Records of the Immigration and Naturalization Service; Microfilm Roll: 9; available online at Ancestry.com).

46 Mary Pickford, telegram to Beaton, 23 February 1931, PCB A1/423. Pickfair, a Hollywood landmark, was demolished in 1990 by its then owner, actress Pia Zadora, who claimed it was infested with termites, but subsequently admitted that she believed it to be haunted by the ghost of a woman who'd had an affair with Douglas Fairbanks.

47 In his diary, Cecil implies (but doesn't state) that they travelled all the way to New York together (describing his miserable feelings 'as we neared NY and the departure of Peter'), and Vickers' biography (*Cecil Beaton*, p. 153) interprets it this way. But Peter's letter from Santa Fe indicates that they had parted somewhere between Arizona and New Mexico.

48 Watson, letter to Beaton, undated (probably March 1931), PCB A1/553/16. Cecil's letter to Peter does not appear to have survived.

49 Beaton, *The Wandering Years*, p. 224; BTP inwards, SS *Europa*, 5 April 1931, New York–Southampton.

50 Beaton, diary, February and end October 1931, PCB.

51 Beaton, diary, end October 1931, PCB.

52 Beaton, *The Wandering Years*, p. 225.

53 Beaton, diary, May 1956, PCB. Charles James was briefly at Harrow, where he was involved in the theatre and began a long friendship with Cecil Beaton, who helped him in his career. James's behaviour was openly homosexual, and some sources claim that he was expelled from Harrow for a 'sexual escapade'. However, there is no record of this, and it is more likely that his father withdrew him from the school because of his behaviour (Reeder, 'Metamorphology', p. 17). Peter later had a very rocky friendship with the erratic James.

6 – PINING FOR GRANDEUR

1 Beaton, diary, end of October 1931, PCB.

2 He sailed on 28 October 1931 aboard the RMS *Olympic*, twin sister of the *Titanic* (BTP outwards, 31 October 1931, Southampton–New York).

3 As announced in, for example, *The Times* court circular, 25 September 1925 and 24 April 1929.

4 Beaton, diary, end of October 1931, PCB.

[5] Beaton, diary, end of October 1931, PCB.

[6] Beaton, diary, end of October 1931, PCB. Probably the young Henry Mond, 2nd Baron Melchett, and his wife. Mond was a Liberal politician and art patron.

[7] Beaton, diary, August 1931, PCB.

[8] Beaton, diary, August 1931, PCB.

[9] Beaton, diary, August 1931, PCB.

[10] Beaton, diary, August 1931, PCB.

[11] The sale was announced in *The Times*, 5 December 1931, p. 3; the buyer wasn't identified. On the 1932–3 electoral registers, Victor William Watson is listed as the sole occupant, with two female servants living in (Electoral Register 1932, City of Westminster Grosvenor Ward N3, p. 213, LMA).

[12] Watson, letter to Beaton, 25 November (probably 1931), PCB A1/553/59. The queen would be Queen Mary, who was in her mid-sixties at this time.

[13] Watson, letter to Beaton, 25 November (probably 1931), PCB A1/553/59. The *Times* critic called the piece 'a work of outstanding imaginative power', but felt that the singing by the National Chorus compared poorly with the 'stalwart quality' of the Yorkshire choir that had performed the cantata's debut at the Leeds Festival the previous month (*The Times*, 26 November 1931, p. 12).

[14] Oliver's sets earned swooning praise from the *Times* critic (who gave the rest of the production a lukewarm appraisal): 'Mr Oliver Messel has given it exquisite scenes which range from the classic lines of the Temple of Jupiter ... to a baroque tapestry of the walls of Troy, and from the snowy whiteness of Helen's first bedroom to the delicate shades of art blue in which she subsequently sleeps with Paris. Mr Messel, too, has produced an unimaginable variety of forms and colours in costumes with which M. Leonide Massine may conjure a welter of movement in the orgy' (*The Times*, 1 February 1932, p. 10).

[15] Watson, letter to Beaton, undated, PCB A1/553/32.

[16] Watson, letter to Beaton, undated (probably 1931 or 1932), PCB A1/553/34.

[17] Tennant, letter to Beaton, undated, PCB A1/520/155, quoted in Hoare, *Serious Pleasures*, p. 158.

[18] Hoare, *Serious Pleasures*, p. 156.

[19] Watson, letter to Beaton, undated (probably mid-1932), PCB A1/553/24.

[20] For instance, Caroline Blackwood, writer and sometime wife of Lucian Freud, thought Tennant 'semi-psychotic' and disliked him intensely (quoted in Hoare, *Serious Pleasures*, pp. 334–5.).

[21] Quoted in Amory, *Lord Berners*, p. 129.

[22] Beaton, diary, 28 June 1932, PCB.

[23] Beaton, diary, 12 July 1932, PCB.

[24] Lady Diana Cooper, quoted in Vickers, *Cecil Beaton*, p. 161.

[25] Beaton, diary, undated (late summer 1932), PCB.

[26] Beaton, letter to Watson, undated (probably mid-September 1932), PCB A2/38.

[27] Beaton, diary, 14 September 1932, PCB.

[28] Watson, letter to Beaton, 17 September 1932, PCB A1/553/15.

[29] Vickers, *Cecil Beaton*, pp. 158–9. In September Eddie Goulding had to flee Hollywood 'after giving a party for eight girls which wound up with two of them having to be sent to the hospital' (Anita Loos, letter to Beaton, 29 September 1932, PCB A1/338/2). William Randolph Hearst suppressed the story, and one newspaperman told MGM that the story wouldn't be printed 'as it was so filthy it couldn't be'.

[30] The *Manchester Guardian*, 9 August 1932, p. 8.

[31] Watson, letter to Beaton, 17 September 1932, PCB A1/553/15.

[32] Hastings, *Nancy Mitford*, pp. 59, 112; Mitford, *Love from Nancy*, p. 109n.

[33] Diana Mosley, *Loved Ones*, p. 156.

[34] Beaton, diary, May 1933, PCB, quoted in Vickers, *Cecil Beaton*, p. 166.

[35] Watson, letter to Beaton, 14 March 1933, PCB A1/553/62.

[36] Watson, telegram to Beaton, 15 March 1933, PCB A1/553/83.

[37] *The Times*, 13 May 1933, p. 12; 15 May, p. 14; 16 May, p. 14; 17 May, p. 19.

[38] Vickers, *Cecil Beaton*, p. 162.

[39] Watson, letter to Beaton, undated (certainly 19 May 1933), PCB A1/553/66. In her biography of Diana, Anne De Courcy (*Diana Mosley*, p. 109) states that Sir Oswald phoned Diana within minutes of Cimmie's death (but doesn't cite a source); Peter Watson's letter to Beaton contradicts this. Robert Byron was particularly close to Nancy Mitford, who once hoped he might marry her – 'but he was a total pederast ... This wretched pederasty falsifies all feelings & yet one is supposed to revere it' (Nancy Mitford, letter to Jessica Mitford, Mitford, *Love from Nancy*, p. 510).

[40] Watson, letter to Beaton, undated (probably 19 May 1933), PCB A1/553/66.

[41] Quoted in De Courcy, *Diana Mosley*, p. 109.

[42] *The Times*, 21 May 1933, p. 15.

[43] Vickers, *Cecil Beaton*, p. 166.

[44] Watson, letter to Beaton, undated (probably 19 May 1933), PCB A1/553/66.

7 – UNDER SOME STRANGE INFLUENCE

[1] Watson, letter to Beaton, dated only 'Saturday tea time' (probably June 1933), PCB A1/553/26. Vickers (*Cecil Beaton*, p. 167n.) dates this letter (and the one of Cecil's to which it was a reply) to May 1933; however, taking Peter's letter about Cimmie Mosley's death (written on 19 May) as a *terminus post quem*,

not enough of May would remain for the events which occurred prior to letter PCB A1/553/26 being written. Cecil wrote (retrospectively) about these events in his diary in July.

[2] Beaton, letter to Watson, undated (probably June 1933), PCB A2/38. The letter has been preserved, unfolded, never having been sent; instead Cecil read it to Peter. Vickers (*Cecil Beaton*, p. 167) states that this occurred one evening. However, Peter's reply seems to indicate that the confrontation had occurred earlier that day, at lunch.

[3] Watson, letter to Beaton, misdated 12 February 1932 (actually 1933), PCB A1/553/14. The letter refers to the operetta *Sissy* by Fritz Kreisler, which premiered in December 1932; therefore the letter must have been written after that date – presumably February 1933.

[4] Watson, letter to Beaton, undated (probably February 1932), PCB A1/553/20.

[5] The character based on Robin Thomas is described thus by Berners in *The Girls of Radcliff Hall* (p. 3).

[6] Watson, letter to Beaton, misdated 12 February 1932 (actually 1933), PCB A1/553/14.

[7] Vickers, *Cecil Beaton*, p. 165.

[8] Beaton, diary, February and May 1933, PCB, quoted in Vickers, *Cecil Beaton*, pp. 163, 167. Peter took a jaundiced view of Viscountess Doris Castlerosse. After attending a party given for her by her husband in early 1932, Peter wrote to Cecil, 'She fancies herself as a movie star and takes herself off to Elstree for tests, which having been hopeless flops she wants to dress the cast. My God, Cecil, isn't she unnerving, I go nearly mad at her sometimes and never off the call-up wire' (Watson, letter to Beaton, undated [probably February 1932], PCB A1/553/20). Cecil believed that Peter was jealously 'incensed' by Cecil's relationship with Doris; in fact, any dislike of her on Peter's part predated the affair.

[9] Beaton, letter to Watson, undated (probably June 1933), PCB A2/38.

[10] Watson, letter to Beaton, dated only 'Saturday tea time' (probably June 1933), PCB A1/553/26.

[11] Watson, letter to Pavel Tchelitchew, undated (probably August 1933), PTC.

[12] Watson, letter to Beaton, undated (probably August 1933), PCB A1/553/69.

[13] According to Vickers (*Cecil Beaton*, p. 168) Cecil was happy at Cannes, but this is not what he told Peter (Watson, letter to Pavel Tchelitchew, undated [probably August 1933], PTC).

[14] Watson, letter to Beaton, undated (probably August 1933), PCB A1/553/5.

[15] Amory, *Lord Berners*, p. 138; the effect was described by Nancy Mitford in *The Pursuit of Love*.

[16] Berners, letter to Beaton, 4 October 1933, PCB A1/53/1.

[17] Berners, letter to Beaton, 15 October 1933, PCB A1/53/2.

[18] Amory, *Lord Berners*, p. 129.

[19] Thomas Messel, personal communication to Adrian Clark, October 2014.

[20] Watson, letter to Beaton, undated (probably late 1933), PCB A1/553/71. This letter was written when Peter was staying at West Dean Park, the country estate of his Eton contemporary Edward James, who had a fortune comparable to Peter's; he was an enthusiastic sponsor of the Surrealist movement and his portrait was painted by René Magritte. At the time when Peter stayed with him, James was working on ballet set designs and was married to the actress and dancer Tilly Losch.

[21] Vickers, *Cecil Beaton*, p. 172.

[22] Beaton, letter to Anita Loos, undated (probably January 1934), PCB A2/40/5.

[23] Edith Sitwell, YCAL, MSS318, Beinecke Rare Book and Manuscript Library, Yale.

[24] Charles Henri Ford, letter to Michael Shelden, 17 February 1985, collection of Michael Shelden.

[25] Watson, letter to Tchewlitchew, undated (1933) from Sulhamstead, PTC.

[26] Ford, letter to Shelden, 13 March 1985, courtesy Michael Shelden.

[27] Watson, letter to Tchelitchew, undated (probably March 1934) from New York, PTC.

[28] Tchelitchew, letter to Watson, 29 June 1934, PCB A1/553/2.

[29] Rose, *Saying Life*, p. 150.

[30] Watson, letter to Beaton, undated (probably 13 February 1934), PCB A1/553/22.

[31] Watson, letter to Tchelitchew, undated from New York (March 1934), PTC.

[32] Watson, letter to Tchelitchew, undated from New York (March 1934), PTC.

[33] Watson, postcard to Tchelitchew, undated from SS *Bremen* (late April/early May 1934), PTC.

[34] Vickers, *Cecil Beaton*, p. 174.

[35] Watson, letter to Tchelitchew, undated from Port-au-Prince (March 1934), PTC.

[36] Watson, letter to Tchelitchew, undated from Port-au-Prince (March 1934), PTC.

[37] Vickers, *Cecil Beaton*, p. 174.

[38] Watson, postcard to Tchelitchew, undated from SS *Bremen* (late April/early May 1934), PTC.

[39] Watson, letter to Beaton, undated (November 1934), PCB A1/553/15.

[40] Fraser, *Night Thoughts*, p. 142.

[41] Peter's physical appearance was captured in many photographs by Cecil Beaton, and there is a series of pictures taken by Pavel Tchelitchew in Paris. Peter's preference for Frances Fox hair ointment is mentioned in a letter to Cecil Beaton (PCB A1/553/18).

[42] John Betjeman, describing a comical scripture reading by a camp Cambridge scholar, observed that the words (from Ezekiel) were read in a manner in which 'Peter Watson would say them at a party' – 'As for the *chariot* the wheels were SO HIGH they were DREADFUL' (Betjeman, letter to Penelope Betjeman, 28 September 1935, in *John Betjeman Letters*, p. 155).

[43] Watson, letters to Beaton, undated (November 1934), PCB A1/553/16, 40.

[44] Watson, letter to Beaton, marked Wednesday (14 November 1934), PCB A1/553/77. Princess Natalia Pavlovna Paley was granddaughter of Tsar Alexander II and cousin of Tsar Nicholas II. She was a favourite model of Cecil Beaton, and had a brief career as a film actress; the following year she was cast in George Cukor's *Sylvia Scarlett*, during which she began a close friendship with the star, Katharine Hepburn.

[45] Watson, letter to Beaton, undated (November/December 1934), PCB A1/553/78.

8 – THE ART OF LIVING

[1] Vickers, *Cecil Beaton*, p. 179.

[2] Beaton, diary, January 1935, PCB. According to Vickers (*Cecil Beaton*, p. 178), Cecil's operation was for appendicitis, but this doesn't seem consistent with Peter's letters from 11 place des États-Unis in November 1934 (PCB A1/553/75–77), indicating that the operation was planned for some time.

[3] Beaton, diary, 16 December 1934, PCB.

[4] The *Autocar*'s reviewer wrote: 'I never thought that I, who had laid it down that the average man over fifty is not safe to drive at over fifty, should ever feel safe driving at eighty' (*Autocar*, 18 January 1935). The popular model that year was the two-seater tourer, but Peter Watson's Bentley was presumably a four-seater, to allow for a chauffeur.

[5] Numbers 1 to 3 Shepherd's Close were built 'to the designs of W. E. Masters; the builders were Pitchers of Hornsey'. Each house was of 'two main storeys with a tall attic' and they were built 'on part of the extensive curtilage which formerly belonged to No. 6 Upper Brook Street. A new private courtyard was laid out and is entered from Lees Place to the east of No. 8' (Sheppard, *Survey of London: vol. 40*, p. 198).

[6] Watson, letter to Beaton, undated (late 1935), PCB A1/553/47.

[7] Watson, letters to Beaton, undated (1935), PCB A1/553/44 & 47.

[8] Electoral Register 1935, City of Westminster Grosvenor Ward N1, p. 213, LMA.

[9] Beaton, diary, January 1935, PCB.

[10] The boxes were so successful they were brought back the following year. 'Merry new Beaton Boxes', said the advertising copy. 'Just say "Wrap them as gifts,

please" and we'll tie them up in amusing boxes that'll make them doubly welcome! A gay catalogue, too ... the cover is patterned with the same Cecil Beaton design' (Harvey Nichols advertisement, *The Times*, 9 December 1935, p. 13).

[11] Beaton, diary, January 1935, PCB.

[12] Friedrich Nietzsche, *The Gay Science* (*Die Fröhliche Wissenschaft*), §290.

[13] Beaton, diary, January 1935, PCB.

[14] Beaton, diary, New Year's Eve 1934–5, PCB.

[15] Quoted by Hoare, *Serious Pleasures*, p. 265.

[16] Watson, letter to Beaton, undated (January 1935), PCB A1/553/64.

[17] Watson, letter to Beaton, undated (13 January 1935), PCB A1/553/60. Drogo can't have been overly concerned by his humiliation, as a few weeks later, on 6 March 1935, he and Janet were married.

[18] Watson, letter to Beaton, undated (possibly 10–15 February 1935), PCB A1/553/53. Sir Alfred's broken leg was reported in *The Times* on 23 January, but his bullying was not; nor did the paper report that the honourable member for South East St Pancras had narrowly avoided a public debagging at the hands of Lord Beaverbrook's daughter. Alfred Beit's other claim to notoriety was his fling with Cecil's flame, Doris Castlerosse – giving rise to the popular *bon mot* that Doris had been 'beaten by Beaton and bitten by Beit'.

[19] Watson, letter to Beaton, undated (January–February 1935), PCB A1/553/72.

[20] Watson, letters to Beaton, January to February 1935, PCB A1/553/63–65.

[21] Watson, letter to Beaton, undated (January/February 1935), PCB A1/553/65.

[22] Watson, letter to Beaton, undated (January/February 1935), PCB A1/553/65.

[23] Watson, letter to Beaton, undated (probably February 1935), PCB A1/553/72. Johann Bernhard Fischer von Erlach was the influential Austrian Baroque architect who designed, *inter alia*, the Schönbrunn Palace and Schloss Klessheim.

[24] Watson, letter to Beaton, undated (probably February 1935), PCB A1/553/72.

[25] Watson, letter to Beaton, undated (probably early February 1935), PCB A1/553/65.

[26] Sergei Diaghilev, letter to *The Times*, 13 July 1929, p. 10.

[27] Benaïm, *Marie Laure*, ch. 2.

[28] Markevitch, *Être*, pp. 319–20. See also Monnard, '*Paradis perdu*', p. 45. The plane would have been a Handley Page HP42, a biplane with huge wings and triple tailfins, which plied the Paris–London route in the 1930s, carrying up to two dozen passengers at a time. It was Markevitch's first time in an aeroplane, and he felt that he was being carried away in the heart of a great bird. Peter had had his first experience of flight the previous year, on Cecil's recommendation, and thought it heavenly – 'I slept and it seemed over in a jiffy' (Watson, letter to Beaton, undated, probably November 1934, PCB A1/553/75).

[29] Markevitch, *Être*, p. 321.

[30] Markevitch, *Être*, pp. 320–21.

[31] *Life*, 15 February 1937, p. 61.

[32] Faringdon guest book, 30 June 1935, via Sofka Zinovieff.

[33] Watson, letter to Beaton, undated (early 1935), PCB A1/553/43.

[34] Watson, letter to Beaton, undated, marked 'Tuesday' (mid-September 1935), PCB A1/553/44.

[35] Quoted in Amory, *Lord Berners*, p. 137.

[36] Berners, quoted in Amory, *Lord Berners*, p. 136.

[37] Watson, letter to Beaton, undated, marked 'Tuesday' (mid-September 1935), PCB A1/553/44.

[38] Berners, *Girls of Radcliff Hall*, p. 30.

[39] Diana Mosley, *Loved Ones*, p. 113.

[40] Amory, *Lord Berners*, pp. 147–8.

[41] Quoted in Amory, *Lord Berners*, p. 148.

9 – *LE PARADIS PERDU*

[1] Beaton, diary, 20 February 1935, PCB.

[2] Watson, letter to Beaton, dated 'Sunday 17', probably 17 March 1935, PCB A1/553/37.

[3] Watson, letter to Beaton, undated (probably June–August 1935), PCB A1/553/44.

[4] Watson, letter to Beaton, undated (probably summer 1935), PCB A1/553/74. Jean Renoir was the son of the painter Pierre-Auguste Renoir. Visconti made a string of important art-house films, culminating in *The Damned* (1969) and *Death in Venice* (1971).

[5] Ford, letter to Shelden, 17 February 1985, courtesy Michael Shelden.

[6] Watson, letter to Beaton, 'Tuesday' (probably September 1935), PCB A1/553/41; Markevitch, *Être*, p. 324ff.

[7] Watson, letter to Beaton, 27 September 1935, PCB A1/553/38.

[8] Homosexuality, which Gorer insisted on placing in quotation marks, was ranked among de Sade's 'class of perverse objects'. Gorer believed that if de Sade had returned in the twentieth century he would have been most surprised by 'the great spread of male "homosexuality," especially among the bourgeoisie. This I imagine to be partly due to the respectability of the new nomenclature, and the aura of martyred literary merit which Wilde, Gide and Cocteau have invested it with, but chiefly to a neurotic fear of life and responsibility' (Gorer, *Marquis de Sade*, p. 208).

[9] Hoare, *Serious Pleasures*, pp. 205–6.

[10] BTP outwards, RMS *Berengaria*, 13 November 1935.

[11] Ford, letter to Michael Shelden, 17 February 1985, courtesy Michael Shelden.

[12] Hoare, *Serious Pleasures*, p. 209.

[13] Tennant, quoted in Hoare, *Serious Pleasures*, pp. 210–11. Oddly, Hoare describes Bankhead as being forty-three years old and 'past the sultry temptress stage'. In fact she was thirty-three (born 1902) and thus only four years older than Stephen.

[14] *The Times*, 20 December 1935, p. 9. That same year, Slobodskaya had starred in a BBC performance of Shostakovich's celebrated opera *Lady Macbeth of the Mtsensk District*. Peter Watson had seen a production of it (under its alternative title *Katerina Izmailova*) in Switzerland in the spring, and wasn't impressed: 'Why they make such a fuss over this I don't understand. Altho' lively and boisterous it is old fashioned and coarse in conception and no advance on Pappa Moussorgsky at all' (Watson, letter to Beaton, undated, probably February/May 1935, PCB A1/553/43).

[15] The *Observer*, 22 December 1935, p. 8.

[16] Markevitch, *Être*, pp. 345–6; also Watson, letter to Hansen, 24 March 1947, CWH.

[17] Watson, letter to Hansen, 24 March 1947, CWH.

[18] SS *Normandie*, arrived New York on 7 December 1936; on this occasion, rather oddly, Peter Watson gave his occupation as 'writer' (PNY: Manifest of SS *Normandie*).

[19] George Plimpton, in Plimpton (ed.), *Truman Capote*, p. 87.

10 – DARK ANGEL

[1] Capote gave this account in the first chapter of his unfinished novel *Answered Prayers*. He knew Denham in the post-war 1940s.

[2] Vidal, in Plimpton (ed.), *Truman Capote*, p. 88. Vidal doesn't give the date of this exchange, but it must have been in 1947, the year Prince Paul of Greece became king and was ill with typhoid fever (Vidal erroneously recalls it being pneumonia).

[3] Details from 1920 and 1930 United States Federal Censuses, 1935 Florida Census, 1930–32 Jacksonville City Directories, and several transatlantic shipping lists from 1935–40 (available online at ancestry.com). On passenger forms, Fouts always gave his date of birth as 9 May 1916; however, the census records indicate that he must have been born in 1914. Sherk's Ice Cream Company was a subsidiary of Southland Dairy Products Inc.; one wonders if dairy-related family heritage came up at all in conversation between Denny and Peter Watson.

[4] Capote, *Answered Prayers*, p. 20. Capote sets this scene in 1936, much later than reality; in fact it would have been 1930 or 1931 (indeed, by 1936 a new Duesenberg would be hard to find – the company was collapsing at this time).

[5] Watson, letter to Hansen, 28 March 1947, CWH.

[6] Rorem, in Plimpton (ed.), *Truman Capote*, p. 89.

[7] Isherwood, *Down There on a Visit*, p. 206. In Isherwood's fictionalised memoir, Denham Fouts appears in the guise of the character 'Paul'.

[8] Isherwood, *Down There on a Visit*, p. 221.

[9] Evidence from the 1920 and 1930 censuses confirms that Denham Fouts had been born in 1914; however, on all his various transatlantic crossings during the 1930s he gave his date of birth as 9 May 1916.

[10] Gore Vidal (in Plimpton, *Truman Capote*, p. 87) says Denham's sexual preference was for 'small boys'; but Peter Watson, who knew him far better, wrote that Denham liked 'boys about 14–16 which I could never understand and which horrifies me now' (Watson, letter to Hansen, 28 March 1947, CWH).

[11] According to Vidal, in Plimpton (ed.), *Truman Capote*, p. 87.

[12] PNY: Manifest of SS *Europa*, Southampton–New York, 4 April 1935; BTP inwards, SS *Europa*, 11 April 1935, New York–Southampton.

[13] Capote, *Answered Prayers*, p. 28.

[14] Watson, letter to Hansen, 28 March 1947, CWH.

[15] Watson, letter to Hansen, 28 March 1947.

[16] Beaton, diary, November 1936, PCB.

[17] Watson, postcard to Beaton, undated (probably 1935–6), PCB A1/553/6. The postcard, depicting a Holbein design for a grandiose cup for Queen Jane Seymour, is clearly selected with some care to appeal to Cecil's baroque sense of style and his dreams of designing for royalty.

[18] Beaton, diary, winter 1936–7, PCB.

[19] Beaton, diary entry marked '1937', PCB.

[20] Passenger lists for SS *Normandie*, arriving New York, 7 December 1936, PNY.

[21] Passenger lists for SS *Europa*, arriving New York, 7 August 1936, PNY. On the passenger list, Louis Denham Fouts gives his address in the USA as 109 Lomax Street, Jacksonville, FL. Whether he actually went there is unknown.

[22] Vickers, *Cecil Beaton*, p. 195.

[23] Marjorie had become involved with Eddy Duchin while taking piano lessons from him; they married in June 1935 (Associated Press report, 6 June 1935). Marjorie was promptly deleted from the Social Register – 'Phooey on the Social Register,' she was quoted as saying. 'It's just a private telephone book, anyway' (United Press report, 3 August 1937). Her happiness was short-lived; on 3 August 1937, after giving birth to a son, named Peter, she died from complications; she was twenty-nine years old. Eddy was unable to cope with the child, so Peter was brought up by friends of Marjorie, the US diplomat W. Averell Harriman and his wife. He became a musician like his father.

[24] Watson, letter to Beaton, undated (January 1937), PCB A1/553/35.

[25] Shelden, *Friends of Promise*, p. 25ff.

[26] They were introduced by their mutual friend, the art critic Herbert Read (Sutherland, *Stephen Spender*, p. 237). Peter Watson's and Stephen Spender's paths had intersected some years earlier in the German gay scene, and before that at Oxford, but they hadn't met.

[27] Watson, letter to Connolly, undated (October 1937).

[28] Watson, letter to Connolly, undated (October 1937).

[29] Watson, letter to Connolly, undated (October 1937), CCP. The engravings were condemned (along with the artist himself) in a piece by Anthony Blunt in the *Spectator* ('Picasso Unfrocked', 8 October 1937, p. 584). Blunt claimed that Picasso was detached from the Spanish conflict, and that his engravings could hardly have any political impact since they would only be seen by a handful of privileged aesthetes. Blunt's fellow critic and occasional sparring partner Herbert Read responded indignantly: 'Mr. Blunt tries to discredit Picasso by picturing him as the idol of a set of emasculated aesthetes. But on the contrary the people associated with Picasso, either as personal friends or as disinterested supporters of his art, have had rather more experience of the actual horrors of war than Mr. Blunt and other ideologists of his generation' (Read, letter to the editor, *Spectator*, 15 October 1937, p. 846).

[30] Metropolitan Museum of Art, object information (provenance) 1996.403.1, available online at www.metmuseum.org/collection/the-collection-online/search/486739 (retrieved 27 September 2014). According to the provenance, Rosenberg acquired the painting from Picasso in March 1936, and sold it to Peter Watson 'probably by 1937'.

[31] From 1937, when travelling abroad, Peter began identifying his occupation (previously 'nil' or 'student') as 'picture dealer'.

[32] Beaton, diary entry marked '1937', PCB.

[33] Watson, letter to Beaton, undated (probably September 1937), PCB A1/553/31.

[34] Watson, letter to Beaton, undated (probably September 1937), PCB A1/553/31.

[35] Beaton, telegram to Watson, quoted in Vickers, *Cecil Beaton*, p. 203.

[36] Vickers, *Cecil Beaton*, p. 202.

[37] Watson, letter to Connolly, undated (autumn 1937), CCP.

[38] Watson, letter to Connolly, undated (November/December 1937), CCP.

[39] Watson, letter to Hansen, 28 March 1947, CWH.

[40] Watson, letter to Connolly, undated (November/December 1937), CCP.

[41] Watson, letter to Connolly, undated (November/December 1937), CCP.

[42] Connolly, review in *The Sunday Times*, 12 December 1937, p. 10.

[43] Watson, letter to Connolly, 11 February 1938, CCP.

[44] 'Bloody Saturday' produced one of the iconic photographs of the era – the image of an injured baby crying amid the rubble of the railway station. It was one of the most viewed – and most controversial – war images of the twentieth century.

[45] Watson, letter to Connolly, 11 February 1938, CCP.

[46] Passenger list, SS *Empress of Canada*, arriving Honolulu 6 January 1938, PHO.

[47] Watson, letter to Connolly, 11 February 1938, CCP.

[48] Watson, letter to Beaton, undated (probably February 1932), PCB A1/553/20.

[49] Watson, letter to Connolly, 11 February 1938, CCP.

[50] Passenger list, SS *Mariposa*, departing Honolulu 19 January 1938, PHO.

[51] Watson, letter to Connolly, 11 February 1938, CCP. *Gone with the Wind* began shooting in January 1939; Cukor, who had spent two years working on the production, was fired by Selznick within three weeks of the start of filming, and replaced by Victor Fleming.

[52] Watson, letter to Connolly, 11 February 1938, CCP.

[53] BTP inwards, SS *Normandie*, 6 April 1938, New York–Southampton.

[54] Watson, letter to Connolly, undated (probably spring 1938), CCP.

[55] Charles Henri Ford, letter to Michael Shelden, 17 February 1985. Ford recalled this visit occurring in 1939, and the magazine idea stalling because of the war. He must have misremembered the date, as there is no evidence of Peter Watson visiting the US in 1939. Ford and Parker Tyler eventually founded the Surrealist magazine *View* in 1940, about the same time as Peter's *Horizon* first appeared.

[56] Watson, postcard to Connolly, May 1938, CCP.

[57] David Gascoyne, diary, 15 March 1938, *Paris Journal*, p. 37.

[58] Watson, letter to Connolly, 11 February 1938, CCP. The Nazis later changed their minds about both Rembrandt and Grünewald (the latter being stamped for approval when his altarpiece at Isenheim church in Alsace became a symbol of German cultural claims to Alsace-Lorraine).

[59] Watson, letter to Connolly, 11 February 1938, CCP. In fact Auden might well have got his few days in Shanghai; far from going back into teaching, he and Christopher Isherwood travelled to China in 1938, observing the Sino-Japanese War; they published their impressions in a joint book, *Journey to a War* (1939).

[60] Hansen, letter to Myers, 1 July 1947, CWH.

11 – A HEAVENLY DWELLING

[1] On one occasion in 1924 Picasso was the honoured guest at a Spanish-themed ball, and was photographed by Man Ray looking slightly uncomfortable in a matador costume, flanked by two glorious señoritas, one of whom was his

wife, the ballerina Olga Khokhlova ('Bal of Etienne de Beaumont' by Man Ray, 1924, Metropolitan Museum of Art 2005.100.326). De Beaumont's *hôtel particulier* (mansion) was the Hôtel de Masseran at 11 rue Masseran, in the 7th arrondissement.

[2] Watson, letter to Beaton, 12 February 1933 (misdated 1932), PCB A1/553/14.

[3] MacLeish, *Reflections*, p. 29; see also Donaldson and Winnick, *Archibald MacLeish*, p. 153.

[4] De Beaumont was certainly the inspiration for the sensational 1924 novel by Raymond Radiguet, *Le Bal du Comte d'Orgel*.

[5] Watson, letter to Lucian Freud, 18 December 1947, PLF.

[6] Artist Michael Wishart, who knew Peter and Denham in the 1940s, wrote in his memoir (*High Diver*, p. 49) that Denham had picked up his opium addiction in China during a trip with Evan Morgan, Viscount Tredegar. This is probably a confused memory of stories told to him by Denham.

[7] A postcard to Stephen Tennant from Istanbul (undated, apparently summer 1938, Hugo Vickers collection) indicates that Peter was closing up 1 Shepherd's Close on 20 September.

[8] Wishart, *High Diver*, p. 54. Tchelitchew painted more than one version of this iconic image between 1935 and 1938), including a number of studies. It is not known which one Peter Watson owned.

[9] Watson, letters to Jean Connolly and Cyril Connolly, undated (respectively late summer and early winter 1938), CCP.

[10] Fraser, *Night Thoughts*, p. 143.

[11] Gascoyne, diary, 27 October 1938, *Paris Journal*, p. 78.

[12] Gascoyne, diary, 10 December 1938, *Paris Journal*, p. 103.

[13] Gascoyne, diary, 19 December 1938, *Paris Journal*, p. 105.

[14] Spender, letter to Isherwood, 1935, quoted in Sutherland, *Stephen Spender*, pp. 168–9.

[15] David Gascoyne, for instance; he noted that 'Brian Howard predicts that she and Christopher Isherwood are going to become the dictators of the British intelligentsia in a few years' time' (Gascoyne, diary, 23 January 1939, *Paris Journal*, p. 113).

[16] Spender, diary, 6 May 1956, *New Selected Journals*, p. 229.

[17] Spender, diary, 5 May 1956, *New Selected Journals*, p. 221–2.

[18] Spender, diary, 30 September 1939, *Journals 1939–1983*, p. 42.

[19] Watson, letter to Jean Connolly, 24 November 1938, CCP.

[20] Gascoyne, diary, 31 December 1938, *Paris Journal*, p. 108.

[21] Gascoyne, diary, 2 January 1939, *Paris Journal*, p. 110.

[22] Gascoyne, diary, 2 January 1939, *Paris Journal*, p. 111.

[23] Gascoyne, diary, 2 January 1939, *Paris Journal*, pp. 111–12.

[24] Peter appears to have been introduced to Stein by Lord Berners. In a sequence of letters to her (undated, possibly 1938), Berners asks if Peter Watson can accompany him when he visits Stein at her country home at Balignin – 'I think you know him. He is an agreeable young man and you will like him' (letters 34, 39, 46, courtesy Berners Trust).

[25] Gascoyne, diary, 23 January 1939, *Paris Journal*, pp. 114–15.

[26] Diana's exact identity has been muddied by various biographies. In biographies of Connolly (e.g. those by Jeremy Lewis, Clive Fisher, and *Friends of Promise* by Michael Shelden), her surname is not given, due to her having given assistance to biographers on the condition that she be identified only as 'Diana'. This was evidently her real name, since she is referred to in at least one letter from Peter Watson by that name (undated, probably December 1938, CCP). In his own diaries, Connolly referred to her as 'Δ' (delta); his friend Peter Quennell called her 'Miss Busybee'. In fact she was Diana Witherby (1915–2006), a budding poet who later worked for Connolly on *Horizon*.

[27] Spender's biographer (Sutherland, *Stephen Spender*, pp. 237, 247) states that there were two trips: one in 1938 and another in 1939. However, the only sources (Spender's recollections in his 1956 diary and an article in *The New Statesman* of 24 June 1939) indicate just one trip: in 1939.

[28] Spender, diary, 5 May 1956, *New Selected Journals*, p. 222.

[29] Spender, diary, 5 May 1956, *New Selected Journals*, p. 222ff.; and unpublished diary, 5 July 1956, PSS. Spender believed Klee's illness was cancer; in fact it was scleroderma. In the 1950s, at a Klee exhibition in London, Spender learned that the gouaches that had been priced at £15 each in 1939 were now worth £750. In recent years, prices for Klee gouaches from the late 1930s have approached £1 million at auction. Why did Peter not buy Spender the paintings he fancied? One can only guess, given Peter's generosity, that he quite possibly did and Spender refused to let him.

[30] Spender, diary, 5 May 1956, *New Selected Journals*, p. 224.

[31] Spender, diary, 9 May 1956, *New Selected Journals*, pp. 229–30.

[32] Shelden, *Friends of Promise*, p. 27.

[33] Cyril Connolly, letter to Jean Connolly, quoted by Shelden (*Friends of Promise*, p. 27) and dated to 10 July 1939.

[34] Watson, letter to Connolly, 17 August 1939, CCP.

[35] Shelden, *Friends of Promise*, pp. 28–9.

[36] Watson, letter to Connolly, 17 August 1939, CCP.

12 – A TIME OF BARBARISM

[1] Watson, letter to Connolly, 17 August 1939, CCP.

[2] Watson, letter to Christophe Bernoulli, undated (September 1939), CCB, B I 391, 1.

[3] RBR records for Peter Watson.

[4] Wishart, *High Diver*, p. 54.

[5] Spender, diary, 9 September 1939, *New Selected Journals*, p. 14.

[6] Beaton, letter to Watson, undated (probably early September 1939), PCB A2/38.

[7] Watson, letter to Christophe Bernoulli, undated (September 1939), CCB, B I 391, 1.

[8] Tippett described Peter Watson as 'a sweet gentle chap ... with an encyclopedic knowledge of art in the widest and best sense' (letter to Fresca Allinson, May 1944, in Tippett, *Selected Letters*, p. 114).

[9] Connolly, manuscript copy for *Horizon*, March 1940, CCP, quoted in Shelden, *Friends of Promise*, p. 29.

[10] Connolly, manuscript copy for *Horizon*, March 1940, CCP, quoted in Shelden, *Friends of Promise*, p. 29.

[11] Sutherland, *Stephen Spender*, p. 257; Shelden, *Friends of Promise*, pp. 31–2.

[12] Shelden, *Friends of Promise*, p. 30.

[13] Connolly, *Enemies of Promise*, p. 94.

[14] The Great House, Lavenham, was bought by Stephen and his brother Humphrey for £1,200 (Sutherland, *Stephen Spender*, p. 239).

[15] Shelden, *Friends of Promise*, p. 32. Spender gave the additional reason that his name 'has been used too much in this [arts editorial] sort of way' (diary, 29 September 1939, *Journals 1939–1983*, pp. 41–2). At this point Spender wanted to focus on being a writer, not an arts journalist.

[16] Spender, diary, 29 September 1939, *Journals 1939–1983*, pp. 41–2.

[17] Spender, diary, 30 September 1939, *Journals 1939–1983*, p. 42.

[18] Spender, diary, 30 September 1939, *Journals 1939–1983*, p. 43.

[19] Shelden, *Friends of Promise*, pp. 39–40.

[20] Watson, letter to Parker, quoted in Shelden, *Friends of Promise*, pp. 39–40. In this instance Peter's carelessness might have been to avoid ruffling his and Charles Henri Ford's feathers, having turned down their magazine idea.

[21] Connolly, 'The Ivory Shelter', *New Statesman and Nation*, 7 October 1939, p. 482.

[22] Lehmann, diary, quoted in Sutherland, *Stephen Spender*, pp. 257–8.

[23] Leeming, *Stephen Spender*, ch. 7.

[24] Connolly, note, 23 October 1939, quoted in Shelden, *Friends of Promise*, p. 38.

[25] Howard, letter to Watson, 11 November 1939, BHC.

[26] The painting had been shipped over before the war, and with the impossibility of returning it, MoMA stored it in their vaults until 1945, when it was handed over to Denham Fouts.

[27] Lefevre Gallery, letters to Watson, 28 January 1938, 2 October 1939, 19 June 1942, TGA 200211.

[28] It is impossible to be definitive on this point; however, if he did have other British works before late 1939, there is no evidence of it.

[29] Lefevre Gallery, letters to Watson, 27 December 1939, 22 February 1940, TGA 200211; and Tate Gallery acquisition record N06190, available online at www.tate.org.uk/art/artworks/sutherland-entrance-to-a-lane-n06190/text-catalogue-entry (retrieved 21 October 2014).

[30] 'Comment', *Horizon*, January 1940, p. 5.

[31] Watson, letter to Beaton, 12 December 1939, PCB A1/553/23. Cecil was caught in the middle of this embarrassing situation, as Stein had told him that 'I had a letter from Peter Watson ... [who] asked me to send them something and I have sent them a little opera poem called Lucretia Borgia' (Stein, letter to Beaton, undated [late 1939], PCB A1/502/14). The work from which the poem came, *Lucretia Borgia*, an 'opera play without songs', was one of Gertrude Stein's oddities; it has been produced occasionally on the fringe.

[32] Woolf, diary, 16 December 1939, quoted in Shelden, *Friends of Promise*, p. 41.

[33] 'Comment', *Horizon*, February 1940, p. 71. The cover was designed by painter John Piper, who had previously collaborated with John Betjeman on the Shell Guides to British counties.

[34] By late 1940 he would be making a personal loss of £100 a month on the magazine, or so he told the artist Robert MacBryde (MacBryde, letter to Fleming, October 1940, CRR).

[35] Watson, notes on February 1940 edition of *Horizon*, CCP.

[36] Spender, 'September Journal', *Horizon*, February 1940, p. 118.

[37] 'Comment', *Horizon*, February 1940, p. 69.

[38] Watson, notes on February 1940 edition of *Horizon*, CCP. It is an indication of how little notice Peter Watson paid to British literature in the 1930s. By this time Orwell had published seven books, including *The Road to Wigan Pier*, *Down and Out in Paris and London*, and *Coming Up for Air*. Orwell did write often in *Horizon*, contributing at least eleven articles and reviews between 1940 and 1946.

[39] Watson, notes on February 1940 edition of *Horizon*, CCP.

[40] Gascoyne, diary, 8–9 January and 22–23 January 1940, *Collected Journals*, pp. 277–9. At the same party Gascoyne met and fell in love with the actor Michael

Redgrave. Also present were Stephen Spender and Tony Hyndman, the boyfriend Spender had finished with before marrying Inez.

[41] Gascoyne, diary, 19 March 1940, *Collected Journals*, p. 298.

[42] Watson, letter to Connolly, undated (probably February 1940), CCP. In the letter, Peter remarks that *Heil Cinderella*, which was a topical pantomime by Cecil Beaton, had just finished its run, and that he was about to see *Desire Under the Elms*; this dates his move to mid-February 1940. Athenaeum Court is now the Athenaeum Hotel, Piccadilly.

[43] Watson, letter to Connolly, undated (probably early 1941).

[44] Thomas, letter to Watson, 2 June 1940, *Collected Letters of Dylan Thomas*, p. 452.

[45] Thomas, letter to Spender, 4 June 1940, *Collected Letters of Dylan Thomas*, p. 453.

[46] Thomas, letter to John Davenport, 8 January 1941, *Collected Letters of Dylan Thomas*, pp. 471–3.

[47] Connolly, quoted in Shelden, *Friends of Promise*, p. 82.

[48] Watson, letter to Connolly, undated (probably February 1940), CCP.

[49] Recollections of Natasha Spender in Sutherland, *Stephen Spender*, pp. 277–8.

[50] Shelden (*Friends of Promise*, p. 51) suggests that Jean Connolly had her ticket booked for the voyage from Galway; in fact her original ticket must have been cancelled, as the voyage of the *Washington* was arranged hastily after the German invasion (see note below).

[51] Who made this decision – Peter or Denham himself, or by mutual discussion – was never recorded.

[52] PNY: Manifest of SS *Washington*, Lisbon–Galway–New York, arriving 21 June 1940. Jean is listed under her first name, Frances; likewise Denham is listed as Louis Fouts. An account of the *Washington*'s voyage and encounter with the U-boat was written by the captain in November 1940 in the *US Naval Institute Proceedings*, reproduced in part at www.usmm.org/washington.html (retrieved 18 October 2014). Film footage of the *Washington*'s departure and arrival at New York is online at www.criticalpast.com/stock-footage-video/ss-washington (retrieved 18 October 2014).

[53] Watson, letter to Connolly, undated (June 1940), CCP.

[54] Watson, letter to Beaton, undated (June/July 1940), PCB A1/553/80.

[55] Watson, letter to Beaton, undated (June/July 1940), PCB A1/553/80.

[56] Spender, *World Within World*, p. 292.

[57] Spender, *World Within World*, pp. 292–3; Sutherland, *Stephen Spender*, pp. 561–2. The last piece of writing Spender published in his lifetime was an elegy for Timothy Corsellis.

13 – SPOILS OF WAR

[1] Watson, letter to Beaton, undated (probably late December 1940), PCB A1/553/73.

[2] ARP report centre messages, 18 September 1940, Westminster City Archives, reproduced online at www.westendatwar.org.uk/page_id__252_path__0p28p.aspx (retrieved 28 September 2014).

[3] 40 Berkeley Square was eventually demolished in 2001, and a new building stands on the site.

[4] Watson, letter to Beaton, undated (probably late December 1940), PCB A1/553/73.

[5] Mitchell, *Nazi Paris*, pp. 37–8.

[6] The records of the Nazi looting (specifically the works owned by Peter Watson) are in several archives – see the Bibliography under Devisenschutzkommando Frankreich and Restitutions Branch Records. Photographs of the ERR at work can be found at www.errproject.org/jeudepaume/photo/ (retrieved 23 October 2014).

[7] Watson, letter to Beaton, undated (probably late December 1940), PCB A1/553/73. The fact that Sidéry contacted Peter so quickly could be seen as exculpating him. If he had instigated and profited from the thefts, he would surely not have informed Peter, as he would have no reason to expect that he would ever have to answer for the crime – the Germans seemed to be winning the war, and Peter would be unlikely ever to come to Paris again. Sidéry (had he been guilty) would merely have had to keep quiet and enjoy his rewards.

[8] The seizure of 702 works of art from the SS *Excalibur* off the coast of Bermuda on 25 September 1940 made international news reports. The shipment was said to be 'an obvious German ruse to secure dollar exchange' (United Press report, 12 October 1940) and there was 'every reason to believe that Fabiani was acting as a German agent' (International News Service report, 9 November 1940). Suspicions of Fabiani strengthened after the war, by which time he was known to have been a collaborator.

Peter Watson appears to have worried that some of his art had been aboard the *Excalibur*; artist Robert MacBryde, who first met Peter at this time, came away with the impression that Peter was certain that his collection was part of the 'loot' (MacBryde, letter to Fleming, 24 October 1940, CRR).

In fact, the paintings in the *Excalibur* shipment were not looted; they were from the collection of prolific art patron Lucien Vollard, and were indeed being sent to America for safety. Eventually, in 1949 the British authorities returned the artworks to Fabiani (di Panzillo, 'Dispersal of the Vollard Collection', p. 260).

[9] Watson, letter to Beaton, undated (probably late December 1940), PCB A1/553/73.

[10] Watson, letter to Beaton, undated (probably late December 1940), PCB A1/553/73.

[11] Watson, letter to Beaton, undated (probably late December 1940), PCB A1/553/73.

14 – THE WAR EFFORT

[1] Quoted in Foss, *War Paint*, p. 9. Foss argues that Clark was being tongue-in-cheek, and that he did at least partly envision a serious artistic purpose for the WAAC.

[2] MacBryde, letter to Fleming, 24 October 1940, CRR.

[3] Bristow, *The Last Bohemians*, p. 89.

[4] MacBryde, letter to Fleming, undated (late October/early November 1940), CRR.

[5] MacBryde, letter to Fleming, undated (late October/early November 1940), CRR.

[6] Bristow, *The Last Bohemians*, p. 89.

[7] MacBryde, letter to Fleming, 22 November 1940, CRR

[8] Watson, letter to Connolly, undated (summer 1940), CCP.

[9] Advertisements in *The Times*, 12 April 1940 and 30 January 1942. Further details of the building's history are in Sheppard, *Survey of London: vol. 38*, pp. 38–48. The building officially opened on 25 May 1939, but took some time to become occupied.

[10] MacBryde, letter to Fleming, undated (January/February 1941), CRR. MacBryde actually states in this letter (and in another, earlier one) that Peter had 'lost 3 flats full of paintings' to the Germans. There is no evidence of Peter having more than one Paris apartment (unless we include the one he is said to have sublet to Buffie Johnson). Either he had paintings on loan in other people's flats at the time of the invasion or (more likely) he was speaking figuratively and MacBryde misunderstood. At this time, if MacBryde can be relied on, Peter seems to have been under the impression that some of his paintings might have been among the load seized by the British at Bermuda.

[11] MacBryde, letter to Fleming, undated (January/February 1941), CRR.

[12] Craxton, letter, 16 June 1986, quoted in Tate Gallery catalogue entry T03838.

[13] Craxton, letter, 16 June 1986, quoted in Tate Gallery catalogue entry T03838.

[14] MacBryde, letter to Fleming, 25–26 March 1941, CRR.

[15] Hoban, *Lucian Freud*, p. 19.

[16] Spender, quoted in Sutherland, *Stephen Spender*, p. 263.

[17] Quoted in Hoban, *Lucian Freud*, p. 22.

[18] Watson, letter to Morris, 2 November 1940, TGA 8317/1/1/3947.

[19] Craxton, interview in *Pallant House Gallery Magazine* 11 (2007), pp. 25–8. Craxton had been given his ticket to the concert by his friend James Iliff, one of his father's piano students, who wasn't well enough to go. One biographer (Collins, *John Craxton*, p. 38) states that the seventeen-year-old Iliff was a friend of Peter Watson, and had been invited to the concert by Peter, but passed his ticket on to Craxton, introducing him to Peter in the process. In fact, James Iliff (who went on to become a composer and music teacher) has no recollection of Peter Watson

(conversation with Adrian Clark), and Craxton's own account suggests that the meeting at the Queen's Hall was a chance encounter.

[20] Evans, 'Craxton', *Oxford Dictionary of National Biography*.

[21] Craxton, quoted in Collins, *John Craxton*, p. 38.

[22] Watson, letter to Piper, 23 October 1941, TGA 200410/1/1/1904/12.

[23] Watson, letter to Craxton, undated (early 1942), CJC.

[24] Colquhoun, letter to Fleming, undated (early 1941), CRR.

[25] Colquhoun, letter to Fleming, undated (early 1941), CRR.

[26] Watson, letter to Craxton, undated (probably April 1941), CJC.

[27] MacBryde, letter to Fleming, undated (April 1941), CRR.

[28] Colquhoun, letter to Fleming, undated (mid-1941), CRR.

[29] MacBryde, letter to Fleming, undated (February 1941), CRR.

[30] Colquhoun, letter to Fleming, undated (mid-1941), CRR.

[31] Colquhoun, letter to Fleming, undated (1941), CRR.

[32] Evans, 'Craxton', *Oxford Dictionary of National Biography*. Also living nearby at Fordingbridge was Augustus John ('your august neighbour Augustus', as Peter referred to him in a letter to Craxton).

[33] Craxton, interview in *Pallant House Gallery Magazine* 11 (2007), pp. 25–8.

[34] Sutherland, quoted in Watson, letter to Craxton, undated (1941), CJC.

[35] The only time in the British edition, at least; in July 1945 a special post-war French edition with the theme 'La Littérature anglaise depuis la guerre' was published, which included an essay by Peter Watson, 'Note sur deux pentres anglais', about Graham Sutherland and John Craxton.

[36] Craxton, interview in *Pallant House Gallery Magazine* 11 (2007), pp. 25–8.

[37] Watson, letter to Craxton, undated (probably 1942), CJC.

[38] Craxton, interview in *Pallant House Gallery Magazine* 11 (2007), pp. 25–8.

[39] Craxton, interview in *Pallant House Gallery Magazine* 11 (2007), pp. 25–8.

[40] Watson, 'Joan Miró', p. 131.

[41] Watson, letter to Freud, 14 September 1941, PLF.

[42] Watson, letter to Craxton, undated (March 1941), CJC.

[43] Watson, letter to Beaton, undated (early 1935), PCB A1/553/64.

[44] Watson, letter to Craxton, undated (probably March/April 1941), CJC. It isn't clear who 'Mrs Wood' was; possibly Christopher Wood's mother; alternatively a confused reference to EQ Nicholson, whose husband was known as 'Kit', as was Christopher Wood, who was associated with Ben Nicholson.

[45] Sutherland, *Stephen Spender*, pp. 263–4. Tony Hyndman was similar in some ways to Denham Fouts, and indeed the two had become friendly in Paris before the war, to the moral benefit of neither of them.

[46] Watson, letter to Craxton, undated (early 1941), CJC.

[47] Watson, letter to Craxton, undated (probably 1942), CJC.

15 – THE WORLD'S COLLAPSE

[1] Nancy Mitford, letter to Violet Hammersley, 26 December 1940, *Love from Nancy*, p. 109.

[2] Quennell, quoted by Shelden, *Friends of Promise*, p. 63. Apparently Connolly lost his insouciance and began to be afraid later in the war when V-1 flying bombs started to hit London and his elderly father was bombed out of the hotel he was living in. Peter too was more fearful of the flying bombs.

[3] Orwell, 'Wells, Hitler and the World State', *Horizon*, August 1941, pp. 133–8.

[4] Watson, letter to Tyler, quoted in Shelden, *Friends of Promise*, p. 64. The letter is of uncertain date, and Shelden places it in 1940; other evidence (including letters to Craxton) suggests that Peter was more likely expressing this view in 1941.

[5] According to Shelden, *Friends of Promise*, p. 64, based on interviews with individuals who were close to Peter Watson during the early 1940s. He rarely wrote down his views on political or social matters, but often talked of them.

[6] Watson, series of letters to Arthur Lett-Haines, probably late 1941, TGA 8317/1/1/3948-3951.

[7] Nicolson, letter to Connolly, cited in Shelden, *Friends of Promise*, p. 85; Watson, letter to Craxton, undated (July 1941), CJC.

[8] Hoban, *Lucian Freud*, pp. 21, 29, 140. Sixty years later Freud still retained his tattooing skill, and executed a pair of sparrows on model Kate Moss, based on some work he'd shown her from 1944.

[9] Collins, *John Craxton*, p. 38.

[10] Watson, letter to Craxton, undated (late 1941), CJC.

[11] Watson, letter to Craxton, undated (late 1941), CJC; and 'Sulhamstead House' in Thames Valley Police booklet, *The History of Thames Valley Police*, available online at www.thamesvalley.police.uk/museum_booklet_a4.pdf (retrieved 28 October 2014).

[12] Watson, postcard to Beaton, 1 March 1936, PCB A1/553/5.

[13] Notices concerning her estate refer to her as Dame Bessie (e.g. *The Times*, 6 November 1942, p. 1), but no record has been found of her having been awarded this title.

[14] Watson, letter to Craxton, undated (early 1942), CJC.

[15] Sulhamstead House and the surrounding estate were sold off between 1943 and 1949.

[16] Watson, letters to Myfanwy Piper, undated (probably mid-1941), TGA 200410/1/1/2942/1–2.

[17] MacBryde, letter to Fleming, undated (January/February 1941), CRR.

[18] Watson, postcard to Craxton, 7 August 1942, CJC.

[19] Watson, letters to Berlin and wife, undated (probably late 1942), TGA 20066/1/20/1-5.

[20] Berlin, *Alfred Wallis*, pp. 7–8. At the time, Sven Berlin (who was British-born, of Swedish ancestry) was a registered conscientious objector. Later, after witnessing naval action in the English Channel, he joined the army and took part in the D-Day landings; his experiences led to a nervous breakdown, and he returned to St Ives to find healing in art (obituaries, *Independent*, 17 December 1999; *Guardian*, 4 January 2000).

[21] Letter from Evelyn Waugh, *Horizon,* March 1943, p. 214.

[22] Waugh, letter to A. D. Peters, February 1940, in *Letters of Evelyn Waugh*, p. 137; Watson, letter to Nicholson, undated (February 1943), TGA 8717/1/2/5291.

[23] Letter from Graham Greene, *Horizon,* May 1943, p. 362.

[24] Watson, letter to Craxton, undated (probably August 1941), CJC. The postcard referred to was sent from St David's, Pembrokeshire, in August 1941. The castle isn't named, but appears to be Plas Llanstephan, which Philipps bought in 1930 (his third Welsh property was Castle Amroth).

[25] Watson, postcard to Craxton, 20 August 1941, CJC.

[26] Watson, letter to Craxton, undated (late 1941), CJC.

[27] Watson, postcard to Craxton, 7 August 1942, CJC.

[28] Watson, letter to Craxton, 20 March 1942, CJC.

[29] Craxton, interview in *Pallant House Gallery Magazine* 11 (2007), pp. 25–8.

[30] Craxton, exhibition catalogue, Whitechapel Gallery, 1967, quoted in Tate Gallery catalogue entry T03838.

[31] Watson, letter to Craxton, 20 July 1944, CJC.

[32] Evans, 'Craxton', *Oxford Dictionary of National Biography*.

[33] Priaulx Rainer, 'Personal Recollections', *ADAM International Review*, issues 385–90, 1975, p. 95. Wyndham's wine collection was left to Cyril Connolly in his will (Lewis, *Cyril Connolly*, p. 416).

[34] Watson, letter to Craxton, undated (1944), CJC.

[35] Watson, letter to Craxton, undated (1944), CJC.

[36] Watson, letter to Connolly, undated (1944), CCP. No record has been found identifying Peter Watson's military duties at this time. He seems only to have referred to it in these two letters, and it does not seem to have lasted long. Most probably he was absorbed for a time into the Home Guard.

[37] Watson, letter to Craxton, undated (1945), CJC.

[38] Watson, letter to Craxton, undated (1945), CJC.

[39] Eduardo Paolozzi, interviewed by Frank Whitford, NLS. Paolozzi, who said of himself and his fellow artists, 'We were all under the shadow of Peter Watson,' added that 'There might one day be a Peter Watson book.' Sadly he didn't live to see it.

[40] Keith Vaughan, diary, 16 May 1942, TGA 200817/1/10.

[41] Keith Vaughan, diary, 16 May 1942, TGA 200817/1/10.

[42] Watson, letter to Craxton, dated 'bank holiday' (probably 7 May 1945), CJC.

[43] Watson, letter to Craxton, dated 'bank holiday' (probably 7 May 1945), CJC.

[44] Watson letter to Craxton, undated (early 1945), CJC.

[45] Watson letter to Craxton, undated (early 1945), CJC.

[46] Watson, letter to Piper, 6 July 1945, TGA 200410/1/1/1904/8.

16 – EVERY KIND OF DISASTER

[1] Shelden, *Friends of Promise*, p. 124.

[2] This incident, recorded on 30 July 1942, is mentioned in a Special Branch report on Stephen Spender, 9 February 1955, contained in Spender's MI5 file. The identity of the person Peter attempted to communicate with is not given. The most likely candidate would be Sherban Sidéry.

[3] Watson, letter to Beaton, 13 October 1945, PCB A1/553/28.

[4] Connolly, letter to Lys, July 1945, quoted in Shelden, *Friends of Promise*, p. 133.

[5] Gascoyne, diary, 31 December 1938, *Paris Journal*, p. 108.

[6] Connolly, letter to Lys, July 1945, quoted in Shelden, *Friends of Promise*, p. 133.

[7] Watson, letter to Craxton, 19 July 1945.

[8] Watson, letter to Craxton, undated (November/December 1945), CJC.

[9] Watson, letter to Craxton, 19 July 1945.

[10] Watson, letter to Freud, 18 December 1945, PLF.

[11] Watson, letter to Craxton, undated (November/December 1945), CJC. Five hundred pounds in 1945 would be equivalent to nearly £20,000 now, and £3,000 then would be almost £100,000 now.

[12] Watson, letter to Craxton, 19 July 1945. Twenty pounds in 1945 would be equivalent to over £700 now.

[13] Watson, letter to Beaton, 13 October 1945, PCB A1/553/28.

[14] Vickers states (in *Cecil Beaton*, p. 397) that Marie-Laure de Noailles 'fell in love' with Peter Watson; presumably this is based on a (unidentified) Beaton source.

[15] Watson, letter to Beaton, 13 October 1945, PCB A1/553/28.

[16] Watson, letter to Craxton, undated (November/December 1945), CJC.

[17] Watson, letter to Craxton, 19 July 1945, CJC.

[18] Watson, letter to Craxton, 19 July 1945, CJC.

[19] Connolly, letter to Lys, July 1945, quoted in Shelden, *Friends of Promise*, p. 135.

[20] Connolly, 'Comment', *Horizon,* February 1946, pp. 77–84.

[21] Watson, letter to Craxton, 19 July 1945, CJC.

[22] Connolly, 'Comment', *Horizon,* February 1946, pp. 77–84.

[23] Connolly, letter to Lys, quoted in Shelden, *Friends of Promise*, p. 136.

[24] Watson, letter to Craxton, 19 July 1945, CJC.

[25] Watson, postcard to Craxton, 4 August 1945, CJC.

[26] Watson, letter to Howard, 4 August 1945, BHC.

[27] Watson, letter to Beaton, 16 September 1945, PCB A1/553/30.

[28] Cooper, 'Investigations into looted works of art and their whereabouts in Switzerland', MFA record T209/25/1. Cooper referred to the painting as 'La Côte'; in fact it was Dalí's *Perspectives* of 1936. This painting was not listed among the records of the ERR and DSK that have survived, so either that part of Cooper's research was guesswork or the German catalogues were not complete. The Kunstmuseum declined to return the painting to Peter Watson; eventually, after the war, an out-of-court settlement was reached, whereby the museum kept the painting in exchange for 3,000 Swiss francs in compensation. It is still part of the Kunstmuseum collection but is owned by the Emmanuel Hoffman Foundation.

[29] Watson, letter to Beaton, 13 October 1945, PCB A1/553/28.

[30] Watson, postcard to Freud, 25 August 1945, PLF.

[31] Watson, letter to Beaton, 13 October 1945, PCB A1/553/28.

[32] Watson, letter to Connolly, 16 September 1945, CCP.

[33] Watson, letter to Connolly, 16 September 1945, CCP.

[34] Watson, letter to Connolly, 5 October 1945, CCP.

[35] Watson, letter to Connolly, 10 October 1945, CCP.

[36] Watson, letter to Connolly, 19 October 1945, CCP.

[37] Watson, letter to Connolly, 26 October 1945, CCP, and letter to Beaton, 25 October 1945, PCB A1/553/48.

[38] Watson, letters to Connolly, 5 and 19 October 1945, CCP. Skira had already been interviewed in March, and had admitted to visiting Paris during the war and purchasing artworks there, but 'denied that he had ever done any traffic in stolen, or even doubtful, pictures or objets d'art of any kind' (letter from the British Legation in Berne to the Ministry of Economic Warfare, 17 May 1945, MFA record FO 837/1156/2).

[39] Watson, letter to Skira, 12 November 1945, RPF.

[40] Memo, Commercial Secretariat, Economic Warfare Department, 16 March 1946, RPF.

[41] Watson, letter to Connolly, undated (November/December 1945), CCP.

[42] Watson, letter to Beaton, 23 December 1945, PCB A1/553/36.

[43] Watson, letters to Commission de Récuperation Artistique, 9 and 14 December 1945, RPF. Eerily, the first of these letters was written five years to the day after the ERR raid on 44 rue du Bac. Confusingly, the list of missing paintings drawn up by Peter Watson in December 1945 does not match the list in the archive of the ERR. There are titles that are on his list but not on theirs, and vice versa. Some of this might be attributable to his faulty memory, some due to inaccurate record-keeping by the ERR, and some due to inconsistent use of titles. Moreover, it cannot be ruled out that some of the discrepancies were due to paintings going missing from the flat before the ERR raided it; it is not impossible that Sherban Sidéry, who apparently disposed of so many of Peter Watson's valuables, also sold some of his paintings.

[44] Watson, letter to Craxton, undated (November/December 1945), CJC. It isn't clear whether this was Otto von Stülpnagel or his cousin Carl-Heinrich von Stülpnagel, both of whom commanded in occupied France during 1942. It was more likely Otto, who had relatively good relations with the French administration in Paris and actually protested to Hitler against the looting of French artworks by the ERR and DSK (to no avail). After the war Otto was put on trial for massacres in France between 1940 and 1942, and committed suicide in a French military prison in 1948. Carl-Heinrich was one of the July 1944 plotters against Hitler, and was executed by the Gestapo in August that year.

[45] Watson, letters to Craxton, undated (November/December 1945), CJC, and to Freud, 18 December 1945, PLF.

[46] Watson, letters to Beaton, October 1945, PCB A1/553/28 & 51.

[47] Watson, letter to Beaton, 23 December 1945, PCB A1/553/36.

[48] Watson, letter to Beaton, 23 December 1945, PCB A1/553/36. Peter refers to Louise as 'Louise Pálffy Esterhazy', in reference to her ex-husband (Count Paul Pálffy) and her then current lover, Paul Esterházy de Galántha, both of whom she had seduced away from the same woman, Austro-Hungarian countess Etti Plesch.

[49] Watson, letter to Beaton, 23 December 1945, PCB A1/553/36.

[50] Watson, letter to Craxton, undated (November/December 1945), CJC.

[51] Watson, letter to Connolly, undated (November/December 1945), CCP.

[52] Parker, *Isherwood*, p. 541.

[53] Parker, *Isherwood*, p. 541.

[54] Fouts, declaration signed 20 September 1945, PCI CI 877.

[55] Metropolitan Museum of Art, object information (provenance) 1996.403.1, available online at www.metmuseum.org/collection/the-collection-online/search/486739 (retrieved 27 September 2014). Mrs Marx kept the painting for fifty

years, lending it occasionally for exhibitions, and finally bequeathed it to the New York MMA in 1995.

[56] Wishart, *High Diver*, p. 49.

[57] Wishart, *High Diver*, p. 50.

[58] Wishart, *High Diver*, pp. 50–51.

[59] Wishart, *High Diver*, pp. 51–2.

[60] Watson, letter to Craxton, undated (mid-1946), CJC.

[61] Watson, letter to Craxton, undated (late 1946, possibly October), CJC.

[62] Watson, letter to Craxton, undated (mid-1946), CJC.

[63] Watson, letter to Craxton, undated (mid-1946), CJC.

[64] BTP outwards, 19 November 1946, SS *Franconia*, Liverpool–New York.

[65] Watson, letter to Craxton, 1 November 1946, CJC.

17 – THE NEW WORLD

[1] This encounter and the subsequent relationship are described in part by Shelden, *Friends of Promise*, p. 209, based on interviews with Waldemar Hansen.

[2] USN muster roll, USS *Herbert C. Jones* (DE-137), 1 December 1945. Norman Richard Fowler MoMM2c (motor machinist second class) had joined the ship on 10 November 1945. Shelden (*Friends of Promise*, p. 209) implies that his first meeting occurred about February 1946; in fact it was more likely late March; Fowler's ship, the USS *Herbert C. Jones*, reached New York on 15 March 1946 after sailing from the Pacific.

[3] US Federal Censuses for 1930 and 1940, Missouri and California. Norman Richard Fowler's date of birth isn't known exactly, but various sources indicate that it must have been between 18 April and 10 July 1926.

[4] Fowler, letter to Hansen, 16 October 1946.

[5] USN muster roll, USS *Skimmer* (AMCU-41/LCIL-1093), 6 March 1945.

[6] USN muster roll, USS *Herbert C. Jones* (DE-137), 1 December 1945.

[7] USN muster roll, USS *Okaloosa* (APA-219), 1 October 1946.

[8] Fowler, letter to Hansen, 16 October 1946, CWH.

[9] Shelden (*Friends of Promise*, p. 209) states that the party was given by Tchelitchew at his apartment, but John Myers (letter to Hansen, undated, probably June 1949, CWH) refers to it as Ruth Ford's party.

[10] Watson, letter to Howard, undated (January 1947), BHC, quoted in Shelden, *Friends of Promise*, p. 171.

[11] Shelden, *Friends of Promise*, p. 171.

[12] Watson, letter to Hansen, 28 March 1947, CWH.

[13] Shelden, *Friends of Promise*, p. 209. Norman Fowler was transferred to the base

at Norfolk, Virginia, for 'Terminal Leave and Discharge' on 25 April 1947 (USN, Daily Personnel Diary of USS *Okaloosa*, 25 April 1947).

[14] Hansen, letter to Shelden, August 1984, quoted in Shelden, *Friends of Promise*, p. 179.

[15] Watson, letter to Hansen, 24 March 1947, CWH.

[16] Watson, letter to Hansen, 28 March 1947, CWH.

[17] Watson, letter to Hansen, 17 March 1947, CWH. Also aboard were David Niven's infant sons, being escorted by a nurse back to England, and the architect George Wornum, who had supervised the design of the ship's interior décor (which Peter thought tasteless) (BTP inwards, SS *Queen Elizabeth*, 13 March 1947, New York–Southampton).

[18] Watson, letter to Hansen, 17 March 1947, CWH.

[19] Watson, letter to Hansen, 18 March 1947, CWH.

[20] Watson, letter to Hansen, 18 March 1947, CWH.

[21] Watson, letter to Hansen, 21 March 1947, CWH.

[22] Watson, letter to Hansen, 28 March 1947, CWH.

[23] Shelden, *Friends of Promise*, p. 180, based on interviews with Hansen.

[24] Bank of England, 'The UK exchange control: a short history', *Bank of England Quarterly Bulletin*, September 1967, pp. 245–60, available online at www.bankofengland.co.uk/archive/Documents/historicpubs/qb/1967/qb67q3245260.pdf (retrieved 5 November 2014). The regulations only applied to countries outside the 'sterling area' (which consisted of countries whose currencies were pegged to sterling), where free exchange was allowed. In 1947 the sterling area mostly consisted of British Commonwealth countries (but not Canada). One hundred pounds in 1945–7 would be equivalent to a little over £3,500 now.

[25] Watson, letter to Hansen, 21 March 1947, CWH.

[26] Watson, letter to Hansen, 24 March 1947, CWH.

[27] Watson, letter to Hansen, 1 April 1947, CWH.

[28] Myers, letter to Hansen, undated (June 1949), CWH.

[29] Watson, letter to Hansen, 13 April 1947, CWH.

18 – TWO AMERICANS IN PARIS

[1] Hansen, letter to Myers, 30 April 1947, CWH.

[2] Hansen, letter to Myers, 30 April 1947, CWH.

[3] Watson, letter to Hansen, 18 April 1947, CWH.

[4] Hansen, letter to Myers, 30 April 1947, CWH.

[5] Hansen, letter to Myers, 30 April 1947, CWH.

[6] Hansen, letter to Myers, 30 April 1947, CWH.

[7] Hansen, letter to Myers, 30 April 1947, CWH. Elizabeth Bowen had inherited the house in 1930, and divided her time between it and her house in Clarence Terrace, London (the venue of the party at which Peter had agreed to fund *Horizon*). In the 1950s she struggled to keep Bowen's Court going, but in the end was forced to sell it; it was demolished in 1961.

[8] Hansen, letter to Myers, 30 April 1947, CWH.

[9] Hansen, letter to Myers, 4 May 1947, CWH.

[10] Hansen, letter to Myers, 4 May 1947, CWH.

[11] Shelden, *Friends of Promise*, p. 156.

[12] Connolly, 'Happy Deathbeds', quoted in Shelden, *Friends of Promise*, p. 77.

[13] Hansen, letter to Myers, 31 May 1947, CWH.

[14] See Appendix – *A Room in Chelsea Square.*

[15] Hansen, letter to Myers, 31 May 1947, CWH.

[16] Hansen, letter to Myers, 31 May 1947, CWH.

[17] Hansen, letter to Myers, 14 June 1947, CWH.

[18] Hansen, letter to Myers, 14 June 1947, CWH.

[19] Hansen, letter to Myers, 14 June 1947, CWH.

[20] Hansen, letter to Myers, 1 July 1947, CWH.

[21] Hansen, letter to Myers, 1 July 1947, CWH.

[22] Hansen, letter to Myers, 1 July 1947, CWH.

[23] Hansen, letter to Myers, 1 July 1947, CWH.

[24] Watson, letter to Craxton, 14 September 1946, CJC.

[25] Hansen, postcard to Myers, 10 July 1947, CWH.

[26] Hansen, letter to Myers, 3 August 1947, CWH.

[27] Hansen, letter to Myers, 3 August 1947, CWH.

[28] Hansen, letter to Myers, 3 August 1947, CWH.

[29] Hansen, letter to Myers, 26 August 1947, CWH.

[30] This quotation is frequently reproduced, and has been attributed to Douglas himself (invariably without a source cited). In fact it originates from book by Paul Fussell (*Abroad: British Literary Travelling Between the Wars*, Oxford University Press, 1980, p. 20). It is possible that Fussell was paraphrasing something Douglas himself wrote.

[31] Hansen, letter to Myers, 26 August 1947, CWH.

[32] Hansen, letter to Myers, 26 August 1947, CWH.

[33] ICA minutes, TGA 955/1/2/1.

[34] Watson, letter to Craxton, 1 November 1946, CJC. The earliest evidence of planning for this project is a letter from Peter Watson to Mesens on 8 December 1945 (PEM), in which he writes that he is stuck in Paris and might not be able to

attend a proposed meeting; this would be the meeting which was eventually held on 22 January 1946.

[35] Herbert Read, 'The Fate of Modern Painting', *Horizon*, November 1947, pp. 242–54.

[36] Watson, letter to Connolly, dated 'Sunday' (5 October 1947), CCP.

[37] Watson, letter to Connolly, dated 'Sunday' (5 October 1947), CCP.

[38] Watson, letter to Connolly, dated 'Tuesday' (14 October 1947), CCP.

[39] Watson, letter to Connolly, dated 'Sunday' (5 October 1947), CCP.

[40] Watson, letter to Connolly, dated 'Tuesday' (14 October 1947), CCP.

19 – THIEVES, DOPE-PEDDLERS AND PURVEYORS OF LOVE

[1] Bank of England, 'The UK exchange control: a short history', *Bank of England Quarterly Bulletin*, September 1967, pp. 245–60, available online at www.bankofengland.co.uk/archive/Documents/historicpubs/qb/1967/qb67q3245260.pdf (retrieved 5 November 2014).

[2] Watson, letter to Hansen, 2 October 1947, CWH. The American Hospital of Paris is a private non-profit hospital that was founded in 1906 as a way of providing American expatriates with access to American-trained doctors.

[3] Watson, letter to Hansen, 8 October 1947, CWH.

[4] Hansen, letter to Myers, 7 October 1947; Watson, letters to Hansen, 7 and 8 October 1947, CWH.

[5] Hansen, letter to Myers, 7 October 1947, CWH. Mopsa Sternheim died of cancer in 1954, aged forty-nine.

[6] Watson, letter to Hansen, 7 October 1947, CWH.

[7] Watson, letter to Hansen, 7 October 1947, CWH.

[8] Watson, letter to Hansen, 8 October 1947, CWH.

[9] Howard, letter to Hansen, 23 February 1948, CWH.

[10] Hansen, letter to Myers, 7 October 1947, CWH.

[11] Hansen, letter to Myers, 7 October 1947, CWH.

[12] Hansen, letter to Myers, 7 October 1947, CWH.

[13] Hansen, letter to Myers, 7 October 1947, CWH.

[14] Hansen, letter to Myers, 14 December 1947, CWH.

[15] Waldemar Hansen, 'Avez-Vous Quelque Chose à Déclarer?', *Poetry* magazine, May 1948, p. 84.

[16] Hansen, letter to Myers, 14 December 1947, CWH.

[17] Hansen, letter to Myers, 6 May 1948, CWH.

[18] Myers, letter to Hansen, 10 May 1948, CWH.

[19] Myers, letter to Hansen, 10 May 1948, CWH.

[20] Watson, letter to Hansen, 23 May 1948, CWH. Peter doesn't specify who this

'illegitimate son' was. Many people were rumoured to be royal bastards – including Peter himself; George Melly, the jazz singer and art connoisseur, was told this rumour by the painter E. L. T. Mesens. Melly thought that Peter, 'a sweet but melancholy man', did bear some resemblance to 'an effeminate and wistful version of the Duke of Windsor' (Melly, *Don't Tell Sybil*, p. 50).

21 Gore Vidal, in Plimpton (ed.), *Truman Capote*, p. 88.

22 Watson, letter to Hansen, 23 May 1948, CWH.

23 Watson, letter to Hansen, 12 May 1948, CWH.

24 Watson, letter to Hansen, 23 May 1948, CWH.

25 Hansen, letter to Myers, 13 June 1948, CWH.

26 Capote, *Answered Prayers*, p. 25.

27 Capote, *Answered Prayers*, p. 28.

28 Capote, *Answered Prayers*, pp. 28–9. Capote disguised Beaton's identity by referring to him anonymously as a young aristocrat.

29 Quoted in Vickers, *Cecil Beaton*, p. 397.

30 Capote, *Answered Prayers*, p. 29.

31 Telegram quoted in Hansen, letter to Myers, 13 June 1948, CWH.

32 Gore Vidal, in Plimpton (ed.), *Truman Capote*, p. 88.

33 Capote, *Answered Prayers*, p. 30.

34 Capote, *Answered Prayers*, p. 34.

35 Hansen, letter to Myers, 13 June 1948, CWH.

36 Hansen, letter to Myers, 11 September 1948, CWH.

37 Watson, letter to Hansen, 20 October 1948, CWH.

38 Hansen, letter to Myers, 11 September 1948, CWH.

20 – EUPHORIA AND DREAD

1 American Foreign Service report on death of Louis Denham Fouts, 17 February 1949, in Reports of Deaths of American Citizens Abroad, 1835–1974, Publication A1 566, ARC ID: 613857, Record Group 59, National Archives at College Park, Maryland, available online at ancestry.com.

2 American Foreign Service letter to State Department, 13 June 1950, in Reports of Deaths of American Citizens Abroad, 1835–1974, Publication A1 566, ARC ID: 613857, Record Group 59, National Archives at College Park, Maryland, available online at ancestry.com.

3 Watson, letters to Beaton, 3 March–7 April 1946, PCB A1/553/17–18. Before the war, Frances Fox (an enormously successful brand of 'scientific' hair treatments and salons) had had a branch in Regent Street, but now the products could only be obtained from America.

[4] Watson, letter to Hansen, 4 January 1949, CWH; BTP outwards, SS *Queen Mary*, 1 January 1949, Southampton–New York.

[5] Watson, letter to Hansen, 4 January 1949, CWH.

[6] Watson, letter to Hansen, quoted in Shelden, *Friends of Promise*, p. 208.

[7] Sonia Brownell, postcard to Hansen, 1 November 1948, CWH.

[8] Shelden, *Friends of Promise*, pp. 208–9, based on interviews with Waldemar Hansen.

[9] Watson, letter to Hansen, 5 February 1949, CWH.

[10] *Horizon*, February 1949.

[11] Watson, letter to Hansen, 5 February 1949, CWH. Existing biographies of Cecil Beaton state that Cecil introduced Peter to Garbo when she stayed at Reddish in 1951 (e.g. Vickers, *Cecil Beaton*, p. 354; Vickers, *Loving Garbo*, p. 158; Souhami, *Greta and Cecil*, p. 197), apparently based on a reading of Cecil's diary, a document that is extremely fluid with chronology, with contemporaneous events mingled promiscuously with reminiscence. Peter's letter of February 1949 indicates that the introduction must have been earlier, perhaps in Paris.

[12] Beaton, diary, summer 1949, quoted in Vickers, *Cecil Beaton*, p. 341.

[13] Beaton, letter to Garbo, 27 June 1949, PCB A2/14a/63.

[14] Watson, letter to Hansen, 5 February 1949, CWH.

[15] Hansen, letter to Myers, 1 March 1949, CWH.

[16] Watson, letter to Hansen, 27 February 1949, CWH.

[17] Watson, letter to Hansen, 27 February 1949, CWH.

[18] Hansen, letter to Myers, 1 March 1949, CWH.

[19] Hansen, letter to Myers, 1 March 1949, CWH.

[20] Watson, letter to Hansen, 27 February 1949, CWH.

[21] Hansen, letter to Myers, 10 March 1949, CWH.

[22] Institute of Contemporary Arts, *ICA Exhibition List*, p. 1.

[23] Watson, letter to Calas, 23 October 1948, CNC.

[24] Watson, letter to Hansen, 27 July 1949, CWH.

[25] 'Don't Be a Gentleman', *TIME* magazine, 27 May 1947.

[26] Watson, letter to Hansen, 28 June 1949, CWH.

[27] Watson, letter to Hansen, 16 May 1950, CWH.

[28] Watson, letter to Sonia Brownell, 4 April (1949), SOP.

[29] Craxton, letters 1984–86, quoted in Tate Gallery catalogue entry T03838.

[30] Hansen, 'London Letter'.

[31] Hansen, letter to Myers, 5 May 1949, CWH.

[32] Hansen, letter to Myers, 5 May 1949, CWH.

[33] Hansen, letter to Myers, 5 May 1949, CWH.

[34] Hansen, letter to Myers, 5 May 1949, CWH.
[35] Hansen, letter to Myers, 11 June 1949, CWH.
[36] Hansen, letter to Myers, 11 June 1949, CWH.
[37] Capote, letter to Andrew Lyndon, 15 July 1949, in Capote, *Too Brief a Treat*, p. 94.
[38] Capote, letter to Andrew Lyndon, 23 August 1949, in Capote, *Too Brief a Treat*, p. 98.
[39] Myers, letter to Hansen, undated (June 1949), CWH.
[40] Ford, letter to Shelden, 13 March 1985, collection of Michael Shelden.
[41] Myers, letter to Hansen, undated (June 1949), CWH.
[42] Spender, diary, 5 May 1956, *New Selected Journals*, p. 223.
[43] Myers, letter to Hansen, undated (June 1949), CWH.
[44] Watson, letter to Hansen, 28 March 1947, CWH.
[45] Hansen, letter to Shelden, 1984, quoted in Shelden, *Friends of Promise*, p. 219.
[46] Watson, letter to Hansen, 5 April 1947, CWH.
[47] Hansen, letter to Myers, 6 September 1949; Watson, letter to Hansen, 24 September 1949, CWH.
[48] Watson, letter to Hansen, 27 July 1949, CWH.
[49] Hansen, letter to Myers, 6 September 1949, CWH.
[50] Watson, letter to Hansen, 6 November 1949, CWH.
[51] Hansen, letter to Myers, 6 October 1949, CWH.
[52] Hansen, letter to Myers, 11 September 1949, CWH.
[53] Watson, letter to Hansen, 12 October 1949, CWH.
[54] PNY: Manifest of SS *Queen Elizabeth*, Southampton–New York, arriving 3 November 1949.

21 – THE GARDENS OF THE WEST

[1] Fowler, letter to Hansen, 13 March 1950, CWH.
[2] Fowler, letter to Hansen, 13 March 1950, CWH.
[3] BTP inwards, SS *Queen Mary*, 9 March 1950, New York–Southampton.
[4] Watson, letter to Hansen, 4 April 1950, CWH.
[5] Fowler, letter to Hansen, 13 March 1950, CWH.
[6] Watson, letter to Hansen, 4 April 1950, CWH.
[7] Watson, letter to Howard, undated (early 1950s), quoted in Shelden, *Friends of Promise*, p. 229.
[8] Watson, letter to Hansen, 10 October 1951, CWH.
[9] Watson, letter to Hansen, 16 May 1950, CWH.
[10] Fowler, letter to Hansen, 21 September 1950, CWH.

[11] Connolly, 'Comment', *Horizon*, November 1949, p. 285.

[12] Connolly, *Ideas and Places*, p. ix.

[13] Connolly, *Ideas and Places*, p. ix.

[14] Watson, letter to Hansen, 6 November 1949, CWH.

[15] Shelden, *Friends of Promise*, p. 213.

[16] Canfield quoted in Shelden, *Friends of Promise*, p. 214.

[17] Watson, letter to Calas, 7 December 1949, CNC.

[18] Watson, letter to Hansen, 16 July 1950, CWH.

[19] Watson, letter to Hansen, 4 April 1950, CWH.

[20] Croft, *Comrade Heart*, p. 202.

[21] Watson, letter to Hansen, 16 July 1950, CWH.

[22] Connolly, 'Comment', *Horizon*, December 1949, p. 362.

[23] Watson, letter to Hansen, 12 January 1950, CWH.

[24] Watson, letter to Calas, 17 July 1948, CNC.

[25] Watson, letter to Hansen, 12 January 1950, CWH.

[26] Peter Townsend, 'Where Do We Go?', *Spectator*, 12 May 1950, p. 643.

[27] Watson, letter to Lord, 21 December 1949, CJL.

[28] Watson, letter to Hansen, 16 July 1950, CWH.

[29] Watson, letter to Hansen, 16 July 1950, CWH.

[30] Chambers, *Continuum Companion to Twentieth Century Theatre*, pp. 332–3.

[31] Watson, letter to Hansen, 14 October 1950, CWH. The Group Theatre of London had no connection with the American company of the same name. Founded in the 1930s, it had produced dramas written by Spender, Isherwood and Auden. Having closed down before the war, the Group was revived in 1950.

[32] Fowler, letter to Hansen, 21 September 1950, CWH. The Leopardi quotation is from R. C. Trevelyan's 1941 translation in *Translations from Leopardi* (Cambridge University Press). Leopardi was a nineteenth-century Italian poet and philosopher, who developed a fixation with the tomb of the earlier poet Torquato Tasso.

[33] Fowler, letter to Hansen, 21 September 1950, CWH.

[34] Watson, letter to Lord, 21 November 1950, CJL.

[35] Watson, letter to Hansen, 2 December 1950, CWH.

[36] Melly, *Don't Tell Sybil*, p. 92.

[37] Melly, *Don't Tell Sybil*, p. 129.

[38] Watson, letter to Hansen, 2 December 1950, CWH.

[39] Institute of Contemporary Arts, *ICA Exhibitions*, p. 3.

[40] Watson, letter to Hansen, 2 December 1950, CWH.

[41] Watson, letter to Hansen, 16 July 1950, CWH.

[42] Watson, letter to Hansen, 29 July 1951, CWH.

[43] Evans, 'Craxton'.

[44] Craxton, letter to Lady Norton, undated (probably February or March 1951) TGA 9113/1/35.

[45] Ian Board, quoted in Farson, *The Gilded Gutter Life of Francis Bacon*, ch. 8. The amount stated is £300; this may be an exaggeration, given the currency allowances still in force.

[46] Watson, letter to Lord, 28 March 1951, CJL.

[47] Letters between Peter Watson and Piers Raymond (Chatto & Windus director), 15 May 1951 to 19 June 1953, RCW.

[48] Baroness Moura Budberg, who had been born into the Ukrainian aristocracy, had started working as a spy for (and against) the Bolsheviks during the Russian Revolution; she had affairs with the British diplomat Robert Bruce Lockhart and was later the mistress and companion of both Maxim Gorky and H. G. Wells. From the 1920s to the early 1950s she was under surveillance by MI5, and became very close to Guy Burgess; the Security Service regarded her as a potentially bad influence on him. As a popular socialite, Baroness Budberg's circle overlapped with that of Peter Watson's; she was a good friend of Cecil Beaton (they shared an enthusiasm for Greta Garbo, among other things) and acquainted with Barbara Skelton, Cyril Connolly, Tom Driberg, Alan Pryce-Jones, Rosamond Lehmann, Laurence Olivier, Harold Nicolson and many others. (See Deborah McDonald and Jeremy Dronfield, *A Very Dangerous Woman: The Lives, Loves and Lies of Russia's Most Seductive Spy*).

[49] Moura Budberg MI5 dossier; see McDonald and Dronfield, *A Very Dangerous Woman: The Lives, Loves and Lies of Russia's Most Seductive Spy*, p.322. Moura's long-term MI5 contact was Klop Ustinov (father of the actor Peter Ustinov), an old friend who is believed to have ultimately recruited her as a British agent.

[50] Auden's file began January 1934; the date of origin of Spender's is not known; only volume 2 (begun in June 1951 during the Burgess and Maclean episode and closed in 1959) is in the public archive. Both Auden and Spender had been either Communists or sympathetic to the Communist cause in the 1930s. Cyril Connolly's MI5 file was begun in October 1940; the cause might have been an incident in Oxford that May; just before Jean Connolly had left for Ireland with Denham Fouts, Connolly tried to phone her from an Oxford hotel. His behaviour, hanging around near the telephone, aroused the suspicions of an army officer, who interrogated him and took exception to his Irish surname and the fact that his passport had been issued in Austria in 1937; the police were called and Cyril had a hard time talking his way out of the situation (Shelden, *Friends of Promise*, pp. 52–3).

[51] Report on telephone transcript, 18 July 1951, SSP Connolly.

[52] Telegram from MI5 operative (name redacted), 20 June 1951, SSP Auden.

[53] Letter from G. T. D. Patterson, British Embassy, Washington, 29 June 1951, SSP Auden.

[54] *The Times*, 8 June 1951, p. 4.

[55] MI5 extract from MI6 letter Y.3270, 20 June 1951, SSP Auden.

[56] *Daily Express*, 13 June 1951, clipping in MI5 file, SSP Auden.

[57] Watson and Hansen, letter to Brian Howard, 28 March 1948, BHC.

[58] This man is still living, and has been interviewed by Adrian Clark; he wishes to remain anonymous.

[59] Peter Watson later told this to Alex Leslie (AFC interview).

[60] Message from R. T. Reed, MI5 section B2a (surveillance), 14 June 1951, SSP Auden.

[61] MI5 numbered their 'PF' files in simple numerical order. For example, Moura Budberg's file, which was begun in 1921, was number 3,736; W. H. Auden's, begun in 1934, was 63,329; many more were added to the watch list during the Spanish Civil War and a huge number after the outbreak of the Second World War, so when Cyril Connolly's file was begun in late 1940, its number was 709,170. Peter Watson's file, at 147,223, must have been opened some time between 1934 and the start of the war.

[62] MI5 minute sheet, 1 February 1955, SSP Spender.

[63] This information came from the Security Service in response to a request for information on file PF 147223 (Security Service, letter to Adrian Clark, 19 October 2012).

[64] *The Times*, 19 September 1955, p. 8.

[65] Fowler, letter to Hansen, 25 March 1952, CWH. A cutter-rigged boat has two headsails (the sails before the mast) and requires particularly skilled handling.

[66] Watson, letter to Hansen, 17 March 1952, CWH.

[67] Watson, letter to Hansen, 17 March 1952, CWH.

[68] Fowler, letter to Hansen, 25 March 1952, CWH.

[69] Davison, *My Ship Is So Small*, p. 37.

[70] Davison, *My Ship Is So Small*, p. 36.

[71] Davison, *My Ship Is So Small*, p. 38.

[72] Edward Allcard, personal communications to Adrian Clark, 20–24 May 2012. Even sixty years later, Allcard retained a fierce loathing of Norman Fowler.

[73] Davison, *My Ship Is So Small*, p. 199.

[74] Fowler, letter to Hansen, 25 March 1952, CWH.

[75] Fowler, letter to Hansen, 25 March 1952, CWH.

[76] Belloc, *The Cruise of the Nona* (1925), pp. 346–7, quoted by Fowler, letter to Hansen, 25 March 1952, CWH.

[77] Fowler, letter to Hansen, 25 March 1952, CWH.

22 – DANGEROUS PURSUITS

[1] Watson, letter to Hansen, 13 July 1952, CWH.

[2] Watson, letter to Calas, 15 February 1954, CNC.

[3] Watson, letter to Hansen, 10 October 1951, CWH.

[4] Watson, letter to Hansen, 10 October 1951, CWH.

[5] Bank of England, 'The UK exchange control: a short history', *Bank of England Quarterly Bulletin*, September 1967, pp. 245–60, available online at www.bankofengland.co.uk/archive/Documents/historicpubs/qb/1967/qb67q3245260.pdf (retrieved 5 November 2014).

[6] Watson, letter to Hansen, 4 April 1950, CWH.

[7] Smith, *British Writers and MI5 Surveillance*, pp. 76–7.

[8] MI5 minute, 2 February 1955, SSP Spender.

[9] Smith, *British Writers and MI5 Surveillance*, p. 78.

[10] Watson, letter to Calas, 15 February 1954, CNC.

[11] Watson, letter to Calas, 2 March 1952, CNC.

[12] Watson, letter to Hansen, 13 July 1952, CWH.

[13] Watson, letter to Calas, 15 February 1954, CNC.

[14] Watson, letter to Calas, 15 February 1954, CNC.

[15] Watson, letter to Hansen, 19 November 1954, CWH.

[16] Watson, letter to Tchelitchew, 30 May 1955, PTC.

[17] Watson, letter to Tchelitchew, 5 January 1956, PCT.

[18] Watson, letter to Hansen, 9 July 1955, CWH.

[19] Watson, letter to Hansen, 17 March 1952, CWH.

[20] BTP inwards, SS *Boskoop*, 3 March 1954, West Indies–Dover.

[21] BTP outwards, SS *Dongedyk*, 10 July 1954, London–Los Angeles.

[22] Houlbrook, *Queer London*, pp. 97–8.

[23] Houlbrook, *Queer London*, pp. 105–7.

[24] In 1952, Alan Turing, the mathematician and computer pioneer, was burgled by an associate of a young man he'd picked up in Manchester; he reported this to the police, and the subsequent investigation revealed the nature of his relationship with the young man. Turing was prosecuted for indecency and sentenced to chemical castration. He died of cyanide poisoning in 1954, apparently suicide.

[25] Quoted in Vickers, *Behind Closed Doors*, p. 174.

[26] According to Alex's recollection, his first meeting could have been either 1951 or 1952; the latter is more likely, as Norman was away from London (AFC interviews).

[27] Richard Hamilton, interview with Adrian Clark, 30 September 2010. The incident probably occurred in July 1951, when Johnson gave a lecture at the ICA and

the 'Growth and Form' exhibition (opened by Le Corbusier on 3 July) was in preparation.

[28] Watson, letter to Spender, 29 May 1953, PSS.

[29] Sutherland, *Stephen Spender*, p. 237.

[30] Watson, letter to Spender, 8 June 1953, PSS.

[31] AFC interview, 12 September 2014.

[32] Raymond Parkes, letter to Shelden, 28 January 1990, courtesy Michael Shelden.

[33] Watson, letter to Spender, 8 June 1953, PSS.

[34] See Cullen, *The Man Who Was Norris*, for an account of the life of Gerald Hamilton.

[35] Quoted in Cullen, *The Man Who Was Norris*, p. 299.

[36] Watson, letter to Spender, 29 May 1953, PSS.

[37] Watson, letter to Spender, 8 June 1953, PSS.

[38] The coronation came during a week of bad weather caused by a freak cold front. On coronation day there were showers and the temperature never got above 12° C.

[39] Watson, letter to Spender, 8 June 1953, PSS.

[40] Watson, letter to Calas, 15 February 1954, CNC.

[41] Watson, letter to Calas, 15 February 1954, CNC.

[42] AFC interview, 18 September 2014.

[43] Watson, postcard to Beaton, 6 August 1955, PCB A1/553/9.

[44] Rorem, *Paris Diary*, p. 193.

[45] Watson, letter to Alice Bernoulli, undated (January 1956), CCB.

[46] Gerald Hamilton, letter to Isherwood, 26 June 1956, PCI.

[47] Watson, letter to Tchelitchew, 5 January 1956, PTC.

[48] Beaton, letter to Hansen, 4–5 May 1956, PCB A2/14a/128; Lys Connolly, letter to Hansen, 8 May 1956, CWH.

[49] AFC interview, 12 September 2014.

[50] Watson, letter to Hansen, 9 July 1955, CWH.

[51] Watson, letter to Tchelitchew, 5 January 1956, PTC.

[52] Wishart, *High Diver*, p. 27. *Limelight* was released in 1952, when Chaplin was sixty-three. Wishart misremembered Chaplin's line as 'Life isn't funny anymore.' He recalled being surprised by Peter's grief, but noted that 'I wouldn't be today.'

[53] Peter Watson had also helped Bacon's rise to prominence by including an essay about him by Robert Melville in the very last issue of *Horizon* (Melville, 'Francis Bacon', *Horizon*, December 1949, pp. 419–23) in which he was declared 'a hope for painting' and compared to Picasso, Duchamp and Goya.

[54] Watson, letter to Hansen, 9 July 1955, CWH.

[55] Watson, letter to Sonia Orwell, 24 February 1956, SOP.

[56] Spender, diary, 7 May 1956, PSS. Peter did write to Sonia (24 February 1956, SOP) that Norman was 'marvellously sunburnt and well and seems enchanted with London'.

[57] This fact came to light during the inquest on 8 May (Spender, diary, 9 May 1956, *New Selected Journals*, p. 230).

[58] BTP inwards, RMS *Queen Elizabeth*, 10 April 1956, New York–Southampton.

[59] Beaton, diary, April 1956, *The Restless Years*, p. 44.

[60] Institute of Contemporary Arts, *ICA Exhibitions List*, p. 11. This meeting must have occurred during the week of 16–20 April.

[61] Beaton, letter to Hansen, 4–5 May 1956, PCB A2/14a/128.

[62] Isherwood, diary, 11 February 1956, *Diaries*, p. 580.

[63] Beaton, diary, 6 May 1956, *The Restless Years*, p. 44.

[64] Beaton, diary, 6 May 1956 (headed retrospectively), PCB.

[65] Beaton, diary, 6 May 1956, *The Restless Years*, pp. 44–5.

[66] Beaton, diary, 6 May 1956, PCB.

[67] Beaton, diary, 6 May 1956, PCB; Beaton, letter to Hansen, 4–5 May 1956, PCB A2/14a/128; Richard Chopping obituary, *Guardian*, 14 June 2008.

[68] Beaton, diary, 6 May and added notes, 1956, PCB; and March 1956, *The Restless Years*, pp. 37–41. The version of *My Fair Lady* on which Cecil had been working was the original Broadway production starring Rex Harrison and Julie Andrews; he later did the designs for the 1964 film with Audrey Hepburn.

[69] Beaton, diary, 6 May and added notes, 1956, PCB. Unless otherwise specified, much of the account that follows is derived by piecing together information gleaned from the unpublished diaries of Cecil Beaton (PCB) and Stephen Spender (PSS), a letter from Beaton to Waldemar Hansen (4–5 May 1956, PCB A2/14a/128), a letter from Richard Roud (American film critic, London correspondent for *Cahiers du Cinéma*) to John Craxton (CJC), and Stephen Spender's account of the evidence given at the inquest (*New Selected Journals*, pp. 229–31). Most of the information comes ultimately from Norman Fowler's account, as told to Spender, Beaton, other friends, and to the inquest. The official records of the inquest no longer exist; like Peter Watson's MI5 file, they were destroyed at some unknown later date.

[70] Spender, diary, 12 July 1956, *New Selected Journals*, p. 249.

[71] Isherwood, diary, 11 February 1956, *Diaries*, p. 580.

[72] *The Times*, 1 May 1956, p. 15. Fire Cross had odds of 25–1 and was an also-ran (*The Times*, 2 May 1956, p. 14).

[73] Norman Fowler's evidence at the inquest, as described by Spender, diary, 9 May 1956, *New Selected Journals*, p. 230.

[74] Personal account given to Stephen Spender (diary, 7 May 1956, PSS).

[75] AFC interview, 12 September 2014. At Palace Gate, Peter would bathe every morning, and then run a bath for Alex, who recalled him being rather mean with the hot water.

23 – THE REALM OF ECSTASY

[1] Beaton, diary, 6 May 1956, PCB.

[2] Beaton, diary, 6 May 1956, PCB.

[3] Spender, diary, 5 May 1956, *New Selected Journals*, p. 221. The editor of Spender's published diaries has labelled this entry '5 May', although it is more likely 4 May, since the wording implies that Peter had died the day before. (In Spender's diaries, like Beaton's, dates were not always clearly or accurately noted.)

[4] Lawson, letter to Craxton, 6 May 1956, CJC.

[5] Spender, diary, 7 May 1956, PSS.

[6] Spender, diary, 7 May 1956, PSS.

[7] Spender, diary, 9 May 1956, *New Selected Journals*, pp. 229–31.

[8] Cecil Beaton had heard this from Freud (Beaton, letter to Hansen, 4–5 May 1956, PCB A2/14a/128).

[9] Spender, diary, 9 May 1956, *New Selected Journals*, p. 230.

[10] In the first stage of drowning (whether the victim is conscious or not), water usually enters the stomach before the lungs.

[11] Spender, diary, 9 May 1956, *New Selected Journals*, p. 231.

[12] United States Navy, *The Bluejacket's Manual*, 10th edition (1940): 'Part 2. – Subjects All Enlisted Men Should Know': Chapter 30: 'Swimming, Life-saving methods, Artificial respiration, Life buoys'. In the 12th edition (1944), the layout was altered, and Chapter 6 was devoted to 'Physical Fitness, Swimming and Lifesaving'.

[13] 'The Brides in the Bath' is the name popularly given to the murders committed by George Joseph Smith between 1912 and 1914, in which he killed three of his wives by drowning them in the bath. Experiments showed that his technique was to fondle the victim's legs while she bathed, then suddenly grab them and pull her underwater – the sudden, gasping inhalation of water was sufficient to cause instantaneous unconsciousness and rapid drowning. Smith's motive in all cases was his wives' money; he was convicted in 1915 and hanged. The 'Brides' case was the subject of many books and articles in subsequent decades, and was very well known by the 1950s.

[14] Spender, diary, 9 May 1956, *New Selected Journals*, p. 231.

[15] Fowler, letter to Hansen, mistakenly dated 'April 13, 1956' (probably 13 May – postmark is 15 May), CWH.

[16] Fowler, letter to Hansen, mistakenly dated 'April 13, 1956' (probably 13 May – postmark is 15 May), CWH.

[17] The source for this is Peter's great-nephew Alasdair Nagle, who does not necessarily subscribe to this theory himself.

[18] Beaton, diary, 6 May 1956, PCB.

[19] Watson, postcard to Beaton, 6 August 1955, PCB A1/553/9.

[20] Beaton, diary, 6 May 1956, PCB.

[21] There were exceptions. Lys Connolly thought Peter seemed 'very happy' in his communications with her since moving to his new flat (Lys Connolly, letter to Hansen, 8 May 1956, CWH). Gerald Hamilton, who lunched with Peter in April, thought he 'seemed very jolly and well at the time' (Hamilton, letter to Isherwood, 26 June 1956, PCI).

[22] Beaton, letter to Garbo, 4–5 May 1956, PCB A2/14a/127.

[23] Watson, letter to Hansen, 12 October 1949, CWH.

[24] Beaton, letter to Garbo, 4–5 May 1956, PCB A2/14a/127.

[25] Hansen, letter to Beaton, 4 May 1956, PCB A1/223. Cecil and Waldemar had kept in touch since the latter's return to America in 1949, and Waldemar had done occasional ghostwriting for Cecil.

[26] Beaton, diary, 6 May 1956, PCB.

[27] Beaton, diary, May 1956, PCB.

[28] Beaton, diary, May 1956, *The Restless Years*, pp. 45–6.

[29] Beaton, diary, May 1956, *The Restless Years*, pp. 45–6.

[30] Spender, diary, 10 May 1956, *New Selected Journals*, p. 231.

[31] Beaton, diary, May 1956, PCB.

[32] Spender, diary, 10 May 1956, *New Selected Journals*, p. 232.

[33] Spender, diary, 10 May 1956, *New Selected Journals*, p. 232.

[34] Spender, diary, 7 May 1956, PSS.

[35] *Art* magazine, vol. 2 no. 13, 18 May 1956, p. 1.

[36] Spender, diary, 6 May 1956, *New Selected Journals*, p. 229.

[37] Spender, diary, 5 May 1956, *New Selected Journals*, pp. 222–3.

[38] Callard, *The Case of Anna Kavan*, p. 78.

[39] Watson, letter to Hansen, 22 November 1948, CWH.

[40] Spender, diary, 10 May 1956, *New Selected Journals*, p. 232.

[41] Spender, diary, 10 May 1956, *New Selected Journals*, pp. 232–3.

[42] Capote, letter to Beaton, 15 May 1956, in Capote, *Too Brief a Treat*, p. 241.

[43] Beaton, diary, 6 May 1956, PCB.

EPILOGUE

[1] Hansen, letter to Beaton, 4 May 1956, PCB A1/223.

[2] Myers, *Tracking the Marvelous*, p. 187.

[3] Furlonger, letter to Hansen, 6 May 1956, CWH.

[4] £120,000 in 1956 would be approximately equivalent to £2.7 million today.

[5] Spender, diary, 28 May 1956, *New Selected Journals*, p. 238.

[6] Vickers notes (*Cecil Beaton*, p. 396) that some people (unnamed) have suggested that Norman murdered Peter. After Vickers' book was published in 1985, Waldemar Hansen received a postcard from a person whose name is unclear (it was signed with two initials, the second of which is clearly *A*). The sender writes of Vickers' biography that 'it says Norman F may have murdered Peter W, which is what I always told you. If only you had come to me in time you could have had your own island instead of Norman' (postcard, unknown sender, CWH). James Lord, who was a close friend of Peter's in the last years of his life, believed he was murdered (Lord, *A Gift for Admiration*). Michael Shelden, who interviewed several people who knew Peter, believed there were grounds to suspect Norman (Shelden, *Friends of Promise*, pp. 230–31).

[7] *The Times*, 17 October 1956, p. 3.

[8] *The Times*, 28 June 1956, p. 1.

[9] Sotheby's sale catalogue, 29 October 1956; also *The Times*, 30 October 1956, p. 10.

[10] *The Times*, 30 October 1956, p. 10.

[11] *The Times*, 22 April 1958, p. 18.

[12] Spender, diary, 16 June 1956, PSS.

[13] Waugh, diary, 11 October 1956, *The Diaries of Evelyn Waugh*, pp. 769–70.

[14] Lancaster, *Brian Howard*, p. 546.

[15] Howard, letter to Banting, quoted in Lancaster, *Brian Howard*, p. 545.

[16] Fowler, letter to Hansen, 30 May 1957, CWH.

[17] Hansen, dream account, 14 November 1957, CWH.

[18] Spender, *New Collected Poems*, pp. 302–3.

[19] Spender, *New Collected Poems*, p. 301.

[20] Eggleston, *Virgin Islands*, pp. 66–7.

[21] Royston Ellis, 'A View from Sri Lanka', roystonellis.com/blog/royston-reports-a-view-from-sri-lanka-number-30/ (retrieved 21 November 2014).

[22] *Island Sun*, 27 March 1971.

[23] Personal communication to Adrian Clark (name withheld), 15 November 2011.

APPENDIX – *A ROOM IN CHELSEA SQUARE*

[1] Hansen, letter to Myers, 31 May 1947, CWH. Waldemar refers to him merely as 'a boy called Michael Nelson' and seems to have had no notion of there being a relationship between him and Peter.

[2] Watson, letter to Hansen, 5 April 1947, CWH.

[3] Gregory Woods, Introduction to 2013 Valancourt edition of *A Room in Chelsea Square* by Michael Nelson; available online at gregorywoodspoet.blogspot.co.uk/2014/01/a-room-in-chelsea-square_29.html (retrieved 19 November 2014).

BIBLIOGRAPHY

Archives and unpublished materials

AFC Interviews with Alexander Fitzroy-Clarence (formerly Alex Leslie) conducted by Adrian Clark, 12–18 September 2014

BTP Board of Trade, Commercial and Statistical Department and successors: Inwards Passenger Lists, BT26; Outwards Passenger Lists, BT27, National Archives, Kew (available online at ancestry.com)

BHC Brian Howard Collection (papers and correspondence), College Library, Eton College, Windsor

CCB Correspondence of Christophe and Alice Bernoulli, UB Basel, NL322, University Library, Basel, Switzerland

CCP Cyril Vernon Connolly papers, Collection 1976-002, Series 1: Correspondence; 20:4, Peter Watson, 1926–1953, Department of Special Collections and University Archives, McFarlin Library, University of Tulsa

CJC Correspondence of John Craxton (from Peter Watson), estate of John Craxton via Richard Riley, trustee

CJL Correspondence of James Lord, Beinecke Rare Book and Manuscript Library, Gen MSS 790, Box 19, Folder 215, Yale University Library, New Haven, Connecticut

CNC Correspondence of Nicolas Calas, the Nicolas and Elena Calas Archive, the Nordic Library at Athens

CRR Correspondence of Robert MacBryde and Robert Colquhoun (letters to Ian Fleming, lecturer, Glasgow School of Art), GMA 21/4, archives of the Scottish National Gallery of Modern Art, Edinburgh

CWH Correspondence of Waldemar Hansen: letters to and from Peter Watson, John Myers, Norman Fowler, Lys Connolly, in possession of Michael Shelden

DKR Records of the Devisenschutzkommando Frankreich, series AJ 40 1036 (Watson), Centre Historique des Archives Nationales, Paris

LMA London Metropolitan Archives, City of London Corporation Libraries, Archives and Guildhall Art Gallery Department (some records available online at ancestry.com)

MFA Reports on looted works of art by the Monuments, Fine Arts and Archives Branch, National Archives, Kew

NLS National Life Stories audio recordings collection: Artists' Lives, C466, British Library, London

PCI Papers of Christopher Isherwood, Huntington Library, San Marino, California

PCB Papers of Sir Cecil Beaton, Correspondence and Diaries, St John's College Library; used by permission of the Master and Fellows of St John's College, Cambridge

PEM Papers of E. L. T. Mesens, 920094, Special Collections, Getty Research Institute Research Library, Los Angeles

PHO Passenger Lists of Vessels Arriving at and Departing from Honolulu, Hawaii, National Archives Microfilm Publication: A3422, Roll 190 and A3510, Roll 121, National Archives and Records Administration, Washington, DC, available online at ancestry.com.

PLF Papers of Lucian Freud, estate of Lucian Freud via Diana Rawstron, Goodman Derrick LLP, executor

PNY Passenger and Crew Lists of Vessels Arriving at New York, 1897–1957. Microfilm Publication T715, 8892 rolls. Records of the Immigration and Naturalization Service; National Archive and Records Administration, Washington, DC (available online at ancestry.com)

PSS Papers of Stephen Spender, Special Collections, Bodleian Library, Oxford

PTC Pavel Tchelitchew Collection, YCAL MSS 318, Beinecke Rare Book and Manuscript Library, Yale University Library, New Haven, Connecticut

RBR Restitutions Branch Records: Records of the Office of Military Government, US Zone (Germany), Property Division, Reparations and Restitutions Branch, Monuments, Fine Arts, and Archives (MFAA) Section, ERR (Einsatzstab Reichsleiter Rosenberg) Card File and Related, RG 260 M1943 Reel 27, National Archives and Records Administration, Washington, DC; Peter Watson listing available online at www.errproject.org/jeudepaume/card_search.php?Query=peter+watson (retrieved 19 October 2014).

RCW Records of Chatto & Windus, correspondence 1953: H–L, CW 129/22, Special Collections, University of Reading

RPF Restitutions à des propriétaires vivant en France: Peter Watson, Archives des Affaires étrangères, Ministère des Affaires étrangères, La Courneuve, France

SOP Papers of Sonia Orwell (Blair), Repository GB 0103, UCL Special Collections, University College Archives, London

SSP Security Service (MI5) Personal Files (PF series) on Wystan Hugh Auden (original ref. PF 63329): KV/2/2588; and Cyril Vernon Connolly (original ref. PF 709170): KV/2/3436, Stephen Harold Spender (original ref. PF 43649 VOL 2): KV/2/3216, National Archives, Kew

TGA Tate Gallery Archive, including papers and correspondence of Sven Berlin, Cecil Collins, John Craxton, Cedric Morris, Ben Nicholson, EQ Nicholson, John Piper, Keith Vaughan, the Institute of Contemporary Arts and the Lefevre Gallery, Tate Britain, London

USN Muster Rolls of US Navy Ships, Stations, and Other Naval Activities, 01/01/1939–01/01/1949; Record Group: 24, Records of the Bureau of Naval Personnel, 1798–2007; Series ARC ID: 594996; Series MLR Number: A1 135, National Archives at College Park, Maryland (available online at ancestry.com)

Books and articles

Aldred, Nanette, 'Art in postwar Britain: a short history of the ICA', in *British Culture of the Post-War*, eds Alastair Davies and Alan Sinfield, pp.146–68 (London: Routledge, 2013).

Amory, Mark, *Lord Berners: The Last Eccentric* (London: Chatto & Windus, 1998).

Bankhead, Tallulah, *Tallulah: My Autobiography* (University Press of Mississippi, 2004; orig. publ. 1952).

Beaton, Cecil, *The Book of Beauty* (London: Duckworth, 1930).

Beaton, Cecil, *The Wandering Years: Diaries, 1922–1939* (London: Weidenfeld & Nicolson, 1961).

Beaton, Cecil, *The Restless Years: Diaries, 1955–1963* (London: Weidenfeld & Nicolson, 1976).

Benaïm, Laurence, *Marie Laure de Noailles* (Paris: Grasset, 2001).

Berlin, Sven, 'Alfred Wallis I', *Horizon* (January 1943), 41–50.

Berlin, Sven, Alfred Wallis: *Primitive* (Bristol: Redcliffe, 1992; orig. publ. 1949).

Berners, Gerald Hugh Tyrwhitt-Wilson, Baron, *The Girls of Radcliff Hall* (London: Montcalm, 2000, first publ. privately, 1937).

Betjeman, John, *John Betjeman: Letters: 1926–1951*, ed. Candida Lycett Green (London: Methuen, 1994).

Bristow, Roger, *The Last Bohemians: The Two Roberts: Colquhoun and MacBryde* (Bristol: Sansom, 2012).

Bryce, Viscount, *The Study of American History: Being the Inaugural Lecture of the Sir George Watson Chair of American History, Literature and Institutions* (Cambridge University Press, 1921).

Byrne, Paula, *Mad World: Evelyn Waugh and the Secrets of Brideshead* (London: HarperPress, 2009).

Callard, D. A. *The Case of Anna Kavan: A Biography* (London: Peter Owen, 1992).

Capote, Truman, *Too Brief a Treat: The Letters of Truman Capote*, ed. Gerald Clarke (New York: Vintage, 2004).

Capote, Truman, *Answered Prayers* (New York: Vintage, 2012; chapter 'Unspoiled Monsters' orig. publ. in *Esquire* magazine, 1975).

Chambers, Colin (ed.), *Continuum Companion to Twentieth Century Theatre* (London: Continuum, 2002).

Clark, Adrian, 'Two British art patrons of the 1940s and 1950s: Sir

Colin Anderson and Peter Watson', *The British Art Journal* 5/2 (Autumn 2004), 73–79.

Clarke, Gerald, *Capote: A Biography*, ebook edn (New York: RosettaBooks, 2013).

Collins, Ian, *John Craxton* (London: Lund Humphries, 2011).

Connolly, Cyril, *Enemies of Promise* (London: Routledge & Kegan Paul, 1938).

Connolly, Cyril, *The Unquiet Grave* (London: Curwen Press for Horizon, 1944).

Connolly, Cyril, *Ideas and Places* (London: Weidenfeld & Nicolson, 1953).

Cranborne, Hannah (ed.) *David Cecil: A Portrait by his Friends* (Wimborne: Dovecote Press, 1990).

Croft, Andy, *Comrade Heart: A Life of Randall Swingler* (Manchester University Press, 2003).

Cross, William, *Evan Frederic Morgan: Viscount Tredegar: The Final Affairs: Financial and Carnal* (William P. Cross with Book Midden Publishing, 2014).

Cullen, Tom, *The Man Who Was Norris: The Life of Gerald Hamilton* (Sawtry: Dedalus, 2014).

Davison, Ann, *My Ship Is So Small* (London: P. Davies, 1956).

De Courcy, Anne, *Diana Mosley* (London: Vintage, 2004).

Di Panzillo, Maryline Assante, 'The Dispersal of the Vollard Collection', in *Cézanne to Picasso: Ambroise Vollard, Patron of the Avant-Garde*, ed. Rebecca A. Rabinow, pp. 259–62 (New York: Metropolitan Museum of Art, 2005).

Donaldson, Scott, and R. H. Winnick, *Archibald MacLeish: an American Life* (New York: Houghton Mifflin, 1992).

Eggleston, George T., *Virgin Islands* (Princeton: T. Van Nostrand, 1959).

Evans, Magdalen, 'Craxton, John Leith (1922–2009)', *Oxford Dictionary of National Biography* (Oxford University Press, 2013), available online at www.oxforddnb.com/view/article/101581 (retrieved 26 October 2014).

Fairbairn's Book of Crests of the Families of Great Britain and Ireland, 4th edn, vol. 1 (London: T. C. & E. C. Jack, 1905).

Farson, Daniel, *The Gilded Gutter Life Of Francis Bacon: The Authorized Biography*, ebook edition (Random House, 2014).

Fisher, Clive, *Cyril Connolly: a Nostalgic Life* (London: Macmillan, 1995).

Ford, Charles Henri, *Water from a Bucket: A Diary* (New York: Turtlepoint, 2001).

Foss, Brian, *War Paint: Art, War, State and Identity in Britain, 1939–1945* (Yale University Press, 2007).

Fraser, Robert, *Night Thoughts: The Surreal Life of the Poet David Gascoyne* (Oxford University Press, 2012).

Gascoyne, David, *Paris Journal, 1937–1939* (London: Enitharmon Press, 1978).

Gascoyne, David, *Collected Journals 1936–1942* (London: Skoob, 1991).

Gorer, Geoffrey, *The Revolutionary Ideas of the Marquis de Sade* (London: Wishart & Co, 1934).

Green, Henry, *Pack My Bag: A Self-Portrait* (London: Random House, 2011; first publ. Hogarth, 1940).

Grimond, Jo, *Memoirs* (London: Heinemann, 1979).

Hansen, Waldemar, 'London Letter', *Poetry* (February 1949), pp. 280–84.

Hastings, Selina, *Nancy Mitford: A Biography* (London: Vintage, 2002; prev. publ. Hamish Hamilton, 1985).

Herbert, David, *Second Son: an Autobiography* (London: Owen, 1972).

Hoare, Philip, *Serious Pleasures: the Life of Stephen Tennant* (London: Hamish Hamilton, 1990).

Hoban, Phoebe, *Lucian Freud: Eyes Wide Open* (New York: Houghton Mifflin, 2014).

Houlbrook, Matt, *Queer London: Perils and Pleasures in the Sexual Metropolis, 1918–1957* (University of Chicago Press, 2005).

Institute of Contemporary Arts, *ICA Exhibitions List, 1948–Present*, available online at http://www.ica.org.uk/sites/default/files/downloads/ICA%20Exhibitions%20List%201948%20-%20Present.pdf (retrieved 12 November 2014).

Isherwood, Christopher, *Down There on a Visit* (London: Vintage, 2012; orig. publ. 1962).

Isherwood, Christopher, *Christopher and His Kind* (London: Vintage, 2012; orig. publ. 1976).

Isherwood, Christopher, *Diaries Volume One: 1939–1960*, ed. Katherine Bucknell (London: Methuen, 1996).

Joyce, Patrick, *The State of Freedom: A Social History of the British State Since 1800* (Cambridge University Press, 2013).

Kewley, Jonathan, *Churches of Mann: Isle of Man Churches, Chapels and Keeills Explored in Words, Pictures and Music* (Ramsey: Lily Publications, 2010).

Knox, James, *Robert Byron* (London: John Murray, 2003).

Lancaster, Marie Jacqueline, *Brian Howard: Portrait of a Failure* (London: Anthony Blond, 1968).

Leeming, David, *Stephen Spender: a Life in Modernism*, ebook edition (London: Macmillan, 2011).

Lees-Milne, James, *Another Self* (London: John Murray, 1970).

Lehmann, John, *The Whispering Gallery: Autobiography I* (London: Longmans, 1955).

Lewis, Jeremy, *Cyril Connolly: a Life* (London: Vintage, 2012).

Lord, James, *A Gift for Admiration: Further Memoirs* (New York: Farrar Straus & Giroux, 1998).

Lowe, John, *Edward James: Poet, Patron, Eccentric: a Surrealist Life* (London: HarperCollins, 1991).

MacLeish, Archibald, *Archibald MacLeish: Reflections*, eds Bernard A. Drabeck and Helen E. Ellis (University of Massachusetts Press, 1986).

Markevitch, Igor, *Être et avoir été* (Paris: Gallimard, 1980).

Mathias, Peter, *Retailing Revolution: A History of Multiple Retailing in the Food Trades* (London: Longmans, 1967).

McDonald, Deborah and Jeremy Dronfield, *A Very Dangerous Woman: The Lives, Loves and Lies of Russia's Most Seductive Spy* (London: Oneworld, 2015).

Melly, George, *Don't Tell Sybil: an Intimate Memoir of E. L. T. Mesens* (London: Heinemann, 1997).

Middleboe, Penelope, *Edith Olivier: From Her Journals* (London: Weidenfeld & Nicolson, 1989).

Mitchell, Allan, *Nazi Paris: The History of an Occupation, 1940–1944* (New York: Berghahn Books, 2013).

Mitford, Nancy, *Love from Nancy: the Letters of Nancy Mitford*, ed. Charlotte Mosley (London: Hodder & Stoughton, 1993).

Monnard, Jean-François, '*Paradis perdu*: Le destin fabuleux d'Igor Markevitch', Dissonance 119 (September 2012), pp. 42–47.

Mosley, Charlotte (ed.), *The Mitfords: Letters Between Six Sisters* (London: Fourth Estate, 2007).

Mosley, Diana, *Loved Ones: Pen Portraits* (London: Sidgwick & Jackson, 1985).

Myers, John Bernard, *Tracking the Marvelous: A Life in the New York Art World* (New York: Random House, 1983).

Neild, R. R. & Robert Neild, *The Financial History of Trinity College, Cambridge* (Cambridge: Granta Editions, 2009).

Nelson, Michael, *A Room in Chelsea Square* (London: GMP, 1986, first publ. 1958).

Nicholson, Ben 'Alfred Wallis II', *Horizon* (January 1943), 50–54.

Parker, Peter, *Isherwood* (London: Macmillan, 2005).

Pearson, John, *The Life of Ian Fleming* (London, Jonathan Cape, 1966).

Plimpton, George (ed.), *Truman Capote: in which Various Friends, Enemies, Acquaintances, and Detractors Recall His Turbulent Career* (New York: Doubleday, 1998).

Powell, Anthony, *To Keep the Ball Rolling* (Harmondsworth: Penguin, 1983; orig. publ. in 4 vols, London: Heinemann, 1976–82).

Pryce-Jones, Alan, *Private Opinion: A Commonplace-Book* (London: Corden-Sanderson, 1936).

Pryce-Jones, Alan, *The Bonus of Laughter* (London: Hamish Hamilton, 1987).

Reeder, Jan Glier, 'Metamorphology: The Personal and Professional Life of Charles James', in *Charles James: Beyond Fashion*, eds Harold Koda and Jan Glier Reeder (New York: Metropolitan Museum of Art, 2014).

Rorem, Ned, *The Paris Diary of Ned Rorem* (London: Barrie & Rockliff, 1967).

Rose, Sir Francis Cyril, *Saying Life: The Memoirs of Sir Francis Rose* (London: Cassell, 1961).

Shelden, Michael, *Friends of Promise: Cyril Connolly and the World of Horizon* (London: Mandarin, 1990).

Sheppard, F. H. W. (ed.), *Survey of London: volume 38: South Kensington Museums Area* (London: English Heritage, 1975), available online at www.british-history.ac.uk/source.aspx?pubid=364 (retrieved 28 September 2014).

Sheppard, F. H. W. (ed.), *Survey of London: volume 40: The Grosvenor Estate in Mayfair, Part 2* (The Buildings) (London: English Heritage, 1980), available online at www.british-history.ac.uk/source.aspx?pubid=298 (retrieved 28 September 2014).

Sitwell, Edith, *Selected Letters of Edith Sitwell*, ed. Richard Greene (London: Virago, 1997).

Smith, James, *British Writers and MI5 Surveillance, 1930–1960* (Cambridge University Press, 2013).

Somerfield, Ferelith, *Mission Accomplished: The Life and Times of Florence Nagle* (Ashford: Dog World Publications, 1999).

Souhami, *Greta and Cecil* (London: Jonathan Cape, 1994).

Spender, Stephen, *World Within World: the Autobiography of Stephen Spender* (London: Random House, 2001; orig. publ. 1951).

Spender, Stephen, *Journals, 1939–1983*, ed. John Goldsmith (London: Faber & Faber, 1985).

Spender, Stephen, *New Collected Poems* (London: Faber and Faber, 2004).

Spender, Stephen, *New Selected Journals, 1939–1995*, eds Lara Feigel, John Sutherland, Natasha Spender (London: Faber & Faber, 2012).

Sutherland, John, *Stephen Spender: The Authorized Biography* (London: Viking, 2004).

Tamagne, Florence, *A History of Homosexuality in Europe: Berlin, London, Paris, 1919–1939*, 2 vols (New York: Algora, 2006).

Tate Gallery, Catalogue entry T03838, *Pastoral for P.W.* by John Craxton, available online at www.tate.org.uk/art/artworks/craxton-pastoral-for-pw-t03838/text-catalogue-entry (retrieved 26 October 2014).

Thomas, Dylan, *The Collected Letters of Dylan Thomas*, ed. Paul Ferris (London: Dent, 1985).

Tippett, Michael, *Selected Letters of Michael Tippett*, ed. Thomas Schuttenhelm (London: Faber and Faber, 2005).

Touche, Rodney, *Brown Cows, Sacred Cows: A True Story of Lake Louise* (Hanna AB: Gorman Brothers, 1990).

Venn, John & J. A. Venn (eds), *Alumni Cantabrigienses: A Biographical List of All Known Students, Graduates and Holders of Office at the University of Cambridge, from the Earliest Times to 1900, vol. 2 part 3* (Cambridge University Press, 1947).

Vickers, Hugo, *Cecil Beaton: the Authorized Biography* (London: Weidenfeld & Nicolson, 1985).

Vickers, Hugo, *Loving Garbo: The Story of Greta Garbo, Cecil Beaton and Mercedes de Acosta* (London: Cape, 1994).

Vickers, Hugo, *Behind Closed Doors: The Tragic Untold Story of Wallis Simpson* (London: Hutchinson, 2011).

Watson, Sir Norman, *Round Mystery Mountain: A Ski Adventure* (London: Edward Arnold, 1935).

Watson, Peter, 'Joan Miró', *Horizon* (August 1941), pp. 131–33.
Waugh, Evelyn, *The Diaries of Evelyn Waugh*, ed. Michael Davie (London: Weidenfeld & Nicolson, 1976).
Waugh, Evelyn, *The Letters of Evelyn Waugh*, ed. Mark Amory (London: Weidenfeld & Nicolson, 1980).
Wishart, Michael, *High Diver* (London: Quartet, 1978).

INDEX

(the initials CB refer to Cecil Beaton, DF to Denham Fouts, NF to Norman Fowler, WH to Waldemar Hansen, OM to Oliver Messel, PW to Peter Watson)

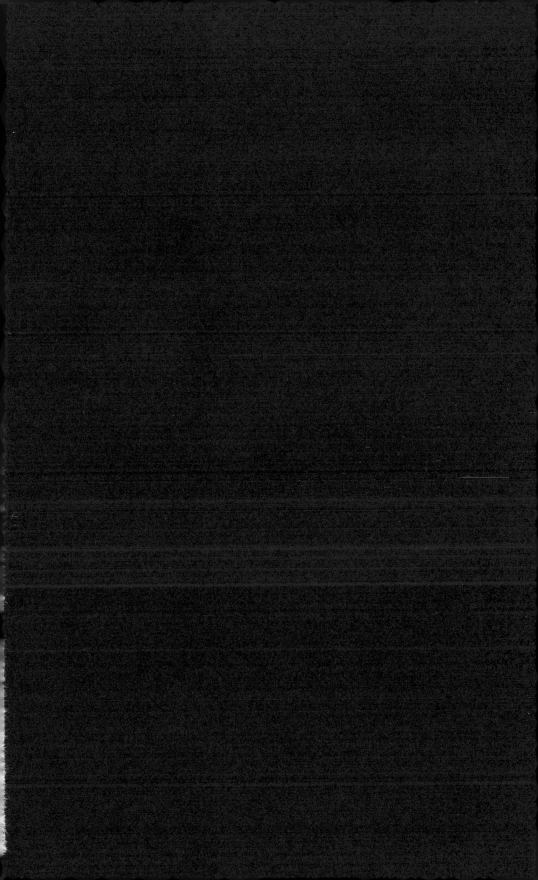